D0204076

Democracy and the mass media

Cambridge Studies in Philosophy and Public Policy

General Editor: Douglas MacLean

The purpose of this series is to publish the most innovative and up-to-date research into the values and concepts that underlie major aspects of public policy. Hitherto most research in this field has been empirical. This series is primarily conceptual and normative; that is, it investigates the structure of arguments and the nature of values relevant to the formation, justification, and criticism of public policy. At the same time it is informed by empirical considerations, addressing specific issues, general policy concerns, and the methods of policy analysis and their applications.

The books in the series are inherently interdisciplinary and include anthologies as well as monographs. They are of particular interest to philosophers, political and social scientists, economists, policy analysts, and those involved in public administration and environmental policy.

Democracy and the mass media

A collection of essays

edited by
JUDITH LICHTENBERG

Published by the Press Syndicate of the University of Cambridge
The Pitt Building, Trumpington Street, Cambridge CB2 1RP
40 West 20th Street, New York, NY 10011-4211, USA
10 Stamford Road, Oakleigh, Melbourne 3166, Australia

First published 1990
Reprinted 1991, 1993

Printed in the United States of America

Library of Congress Cataloging-in-Publication Data
Democracy and the mass media: a collection of essays / edited by Judith Lichtenberg.
p. cm. – (Cambridge studies in philosophy and public policy)
ISBN 0-521-38122-3 – ISBN 0-521-38817-1 (pbk.)
1. Freedom of the press. 2. Government and the press.
3. Journalism – Political aspects. I. Lichtenberg, Judith.
II. Series.
PN4735.D46 1990
323.44'5–dc20 89-28871
CIP

A catalogue record for this book is available from the British Library.

ISBN 0-521-38122-3 hardback
ISBN 0-521-38817-1 paperback

Contents

Preface

The Institute for Philosophy and Public Policy was established in 1976 at the University of Maryland at College Park to conduct research into the values and concepts that underlie public policy. Most research into public policy is empirical: It assesses costs, describes constituencies, and makes predictions. The Institute's research is conceptual and normative: It investigates the structure of arguments and the nature of values relevant to the formation, justification, and criticism of public policy. The results of its research are disseminated through publications, lectures, conferences, and teaching materials.

The present volume grew out of intensive discussions by the Institute's Working Group on News, the Mass Media, and Democratic Values, which met on three occasions in 1985–6 to discuss the moral, philosophical, and legal foundations of mass media regulation. All but one of the papers were written specifically for this group. Papers were subjected to criticism and comment by the whole group and were revised and rewritten for this volume.

In addition to thanking the authors of the essays in this book, who gave generously of their intelligence and energy, the editor wishes to thank Sara Engram, Jack Landau, and Anthony Smith, whose participation at the meetings added substantially to the value of the discussions and to the quality of the essays in this book.

Financial support for the Institute's project on news, the mass media, and democratic values was provided by the

Markle Foundation, and it is a pleasure to acknowledge its generosity. The views expressed by the contributors are, of course, their own and not necessarily those of the Institute, the Markle Foundation, or the institutions with which the contributors are affiliated.

The successful completion of this project is due in no small measure to several other members of the Institute's staff. Douglas MacLean, its director, provided guidance both at the meetings and at earlier and later stages of the project. Claudia Mills's expert editorial skills were extremely useful. Lyndal Andrews, Lori Owen, and Kathleen Wiersema were at various stages responsible for the financial management of the project. And Carroll Linkins provided invaluable assistance, both secretarial and organizational, at every step along the way.

JL

Contributors

Jeffrey B. Abramson is associate professor of politics at Brandeis University, where he teaches political philosophy and constitutional law. He is the author of *Liberation and Its Limits: The Moral and Political Thought of Freud* and coauthor (with F. Christopher Arterton and Gary R. Orren) of *The Electronic Commonwealth: New Media Technologies and Democratic Politics*. Professor Abramson is currently working on a study of the American jury as a democratic institution.

Jay G. Blumler is director of the Leeds University Centre for Television Research, where he holds a Personal Chair in the Social and Political Aspects of Broadcasting, and professor of journalism at the University of Maryland. Author of many books and articles on political communication, he is president of the International Communication Association, a coeditor of the *European Journal of Communication*, and a specialist adviser to the British Select Committee on Televising the Proceedings of the House of Commons.

Lee C. Bollinger is professor of law and dean of the law school at the University of Michigan. He has written widely on First Amendment issues and is the author of *The Tolerant Society: Free Speech and Extremist Speech in America*.

Roger Donway is managing editor of *Orbis*. He is coauthor (with David Kelley) of *Laissez Parler: Freedom in the Electronic Media*.

Owen M. Fiss, Alexander M. Bickel Professor of Public Law at Yale University, has written widely on constitutional and free speech issues.

Henry Geller is director of Duke University's Washington Center for Public Policy Research, which focuses on telecommunications policy. He was general counsel to the Federal Communications Commission from 1964 to 1970 and assistant secretary of commerce for communications and information from 1978 to 1981.

Michael Gurevitch is professor at the College of Journalism, University of Maryland. He is coauthor (with Elihu Katz) of *The Secularization of Leisure* and (with Jay Blumler) of *The Challenge of Election Broadcasting* and is the author of many essays on media "uses and gratifications" and political communication. He is currently conducting a comparative analysis of meanings in television news.

Stephen Holmes is professor of political science at the University of Chicago and the author of *Benjamin Constant and the Making of Modern Liberalism.*

David Kelley is an independent writer and scholar who has taught philosophy at Vassar College. With Roger Donway he wrote *Laissez Parler: Freedom in the Electronic Media.*

Judith Lichtenberg is senior research scholar at the Institute for Philosophy and Public Policy, University of Maryland. She has written widely in the areas of ethics and journalism ethics and is working on a study of objectivity in journalism.

Onora O'Neill teaches at the University of Essex and writes on Kantian problems and political philosophy. Among her works are *Faces of Hunger: An Essay on Poverty, Justice and Development* and *Constructions of Reason: Explorations of Kant's Practical Philosophy.*

T. M. Scanlon, Jr., is professor of philosophy at Harvard University. Among his many writings in moral and political philosophy are several influential articles on freedom of expression.

Frederick Schauer is professor of law at the University of Michigan. He is the author of *The Law of Obscenity* and *Free Speech: A Philosophical Inquiry,* as well as many articles on freedom of speech, the structure of rights, and the analysis of rules.

Carl Sessions Stepp is associate professor at the University of Maryland College of Journalism and senior editor of the *Washington Journalism Review.* He spent twelve years as a reporter and editor for the *Charlotte Observer,* the *St. Petersburg Times,* and *USA Today.* He is the author of *Editing for Today's Newsroom.*

Sanford J. Ungar is dean of the School of Communication at The American University and former host of *All Things Considered* on National Public Radio. He has written several books, including *The Papers and the Papers: An Account of the Legal and Political Battle over the Pentagon Papers* and *Africa: The People and Politics of an Emerging Continent.*

Introduction

JUDITH LICHTENBERG

It is hardly more than a platitude to say that the press has always played an important role in the political process. This role is, after all, a primary reason freedom of the press has been thought a necessary safeguard in a democratic society. But never before has the press been as critical to the political process as it is today, and never before has its importance been so widely and publicly recognized. Each election year renders these truths more self-evident.

The increased importance of the press in the political process brings out an ambiguity in its role. Traditionally, the press has been conceived as an observer – ideally, a neutral observer – of the political scene. On this view, the press is part of the political process but it is also not part; it stands outside. But events of the last few decades have demonstrated the inadequacy of this view. The press today – the mass media in particular – is one of the primary actors on the political scene, capable of making or breaking political careers and issues.

The seeming undeniability of the idea that the media are agents in the political process and not simply observers of it provides one important reason for rethinking the traditional prerogatives and responsibilities of the press. Is regulation of the press justified? In the American system, at least, the First Amendment grants the press a privileged place: "Congress shall make no law abridging the freedom of speech, . . . or of the press." The only question this unqualified statement seems to leave open is what counts as "press." But this *is* a big question. From their inception early in the century, the electronic media have never enjoyed the privileges, the immunity from government regulation, of the print press. Are television reporters not "press"? It may have been easy in the early years to fail to recognize the potential reportorial role of the electronic media. Broadcasters, it has been said, were the "lineal descendants of operators of music halls and peep shows."[1] That may partly explain why from the beginning government regulation of broadcasting was not seen as trampling freedom of the press. Today, of course, when most people rely heavily on television for news, no one doubts that the electronic media are a mainstream part of the press. But that leaves us with a dilemma about the proper objects of media regulation.

PRINT VERSUS ELECTRONIC MEDIA?

Radio and television stations are licensed by the Federal Communications Commission (FCC). They are subject to a variety of regulations, including equal time rules and, until recently, the fairness doctrine. Abandoned by the Reagan administration's FCC, but possibly to be enacted by Congress as law in the future, the fairness doctrine required that radio and television stations devote a reasonable amount of broadcast time to controversial issues of importance to the public, and that they offer adequate opportunity for opposing viewpoints.[2] The equal time rules, which were enacted by Congress in Section 315(a) of the Communications Act, require that all equally qualified candidates for public offices be afforded equal opportunities for broadcast time. (This rule contains four significant exemptions, however.)[3] Any suggestion that such rules also fall on newspapers or magazines is taken – by the vast majority of journalists, among others – to be fundamentally inconsistent with the First Amendment and more generally with a commitment to freedom of the press.

The constitutional asymmetry between print and broadcasting is codified in two pivotal Supreme Court decisions: *Red Lion Broadcasting v. FCC* (1969)[4] and *Miami Herald v.*

Tornillo (1974).[5] *Red Lion* concerned a Pennsylvania radio station that in 1964 aired a broadcast by the Reverend Billy James Hargis as part of a "Christian Crusade" series. Hargis attacked Fred Cook, the author of a book called *Goldwater – Extremist on the Right.* He charged, among other things, that Cook had worked for a Communist-affiliated publication (*The Nation,* as it turned out), and that he had now written "a book to smear and destroy Barry Goldwater."[6] Cook demanded free reply time, which the station refused to give him. The Supreme Court unanimously upheld the FCC's requirements that under the fairness doctrine radio and television stations provide free reply time to those attacked in station broadcasts.

Several years later, the *Miami Herald* published editorials criticizing Pat Tornillo, a candidate for the Florida House of Representatives. Tornillo demanded that the paper print his replies, which it refused to do. He brought suit, relying on a Florida right-of-reply statute that provided that if a candidate for nomination or election is attacked "regarding his personal character or official record by any newspaper, the candidate has the right to demand that the newspaper print, free of cost to the candidate, any reply the candidate may make to the newspaper's charges."[7] The statute also required that the reply appear as conspicuously as the charges prompting it. The Supreme Court held that such statutes violate the First Amendment guarantee of a free press. Its decision was once again unanimous, and it failed even to mention *Red Lion.*

Are there significant differences between print and broadcasting that explain and legitimize this deeply entrenched split? (We speak of broadcasting because for most of the history of electronic media, the electronic press was the broadcast press – radio and television. The development and penetration of cable and other communications technologies in the last decade or so have altered the landscape once more and complicated the policy questions confronting us.) If not – if the similarities between print and electronic media are more relevant than their differences – is the current system irrational and wrong? Even if it is, that alone doesn't tell us which way to go: whether we should regulate the print media or deregulate the electronic.

"Our views on broadcasting technology were formed," R. H. Coase has said, "in the shadows cast by a mysterious technology."[8] The earliest rationale for the regulation of electronic media – specifically radio – was the "etheric bedlam," as the Department of the Navy quaintly described it in 1910, resulting from the unregulated operation of several stations on the same frequency at the same time.[9] Government was called upon to act as traffic cop. Yet it could have performed this function without engaging in the much more extensive regulation it undertook from the beginning. Instead of granting licenses free on the basis of criteria imposed and interpreted by the government – such as that licensees serve as public trustees – the state could have created a market in the spectrum, granting licenses to the highest bidder. Advocates of the free market endorse such a system today.

The most common rationale given for government's performing a regulatory role has always been scarcity. The spectrum is a finite and very limited resource. Perhaps because the inherent limit of the airwaves is so obvious, it was natural to think of the spectrum as belonging to the public, on whose behalf the government could presume to regulate.

But further reflection as well as developments over the last half century call this assumption into question. In the first place, as economists are quick to note, *all* resources are scarce; in this the airwaves are no exception.[10] (The only thing that's not scarce is scarcity itself.) Newspapers are scarce too – although for somewhat different reasons than spectrum space. The number of newspapers that can survive in a given area is extremely small, and the price of owning one is prohibitive for all but very few. Here the cause of scarcity is not the physical limits of the spectrum but certain economic facts, especially the economics of newspaper advertising, which cause not simply scarcity but often monopoly.

How does this happen? To put it briefly, advertisers constitute the economic lifeblood of a newspaper, and the largest among them – such as supermarkets and department stores – may spend vast amounts of money on newspaper advertising. The newspaper with the largest circulation in a given market can charge the lowest price per household to advertisers. The lower price per household attracts more advertisers, thus benefiting the newspaper with larger circulation, which, in just another instance of the "rich get richer" syndrome, may therefore come to dominate even more strongly. The result is often that the paper with smaller circulation eventually goes out of business.[11]

But although the reasons for newspaper scarcity are purely economic, while broadcasting scarcity results from physical facts as well (we may assume) as economic ones, the result is the same: a small number of media outlets within a given market.

These abstract truths have been made concrete in the last few decades by two trends: on the one hand, the rapidly declining number of major newspapers and, more significantly, the more areas served by only one major newspaper; on the other hand, the development of new electronic communications technology, especially cable television, which vastly increases the number of channels available to viewers. These facts demonstrate that if scarcity is the only rationale for regulation, we ought to regulate both print and electronic media, or neither.[12]

It might nevertheless be argued that print outlets are still much more abundant than electronic ones. A cable operator might allocate a couple of channels to public access; that is not many, and one must still rely on other people and organizations to get one's message out. Yet almost anyone can crank out a pamphlet or a newsletter without dependence on others. Whether this seems a convincing argument for treating print and electronic media differently depends on how important we think the distinction between mass and nonmass media is. That one can produce a leaflet and distribute it – even relatively broadly – in a community may seem a trivial exercise when compared with the product of a large, sophisticated metropolitan newspaper or television station. Publishing a pamphlet may fulfill the need for self-expression, but it does little to advance the quest for truth or the strengthening of democracy.

But other arguments besides scarcity have been advanced for regulating the electronic media while leaving print untouched. One is that television has a power to shape beliefs and opinions that is not possessed by the printed word: One (moving) picture is worth ten thousand words. Television's effects can be visceral and direct, and it has been held responsible for increased violence, the collapse (or, alternatively, the entrenchment) of traditional sex roles, the end of the Vietnam War, and other significant events and trends. Establishing a causal connection between television viewing and specific behavior, or the formation of particular attitudes or beliefs, is extremely difficult, however, and the evidence for such effects is conflicting. Even if we assume that some such effects exist, there have been, as far as we know, no studies comparing the impact of television with, say, that of newspapers.

There is another important reason to doubt the power argument. Television – particularly in its news and public affairs programming, which is the primary focus of this volume – is likely to exert its power most strongly on the less well-educated and influential in American society, at least partly because such groups are the most frequent viewers of network news.[13] (The audience for the *MacNeil/Lehrer NewsHour* and other public television programs is richer and better educated.) Yet newspapers like the *New York Times* and the *Washington Post* may have much more influence on the political process because they are avidly read by politicians, public officials, corporate executives, and other decision makers and agents of change in the society.

So the argument from power is inconclusive, for television exerts most power on the least powerful. A related argument is that even if the electronic media are not more powerful than print, they are more intrusive and less escapable. Reading takes effort and active participation, but television's messages thrust themselves upon us. Television's capacity to bring messages into the home uninvited surely bears on the appropriateness of regulation in the interest of children, and perhaps more broadly on questions of obscenity and offensiveness. As for regulation in the interest of fairness, liberty, and the political process – the questions to which most of the writers in this volume are primarily addressing themselves – its relevance as an argument independent of the question of television's power is unclear.

Some scholars have acknowledged the parity between print and broadcasting but still maintain that they ought to be treated differently. In an influential 1976 article, Lee Bollinger argued that the Supreme Court "should now acknowledge that for first amendment purposes broadcasting is not fundamentally different from the print media. Such an admission would not compel the Court either to permit access regulation throughout the press or to disallow it entirely. There is . . . an alternative solution."[14] The alternative solution, according to Bollinger, rests on recognizing two facts. One is that society "obviously has *thought differently* about broadcasting than it has about the print media."[15] The other is that "broadcast regulation involves only a *part* of the press."[16] Regulation of broadcasting (or, more generally, of the electronic media) allows us to have the best of both worlds: Since there is good reason to regulate and good reason not to, we can split the difference by regulating some media (the newer ones, where regulation accords with tradition and social attitudes toward it are accepted) while leaving the print press – and our well-formed attitudes about freedom of the press and the First Amendment – untouched.

This argument is satisfying because it lets us have our cake and eat it too. The main objection to it – one that broadcasters can hardly be blamed for raising – is that if no relevant differences between print and broadcasting can be offered, imposing a burden on broadcasting that is not shouldered equally by the print media constitutes invidious discrimination. Unless we can answer this objection, Bollinger's otherwise attractive solution remains problematic.

THE POWER OF THE PRESS

Whatever the similarities and differences between print and electronic media, the desire to impose constraints of one sort or another on the media clearly derives from a general belief in their power to condition people's beliefs, attitudes, opinions, values, worldview. If we did not believe the press was a potent force in the world, we would not think curbing its freedom worth the price. (At the same time, ironically, if we did not believe the press was potent, we would not think protecting its freedom worth the price.)

Yet the precise nature and extent of the media's influence have been matters of dispute for as long as the field of mass communications research has existed – around sixty to seventy-five years.[17] The dominant view has swung widely from the belief that the media heavy-handedly shape human attitudes, to great skepticism about their effects, and back again to a belief in their power. In the 1910s and 1920s, the prevailing belief was that the media have powerful effects on the human mind. This view exemplified a more general picture of society as *mass* society, divided between a large populace and a small elite that was able to manipulate it. The appeal of this view was rooted partly in external events: the impressive rise of the mass press, radio, and moving pictures, on the one hand, and the ways mass political movements, especially fascist movements, used these new tools as powerful instruments of propaganda, on the other.[18]

The early belief that the media are powerful was based less on scholarly research than on anecdotal observation and common sense. In the 1930s, social scientists began to study mass communications in a more systematic way. And so began the era of the "minimal effects" thesis: the view that by themselves the media were virtually powerless to change minds, that it was rather the context of family, friends, colleagues, and co-workers that was primarily responsible for people's opinions and attitudes.

Perhaps this conclusion was due in part to the difficulties of establishing interesting conclusions about such large and seemingly vague issues with the tools of social science, which, when they do not merely confirm common sense, often seem to confound it. Perhaps it was due also to the absence of deep social conflict, and the existence of a kind of consensus (if only skin deep) during the main period of this phase of research – the 1940s and 1950s. In any case, the intuitively powerful view that the media *do* shape consciousness began to make itself felt again in the 1960s. Several explanations for its resurgence can be offered. One is the upheavals of the 1960s themselves. The presence of striking political events allows the media to exert more effectively any power they have. A related development is increased political skepticism and alienation (what we might call the Vietnam–Watergate syndrome) and the concomitant erosion of political loyalties. Obviously the power of the media increases relatively as other forces lose strength. Finally, there is the rise of television. Television, of course, dates from the late 1940s. But early television newscasts barely realized the visual component of their medium; they much more resembled radio broadcasts, just as the first moving pictures emulated theater. It took some time before television's possibilities were fully realized and exploited.

In any case, during the third and current period, the predominant view is that the mass media exert great power: not simply economic or political power but the power to shape how we think about the world. Predictably, perhaps, the current view does not simply rehash the first wave of belief in media effects. The original view held that the media influence attitudes: what we like or dislike, favor or reject. The contemporary version is more complex. First of all, it tends to emphasize cognition rather than affect. The media provide not only information but also the conceptual frameworks within which information and opinions are ordered – not just facts, but a worldview. Contemporary mass communications researchers also emphasize the "agenda setting" function of the press. As Bernard Cohen puts it, the press "may not be successful much of the time in telling people what to think, but it is stunningly successful in telling its readers what to think *about*."[19] Finally, political actors are forced to shape their messages and their images to the contours of the contemporary press, and this affects the public's perceptions and the political process.[20]

To many people these conclusions hardly warrant the strenuous efforts social scientists have employed to establish them: They are just the plain offerings of common sense and, increasingly, the conventional wisdom of politicians and even journalists. The question, one might say, is not whether the press exerts a great deal of power – not always in beneficial ways – but what, if anything, to do about it.

In his essay in this volume, however, Jeffrey Abramson does question the conventional wisdom. In considering four criticisms of press ethics – all bearing, in one way or another, on the press's power – he takes on the view not only that the press is powerful but also that it is weak and manipulated. Yet even this view, which seems to deny the hegemony of the press, in a sense ironically acknowledges it: If the press does the government's bidding – if it could *succeed* in doing the government's bidding – then to that extent the press is powerful. The controversy between those who say the media are powerful and those who say they are weak and manipulated can then be seen as a dispute mainly about the source and content of the media's messages; the power of the media themselves is not so much in dispute.

This is not to say that the difference is trivial. But even if government's agenda does not drive the media's messages, it does not follow that the press is independent of outside pressures. In fact, the criticism Abramson takes most seriously is that what most severely compromises contemporary journalism is the economic pressures on it.

However we resolve questions about the precise nature and source of the press's power, the larger issue, which Michael Gurevitch and Jay Blumler's essay explores, is how to resolve the tensions "between the ostensibly democratic ideals which the mass media are supposed to serve and the communication structures and practices that actually tend to prevail."

REGULATION AND ITS ALTERNATIVES

That a diversity of perspectives or a multiplicity of voices in the public forum is desirable is perhaps beyond dispute. And that in contemporary society the mass media constitute the public forum may be equally uncontroversial. But how to achieve the multiplicity of voices if it doesn't come about naturally? – that is the question. The problem can be framed in terms of the legitimate constraints on press behavior, and this question is perhaps the guiding theme of the essays in this volume. Henry Geller provides a context by describing current government policy – and plausible alternatives – concerning the regulation of mass communications.

One issue, addressed by Frederick Schauer, is to what degree the press should be insulated from popular choices and decision making. How far, constitutionally and morally, does the First Amendment protect the press from the wishes and goals of the electorate? A related question concerns the legitimacy and appropriateness of regulation of the press. The essays by Stephen Holmes, David Kelley and Roger Donway, Judith Lichtenberg, Owen Fiss, Onora O'Neill, Carl Sessions Stepp, and Lee C. Bollinger all address this question directly. Onora O'Neill argues that regulation of communicators is inevitable; for "legal, economic, and social structures and traditions as well as conversational and literary forms and conventions regulate who communicates with whom, and the topics and occasions on which they communicate." On this view, the question is not whether the press shall be regulated but who shall do it and how conscious and explicit a process it will be. Obviously this view conflicts with the common belief that genuine freedom of the press is possible and that it is incompatible with regulation.

In any case, we need to analyze the notion of explicit government regulation more carefully. Understood broadly, all law is regulation, governing the actions of and relations among individuals, groups, and organizations in a society. In this sense, libel law is a form of regulation. But libel law is part of private law, governing disputes between private parties. Even the most zealous advocates of deregulation or freedom of the press do not argue for the total abolition of libel law – or private law more generally. Indeed, they are likely to believe that private law is exactly where conflicts in a society should be resolved. The controversy over regulation is about the limits of public law, which governs the behavior of public agencies.[21] The question is how much and what kind of power these public agencies – which in turn regulate the behavior of private parties – should have.

With respect to communications media, we can distinguish three abstract modes of regulation in this narrower sense: content regulation, structural regulation, and subsidy. Content regulations – the paradigm case is the fairness doctrine – make specific demands of press institutions to cover certain kinds of issues or to provide access to certain points of view. Structural regulations – like limits on cross-ownership of media – build restrictions into the structure and organization of media ownership and management; they do not meddle explicitly in ideas or "content." With subsidy, funds are used to promote programming or material that would fail to be provided in the unrestricted marketplace.

But these categories, although standard in the literature of media regulation, are rather artificial: In practice they cannot always be easily separated. Subsidies are always given for a certain purpose; to that extent they are not wholly content-neutral. Access requirements, usually considered a form of structural regulation, presuppose criteria for sorting and choosing among those who seek access, except where access is offered entirely on a first-come, first-served basis. We must know whether a view has been aired before, or how far it diverges from other positions that have been presented. Such decisions cannot avoid judgments about content. On the other hand, the term "content regulation" is also misleading: So-called content regulations like the fairness doctrine do not prescribe that any particular issues or particular viewpoints be represented, only that issues of "public importance" be covered and that a diversity of views be aired.

Still, the distinction between content regulation and other forms reflects a fundamental intuition, codified in First Amendment law: the idea that "above all else, the First Amendment means that government has no power to restrict expression because of its message, its ideas, its subject matter, or its content."[22] An investigation of the meaning of this core idea forms the basis of T. M. Scanlon's essay.

What are the alternatives to government regulation of the press? The most obvious is no regulation at all. One view is that "nothing is broke" and so no change is called for. Even many journalists today find this position (or at least admitting it openly) a bit too smug. Carl Sessions Stepp endorses what he calls the professional responsibility model of journalism, which involves educating, or reeducating, journalists to make them more responsive to the kinds of criticisms commonly raised against them.

A position less intrusive than government regulation (which, it must be emphasized again, is a broad category that includes a great variety of possible policies) but more intrusive than the professional responsibility model would endorse the use of ethics codes or press councils. The crucial question is, What sanctions would be attached to violations? Is peer disapproval (if indeed that is forthcoming) enough? Would the journalism profession permit anything more? If not, are codes or councils simply empty symbols?[23]

POLITICAL THEORY AND FREEDOM OF EXPRESSION

One's view about the legitimacy and appropriateness of government regulation of the media depends on how one resolves several underlying issues:

1. The legitimacy of state action generally: Under what circumstances may the state interfere with the activities of nongovernmental agents (individuals, groups, corporations)?

2. The nature and importance of the values and interests at stake in freedom of speech and press. What rights, if any, are at stake?
3. The particular risks and disadvantages of government regulation of the press.

Let us consider each of these in turn.

1. Some people oppose regulation of the press on general laissez-faire grounds. Robert Nozick succinctly expresses this libertarian view: "A minimal state, limited to the narrow functions of protection against force, theft, fraud, enforcement of contracts, and so on, is justified. . . . Any more extensive state will violate persons' rights not to be forced to do certain things."[24] On such a view, freedom of speech or press possesses no special prerogatives, but liberty-in-general should be extensive. As Kelley and Donway argue in their essay, "the primary rationale for insisting that government respect and preserve [freedom of expression is] the basic rationale for government: the protection of freedom in general."

Stephen Holmes, in his contribution to this volume, challenges the view, which he calls the "storybook account," that the European theorists on whose views the American political system was founded were "tenaciously antistatist." He argues that the early liberal theorists were fully convinced that "private power poses as great a threat to liberty as does public power." Owen Fiss puts this point in contemporary perspective by arguing that "the power of an agency, like the FCC, is no greater than that of CBS . . . there is no reason to assume that one kind of power will be more inhibiting or limiting of public debate than the other."

Lee Bollinger provides a different argument for the legitimacy of state involvement. People can express values through the state, he believes, that cannot or will not get expressed through the marketplace. Just as individually, in my role as citizen, I may vote for a recycling bill at the same time as, in my role as consumer, I throw away bottles and cans, collectively we may support a fairness doctrine as a way of institutionalizing values that will be "undervalued by any other method of social decision making."[25]

2. Whatever position one takes on the legitimate limits of state activity in general, one's view about the proper role, if any, of government in regulating the press depends on how one understands the values underlying freedom of expression. Probably the standard view is that although the state is justified in regulating many kinds of activities, speech and press have a special place and are protected from government intrusions legitimate or appropriate in other areas. The First Amendment makes it difficult not to grant that, at least in the United States, speech and press are afforded a large degree of insulation from government interference, whatever one thinks about the legitimacy of regulation in general. But there is still a lot of disagreement about just how much protection is or should be afforded. Many, like Carl Stepp, would argue that government should keep its hands entirely off the press.

Traditionally many different arguments have been advanced for freedom of speech and of the press – that it is a means to attaining truth or individual self-realization, a necessary element in a democratic society, a precondition of personal autonomy, a watchdog of government. One important question is whether one of these values is preeminent or whether they are coequal underpinnings for freedom of expression. Owen Fiss takes the line, first set out by Alexander Meiklejohn, that the need for "rich public debate" in a democratic society – enabling citizens to make intelligent decisions about public policy – is the preeminent value in freedom of expression, and trumps other free speech–related interests, such as the interest in personal autonomy. Judith Lichtenberg argues against a monistic view of free speech interests – granting the importance of individual autonomy, as well as the various other arguments for freedom of expression – but argues that nevertheless government regulation is not precluded. Kelley and Donway distinguish (what is not often clearly separated) the watchdog function from the other political functions of freedom of expression, and argue that the watchdog function is historically and philosophically the most important for the press (much more important than the educative one emphasized by Meiklejohn), and that it does preclude government involvement. Sanford J. Ungar's account of the importance of freedom of speech and of the press even in nondemocratic countries brings together a variety of the political functions of these freedoms.

We can parse the standard rationales for freedom of expression in a variety of ways; how we do so influences our views about the legitimacy and appropriateness of regulation. Even the traditional way of framing the issues, in terms of freedom of *expression*, is open to challenge. Onora O'Neill argues that the central issues have more to do with communication than with expression. As she points out, "the media are important, especially in democracies, not simply because they are organs for self-expression (for most they are no such thing) but mainly because they are organs of communication." Emphasizing communication rather than expression makes questions of *access* to the media a pressing concern.

Relatedly, we can think of the interests of *speakers* or *audiences* or society at large.[26] It seems clear that freedom of expression or communication encompasses all of these, but the ones we emphasize will affect our conclusions. An emphasis on the interests of audiences or society at large – in being politically informed or attaining truth – will suggest different responsibilities for the press and a greater role for government than an emphasis on speakers' interests in autonomy or self-expression. Despite the fact that those arguments most commonly cited in support of the First Amendment – the arguments from truth and from democracy – clearly emphasize the interests of audiences more than those of speakers, the popular view of free speech suggests that it is the interests of speakers that are fundamental. ("It's a free country and I can say what I want.")

The question can be subdivided even further: To the extent that we focus on speakers' interests, do we focus on their interests in speaking or on their interests in being heard? Again, the popular view suggests the former, although a deeper look at the rationales for freedom of expression seems to imply that the latter matters more. Most of us are not interested simply in hearing ourselves talk.

Also significant is whether we frame these issues in terms of rights. What is perhaps the most common assumption about freedom of expression holds that the rights of speakers (including newspapers and the like) are fundamental, and thus that attempts to interfere with their activities violate rights and are therefore impermissible. One way of attacking this view is to argue that those now excluded from the mass media have certain positive rights, rights of access to the media.[27] But such a strategy encounters obvious problems, which libertarians are quick to point out. To suppose that everyone has rights to communicate in the mass media is to open the way for such overload and chaos as to constitute a virtual reductio ad absurdum. An intermediate position is to argue for "contingent" rights of access: rights triggered by press actions. On this view, for example, a person attacked in a newspaper would have a right of reply in that newspaper. It is these kinds of rights that are at issue in *Red Lion* and *Miami Herald*.

Judith Lichtenberg offers a different strategy for showing that regulation to achieve greater access is permissible. Instead of claiming that those now not heard have a positive right of access, she argues that providing access does not violate rights of those who own or control the media. Onora O'Neill takes yet another tack. She argues that we ought to begin not with the perspective of rights but, rather, with what she takes to be the more fundamental perspective of obligations: Ask not what rights we have with respect to communication, but what duties.

3. Respect for tradition and legal precedent leads many people to agree that regulation of the print media ought to be avoided; at the same time they have no objection in principle to regulation of the electronic media. Nevertheless, they may believe that experience proves that government does a bad job when it regulates the electronic media and that, despite the problems that regulation is designed to solve, as a matter

of fact government intrusion hurts more than it helps – or at best does neither harm nor good. In such cases, a view that appears to be founded on deep philosophical grounds may turn instead on empirical beliefs about the effects of this or that kind of policy. So, for example, disputes about whether we should have a fairness doctrine often rest on disagreement not about rights or about ultimate values but, rather, about whether in fact a policy like the fairness doctrine promotes or inhibits the multiplicity of voices.[28]

One might be skeptical of the efficacy of regulation for any number of reasons: the danger in government interference because of the state's inherent conflict of interest in regulating the press and the likelihood that it will suppress points of view contrary to its interests and promote those sympathetic to it; the extreme difficulty of interpreting and enforcing regulations like the fairness doctrine; or a special incompetence of government agencies in such matters. Although he does not take a pure antiregulatory line, Henry Geller's essay in this volume expresses many of the sentiments associated with the view that whatever its merits in principle, government regulation of broadcasting, at least in the form of so-called content regulation, doesn't work very well. The essays by Holmes, Fiss, and Lichtenberg attempt to rebut some of these worries.

NOTES

1 V. O. Key, *Public Opinion and American Democracy* (New York: Knopf, 1963), p. 389.
2 See Fred Friendly, *The Good Guys, the Bad Guys and the First Amendment: Free Speech vs. Fairness in Broadcasting* (New York: Random House, Vintage, 1977), chap. 2.
3 Ibid., p. 213, note.
4 395 U.S. 367.
5 418 U.S. 241.
6 395 U.S. 367, 371.
7 418 U.S. 241, 244.
8 R. H. Coase, "The Federal Communications Commission," *Journal of Law and Economics* 2 (1959): 40.

9 Quoted in Coase, ibid., p. 2.

10 See, e.g., ibid., p. 14, and Kelley and Donway, "Liberalism and Free Speech," this volume.

11 For a detailed discussion of this process with reference to the *Washington Post* and its former competitors, see Ben H. Bagdikian, *The Media Monopoly* (Boston: Beacon, 1983), pp. 120–5. According to Bagdikian, newspapers, magazines, and broadcasters are five times more dependent economically on advertisers than on audiences; in 1981, for example, they "collected $33 billion a year from advertisers and only $7 billion from their audiences" (p. 123).

12 For an attack on the scarcity rationale, as well as the other arguments considered here, see Lucas A. Powe, Jr., *American Broadcasting and the First Amendment* (Berkeley: University of California Press, 1987), pp. 200–9, and Lee Bollinger, "Freedom of the Press and Public Access: Toward a Theory of Partial Regulation of the Mass Media," *Michigan Law Review* 75 (1976).

13 See Shanto lyengar and Donald R. Kinder, *News That Matters: Television and American Opinion* (Chicago: University of Chicago Press, 1987), chap. 6, for careful empirical studies showing that viewers with little formal education, the politically uninvolved, and the politically independent are more likely to be influenced by the agenda set by television news than those with more education, those more involved in politics, or those more politically partisan.

14 "Freedom of the Press and Public Access," p. 2.

15 Ibid., p. 17.

16 Ibid.

17 I am indebted for this account to Michael Gurevitch, and to Denis McQuail, *Mass Communication Theory* (Beverly Hills, Calif.: Sage, 1983), pp. 176–8.

18 Walter Lippmann's *Public Opinion*, published in 1922, is an influential example of this view.

19 *The Press and Foreign Policy* (Princeton: Princeton University Press, 1963), p. 13. See also Maxwell McCombs and Donald Shaw, "The Agenda-Setting Function of the Press," *Public Opinion Quarterly* 39 (1972), and lyengar and Kinder, *News That Matters*.

20 See, for some examples from a very large literature, Thomas Patterson, *The Mass Media Election* (New York: Praeger, 1980); Dan Nimmo and James E. Combs, *Mediated Political Realities*

(New York: Longman, 1983); Todd Gitlin, *The Whole World Is Watching: Mass Media in the Making and Unmaking of the New Left* (Berkeley: University of California Press, 1980); Gladys Engel Lang and Kurt Lang, "The Unique Perspective of Television: MacArthur Day," in *Politics and Television Re-viewed* (Beverly Hills, Calif.: Sage, 1984).

21 This is not to deny that there is a great deal of controversy today about libel law and its reform; there is. But that is a subject in itself, which we do not tackle here.

22 *Police Department of Chicago v. Mosley,* 408 U.S. 92 (1972).

23 The one attempt at a press council in the United States, the National News Council, which existed from 1972 to 1984, was a failure, at least in part because it lacked the support of major news organizations, most notoriously the *New York Times.* See Patrick Brogan, *Spiked* (A Twentieth Century Fund Paper, New York: Priority Press, 1985).

24 *Anarchy, State, and Utopia* (New York: Basic, 1974), p. ix.

25 For an extensive defense of this kind of view (with particular application to environmental issues), see Mark Sagoff, *The Economy of the Earth* (Cambridge: Cambridge University Press, 1988), chap. 5.

26 For a good discussion, see T. M. Scanlon, Jr., "Freedom of Expression and Categories of Expression," *University of Pittsburgh Law Review* 40 (1979): 520–8.

27 See Jerome Barron, "Access to the Press: A New First Amendment Right," *Harvard Law Review* 80 (1967). Kelley and Donway's essay criticizes this approach.

28 Often, however, we find a neat coincidence between people's philosophical or ideological views and their beliefs about how the world works: Those who believe in rights of access find that policies intended to promote diversity, like the fairness doctrine, work; those concerned with the property rights of media owners happen to think that such policies don't work.

Chapter 1

Liberal constraints on private power?: reflections on the origins and rationale of access regulation

STEPHEN HOLMES

The long debate over federal regulation of commercial broadcasting has focused largely on constitutional, administrative, technological, and economic questions. But the fairness doctrine, right-of-reply laws, and equal opportunity provisions cry out for a treatment that is simultaneously more historical and more theoretical. They raise questions as fundamental as, What are the legitimate purposes and proper limits of state action? What is the basic rationale for press immunity from government control? For what purposes can this special freedom be curtailed? Even a superficial answer to such questions presupposes a historical understanding of the political traditions encoded into the U.S. Constitution, not to mention a theoretical analysis of the preconditions for effective democratic government.

PRIVATE POWER AND EQUAL ACCESS

According to the storybook account, the European theorists who most influenced the American Founding Fathers were tenaciously antistatist. If they viewed the state as an agent of coercion that must be restricted, they saw civil society as a sphere of freedom that must be enlarged. While they perceived the public sector as posing a threat to liberty, and therefore advocated its strict regulation, they considered the private sector to be utterly harmless, inviting only benign neglect. But how accurate is this portrait of those great European theorists esteemed and emulated by the framers of the American Constitution?

Rereading, say, Locke and Montesquieu, we find no trace of blanket hostility to the state; nor do we encounter any veneration of an unregulated private sphere. Without authority, we learn, society would eventually collapse into a more or less unlivable "state of nature."[1] Anarchy poses as great a threat to freedom as tyranny. Civil society, indeed, is society "civilized" by the state. As seventeenth- and eighteenth-century theorists were all too painfully aware, a crippled government exposes its subjects to highway murder-gangs. For the sake of security, the "private sector" had to be severely contracted. Candidates for justified public suppression included *private* armies, *private* courts, and *private* taxation, as well as the *private* right to declare war and the *private* right to prosecute criminals. Freedom can be achieved only if public authorities are granted a monopoly over such crucial and delicate functions.

Not Locke and Montesquieu, but rumbustious barons and disloyal papists displayed uncompromising hostility to the state. The writers admired and echoed by the American framers were not opposed to authority in general, but only to arbitrary and unruly authority, authority unjustified by reference to the public good. Although sovereignty was dangerous and deserved distrust, a sovereignless condition was no less frightful. The main problem an effective government was designed to solve was not merely "disorder," moreover. Chaos and anarchy were euphemisms for *private oppression,* for harm inflicted by the strong upon the weak. The main reason why "it is impossible for the human race to subsist, at least in any comfortable or secure state, without the protection of government"[2] is that an ungoverned community is a community at the mercy of private oppressors.

The redistributionist dimension of social contract theory often is, but should not be, overlooked. The move from the state of nature to civil society presupposes a state-orchestrated *redistribution of security.* The security of warrior magnates is decreased (e.g., their fortresses are torn down) to increase the security enjoyed by the majority of their fellow citizens. In other words, the social contract not only produces order and imposes peace; it also redresses a serious inequality in the capacities of individuals to defend themselves.

Private power poses as great a threat to liberty as does public power. That is a faithful restatement of the basic principle bequeathed to James Madison and Thomas Jefferson by their French and English predecessors.[3] Strict noninterference by the state would produce not wholesome competition but an outcropping of brutal monopolies. Only a sovereign, bureaucratic, and centralized authority can hope to tame private power. The freedom prized by Locke and Montesquieu is thus seriously distorted when described as exclusively "negative." Such theorists were not concerned to wall off a private sphere beyond the competence of public officials. The "privacy" of a home or a church, Locke insisted, does not shield malefactors from the arm of the law.[4] Wherever they find themselves, in fact, victims of violence and fraud can seek remedy from public authority. Lockean freedom implies universal *access* to the power of the state. Lockean rights are not merely shields against governmental involvement; they include explicit *entitlements to affirmative state action* to protect individuals from harm by third parties.

In the seventeenth and eighteenth centuries, protecting the weak against the strong meant, among other things, abolishing tax immunities and distributing fiscal burdens more equitably. The state of nature was not merely disorderly; it was also unjust. Conversely, public authority was meant to establish not simply order but rather a *just order.* Madison is unequivocal on this point: "Justice is the end of government. It is the end of civil society."[5] Justice, of course, is a slippery concept, notoriously difficult to define. For the Founders, however, it did not mean merely the prevention of mutual harm (by force or fraud) and the enforcement of contracts. At the very least, it also included the more ambitious idea of *equal access to the law,* a norm incompatible with many ostensibly "contractual" relations (e.g., those involving indentured servitude). Etymologically, "privileges" referred to "private laws." The abolition of privileges, too, meant that the private must be sacrificed to the public and (as a matter of principle) special access should yield to equal access. The Sixth Amendment to the U.S. Constitution is a useful symbol of this positive dimension of modern liberty. Trial by jury cannot plausibly be conceived as withdrawal into a nonpolitical sphere, but only as a (universally available) opportunity to exploit the resources of public institutions.

A PUBLIC RATIONALE FOR PRIVATE PROPERTY

But what about the sacredness of private property? Does it not suggest, contrary to the line of argument I have been pursuing, that an unregulated private sphere was highly valued by the intellectual precursors of the American framers? Not exactly.

Despite the rhetoric of "natural rights," property rights against the state were granted only conditionally: Private individuals, for example, were barred from building armed fortresses on their land.[6] Spheres protected *from* government were simultaneously regulated *by* government. As campaigns against excessive taxation and the quartering of soldiers in private homes demonstrate, the "inviolability" of private property was associated with resistance to oppression. But even the most vehement enemies of confiscatory authority recognized that *property was a source of power* as well as an instrument of freedom: "Where the riches are in a few hands, these must enjoy all the power."[7] It is inconceivable that eighteenth-century writers could have overlooked the threat to liberty and justice posed by massive accumulations of wealth, because political power had only recently begun to be separated in any degree from ownership of land.

According to Locke, a person's exclusive property rights are valid only "where there is enough and as good left in common for others."[8] Your right to deny others access to your property is rescinded in case of dire necessity. In other words, Locke explicitly and unmistakably advocated a universal entitlement to welfare.[9] True, by advertising its "presocial" origin, Locke made private property seem almost untouchable. But his rhetoric here was merely a sensible adaptation to contemporary political struggles. Kings, popes, and other potentates frequently invoked the divine origins of their authority. Countersacralization was a plausible response. Locke focused on the "presocial" origins of property in order to outbid the presocial credentials of confiscation-prone divine right rulers: one you-can't-touch-me ideology deserved and provoked another. To this extent, his position was essentially wedded to the theological premises of seventeenth-century political debate.[10]

By the eighteenth century, apologists for political authority had ceased to insist on the government's presocial origin and were content to justify its rule by appeal to the public interest. Theorists who *opposed* authority in the name of property naturally followed suit. Both Hume and Montesquieu, for example, justified private property in a consequentialist fashion, by reference to the advantages of the institution for the community as a whole.[11] Contrary to Locke's fanciful "labor theory" of initial appropriation, *private property was understood as a monopoly granted by the government for the sake of the public interest.*[12] Public security and "the common wealth" could be maximized only on the basis of a legally enforced system of private ownership.

Madison echoed these public rationales for private property in *Federalist* 10 and 51. Debt cancellation was unjust, of course, because it allowed present debtors to deprive future potential-debtors of the chance to receive favorable loans. But Madison's essential argument against submitting property to majority control was that such an arrangement would produce a climate of hysteria and mutual fear incompatible with the proper functioning and even endurance of a republican regime. Civil war and an eventual relapse into royalism were the predictable consequences of abolishing legal barriers against uncompensated confiscation.

Madison did not endorse property rights solely because of their contribution to the stability of popular government. I am speaking here of a partial justification only. But he *did* partly justify private property by invoking its democracy-reinforcing consequences.[13] As a result, when the unregulated exercise of property rights obviously subverts democratic processes, proponents of regulation can plausibly adduce some of the same principles Madison originally used when defending private property itself.

Harold Laski argued that advocates of private rights accepted regulation and, of course, taxation of property only because they believed such "meddling" indirectly helped increase profits and stabilize markets.[14] One piece of evidence suggesting that Montesquieu, for example, valued political arrangements only when they subserved economic interests is his advocacy of the restricted suffrage. How can we explain his defense of a property qualification for voting unless we assume that he wanted to keep power in the hands of the wealthy and to defend their property against the hungry and dispossessed? The best answer to this question comes from Montesquieu himself: The propertyless should not be given the franchise because, if they were, they would not hesitate to sell their vote for a solid meal.[15] In other words, the restricted suffrage was justified because money is power, and *a republic must restrict the buying power of money* in order to guarantee the principle of majority rule.[16] In changed circumstances, needless to say, this same rationale might be invoked to justify significant government regulation of the private sector – including, for example, the press.

INHIBITING EFFECTS OF PRESS FREEDOM

Immanuel Kant celebrated what he abstrusely called "the transcendental principle of publicness" by opposing it to the "secretive system of politics."[17] In praising open at the expense of closed politics, he was faithfully echoing numerous predecessors and contemporaries. Enlightenment theorists in general tended to contrast *publicity* with the obscurantism of priests, the intrigues of courtiers, and the secret cruelties of tyrants, petty or enthroned. Wide-open, visible, and criticizable rule was widely seen as the enviable alternative to "a back-stairs influence and clandestine government."[18] Sunlight, as Brandeis later noted, is the best disinfectant. Exposure to the light of day was extraordinarily effective for flushing out corruption and revealing abuses of office. Compelled to expose their activities to public scrutiny, political figures are more reluctant to swindle and steal. With the same idea in mind, Montesquieu mounted a searing attack on secret accusations, unsigned denunciations of fellow courtiers delivered by stealth to the king.[19] Here again, *publicity* was advocated as a cure for abuses of power. Accusations that were made publicly allowed the accused a civilized chance for explanation and rebuttal.

Cleansing, inhibiting, and abuse-preventing functions were also assigned to freedom of speech and of the press. As Cato poetically wrote: "Liberty of Speech . . . drags [guilt] out of its lurking Holes, and exposes its Deformity and Horror to Day-light."[20] Montesquieu, too, welcomed "political newspapers" on these grounds, optimistically asserting that sinister conspiracies had become almost impossible due to the combined effect of the postal service and the press.[21] Mme de Staël, a European theorist of the Founders' generation, was merely echoing the common view when she described freedom of the press as "the right on which all other rights depend."[22] How could the right to a jury trial be effectively guaranteed, for example, if violations of that right were never publicized?

Hume laid particular emphasis on the intimate connection between distrust of government and freedom of the press. England tolerated more liberty of the press than any other European nation because the English regime was based on "mutual watchfulness and jealousy."[23] A tyrant is most successful when, in divide-and-rule fashion, he can prevent his subjects from communicating effectively with one another. Independently operated newspapers paralyze a potential oppressor because they make disgruntled citizens aware of each other's disgruntlement and of their collective strength. As an open channel of communication, a free press can coordinate popular resistance:

> Arbitrary power would steal in upon us, were we not careful to prevent its progress, and were there not an easy method of conveying the alarm from one end of the kingdom to the other. The spirit of the people must frequently be rouzed, in order to curb the ambition of the court; and the dread of rouzing this spirit must be employed to prevent that ambition. Nothing so effectual to this purpose as the liberty of the press, by which all the learning, wit, and genius of the nation may be employed on the side of freedom, and everyone be animated to its defense.[24]

The prohibitive effects of a free press explain its close association with free government. By threatening to bugle awake a drowsy public, newspapers can *curb* the ambition of rulers and *prevent* the worst excesses of arbitrary power. But freedom of the press was also viewed in a more positive light, as a stimulant rather than merely a depressant.

THE PUBLIC-DEBATE RATIONALE FOR PRESS FREEDOM

Underlying a more positive evaluation of press freedom was the historically astonishing[25] principle that *public disagreement is a creative force.* Those who quarreled with the authorities were not merely adjunct "checks and balances," supplementary dikes raised against oppression. Rather, they nourished the government with counterarguments, unsettling information, novel suggestions, and fresh perspectives, even while highlighting inconsistencies and unnoticed side effects of current policy.

Publicity, in other words, was not merely a paralyzing spotlight. It was also an arena for give-and-take, for mutual criticism and mutual stimulation, for acquiring new ideas and advancing proposals for reform. This notion, which eventually became the leading rationale for press freedom, was originally introduced to explain the superiority of parliamentary over monarchical rule. Autocratic governments are typically misserved by their own hirelings who, in private council, embroider facts with flattery and thereby unintentionally weaken the regime. An uncriticizable ruler hears only one side of the story and never learns about serious problems until they have gotten out of hand. Issuing commands and expecting its citizens silently to obey, a closed and repressive regime deprives itself of a powerful resource locked within its own citizens. Such a state is self-impoverishing. Even an unwavering advocate of absolute monarchy, such as Jean Bodin, could appreciate the many uses of open debate in a public assembly.[26] By the eighteenth century, the self-defeating nature of censorial government and the political benefits resulting from an unimpeded flow of information were widely recognized.[27] According to Hume, for example, a free press strengthens the government by making magistrates aware of "murmers or secret discontents" before they become unmanageable.[28] Kant agreed: "To try to deny the citizen this freedom [i.e., "the *freedom of the pen*"] means withholding from the ruler all the knowledge of those matters which, if he knew about them, he would himself rectify, so that he is thereby put in a self-stultifying position."[29] Much earlier, Milton had actually defined "civil liberty" as the capacity of government, on the basis of a free press, to correct its own mistakes.[30] If policies are set publicly and public criticism is encouraged, a government can avoid self-contradictory legislation, nip crises in the bud, and remedy its own blunders.

For this reason, the central institution of representative government became the opposition. As one close observer of British politics wrote in the 1760s: "Opposition is of use in this country whether upon good or bad motives."[31] Lack of moral virtue and noble intentions does not detract from the regime-stabilizing effects of vocal political opposition to the ruling clique. Locke had drawn attention at the close of the seventeenth century to the advantages of making political decisions in an atmosphere of public disagreement: When legislators hear "all sides" on a controversial question, they are more likely to make an intelligent decision. We elect our deputies so that they may "freely act and advise, as the necessity of the Commonwealth, and the Publick good should, upon examination, and mature debate, be judged to require. This, those who give their Votes before they hear the Debate, and have weighed the Reasons on all sides, are not capable of doing."[32] Good political advice requires the advisers to hear all sides of a question. In other words, rationality depends on exposure to a *multiplicity of voices*. Elected representatives are particularly well placed to benefit from the clash of rival views.[33]

At the beginning of the nineteenth century, Mme de Staël discovered the same utility in an oppositional press. She claimed, first of all, that "political newspapers began at the same time as representative government; and such a government is inseparable from them."[34] The connections between political journalism and popular government in a large country were numerous. For one thing, the press served as a transmission belt, conveying information across great distances, connecting citizens with each other and with their representatives. Furthermore, no citizen would bother to read daily accounts of political affairs unless he considered these affairs to be in some way his own. Under the Constituent Assembly, she continued, journalistic freedom caused serious problems: "But if, to maintain its power, [the government] had gagged its adversaries and granted freedom of the press to its friends alone, representative government would have been destroyed."[35] Censorship destroys representative government because the voting public will never have confidence in a regime that refuses to expose itself to criticism.

Throughout the Enlightenment, however, the clinching argument for press freedom was that public disagreement sharpens the minds of all parties, producing decisions that are much more intelligent than any proposals presented at the outset. The optimistic notion that truth will always defeat falsehood in open combat was originally invoked against censorship in the seventeenth century.[36] By the eighteenth century, the truth-generating capacity of uncensored debate had become a standard rationale for freedom of the press: "If we should be sure of the truth of our opinions, we should make them public. It is by the touchstone of contradiction that we must prove them. The press should therefore be free."[37] Despite extreme bitterness toward his critics, Jefferson agreed that, of all the instruments useful for discovering the truth, the "most effectual hitherto found, is freedom of the press."[38] As is well known, this very argument resurfaced in Mill's fallibilistic doctrine that the only foundation we have for our beliefs is a standing invitation to the whole world to refute them.[39] Such an epistemological principle rules out, among other things, any restraint on criticisms that journalists might make of those in power. As these passages show, Milton, Locke, Trenchard and Gordon, Helvétius, Jefferson,[40] and (later) Mill all advanced an "instrumental" justification of freedom of speech and the press, appealing to its overall social utility. In other words, the public-debate rationale for freedom of the press, associated with the names of Holmes and Brandeis and later popularized by Alexander Meiklejohn,[41] was a commonplace at the time of the Founding.

Democracy, as we understand it today, is not simply a matter of majority rule. Democratic procedures supplement majoritarianism with constitutional restraints that, in turn, oblige majorities to submit their decisions to ongoing criticism. Not any "will," but only a will formed in uncensored public discussion, is (and should be) granted sovereign authority.[42] The First Amendment, one might say, ensures that the electoral majority will remain a majority capable of learning. Stated differently, a legally guaranteed right of opposition provides an essential precondition for the formation of a democratic public opinion. Popular sovereignty is meaningless without rules organizing and protecting disagreement: Consent confers no authority unless the possibility of unpunished dissent is institutionally guaranteed. Indeed, unanimity on political questions may be a sign of irrationality rather than of rational agreement. As Mill wrote, "unity of opinion, unless resulting from the fullest and freest comparison of opposite opinions, is not desirable."[43] For the sake of collective rationality, "a perpetual and standing Opposition" must be kept up.[44] This way of thinking implies that *the government has an affirmative obligation to protect and even encourage the expression of rival views.* In the absence of public disagreement, of a civil kind, policies are likely to be unintelligent as well as badly skewed toward private interests.

The "collision"[45] or "jarring"[46] of ideas yields suggestions no one would have dreamed of in isolation. But the perceived legitimacy of public disagreement also serves to enlist the creative energies and decentralized intelligence of citizens in solving common problems. This, at any rate, is the basic idea underlying the Holmesian metaphor of a free trade in ideas.[47] Like an economic market, a nationwide network of public debate can mobilize resources that would otherwise lie dormant (e.g., minds working at one-half capacity), but which can be stimulated into use and thereafter contribute to making government policy more intelligent and government policymakers more aware of alternatives and disturbing side effects. As Hume noted in the passage already cited, a free press can rouse "all the learning, wit, and genius of the nation."[48] Such human resources will presumably improve the performance of government, not merely intimidate ruling elites back onto the narrow paths of legality.

One might, in fact, distinguish *three* functions of the free market of ideas: An independent and uncensored press can help (1) provide an incentive for citizens to develop new ideas, (2) mobilize preexistent ideas and bring them to public attention, and (3) improve all ideas through a process of mutual criticism. The market analogy is not fully satisfying, however. For one thing, competition among firms is justified by the satisfaction of consumer demand. Competition among would-be policymakers, by contrast, is justified by the education of speakers and listeners in the practice of democratic government and by the expectation that public learning will occur so that collective decisions will be *better* (more intelligent, better informed) than decisions made without benefit of debate.

In any case, the public-debate rationale for freedom of the press makes no reference to property rights, personal autonomy, or the right of self-expression. A multiplicity of voices and an open clash of views are said to serve a public purpose. Freedom of the press, according to this powerful tradition, is justified by its beneficial effects on the quality of collective decisions. As is well known, however, the public-debate rationale leaves an important question unanswered: What if an improvement of collective decision making through exposure to a diversity of views could be achieved only by imposing some sort of regulative regime on the press?

COUNTERWEIGHTS AND CHILLING EFFECTS

Publicity is not as innocent as the preceding section has made it sound. The semantic career of the word itself drives this point home: *Publicity* can poison the air as well as cleanse it. Even the most radical thinkers in early modern Europe had conceded that some "affairs of state cannot be communicated publicly without danger to the common interest."[49] The need to protect national security is not the only case in point. The publicity of parliamentary debates, for example, while often creative, can also foster playing to the gallery. In representative systems, politicians are confronted with their mistakes in the presence of their enemies, not exactly an environment congenial to learning. Hobbes, perhaps the most brilliant opponent of public government, pressed these considerations with unrivaled force. Publicity, far from ensuring rationality, is a display case for human vanity and an arena for envy and resentment. Public debate is very much like public dueling: "a trial of a little vain glory."[50] Kings should receive advice in private, because public speech is necessarily infected by the fear of displeasing others and the desire to stir the passions of one's listeners.[51] Public discussion is additionally dangerous because the humiliation of public defeat gives losers a powerful incentive to undermine the policy that, against their well-publicized advice, is now being implemented.[52] Such doubts about the connection between publicity and rationality, far from being "refuted," left a significant trace on American constitutional thought. It does not seem at all strange that a "rule of secrecy" was imposed at the Federal Convention in 1787. Still today, in the same spirit, the press may be excluded from certain pretrial hearings and, of course, jury deliberations are carefully withdrawn from the distorting light of publicity.

When ideas are tested in public, moreover, truth may *not* necessarily prevail over error. Why shouldn't the free market of ideas display the same defects as the commodity market? People sometimes buy a product less for its intrinsic merits than, on a conformist impulse, because a neighbor had already purchased one. Ideas, too, are frequently diffused by osmosis, imitation, contagion, or "group think." But if the hopes of Milton, Trenchard and Gordon, Jefferson, and Mill were exaggerated, they were not therefore without a realistic core. Even if publicity does not guarantee the triumph of truth, it may still be the best means known for correcting mistakes and discovering untried solutions. On the other hand, the lack of an attractive alternative to publicity does not imply that publicity must remain completely immune to regulation.

The sometimes poisonous character of publicity is nowhere more manifest than in cases of defamation. In the common law that British settlers brought to America, libel was a criminal as well as a civil offense, an injury against the public, not merely against the defamed individual. Because insults, even if true, predictably ignited a yearning for violent revenge, libel was originally considered a conspiracy to break the public peace.[53] Unfortunately, criminal penalties for defamation allowed public officials to allege sedition and use the courts to punish their critics. Eighteenth-century predecessors of the American Founders expressed grave doubts about the common law of libels for this reason.[54] Unfortunately, it is impossible both to protect innocent reputations and to expose the powerful to effective criticism. In this case, too, the private good has to be sacrificed to the public: "It is certainly of much less Consequence to Mankind, that an innocent Man should be aspersed, than that all Men should be enslaved."[55]

Accountable government is impossible if authorities can terrorize the press into meekness by threatening indictment for seditious libel. That was Madison's inspiring response to the Sedition Act of 1798.[56] Freedom of the press is "the only effectual guardian of every other right."[57] But it is also an essential instrument of self-rule, providing voters with indispensable information about candidates and issues. Indispensable to any republican government, press freedom cannot be secured, as Blackstone claimed, by the mere abolition of prior restraint. The anticipation of future punishment will curtail bold criticism of public officials as surely as the detested system of licensing. Critics *intend* to bring abusive rulers into disrepute. Punishing this intention will thus destroy "the right of freely discussing public characters and measures."[58] The free expression protected by the First Amendment requires immunity from subsequent prosecution for all critics of the performance of public officials; a republican system has no place for laws punishing defamation of the government.[59]

Madison, too, justified press freedom instrumentally, by invoking its contribution to creating an informed electorate. The belief that defamation of public officials deserved First Amendment protection resurfaced spectacularly in the unanimous Supreme Court ruling in *New York Times v. Sullivan*,[60] which made it next to impossible for public officials to collect damages for false statements about their official conduct. According to the *Sullivan* Court, the "central core" of the First Amendment was the protection it afforded critics of the governmental acts of public officials. In throwing constitutional protection around newspapers engaged in good-faith criticisms of public officials, the Court drew a striking analogy between federal officeholders and the press.[61] In order to ensure vigorous prosecution of public business, federal officials are granted immunity from libel actions for statements made pursuing their duty.[62] The press, or so the Court argued, should be given the same immunity for the same reason.[63] This private press–public official analogy is elaborated with some eloquence, leaving the impression that an adversary journalist *is* a public official or that the media should be considered an unofficial "fourth branch" of the American government. Freedom of the press, on this understanding, protects not a private right but, rather, a public function.[64]

Amazingly enough, several eighteenth-century writers drew opposite conclusions from the same premises. Writing in a period of intense political turmoil fueled partly by incendiary journalism, Mme de Staël argued that newspapers, while "the greatest means to counter oppression and propagate enlightenment," should be regulated precisely because the daily press is a "public" not a "private"' institution.[65] In a hilarious spoof of 1789, Benjamin Franklin had made the same point. Because the press is a *public power* similar to the three branches of government, it should be shackled with serious legal restrictions. What concerned Franklin, of course, was not criticism of public officials but, rather, the capacity of false accusations to ruin the reputation of private individuals for life. His assumption, common at the time, was that readers are basically malicious and that, as a consequence, scandalous rumors will travel quickly and be remembered clearly while boring retractions, however true, will soon slip from the public mind.[66] Against an anarchical freedom of the press, Franklin appeals to the liberal principles of publicity and the rule of law. Before "the court of the press," he says, there are no laws.

> The accused is allowed no grand jury to judge of the truth of the accusation before it is publicly made, nor is the name of the accuser made known to him, nor has he an opportunity of confronting the witnesses against him, for they are kept in the dark as in the Spanish court of Inquisition.[67]

If Montesquieu invoked the principle of publicity against the ancient abuse of secret denunciations, Franklin, in turn, attacked the press for *its* use of anonymous accusations. A beneficial publicity was not guaranteed by the freedom to publish: It also required identifiable (i.e., accountable) speakers and an opportunity for rebuttal. The unrestricted freedom of the press is actually the unreviewable power of the press, the arbitrary power of an unelected minority to inflict harms free from any rule or regulation. Anyone who proposes civilizing constraints on the press, however, not only has his face blackened by printer's ink but is also accused of being an enemy of liberty.[68] This state of affairs provoked Franklin to reply that, if the press wants to exist free of all rule, that is, in an anarchical state of nature, citizens are justified in reclaiming their presocial rights:

> My proposal then is to leave the liberty of the press untouched, to be exercised in its full extent, force, and vigor; but to permit the *liberty of the cudgel* to go with it *pari passu*. Thus, my fellow citizens, if an impudent writer attacks your reputation, dearer to you perhaps than your life, and puts his name to the charge, you may go to him as openly and break his head.[69]

Despite its obvious frivolity, this passage contains a serious point. Liberty is not identical to a ruleless state of individual license. The disciplining of speech through tort law has never implied the extinction of freedom. For all its immunity to political censorship, the press cannot pretend to a liberty from all the obligations of mutual self-restraint imposed by the social contract. If it isn't willing to grant defamed citizens the right of the cudgel, Franklin concludes, the legislature ought to consider imposing enforceable regulations on the press.

The continuing debate about libel law helps us focus attention on a dilemma bedeviling all regulation of the media. The freedom of the press is also the power of the press, including the power to harm. Any institution strong enough to act as an effective counterweight to government is also strong enough to inflict serious damage on innocent bystanders. Those harmed by private power wielders naturally turn to government for remedy; for instance, defamed parties inevitably ask the courts for compensatory damages. The common law of libel has traditionally aimed at balancing the speaker's interest in freedom with the interests protected by rules inhibiting communication. Unfortunately, this is a very unstable balance. Above all, there is no way to *check* the power of the press without exerting a *chilling effect* on the press's vigorous pursuit of its investigatory and reportorial missions. Some journalistic negligence deserves to be chilled. But how can this reasonable goal be achieved without overprotecting malefactors, private as well as public, from their most annoying critics?[70]

PRIVATE MONEY AND DEMOCRACY

Money talks. Noticing the recent proliferation of business-financed think tanks, one journalist added: Money thinks. The disproportionate influence of the wealthy on public policy, in any case, seems incompatible with majority rule. But the strong democratic reasons for public regulation of wealth-based speech are balanced by strong democratic reasons against. Gagging the rich is both useful and destructive to representative government. This ambiguity is obviously relevant to the question of regulating the media, which are – after all – owned by the rich. Before turning directly to access regulation, however, it will be useful to examine the imaginative balance between competing constitutional claims struck in *Buckley v. Valeo*.[71] This decision clarifies the problem that inevitably emerges whenever the state attempts to contain the abusable power of those private entities that may, in turn, challenge the authority of public officials.

Upholding part of the Federal Election Campaign Act (1971, amended 1974), the *Buckley* Court overturned several of the act's key provisions. While sustaining the limits that Congress had placed on "contributions" to candidates and campaigns, the majority struck down the limits placed on "expenditures." (If you simply write a thousand-dollar check and give it to a candidate's campaign manager, you are making a contribution; if you take out a newspaper advertisement in his favor without consulting his staff, you are making an expenditure.) Before the *per curiam* decision is analyzed a word should be said about the dissents of Burger and White. Both argued emphatically that the distinction between contributions and expenditures is fuzzy, arbitrary, and ultimately untenable. As White asked: What sense does it make to limit how much I spend with a candidate's approval, while refusing to limit how much I spend on his behalf?[72] Burger agreed, saying – and what he meant will be explained shortly – that contributions and expenditures are two sides of the same First Amendment coin.[73] But although Burger and White agreed on the untenableness of the distinction on which the majority of the Court built its case, they disagreed about almost everything else.

Principally at stake in *Buckley,* according to Burger, was the First Amendment. Money may not *be* speech; but it certainly helps communicate ideas. In a large industrial society, effective political speech can be enormously costly. In effect, to regulate money is to regulate speech. To prevent contributions is also to interfere with freedom of association (crucial for those wishing to advocate unpopular or controversial views). Burger therefore argued that the act was a serious threat to democracy because it allowed Congress to restrict First Amendment rights in the electoral process where the public has its only chance to consider the issues and get to know the candidates. As Brennan had argued earlier, the Constitution was designed to protect the "unfettered interchange of ideas for bringing about social and political changes desired by the people."[74] The act obstructed this interchange. Thus, Burger wanted *both* contribution and expenditure limitations overturned.

White, by contrast, wanted *both* limitations upheld. At issue in *Buckley,* in his view, was corruption. Money is used principally not to communicate ideas but, rather, to purchase influence. If a candidate is elected with massive financial backing from a few rich individuals, he will necessarily favor their views and interests over the views and interests of less forthcoming constituents. At the very least, massive contributions will buy cordial access to an elected official, providing opportunities for persuasion not available to the noncontributor. Congressmen did not believe that bribery and disclosure laws were adequate for preventing this sort of abuse. And who is in a better position to know what procures favors than they?

White was also concerned with the effect of the act on democratic government. If the public gets the idea that offices can be purchased, the moral basis of the representative system will be permanently eroded: "The evils of unlimited contributions are sufficiently threatening to warrant restrictions regardless of the limits on the contributor's opportunity for effective speech."[75] Thus, the state's interest in suppressing corruption (and even the appearance of corruption) is so great that the act should be allowed to stand without being subjected to strict scrutiny for possible violations of the First Amendment.

Essentially, the majority accepted both arguments, allowing them to modify each other. Although the dissents were manifestly one-sided, the *per curiam* opinion attempted to balance the conflicting claims they contained. The Court upheld the contribution limitation because it saw corruption as a real threat to democracy; and it invalidated the expenditure limitation because it saw the violation of First Amendment rights as an equally genuine menace. If I were asked to provide a rationale for the majority's decision, I would say this: The distinction between contributions and expenditures is admittedly shaky, but it allowed the Court to convey a double message, a message *almost adequate* to the complexity of the problems involved – that (1) the American system is hostile to the purchase of political favors and that (2) elected officials cannot be allowed to regulate political speech or its preconditions.

The Court's job would have been much easier if there had been two sorts of money: blue chits for buying influence and green chits for enabling citizens to communicate their views. But there is no such distinction – and no magic bullet capable of destroying the harmful uses of private money while leaving the beneficial uses untouched. It is not written on a dollar bill what you must use it for. The Court would have liked to draw a line between corruption, on the one hand, and financial backing for the communication of ideas, on the other. Because it could nowhere locate this phantom line, it chose a second best solution: the almost-real, much-easier-to-draw line between expenditures and contributions. *The drawable line symbolized the undrawable one.* By sustaining the act's contribution limitations, and overturning its expenditure limits, the Court conveyed its commitment to the complex (and to some extent inconsistent) pattern of values implicit in the Constitution.

Justice White also suggested that the regulation of campaign financing is partially analogous to antitrust law. Just as we can dissolve big monopolies to reestablish competition on the market, so we can break up monopolies in the political marketplace, restoring competition by limiting expenditures as well as contributions. The Court did not take this argument to be decisive because money, although useful for establishing monopolies, can also be useful for disrupting monopolies. More specifically, money may be the only resource capable of challenging the monopoly on public attention possessed by incumbents, famous public figures, newspaper owners, and so forth. Burger, too, recognized the importance of money as a trust buster that may, in certain circumstances, be more effective than government. How can we allow incumbents to structure campaign finance laws preventing challengers from using the one tool that might outweigh the advantages of office?

The Court also invalidated another provision of the act, one placing a ceiling on how much of his own money a candidate may spend during a campaign. Arguing to uphold the provision, White wrote that there is no constitutional right to purchase office, and that a cap on personal expenditures would also help avoid the impression that elections are "purely and simply a function of money."[76] The majority, in striking down this provision, said that Congress must make no law hindering individuals from advocating their views as vigorously as possible. It is completely foreign to the First Amendment to restrict the speech of some to enhance the relative voice of others. The First Amendment was designed, as Justice Black once wrote, to protect "the widest possible dissemination of information from diverse and antagonistic sources."[77] As *Red Lion* demonstrated, however, this same principle can be invoked to justify restricting the speech of some to enhance the voice of others.

The *Buckley* Court's most significant argument was this: to restrict personal spending would *not* neutralize disparities or equalize political influence. It would simply throw the advantage entirely to the side of elected officials, making them unchallengeable from the outside. Because incumbency, fame, and a telegenic personality are also unequally distributed sources of power, to limit money alone would not equalize or diffuse power but would, rather, concentrate it further still.

There are no purely defensive weapons. As our discussion of libel law suggested, any power strong enough to serve as an effective counterweight is also strong enough to need counterbalancing itself. The problem of regulating campaign contributions revolves around the same dilemma. On the one hand, if we try to protect the political process against overrepresentation of the rich, we end up giving an unfair advantage to incumbents (i.e., the incumbents are happy to give an advantage to themselves). On the other hand, if we make it possible for outsiders to challenge incumbents fairly, we expose the process to the dangers of unfair overrepresentation of the rich. If private wealth is placed completely beyond the scope of public control, democracy can quickly become discredited. But democracy can also be subverted if democratically elected officials are free to regulate the political use of private funds.

Buckley thus provides a very illuminating commentary on the central problem of our concern. Government intervention in the private sector is both necessary and dangerous because, for any democracy, private power is both dangerous and necessary. A variety of cases touching directly on press freedom also reveals the Court's awareness that effective counterweights can be serious abusers of power. On the one hand, the investigative press serves to inform citizens of military and intelligence activities and thereby exerts a "chilling effect" on illegality and corruption. On the other hand, there *are* some cases (even if we cannot trust the CIA to tell us which ones) in which freedom to publish can cause permanent harm to national security. Similarly, media presence at pretrial hearings set to discuss the suppression of illegally obtained evidence might prevent various forms of judicial impropriety; but it might also make a fair trial unlikely if not impossible. The Court has not been terribly consistent on either of these questions.[78] It is certainly easier to oscillate back and forth between obviously contrary principles than to strike a "delicate balance" between them. Indeed, the most outstanding example of splitting the difference, of refusing to choose between antithetical principles, occurs in the Court's decision to uphold access rights for the broadcast media while overturning almost identical arrangements for the printed press.

REEXITING THE STATE OF NATURE

Individuals cast into a state of nature do not celebrate their immunity from government interference. Indeed, anarchy produces a near-universal clamor for government involvement. Such was the predictable result, in the 1920s, of the "etheric bedlam" besetting the unregulated electromagnetic spectrum. In passing the Radio Act (1927) and the Communications Act (1934), Congress made laws abridging press freedom. Despite the Miltonian legacy enshrined in the Constitution, the legislature instituted a licensing system for broadcasters. By adhering to the letter of the First Amendment, however, Congress would have made all communication through the airwaves impossible – a consequence obviously irreconcilable with the framers' desire to maintain and enrich freedom of the press.

My right to speak is useless unless my speech can be heard. In the absence of regulation, a cacophony of voices would make all broadcasting inaudible. For this reason, the Federal Communications Commission[79] was welcomed as a traffic cop, able to allocate frequencies and help broadcasters avoid mutual disruption. State action of this interference-preventing sort is rarely considered illegitimate. In acting as a coordinator, the government is merely an instrument for the efficient achievement of private purposes. But even this minimal sort of intervention shatters the myth that the First Amendment is exclusively an obstacle to governmental censorship. Property rights do not merely set limits to state infringement; they also require, among other things, government enforcement of trespass laws. Analogously, the free speech and free press provisions do not merely limit the state; they also require affirmative state action aimed at securing the preconditions for effective freedom of expression.

As the Court recognized, however, the avoidance of anarchy was only a partial concern. The FCC was always more than a "traffic officer."[80] If the government's aim had been merely to prevent mutual interference, it could have allocated frequencies by lottery or to the highest bidder. Instead, it granted licenses on the basis of an explicit public interest standard. Declaring the spectrum to be an inalienable part of the public domain, Congress nevertheless refused to confer public-utility or common-carrier status on broadcasters. Instead, it established an administrative agency to award temporary and renewable broadcasting rights to some applicants and to withhold them from others, but only on the condition that each licensee agree "to share his frequency with others and to conduct himself as a proxy or fiduciary with obligations to present those views and voices which are representative of his community."[81] To prevent media potentates from single-handedly disqualifying an office seeker or skewing the political process by denying vital information to voters, various access rules were developed. Not only did broadcasters have to operate in the public interest and devote coverage to various sides of controversial issues; they were also required to provide access to candidates for political office.[82]

Government action, in other words, was not justified solely by the desirability of escaping from the "state of nature" of unregulated spectrum use. Regulation was meant to establish not mere order but, rather, a certain kind of order, maybe even a *just order.* At stake in public oversight of broadcasting was not merely efficient coordination but also some sort of moral norm: perhaps fairness,[83] but certainly an obligation to serve the public interest. Temporary monopolies granted to some had to be justified by benefits which accrued to all. In classical contractarian theory, individuals who became policemen could keep *their* weapons even after the all-transforming transition from the state of nature to civil society; but they could do so only on the condition that they would use these weapons to protect their fellow citizens. The implicit analogy here seems strained because it associates private broadcasters with public officials. But that is precisely the analogy drawn by the *Sullivan* Court. Moreover, a cost-free award of monopoly rights over a portion of the public domain gives at least minimal credibility to the comparison. Licensees are not public officials; but, as nonpaying recipients of administratively awarded spectrum rights, they *are* public trustees. As several commentators have argued, programming bound in some way to respect the public interest seems inevitable so long as we retain a nonmarket system for allocating the electromagnetic spectrum.[84] Trusteeship means that licensees must guarantee that excluded parties are not entirely excluded, that, at a minimum, everyone has a chance to hear rival groups express viewpoints free from the broadcaster's own one-sided and censorial regime. Variety for the onlookers compensates for exclusivity among the participants.

MEGAPHONES AND MONOPOLISTS

The hotly disputed *Red Lion* decision of 1969 upheld the constitutionality of various forms of broadcast regulation, including the mandatory provision of free reply time to those whose personal honesty or integrity was attacked during the discussion of controversial public issues. The Court's ruling was grounded on the premise that the First Amendment protects citizens not only from government but also from private monopolists and oppressors. In subsequent decisions, the Court seems to have denied this basic assumption, asserting flatly that "the First Amendment does not reach the acts of private parties."[85] Underlying the notion that rights restrict public authorities but not private monopolists is a bizarre historical theory articulated most succinctly by Justice Douglas: "The struggle for liberty has been a struggle against Government."[86] Freedom means only freedom *from* government, not at all freedom from private oppressors *by means of* government. As explained earlier in this essay, however, neither the great European theorists who influenced the American Founders nor the Founders themselves held this implausible view. They all knew that liberty would be wholly impossible without an effective state. The capacity of public officials to violate rights does not entail the incapacity of private power wielders to do the same.

The *Red Lion* Court was much more faithful to the intellectual origins and basic meaning of the Constitution than its many detractors have allowed. The Court argued, quite persuasively, that the broadcaster's right to freedom of speech "does not embrace a right to snuff out the free speech of others."[87] No licensee, it claimed, has a constitutional right "to monopolize a radio frequency to the exclusion of his fellow citizens."[88] Noting that the First Amendment provides no sanctuary for "private censorship,"[89] the Court summarized its case by citing the pivotal thesis of *Associated Press v. United States:* "Freedom of the press from governmental interference under the First Amendment does not sanction repression of that freedom by private interests."[90]

Trust-busting is a legitimate liberal goal because private power wielders can inflict terrible harms on individuals. Libel law has always restricted the freedom of the press (i.e., the power of private parties) for this reason alone. More significantly, private power can inflict damage on what can only be called "the commons," that is, on "public space." To make this point, the *Red Lion* Court resorted to the famous megaphone analogy:

> Just as the Government may limit the use of sound-amplifying equipment potentially so noisy that it drowns out civilized private speech, so may the Government limit the use of broadcast equipment. The right of free speech of a broadcaster, the user of a sound truck, or any other individual does not embrace a right to snuff out the free speech of others.[91]

According to *Buckley,* the government cannot restrict the speech of some to enhance the speech of others. By upholding contribution limitations, however, the *Buckley* Court did exactly that. The *Red Lion* Court's megaphone analogy clarifies the rationale for such an arrangement. One person's right of free speech must be limited by the coequal right of others to free speech, and not only in the context of political campaigns.

But the rationale for the Court's decision in *Red Lion* is not captured by the notion of reciprocally limiting private rights. It is not simply a question of balancing the rights of station owners with the rights of those excluded from expressing their views on the air. Indeed, the Court was quite clear that what overrode the right of broadcasters to complete editorial control was the right of the audience to hear conflicting views.[92] The First Amendment does not merely have the *negative* purpose of liberating individuals from government censorship. It also has the *positive* purpose of creating an informed public capable of self-government. As Madison argued, the liberal taboo on government censorship is based, among other things, on a desire to keep the citizenry well informed. But to accomplish this purpose, or so the Court alleged, the government had to prevent "private censorship" from prematurely narrowing the range of voices incorporated into public debate. Unrestricted "editorial autonomy for megaphonists" would obstruct the free flow of information and subvert the basic purpose of the First Amendment.

Note the unusual nature of the "right" that the Court here affirmed: "the right of the public to receive suitable access to social, political, esthetic, moral, and other ideas and experiences."[93] The FCC granted broadcasters a monopoly over a certain frequency in exchange for a public service, that is, coverage of public issues and a fair presentation of the various sides in significant debates. In this way, the broadcast media were legally required "to present representative community views on controversial issues."[94] At issue, in other words, is the access of listeners to information not the access of speakers to the microphone. Listeners and viewers are privileged because they constitute the public engaged, it is assumed, in an attempt at rational self-rule. Democratic decision making is attractive only when alternatives are canvassed and a chance for rebuttal is made available. The right of all citizens to exercise their rational capacities by participating in collective deliberation is meaningless unless individuals inhabit a public space where significant alternatives are open to consideration. As the *Red Lion* Court saw it, editorial autonomy must be limited to preserve the public's right to know and, thus, to form its opinions in a rational way, that is, to preserve its capacity for self-government.

Five years later, in *Miami Herald v. Tornillo*,[95] the Court struck down a Florida statute requiring newspapers to provide politicians, attacked in the course of an electoral campaign, with a free opportunity to reply. Apparently the First Amendment *did* create privileged monopolists able to deny people, even candidates for public office, freedom of expression. In a telegraphic ruling, the Court asserted that right-of-reply statutes inhibit robust debate. Two years earlier, upholding a law that required reporters to divulge confidential sources at grand jury proceedings, the Court had seemed relatively indifferent to the chilling effect of governmental controls on the press.[96] But *Miami Herald* introduced the chilling effect rationale into the heart of First Amendment jurisprudence. As is well known, no mention at all was made of *Red Lion*, leaving unclear the constitutionality, under the equal protection clause, of regulating the broadcast media but not the printed press.

The two-part doctrinal premise underlying *Miami Herald* was that (1) the First Amendment serves as a shield protecting editorial autonomy, and (2) that it affords no protection at all against private censorship. From a constitutional standpoint, obligatory speech is not very different from forbidden speech. Representing the majority, Burger suggested that editors have a First Amendment right to be unfair: "A responsible press is an undoubtedly desirable goal, but press responsibility is not mandated by the Constitution and like many other virtues it cannot be legislated."[97] That journalistic responsibility *can* be legislated is demonstrated by the persistence (however attenuated) of libel law. Nonetheless, the Court held that government agents cannot, on the basis of the public's right to a free flow of information, compel a news editor to publish an item he prefers to withhold. In concurring, White wrote:

> Of course, the press is not always accurate, or even responsible, and may not present full and fair debate on important public issues. But the balance struck by the First Amendment with respect to the press is that society must take the risk that occasionally debate on vital matters will not be comprehensive and that all viewpoints may not be expressed.[98]

The government and its agents merit distrust. As a result, "we have never thought the First Amendment permitted public officials to dictate to the press the contents of its news columns or the slant of its editorials."[99] To avoid the hassle associated with enforced access, newspapers would refrain from discussing the most important issues and individuals. Enforced access would penalize the press, inhibit criticism of government officials, and intrude on the function of editors. Referring to "the heavy hand of the government," White concluded that the very sort of interference with editorial autonomy he had ringingly endorsed in *Red Lion* is constitutionally disallowed.

According to Lee Bollinger, the juxtaposition of *Miami Herald* and *Red Lion* did not necessarily signal judicial incoherence, the murkiness of First Amendment law, or the Court's proclivity to mindless incrementalism. Instead, the Court was even more intelligent than it knew, striking "a delicate balance" between rival First Amendment values.[100] To paraphrase Bollinger's by-now famous claim: The Court would have liked to distinguish between the media as a democracy-reinforcing exercise of freedom and the media as a democracy-disabling exercise of power. But the unregulated media *simultaneously* foster and restrict the variety of debate. Although networks and newspaper chains are powerful business conglomerates restricting competition, they also continue to exercise important trust-busting powers (notably, they prevent the government from having a monopoly on information flow). As a result, the Court was placed in a dilemma. It again solved the problem poetically. The distinction it made between the electronic and print media was undoubtedly shaky. Although highly dubious in itself, the drawable line nevertheless symbolized the undrawable one. An implausible distinction allowed the Court to affirm two important constitutional principles: (1) the government deserves distrust, and (2) so do wielders of private power.[101]

SOME PROBLEMS OF ACCESS REGULATION

There are a number of troubling aspects to *Red Lion,* however, other than the unresolved conflict with *Miami Herald* (if we should still consider it unresolved). I will summarize these problems by way of a commentary on Judith Lichtenberg's interesting argument in favor of access regulation.[102] None of my criticisms entails the unconstitutionality of access regulation; but they do (I think) raise some important questions about its wisdom as policy.

The basic argument against Lichtenberg's position, which is attractive in many ways, is that she tends to underestimate the rationale for liberal mistrust of government. As a result, she seems to ask more of government than government is likely to give. Certainly the government cannot, as she sometimes suggests, guarantee the *realization* of First Amendment values. No regulatory commission, for example, can ensure an equally distributed capacity to communicate or guarantee that everyone will have something interesting to say, or that when people publicize their views, listeners will understand them. Moreover, it seems unlikely that FCC regulation will contribute toward making the media *more representative* than any branch of our government has ever been. Not even strict PR will guarantee the representation of all minority views in a national assembly.

At times, Lichtenberg suggests that an increase in government intervention will actually foster increased media independence from the government, that is, prevent the media from toeing the government line. But doesn't every regulation converting the media into a "neutral forum" lessen its capacity to act as a partisan gadfly, investigating and criticizing government in an aggressive way? Even a partial regulation scheme permits retaliation against newspapers: A criticized administration can threaten not to renew the license of a broadcasting station that is the property of the newspaper's owner.[103] Finally, how can personal-attack rules, requiring notification, provision of the offending manuscript, and arrangement for a reply avoid reducing the level of electoral coverage? Even when the FCC judges broadcasters on their overall performance rather than on a program-to-program basis, long-term monitoring is bound to have an inhibiting effect.

Lichtenberg correctly says that the press should be independent not only of government but also of the power of money. To blame the one-sidedness of press coverage on "money," however, is both ambiguous and incomplete. As she herself notes, the manipulation of the press by wealthy individuals is quite different from the decision by station managers to provide programming that viewers want (and that, therefore, advertisers will support). The liberal-constitutionalist tradition makes it clear that private power may be limited for public purposes. In the second case, however, media regulation does not seem constitutionally compelled. I find it hard to believe that broadcasters perceive "blandness" as a surefire technique for increasing their ratings. But if the majority of the American people want blandness, who empowers the government to shower them with raciness and pungency?[104] Moreover, media coverage of important issues may be one-sided even when money does not exert its distorting influence. Broadcasters may simply be too stupid, unimaginative, or ideologically rigid (for psychological not economic reasons) to get a firm handle on the full diversity of reasonable viewpoints. But government intervention to compensate for the dim-wittedness of reporters doesn't seem as consonant with liberal values as intervention to prevent the wealthy from drowning out the voices of the poor. Moreover, as Lichtenberg notes, "All news media favor the more articulate over the less articulate."[105] Life does this too, of course, as does (more pertinently) the town-meeting style of direct democracy. But can government actually compensate for disparities of credibility because of such extraneous factors as good looks and euphonious diction?

Lichtenberg's basic argument, if I've understood her correctly, is that there are no conflicting constitutional principles in the domain of media regulation.[106] There is only one value (i.e., fairness or diversity or the multiplicity of voices) and the dispute is merely about the best means for ensuring its realization. I prefer to say that there are two principles at stake here (distrust of government power and distrust of private power) and that the liberal-constitutionalist tradition compels us to strike some sort of balance between the two. But this is largely a verbal question, for these two principles could probably be redescribed as one.[107] More to the point: The rationale Lichtenberg invokes for access regulation does not actually mandate either fairness or diversity. What we want, after all, is not to have *all* views fairly presented or even to have a variety of views. For the democracy-enabling function of free speech to be achieved, the media must present a wide spectrum of *intelligent, informed, and thoughtful* views.[108] Lichtenberg recognizes this herself when she distinguishes, quite helpfully, between the informative, representative, and critical functions of the press.[109] The best critic may be wholly unrepresentative, even wholly unpopular.[110] Contrariwise, if my view is not "worth saying," should the press be compelled to print it on the grounds of fairness to me? To be sure, to say that the media should only be required to air "intelligent" viewpoints considerably weakens the case for access regulation. Unintelligent regulators may be able to impose somewhat mechanical standards such as diversity and fairness; but they surely cannot be trusted to decide which viewpoints are interesting or intelligent.[111]

Sometimes Lichtenberg accuses the media of being too representative (giving viewers what they want) and other times of not being representative enough (neglecting minority viewpoints). But the fundamental question may be, What sort of representative should the press be – a delegate or a trustee? If the media are delegates, their functions are fulfilled when they perform "constituency services," that is, when they speak out for their own special "electorates." But if the media are to be accountable trustees – which is what the term "fiduciary" implies – then must not editors be granted some independent right to decide which viewpoints are worth hearing?

BEYOND ACCESS REGULATION

If a government lists food prices in a conspicuous place outside a bazaar, sellers will be unable to profit unfairly (i.e., uncompetitively) from consumer myopia. Like other markets, the free market of ideas can be made more competitive by government intervention. The history of copyright law, not to mention tax-financed education, demonstrates that a prophylactic theory of the free press clause is inadequate. The First Amendment is not merely a shield against unwanted government intrusion. Even a minimal or nightwatchman state must play *an important positive role in facilitating communication,* that is, in increasing the productive power of intellectual exchange.

Markets do not simply give people what they want. Rather than merely satisfying preferences, sellers shape preferences. As a result, we cannot plausibly justify a market system by invoking (ostensibly independent) preferences which the market satisfies.[112] Because preferences today are shaped by all sorts of private powers (including, for example, the mass media), there is no good reason why the majority, through its elected representatives, should be constitutionally barred from exerting all preference-shaping influence. The extension of the franchise itself was originally justified as a technique for creating an interest in public affairs unknown among nonvoters. Politics is an acquired taste – acquired under the stimulus of legal reforms. Supply creates demand and opportunity emboldens people to cultivate their capacities. Even a small chance to influence political decisions provides an incentive to develop informed opinions and preferences for the first time. To help the population as a whole cultivate a taste for educated debate about political affairs, a majority might establish, say, tax-funded public libraries. On the theory that preferences are more rational if shaped in the presence of information about alternatives, a democratic state might use its authority to extend the number of worthwhile viewpoints to which its citizens are exposed.

In other words, both access regulation and the fairness doctrine are well within the spirit of the liberal political tradition inspiring the U.S. Constitution. Nevertheless, such controls on broadcasting can be, and have been, effectively criticized on practical grounds. Indeed, the most devastating argument against such regulations is that they exert an inhibiting effect on robust, wide-open debate, and especially on the unsparing criticism of public officials. If it actually *decreases* the variety of viewpoints to which the listening and viewing public is exposed, then the fairness doctrine is defeated by its own rationale.

Fortunately, the FCC has at its disposal less intrusive means to achieve the same desirable end. Cross-ownership rules, for one thing, do not involve the government in editorial functions; and the Sherman Act can be invoked to prevent group boycotts of controversial speakers. Moreover, Henry Geller's proposal of a spectrum fee, levied on the networks and used to subsidize public television, seems to be a much more effective technique for guaranteeing diversity than any form of content regulation. The idea of taxing spectrum users and using the proceeds to encourage alternative outlets freed from the demands of profit-making draws support from one of the most powerful defenders of free speech. Skeptical about state power, John Stuart Mill nevertheless advocated "the greatest possible centralization of information, and diffusion of it from the centre."[113] Mill deliberately employed the scare word "centralization" here to demonstrate that effective government intervention need not be intrusive. Indeed, he clearly distinguished his favored information-providing and alternative-creating functions of government from its coercive capacity to prohibit certain actions or to prescribe what is to be done and how to do it:

> There is another kind of intervention which is not authoritative: when a government, instead of issuing a command and enforcing it by penalties, adopts a course so seldom resorted to by governments, and of which such important use might be made, that of giving advice and promulgating information; or when, leaving individuals free to use their own means of pursuing any object of general interest, the government, not meddling with them, but not trusting the object solely to their care, establishes side by side with their arrangements, an agency of its own for a like purpose.[114]

The least drastic means for the FCC to guarantee diversity in broadcasting is to abandon all forms of content regulation and substantially to increase subsidies to public television and radio.[115] This was more or less the proposal favored by Thomas Emerson: Forget fairness and concentrate on providing more outlets.[116] Unfortunately, content regulation promotes self-censorship and issues in a net reduction of diversity. Fortunately, the demand for positive state action implicit in the free-press provision of the Constitution can be satisfied in other ways.

NOTES

1 "Une société ne sauroit subsister sans un gouvernement" (Montesquieu, "De l'esprit des lois," in *Oeuvres complètes,* vol. 2 [1, 3], p. 237).

2 David Hume, "Of the Original Contract," in *Essays: Moral, Political, and Literary* (Oxford: Oxford University Press, 1963), p. 453.

3 Herein, one might argue, lies the essential superiority of the Lockean and Montesquieuist over the Marxist tradition. Because of their one-sided distrust of the owners of the means of production, Marxists have tended to minimize the independent threat to freedom posed by the wielders of the means of destruction. Despite their intense concern with *political* tyranny, by contrast, heirs of Locke and Montesquieu cannot (if faithful to their intellectual ancestors) lose sight of extra-political or nonstate forms of oppression.

4 John Locke, *A Letter Concerning Toleration* (1689) (Indianapolis: Bobbs-Merrill, 1955), pp. 39, 56.

5 *The Federalist Papers,* no. 51 (New York: Mentor, 1961), p. 324.

6 J. A. W. Gunn, *Politics and the Public Interest in the Seventeenth Century* (London: Routledge & Kegan Paul, 1969), p. 304.

7 David Hume, "Of Commerce," in *Essays,* p. 271.

8 John Locke, *Two Treatises of Government* (New York: Mentor, 1965), p. 329 (2, 27).

9 Ibid., pp. 205–6 (1, 42).

10 It is thus anachronistic and obfuscatory to speak, for example, with Robert Nozick, of a sacred or inviolable or natural right to property in a society where government no longer boasts a divine sanction.

11 David Hume, *A Treatise of Human Nature* (Oxford: Clarendon Press, 1967), pp. 484–501; Montesquieu, "Lettres persanes," in *Oeuvres complètes,* vol. 1, p. 159 (letter 19); "De l'esprit des lois," ibid., vol. 2, p. 294.

12 Those who doubt that private property is a *government-granted monopoly* should ask the question, What would be the distribution of property in our society if there were no state? (One feasible answer is that the Mafia would have it all.)

13 A similar democratic rationale can be provided for the principle of nonentanglement between church and state: to privatize

emotionally charged religious questions is to prevent them from overloading the public agenda and crippling the community's capacity to resolve its other problems democratically.

14 Laski, *The Rise of Liberalism* (New York: Harper, 1936).

15 Montesquieu, "De l'esprit des lois," p. 400.

16 To put the eighteenth-century defense of the restricted suffrage in proper perspective, we should recall the medieval practice of *selling* the right to be represented as if it were "a piece of property" (Guido de Ruggiero, *The History of European Liberalism* [Boston: Beacon Press, 1959], p. 2). Classes that contributed to the king's coffers and war efforts were rewarded with a voice in the Estates General or the House of Lords or Commons. Modern voting rights, by contrast, are distributed universally, not bought or sold. The universality of political rights signals a crucial decision to restrict the power of money: not in practice but *in principle* (and principles constrain without dictating practice), money cannot buy political influence any more than it can buy religious salvation, for example, by purchasing indulgences. The restricted suffrage established a threshold for entrée into political life; but it did *not* involve any exchange, any purchase of the right to vote. It was a second-best solution, based (contrary to first appearances) on the principle that *access to the state is not for sale.*

17 Immanuel Kant, "Perpetual Peace" (1795), in *Kant's Political Writings*, ed. Hans Reiss (Cambridge: Cambridge University Press, 1970), pp. 126, 130.

18 Edmund Burke, "Thoughts on the Cause of the Present Discontents" (1770), in *Selected Writings and Speeches*, ed. Peter Stalis (Chicago: Regnery, 1963), p. 114.

19 Montesquieu, "De l'esprit des lois," pp. 452–3.

20 John Trenchard and Thomas Gordon, "Of Freedom of Speech: That the same is inseparable from Publick Liberty" (1720), in *Cato's Letters: Essays on Liberty, Civil and Religious, and Other Important Subjects* (New York: Da Capo, 1971), vol. 1, p. 98.

21 "Causes de la grandeur des Romains" (1734), in *Oeuvres complètes*, vol. 2, pp. 193–4.

22 Madame de Staël, *Considérations sur les principaux événements de la Révolution française* (Paris: Delaunay, 1818), vol. 1, p. 292; cf. Cato: "Liberty of Speech and Liberty of Writing . . . secures all

other Liberties" ("Discourse on Libels" [1722], in *Cato's Letters*, vol. 3, p. 294).

23 Hume, "Of the Liberty of the Press," in *Essays*, p. 10.

24 Ibid., 10–11.

25 Ostensibly the most "democratic" theorist of the eighteenth century, Rousseau denied that public disagreement could be politically creative just as ardently as any advocate of absolute monarchy.

26 "For where can things for the curing of the diseases of the sicke Commonweale, or for the amendment of the people, or for the establishing of lawes, or for the reforming of the Estate [i.e., the state], be better debated or handled, than before the prince in his Senat before the people? There they conferre of the affaires concerning the whole bodie of the Commonweale, and of the members thereof; there are heard and understood the just complaints & greevances of the poore subjects, which never otherwise come unto the princes eares; there are discovered and laid open the robberies and extortions committed in the princes name; whereof he knoweth nothing, there the requests of all degrees of men are heard." Jean Bodin, *The Six Bookes of a Commonweale* (1576) (Cambridge, Mass.: Harvard University Press, 1962), p. 184 (3, 7).

27 Significantly, the government-strengthening rationale for press freedom depends on a sharp distinction between public and private interests: An uncensored press can benefit the government as a whole while nevertheless doing permanent damage to the particular officeholders of the moment.

28 Hume, "Of the Liberty of the Press," p. 11.

29 Kant, "On the Common Saying: 'This May Be True in Theory, but It Does Not Apply in Practice,' " in *Kant's Political Writings*, p. 85.

30 John Milton, "Areopagitica (1644)," in *Complete Prose Works* (New Haven, Conn.: Yale University Press, 1959) vol. 2, p. 487.

31 Cited in John Brewer, *Party Ideology and Popular Politics at the Accession of George III* (Cambridge: Cambridge University Press, 1976), p. 75.

32 John Locke, *Two Treatises of Government*, pp. 461–2 (2, 222).

33 The classical distinction between delegate and trustee hinges precisely on this advantage of the legislative situation. Because a delegate is subject to immediate recall if he deviates

an iota from his explicit mandate, he is legally prevented from learning anything from his fellow deputies or exposing his views to their criticisms. A trustee is granted more leeway, and not because he is better or wiser by nature. What matters is that he is favorably placed for hearing all sides of an issue: "If he devotes himself to his duty, [a representative] has greater opportunities of correcting an original false judgment, than fall to the lot of most of his constituents" (J. S. Mill, "Considerations on Representative Government," in *Essays on Politics and Society* [Toronto: University of Toronto Press, 1977], p. 509). Ordinary voters are parochial and seldom exposed to the viewpoints of fellow citizens who live in distant places. Constituents owe some degree of deference to their representative not because of his noble character but because his colleagues are rewarded for proving him wrong and disclosing his follies.

34 Mme de Staël, *Considérations sur la Révolution française,* vol. 1, p. 292; Mill also wrote that "the newspaper press" made popular government in a large country possible for the first time (Mill, "Considerations on Representative Government," in *Essays on Politics and Society,* p. 378).

35 Mme de Staël, *Considérations sur la Révolution française,* vol. 1, p. 291.

36 "Let [Truth] and Falsehood grapple; who ever knew Truth put to the worse in a free and open encounter" (Milton, "Areopagitica," in *Complete Prose Works,* vol. 2, p. 561). Locke modestly echoes this claim, writing that "the truth would do well enough if she were once left to shift for herself" (Locke, *A Letter Concerning Toleration,* p. 45); Cato continued this tradition: "Truth has so many Advantages above Error, that she wants only to be shewn, to gain admiration and Esteem" ("Discourse Upon Libels," in *Cato's Letters,* vol. 3, pp. 298–9); Jefferson also concurred, somewhat more robustly: "Truth is great and will prevail if left to herself" (Thomas Jefferson, "A Bill for Establishing Religious Freedom" [1777], in *Writings,* ed. Merrill Peterson [New York: Library of America, 1984], p. 347).

37 Helvétius, *A Treatise on Man,* vol. 2 (sec. 9, chap. 12), p. 328.

38 Thomas Jefferson, letter of June 28, 1804, *Writings,* p. 1147.

39 Mill, "On Liberty," in *Essays on Politics and Society,* p. 232.

40 And Madison, too, as we shall see.

41 Alexander Meiklejohn, *Political Freedom* (New York: Harper, 1960).

42 Cf. A. D. Lindsay, *The Essentials of Democracy*, 2nd ed. (London: Oxford University Press, 1951).

43 "On Liberty," in *Essays on Politics and Society*, p. 260.

44 Mill, "Bentham," in *Essays on Ethics, Religion and Society*, ed. J. M. Robson (Toronto: University of Toronto Press, 1969), p. 108.

45 Mill, "On Liberty," in *Essays on Politics and Society*, p. 229.

46 Alexander Hamilton, "Federalist, No. 70," in *Federalist Papers*, p. 427.

47 *Abrams v. United States*, 250 U.S. 616, 630 (1919).

48 Hume also stressed the contribution of press freedom to public education: "It is to be hoped that men, being everyday more accustomed to the free discussion of public affairs, will improve in the judgment of them" (Hume, "Of the Liberty of the Press," p. 11).

49 Philippe du Plessis-Mornay, "Vindiciae contra tyrannos" (1579), in *Constitutionalism and Resistance in the Sixteenth Century*, ed. Julian Franklin (New York: Pegasus, 1969), p. 150.

50 *De Cive* (1642), in *Man and Citizen*, ed. Bernard Gert (New York: Doubleday, 1972), p. 230.

51 Furthermore, "the Passions of men, which asunder are moderate, as the heat of one brand; in Assembly are like many brands, that enflame one another, (especially when they blow one another with Orations) to the setting of the Commonwealth on fire, under pretence of Counselling it" (*Leviathan* [1651] [Oxford: Oxford University Press, 1965], Part 2, chap. 25, p. 309); conceding the partial truth of this Hobbesian argument for restricting public speech, Hume converted it into a roundabout justification for freedom of the press: "A man reads a book or pamphlet alone and cooly. There is none present from whom he can catch the passion by contagion" ("Of the Liberty of the Press," p. 11).

52 "When equal orators do combat with contrary opinions and speeches, the conquered hates the conqueror and all those that were of his side, as holding his council and wisdom in scorn, and studies all means to make the advice of his adversaries prejudicial to the state: for thus he hopes to see the glory taken from him, and restored unto himself" (*De Cive*, p. 231 [10, 12]).

53 William Blackstone, *Commentaries on the Laws of England* (1765–9) (Chicago: University of Chicago Press, 1979), vol. 4, p. 150.

54 "What are usually called Libels, undoubtedly keep Great Men in Awe, and are some Check upon their Behavior, by showing them the Deformity of their Actions, as well as warning other People to be on their Guard against Oppression" (Trenchard and Gordon, "Discourse upon Libels" [1722], in *Cato's Letters*, vol. 3, p. 292).

55 Ibid., p. 294.

56 James Madison, "Report on the Virginia Resolutions," in *Mind of the Founder*, ed. Marvin Meyers (Indianapolis: Bobbs-Merrill, 1973), pp. 328–42.

57 Ibid., p. 315.

58 Ibid., p. 340.

59 See Harry Kalven, Jr., "The New York Times Case: A Note on 'the Central Meaning of the First Amendment,' " reprinted in *Free Speech and Association*, ed. Philip Kurland (Chicago: University of Chicago Press, 1975).

60 376 U.S. 254 (1964).

61 376 U.S. 254, at 282 (Brennan, for the majority), and 304 (Goldberg, concurring in result).

62 *Barr v. Matteo*, 360 U.S. 564 (1959).

63 "It would give public servants an unjustified preference over the public they serve, if critics of official conduct did not have a fair equivalent of the immunity granted to the officials themselves" (376 U.S. 254, 283).

64 Cf. Potter Stewart, "Or of the Press," *Hastings Law Journal* 26 (January 1975): 631–7.

65 Mme de Staël, *Des circonstances actuelles qui peuvent terminer la Révolution et des principes qui doivent fonder la République en France* (1798) (Paris: Droz, 1979), p. 113; "faire un journal est un emploi public, tandis qu'écrire un livre n'est que l'exercice d'un droit consacré" (pp. 115–16).

66 To underline his belief that honest counterargument was not a sufficient remedy to slander because the truth will never catch up with a lie, Franklin quotes Dryden: "There is a lust in man no charm can tame, / Of loudly publishing his neighbor's shame. / On eagle's wings immortal scandals fly, / While virtuous actions are but born and die."

67 Benjamin Franklin, "An Account of the Supremest Court of

Judicature in Pennsylvania, viz., The Court of the Press" (1789), in *American Political Writing During the Founding Era*, ed. C. Hyneman and D. Lutz (Indianapolis: Liberty Classics, 1983), vol. 2, p. 708.

68 Ibid., p. 709.

69 Ibid., p. 710.

70 Making it difficult for public officials but easy for private citizens to bring libel suits is only a partial answer due to the Court's confusion about exactly who is a public figure.

71 424 U.S. 1 (1976).

72 424 U.S. 261–2.

73 424 U.S. 241.

74 *Roth v. United States*, 354 U.S. 476, 484 (1957).

75 424 U.S. 260.

76 424 U.S. 265. J. S. Mill had already posed the fundamental question here: "Of what avail is the most broadly popular representative system, if the electors do not care to choose the best member of parliament, but choose him who will spend most money to be elected?" ("Considerations on Representative Government," p. 389).

77 *Associated Press v. United States*, 326 U.S. 1, 20 (1945).

78 On the press's right to be present at criminal trials, compare *Gannett v. De Pasquale*, 443 U.S. 368 (1979) with *Richmond Newspapers v. Virginia*, 448 U.S. 555 (1980); on the press and national security, compare *New York Times v. United States*, 403 U.S. 713 (1971) with *Snepp v. United States*, 444 U.S. 507 (1980).

79 Originally the Federal Radio Commission.

80 *National Broadcasting v. United States*, 319 U.S. 190, 215–16 (1943).

81 395 U.S. 389.

82 Although candidates for federal office have affirmative access rights, candidates for local and state office are only guaranteed contingent access, in other words, equal opportunity must be made available to one candidate *if* it has already been made available to his rival.

83 Lee Bollinger ("Freedom of the Press and Public Access: Toward a Theory of Partial Regulation of the Mass Media," *Michigan Law Review* 75 [November 1976]), while noting the crucial distinction between overcoming anarchy and achieving fairness, argues persuasively that the physical necessity of order-imposing government regulation of the airwaves prepared

broadcasters psychologically for the more ambitious content regulation imposed by the fairness doctrine (p. 20).

84 Benno Schmidt, Jr., *Freedom of the Press vs Public Access* (New York: Praeger, 1976).

85 *Columbia Broadcasting System v. Democratic National Committee,* 412 U.S. 94, 119 (1973) (Burger, for the Court); also: "That 'Congress shall make no law . . . abridging the freedom of speech, or of the press' is a restraint on government action, not that of private persons" (412 U.S. 114).

86 *CBS v. DNC,* 412 U.S. 94, 162 (concurring in judgment).

87 395 U.S. 367, 387.

88 395 U.S. 389.

89 395 U.S. 392.

90 *Associated Press v. United States,* 326 U.S. 1, 20 (1945).

91 395 U.S. 387.

92 "It is the right of the viewers and listeners, not the right of the broadcasters, which is paramount" (395 U.S. 390).

93 395 U.S. 390.

94 395 U.S. 394.

95 418 U.S. 241 (1974).

96 *Branzburg v. Hayes,* 408 U.S. 665 (1972).

97 418 U.S. 256.

98 418 U.S. 260.

99 418 U.S. 261.

100 Bollinger, "Freedom of the Press and Public Access," p. 27.

101 In *Columbia Broadcasting System v. Democratic National Committee,* the Court agonized about whether or not the censorial behavior of the government-licensed media qualified as "state action" and should thus be forbidden under the First Amendment. This debate seems particularly sterile. For one thing, the enjoyment of any private right presupposes some form of state action (e.g., the preservation of public peace or the enforcement of trespass and contract law). The "taking" of property is constitutionally forbidden whether the "takers" are public officials or private thieves (does the eminent domain clause raise private theft to constitutional status?). What prevents us from saying, analogously, that the suppression of speech is regulable if done by either the government or the press?

102 Judith Lichtenberg, "Foundations and Limits of Freedom of the Press," this volume.

103 For this argument and other criticisms of Bollinger from a

"free market" perspective, see Matthew L. Spitzer, *Seven Dirty Words and Six Other Stories* (New Haven, Conn.: Yale University Press, 1986), pp. 43–66.

104 On the FCC ruling against blandness in political coverage, see *Columbia Broadcasting System v. Democratic National Committee,* 412 U.S. 94, 112 (1973).

105 Ibid., p. 10.

106 Ibid., p. 28.

107 All power (private or public) is likely to be abused and, as a consequence, should be distrusted.

108 Alexander Meiklejohn, *Political Freedom,* p. 26.

109 Lichtenberg, "Foundations," this volume.

110 Justice Brennan argued for the insufficiency of the fairness doctrine in precisely this manner: ". . . by definition, the Fairness Doctrine tends to perpetuate coverage of those 'views and voices' that are already established, while failing to provide for exposure of the public to those 'views and voices' that are novel, unorthodox, or unrepresentative of prevailing opinion" (*Columbia Broadcasting System v. Democratic National Committee,* 412 U.S. 94, 190, Brennan dissenting).

111 Jeremy Bentham defended press freedom not on a priori or doctrinal grounds but only after weighing costs and benefits: "The liberty of the press has its inconveniences; nevertheless, the evils which result from it are not to be compared to those of a censorship." Censorship will prevent the discovery and diffusion of important truths and thus impede "the whole progress of the human mind." But Bentham's basic argument against censorship was that the censors themselves will almost surely be "inferior men," too stupid to be entrusted with the task of deciding in secret what should and what should not be published (Bentham, "Principles of the Penal Code," *A Theory of Legislation* [Bombay: Tripathi, 1975], p. 228). For almost all writers in the liberal-constitutionalist tradition, in fact, the basic argument against government regulation of the press was *distrust* of government. Officials are often self-interested and even malicious. But a more important justification for "watchfulness and jealousy" is that agents of the state are usually short on brains.

112 On this point, see Cass Sunstein, "Legal Interference in Private Preferences," *University of Chicago Law Review* 53 (1986): 1129–74.

113 J. S. Mill, "On Liberty," in *Essays on Politics and Society,* p. 309.
114 J. S. Mill, *Principles of Political Economy,* 1848, vol. 2, p. 443.
115 According to Geller, broadcasters might be willing to accept a spectrum fee without protest if, in exchange, they were liberated from various forms of FCC oversight.
116 Thomas Emerson, *The System of Freedom of Expression* (New York: Random House, Vintage, 1971), p. 671.

Chapter 2

Liberalism and free speech

David Kelley and Roger Donway

The First Amendment says that Congress shall make no law abridging the freedom of speech or of the press. Our laws and courts take an expansive view of the liberty of the printed press. Its principal organs are in private hands, owned and operated as private property. No government agency evaluates their product as better or worse, as more or less "in the public interest." A long and honored national tradition, from the Founding Fathers to the present, declares that the printed press should not be regulated by government, outside a few narrowly drawn areas such as national security and obscenity.

But the electronic press enjoys no such protection. Governments at various levels own, license, or franchise the principal means of communication: radio, television, cable systems. The Federal Communications Commission (FCC) is charged with regulating all of these in the public interest, and many states and municipalities have a hand in the matter as well. The fundamental decisions of the Supreme Court have upheld the power of the government to engage in these activities. Indeed, the Court has held that the constitutional ban on abridging freedom of speech – which forbids regulation of newspapers or magazines – may actually require regulation for electronic media.

This double standard is anomalous in principle, and increasingly difficult to implement in practice, as the two forms of media coalesce. Major newspapers use electronic means to distribute copy to printing plants, and various promising electronic services, such as videotext and teletext, deliver information in a print format. Partly for these reasons, the recent trend has been toward deregulating the electronic media, extending to them more of the protections that print has enjoyed. The FCC has relaxed its license-renewal procedures and program guidelines for broadcasters, and repealed the fairness doctrine. Recent laws and court decisions have put limits on what cities can extract from cable companies and on how much they can interfere with programming.

This trend has been welcomed by most advocates of a free market economy, who believe, like their predecessors in the classical liberal tradition, that economic and intellectual freedom go hand in hand. Contemporary liberals, who advocate a much larger role for government in the economic realm, are divided. Some are wary of any government involvement in matters of speech, and support deregulation. Others oppose it, seeking to maintain the double standard, or even to move in the opposite direction, by extending government controls to the print media. Those in the latter group, unlike traditional advocates of media control, argue that the controls they have in mind actually enhance and protect the very values that have made freedom of speech a central tenet of liberalism.

This is the new case for regulation of the press, and it can be divided into three basic arguments. The argument from positive rights holds that speakers have certain rights of access to the media, and the public as audience has certain rights to receive information and other goods; it says that government must intervene to secure these rights. The teleological argument maintains that freedom of speech is not an end in itself but an instrument for achieving certain values such as truth and fairness, and that positive government action can sometimes achieve these values more effectively than noninterference. The argument from democracy holds that government regulation may be necessary to ensure that the media provide the kind of information and debate required for an informed electorate.

Our goal in this essay is to examine these arguments and

to show why they should be rejected. We will try to show why the proposals would be neither fair nor effective. Our argument throughout, however, rests on certain basic philosophical premises – as do the arguments we oppose. No conclusion about rights to freedom of speech and press can be supported without placing them within a systematic view of rights and government, and any systematic view in turn rests on assumptions about human nature and basic values. Because our own position is that of the classical liberals, as revived and amended by recent thinkers such as Ayn Rand and Friedrich von Hayek, this essay is largely a debate between classical and modern liberalism. Before we turn to the arguments themselves, therefore, we need to put these positions in historical perspective.

CLASSICAL AND MODERN LIBERALISM

The doctrine of freedom of speech and press embodied in the First Amendment was the product of the classical liberal political philosophy that emerged late in the seventeenth century. In defense of these freedoms, the classical liberals drew on various strands of political experience.

The Renaissance engendered an appreciation of individuality in thought and style, and an ever widening range of issues came to seem discretionary or debatable. The sanguinary religious wars of the sixteenth century convinced many that tolerating even fundamental differences in belief was preferable to endless strife. The new science and philosophy showed that positive benefits could be gained from challenging orthodoxy, and made martyrs of those executed, repressed, or "chilled" by the Inquisition and its ilk. The growing role of Parliament in Britain suggested that publicity and debate could be effective weapons against a power-hungry executive.

Such trends were evidence that intellectual and artistic activity flourishes only in a climate of freedom. Classical liberals incorporated this idea in the broader framework of natural rights theory. The theory, as formulated by Locke and adopted by classical liberals during the next century and a half, transformed the older tradition of natural law into a philosophy of individualism. The concept of rights reflected a view of individuals as independent agents. The "Law of Nature," said Locke, "teaches all Mankind, who will but consult it, that being all equal and independent, no one ought to harm another in his Life, Health, Liberty, or Possessions."[1]

This independence had two dimensions. Ethically, each individual is an end in himself; as Locke put it, we are not made for one another's uses.[2] The moral basis of rights is teleological, the ultimate value being the individual's life and happiness; the basic right is that of self-preservation. This value was regarded as common to all mankind, but not as collective in the later, utilitarian sense. The standard is the good of each, not the good of all. Hence there can be no moral justification for sacrificing one individual to another, or to the group. Ontologically, moreover, the individual acts primarily *as* an individual in pursuit of values. Human action is rational action, and reason is a faculty possessed and exercised in the state of nature, prior to social organization. All cooperative action, with all of its benefits, from the cumulative growth of knowledge to the division of labor in production, derives from the individual exercise of reason.

The individual, in short, is the unit of value and action. This does not imply that man is not a social animal, and none of the classical liberals denied it. But it does imply that social interaction must be voluntary; individuals must remain free to act on their judgment in pursuit of their values. The rights to life, liberty, property, and the pursuit of happiness are principles that protect this freedom. They are not conditioned on the individual's acceptance of any obligation beyond that of respecting the rights of others. The principles expressed by the concept of rights are true in virtue of human nature and the natural autonomy of the person; they are not the product of positive law or government grant. On the contrary, they define the purpose of government. The state is an instrument, a common agent whose function is to preserve the rights of individuals against depradation by each other, and it must not itself encroach on those rights.

Within this framework, the right to think, speak, and publish freely are important elements of the more general freedom to pursue one's ends by exercising one's reason. They play the same role in the intellectual sphere that the freedom to acquire and dispose of private property plays in material production. Without freedom of speech and press, wrote "Cato," there could be "neither Liberty, Property, true Religion, Arts, Sciences, Learning, or Knowledge."[3] Thus the primary rationale for insisting that government respect and preserve this freedom was the basic rationale for government: the protection of freedom in general.[4]

Of course, the classical liberals recognized that freedom of speech, especially in the form of freedom of the press, also had an important political role. A press that is free to publicize the actions of government can perform the *watchdog* function of protecting against the tendency of the state to aggrandize its power and abuse the rights of its citizens. It can also perform the *democratic* function of providing information to the electorate and fostering debate on the issues they would be voting on; in this respect, freedom of public discussion was an extension of earlier arguments for freedom of parliamentary debate.[5]

Of these two functions, the first was clearly the more important. The watchdog function is set by the end of government, the protection of liberty, and would be required no matter what form of government – democratic or otherwise – were chosen as a means to this end. As Martin Diamond observes, "for the founding generation [in America], it was liberty that was the comprehensive good, the end against which political things had to be measured; and democracy was only a form of government which . . . had to prove itself adequately instrumental to the securing of liberty."[6]

But both political functions derive from the primary function of allowing individuals to pursue knowledge and enlightenment in the manner required by their rational nature. It is because the basic role of government is to protect such liberty that we need a watchdog in the first place to guard against deviations from that role. Just as government is a limited and derivative phenomenon, an instrument allowing individuals to pursue the primary values and activities of life, so the political functions of freedom of speech and press were subordinate to the primary intellectual, religious, and aesthetic functions. In this respect, freedom of speech was like property or freedom of association, whose primary function was to enable individuals to pursue their private ends, but which also had the secondary virtue of serving as a check on government.

The classical liberals' conception of rights, as we noted, is inherently individualist. Rights protect the individual's freedom to act on the basis of reason, alone or in cooperation with others, in pursuit of his own life and happiness. Rights therefore have a teleological foundation. In making the protection of rights the end of government, however, they implicitly denied that the deeper values in which rights are grounded are collective values to be sought by society acting as a unit. This implication was not always stated, and perhaps not even grasped, very clearly by the liberals themselves. But it was clearly identified by their critics, including the utilitarians.[7]

John Stuart Mill's *On Liberty* is usually seen as continuous with classical liberal doctrine, and in one sense it is. Versions of the arguments for tolerance in Chapter 2 can be found in earlier works such as Jefferson's "Bill for Establishing Religious Freedom." But Mill rejected the framework of natural rights, replacing it with the standard of the greatest good for the greatest number.[8] His substitution of a collectivist for an individualist teleology marks the watershed between classical and modern liberalism. Because utilitarians abandoned the enlightened egoism of the classical liberals, they removed the fundamental basis for resisting government control over the individual. Because the ultimate standard was now the good of society, all values were potentially within the ambit of collective action, and it became a practical matter for the state whether to pursue a given value directly, through its coercive powers, or indirectly, by allowing individuals a measure of freedom.

In making this practical decision, the modern liberals relied on a distinction between an inner realm, comprising matters of belief, values, "life-style," family and other personal relationships; and an outer realm embracing economic activity and nonpersonal associations with others. In the outer realm, the early utilitarians believed that a market system, based on private property and freedom of contract, would best promote the general welfare. Their "policy" views were therefore similar to those of classical liberals, despite the change in basic principles. Over time, however, liberals came to advocate extensive government involvement in the economy: transfer payments, social insurance, control of money and banking, regulation of business and labor relations. In effect, they came to see the group rather than the individual as the unit of action.

This shift occurred for a number of reasons, four of which are worth mentioning here, as we will encounter them again in later sections. The first was a belief in the rationality and efficacy of collective action – the social use of intelligence, as John Dewey described it[9] – on the model of technological control over nature. The second was a shift from a negative to a positive conception of freedom. The negative liberty defended by classical liberals is the freedom to choose among a range of alternatives. It does not depend on what alternatives one has available, or how many there are; that is determined by one's abilities, the physical environment, and the willingness of others to engage in various transactions with one. Positive freedom, by contrast, is the freedom to succeed in exercising and developing one's capacities, and this does depend on the number and types of alternatives one has to choose from – opportunities that may have to be supplied by other people.

The third point was that interference with such freedom need not take the form of a positive act of compulsion. It could take the form of a failure to act, a failure to provide someone with the relevant opportunities. Employers who do not offer wages above a low level, bankers who do not make loans, the public at large when it refuses to make education, medical care, housing, and other goods available – all these may be accused of interference. From this standpoint, there is no essential difference between coercion and other forms of influence one person may exert on another, between political and economic power, nor between regulation or censorship by the state and the exercise of property rights by private owners. Fourth, and finally, owners cannot object if the state acts to achieve positive freedom by taking or regulating property, since property is social in origin: Wealth is a collective product, and title to it is granted and protected by the state.

These four principles lay behind the liberal crusade for government action in the outer realm. In the inner realm, however, liberals typically retained an individualist ontology. For reasons such as those given by Mill, they saw coercion as an ineffective and destructive instrument; matters of belief and personal happiness should be left to the individual. But even in the inner realm, the good of each is part of a social value, the good of all. As L. T. Hobhouse put it, "The limit to the value of coercion thus lies not in the restriction of social purpose, but in the conditions of personal life."[10]

This shift in basic premises has affected the liberal view of free speech. The benefits of freedom identified by the classical liberals – the discovery of truth, progress in the arts and sciences, the salutary moral effects of the free exercise of religion – have been transformed into social values, and freedom itself into a social instrument. This view is reflected in the leading free speech decisions of the U.S. Supreme Court, which has largely adopted the pragmatism of Holmes and Brandeis. As Benno Schmidt observes:

> Holmes and Brandeis sought to persuade their brethren on the Court to protect speech largely on pragmatic grounds of social value. The marketplace of ideas was the result, and it remains the dominant imagery in the rhetoric of freedom of expression. Individual speech must be protected because it

> brings diversity, competition, and therefore efficiency to the collective search for truth, not because it is a manifestation of personal autonomy on which the state may not impinge.[11]

One effect of this new foundation is to elevate the importance of the democratic function of speech. Indeed, Alexander Meiklejohn saw this as the sole justification of freedom of speech and press, which may be abridged when they do not serve that purpose.[12] Even liberals who find this view too narrow place far more importance on the democratic function than did the classical liberals. For one thing, they do not restrict the state to the end of protecting rights, but give it a much broader mandate. Democracy for them is not merely a means of deciding how to achieve purposes that are antecedently given, but a way of deciding what ends government should pursue in the first place. Thus the scope of public discussion is broadened immeasurably. But there is a deeper reason as well. The democratic function of free speech is not a secondary or subordinate function, because political life is not subordinate to private. Liberals typically regard democratic participation as a way of life, an activity no less important to individual self-realization than private, inner expressions of the self.

Another consequence follows from the distinction between inner and outer realms. Although the content of speech reflects its intellectual basis, and must therefore be left free, its material or economic aspects may be regulated or subsidized by government. Thus liberals have endorsed regulation of advertising, investment advice, and other types of "commercial speech"; antitrust actions against media corporations; subsidies for education, research, art, and even some political advocacy; and public ownership of the airwaves and regulation of broadcasting.

These are significant changes from the classical liberal conception of free speech. On the core issues involving the content of speech, however, at least where the print media are concerned, the liberal position has been analogous to that of the early utilitarians regarding the economy. Despite a collectivist standard, they have generally held to an individualist ontology, and opposed government regulation as a matter of policy. But the new arguments for retaining regulation in broadcasting, and extending it to the print media, reflect the same shift that occurred a century ago on economic matters. They follow the same pattern and rely on the same basic premises, although, as we shall see, different proponents of regulation put different emphases on the different premises.

POSITIVE RIGHTS

The first argument is based on the familiar distinction between positive and negative rights. For our purposes, the distinction may be drawn on two related dimensions. Negative rights are rights to freedom of action (speaking, using one's property), while positive rights are rights to goods (food, education, medical care). And negative rights impose only negative obligations on others not to interfere with the action, while positive rights impose positive obligations to provide the good. The concept of positive rights obviously reflects the positive conception of freedom. And insofar as any right is understood partly in terms of the actions regarded as interfering with it, the concept of positive rights also reflects the expanded notion of interference: Failure to provide the goods is a restraint on the person, a violation of the right.

In the realm of communication, positive rights are not often applied to the simplest case: direct, face-to-face communication. With the possible exception of some radical activists, no one claims that a speaker has a right to a captive audience in this context, or that one's right to listen may be violated by the failure of others to speak. But where communication takes place through a medium – a publication, broadcast station, lecture hall, or the like – positive rights have been attributed to its audience: rights to receive information or other goods. And positive rights have been attributed to potential speakers: rights of access to the use of the medium for reaching the audience. In both cases, the positive obligations fall on the owners of the medium, typically regarded as performing "merely" economic functions.

The FCC has always defended its regulation of broadcasting on these grounds. "Licensee discretion [i.e., freedom] is but a means to a greater end, and not an end in and of itself, and [is justified] only insofar as it is exercised in genuine conformity with the paramount right of the listening and viewing public to be informed."[13] The same rationale is frequently offered for municipal regulation of cable television.[14] The Supreme Court has held that these positive rights of the audience derive from the First Amendment: "It is the right of the public to receive suitable access to social, political, esthetic, moral, and other ideas and experiences that is crucial here."[15] Under the fairness doctrine and equal opportunity rule, speakers have also been granted positive rights of access in various circumstances. A number of law journal articles have suggested that these access rights be broadened and extended to the print media.[16]

Positive rights do not simply "expand" negative rights, as their advocates often claim. The two kinds of rights are necessarily incompatible. For one thing, regulations imposed to enforce positive rights involve a redistribution of wealth, in violation of property rights. The fairness doctrine requires that if a broadcaster takes a position on a controversial issue, he must offer spokesmen for competing views, free of charge, the use of expensive broadcasting equipment, valuable time, and the services of highly trained employees. Media access groups often boast of their ability to extract airtime worth hundreds of thousands of dollars.[17] The regulations also curtail the freedom of association; they are imposed precisely for the purpose of forcing media owners to do business with people with whom they would not otherwise choose to associate.

But the most significant cost of positive rights, for our purposes, is that enforcing them restricts freedom of expression and communication – principally that of broadcasters, secondarily that of the audience and speakers they would otherwise have brought together. Owners and managers of a medium do not perform a "merely" economic function.

Many are in the business because they have information, ideas, ideologies, and artistic visions they want to communicate. Even those whose purpose is entirely commercial must make daily judgments about content in order to build an audience and attract speakers. Regulations prohibit owners from acting on these judgments.

Nor is this an unfortunate side effect. It is the point of the regulations, and often the goal of those who seek access. The essence of free speech is advocacy, and that includes the right to reject opposing views – by explicit critique or by silence, depending on one's judgment about the views and about the audience one is trying to convince. From the very beginning of broadcasting, regulators were hostile to this exercise of freedom. In one case, the FCC declared flatly that "the broadcaster cannot be an advocate."[18] The fairness doctrine relaxed this ban, but only on condition that advocacy be muted by airing alternative views, regardless of the broadcaster's judgment of their merit. The clear intent was to limit the effectiveness of any message or cause. And that is clearly the intent of many activists who use the fairness doctrine. Environmentalists, for example, have been especially successful in obtaining airtime for opposing nuclear power and advocating solar and other types of energy. They hardly needed the time of the target stations in order to express their views, which have been widely covered and debated. The goal was obviously to neutralize the public opposition of the station owners.[19]

The question is, What could justify all this? What grounds are there for attributing positive rights to speakers or audience, when these rights are incompatible with the negative rights to property, association, and speech? The primary rationale offered by the courts is an alleged peculiarity of the broadcasting medium. The electromagnetic spectrum is supposed to be a kind of commons owned by the public. Too many people want to use this medium, however, for it to function *as* a commons. On behalf of the public, therefore, the government licenses certain users to the exclusion of others, but only on condition that they serve various interests of the public. In effect, the positive rights of nonlicensees – both speakers and hearers – derive from their negative rights as ultimate owners.[20]

This argument is irrelevant here, for two reasons. First, it is unsound. There is nothing physically peculiar about the spectrum that distinguishes it from other resources such as land. Precisely because the spectrum cannot function as a commons, there is no reason to treat it as such. Private property rights – the rights of exclusive use and control over frequency bands in delimited geographical areas, including the rights to buy, sell, and subdivide them – can be defined and protected in the same way as private property rights in land or other resources. Nothing in the nature of the medium forced Congress to declare the spectrum public property and erect a licensing scheme.[21] Second, the argument has no bearing on the print media, to which many proponents of positive rights would like to extend regulation. Insofar as they want to use broadcasting regulation as a precedent for all media, they are assuming with us, and against current law, that broadcasting is not unique.

So let us turn to a deeper argument regarding property. Judith Lichtenberg observes that "the typical claim of editorial autonomy by publishers and editors is really a disguised property claim – it is the assertion of a property right in the guise of a free speech right."[22] This is true, though the reference to disguises is misleading. The freedom in question can be described either as the freedom of media owners to use and dispose of their property as they see fit, or as the freedom to decide what contents will be published or broadcast. Lichtenberg goes on to argue that once the right of free speech depends on property rights, it loses some of its force, since she takes it for granted that property may be regulated in various ways (licensing, zoning, etc.). Thus, if we decide – say, on grounds of broadening public debate – that media owners should not be granted the exclusive property rights they claim in their facilities, then they do not have the exclusive right they claim to editorial autonomy. Having cleared the ground, so to speak, we may decide that would-be speakers have a right of access to those facilities (although Lichtenberg herself does not employ the concept of positive rights here).

The flaw in this argument is the assumption that free speech rights which depend on property are a special class, of less significance than "pure" free speech rights. In fact, the latter class is empty. Any action whatever involves the use of physical resources; at a minimum, any action takes place at some location. The exercise of any right, therefore, involves an exercise of property rights, and some system of property is required in order to define any category of rights, including those of speech. Even the freedom to think as one pleases in the privacy of one's home depends on a property claim in the home. In the case of editorial autonomy, it is not only the editors who are claiming a property right. Those who demand a right of access are making a competing property claim to control over the same facilities. To decide between these claims, we must adopt some comprehensive position on property.

One cannot defend a position on property merely by appealing to the current practice of the state, shaped as it is by a century of liberal legislation. A philosophical defense must rest on philosophical premises. Liberals will presumably appeal to some form of the premise we mentioned in the last section: that property is social in origin, a collective product whose distribution may be governed by social needs. In opposition, we would appeal to the individualist view that wealth is created by the productive activity of individuals, who acquire thereby the right to use it as they see fit, in the service of their own lives and happiness. This is not the place to discuss the matter in depth, but we do want to make several observations.

No one claims a positive right of access to someone else's home, or, to use Lichtenberg's example, a right to orate in a dentist's waiting room. Lichtenberg offers two distinctions to explain why property rights prevail in these cases but not in the case of the media.

The first point is that a home falls within a private sphere, whereas the major media are engaged in a public business; and that we assign a greater value to autonomy of action within the private sphere. This version of the private–public distinction is an incarnation of the liberal distinction between inner and outer realms, and reflects the liberal tendency to regard the outer realm as a field of collective action, distant from the inner springs of personality and the autonomous pursuit of values. This is not a view we share. Productive activity may not require privacy in the same way as other activities. But that says nothing about its importance. "The goal of reshaping the earth in the image of [one's] values," as Ayn Rand put it,[23] is a central source of meaning in life. And for reasons we will develop more fully in the next section, it requires the same autonomy, the same control over the physical means, the same freedom to associate with others or go one's own way, as any private activity. Privacy and autonomy are distinct values. Indeed, the function of rights in our view is not only to protect a private sphere around the individual, but also to protect his autonomy when he acts in public, to protect the outer expression of individuality.

The second point of difference pertains to alternatives. No one needs the positive right to "harangue a captive audience" in the dentist's office, Lichtenberg says, because public streets and parks are available as an alternative; whereas "small journals and pamphlets are not reasonable alternatives to CBS and the *New York Times*."[24] But there is a switch of standards in this argument. Are we concerned with alternative means of expressing oneself, or of reaching a given audience? Public streets and parks provide alternative means of expression but not of reaching the particular people who are in the waiting room. In exactly the same way, small journals and pamphlets *do* provide an alternative means of expression, but not of reaching the same audience as CBS or the *Times*.

The idea that rights are determined by the presence or absence of reasonable alternatives derives from the basic notion of positive freedom – the notion that freedom means having certain opportunities available to one. Appealing to this concept in the present context makes it especially clear that it has nothing to do with freedom. It is a demand on the time, ability, and achievements of others. Access to the major media cannot by any stretch be regarded as a basic necessity, on the order of food and shelter. It is not even necessary for the act of expressing oneself. Means of expression can be obtained easily and cheaply, in the form of pamphlets, sound trucks, airtime on small radio stations. Flourishing national magazines have been started recently for under five thousand dollars. But proponents of positive rights are not satisfied with the cheap and easy vehicles, or the ones requiring a great deal of work. These, they argue, do not reach the same audience as the television networks, or the major newspapers or newsmagazines, which are seen and read by millions of people.[25] But these national media had to be created by enormous investments of effort and money, and the audience they enjoy was earned by years – usually decades – of productive work. Here, if anywhere, is a case for the Lockean argument that the product belongs by right to the producer. For someone who contributed nothing to this achievement to claim a property right in these media is a particularly egregious example of demanding a right to the labor of others.

We have examined the positive rights rationale at some length because of its importance in the history of broadcast regulation and its potential as precedent for the print media. But it is not the primary rationale of those who want to continue and expand such regulation. The concept of positive rights is an attempt to put collectivist premises in the language of individualism. The major arguments for media regulation appeal to those premises directly.

THE TELEOLOGICAL ARGUMENT

The case for freedom of speech and press is normally put in teleological terms. Such freedom promotes the free flow of information, open and robust debate, a multiplicity of voices. These conditions are necessary in turn for winnowing truth from error and for democracy to function. Truth and democracy are the *summa bona,* the sources of the value we place on open and robust debate and the other conditions. The teleological arguments for regulation claim that these conditions can sometimes be achieved more fully or effectively through government regulation than through noninterference.

Owen Fiss argues that the primary purpose of the First Amendment is to guarantee "rich public debate." If the government pursues that goal by leaving speakers autonomous, the content of the debate will be determined by the free market, and thus, he assumes, will be disproportionately affected by certain speakers – media owners and the kinds of consumers that advertisers want to attract – and by considerations such as profitability that bear no relation to the information needs of the electorate. Instead, he argues, we should reject the presumption against state interference with speech. Under this principle, the state "is allowed, encouraged, and sometimes required to enact measures or issue decrees designed to enrich public debate, even if that action entails an interference with the speech of some and thus a denial of individual or institutional autonomy."[26]

Lee Bollinger offers a somewhat different version of the argument. We may recognize, he says, that the mass media do not prevent other speakers from entering the marketplace of information and ideas, and that these media have attained their position by giving the audience what they want. We may nevertheless decide that our decisions as individuals in the marketplace reflect intellectual sloth and a desire to hear only those voices that agree with us. "And we may, accordingly, decide together, through public regulation, that we would like, to some extent, to alter or modify the demands we find ourselves making in that free market context."[27]

In short, the teleological argument is that freedom of speech as traditionally conceived – the right to autonomy of action in a free market – is merely a social instrument, which may not always achieve its end as well as government could by pursuing those ends directly. Such government action might take the form of subsidies, which regulate demand: The government takes control of decisions about how some portion of the earnings of its citizens will be spent. Or the government may regulate suppliers of speech by maintaining the licensing scheme, fairness doctrine, and other controls on broadcasters, and perhaps extending them to the print media as well. As we observed, the fundamental values underlying this argument are truth and democracy. The proponents of the argument do not always distinguish clearly between them, presumably because the same intermediate values – the free flow of information, open and robust debate – are necessary for both.[28] For reasons that will emerge in what follows, however, we believe that different considerations are relevant depending on which basic value is at stake. We will therefore concentrate on truth in this section, and discuss democracy in the next.

No one would deny that truth is a value – at least, no one in the broad liberal tradition in which we include ourselves. And we certainly recognize the insight embodied in the metaphor of the marketplace of ideas: that truth can be expected to emerge only when all ideas are free to compete for rational acceptance, and that certainty is possible, on matters of any depth and complexity, only when one has submitted one's ideas to such competition. But the question is: To whom are these things values?

Ultimately, we would argue, all values are values *to* individuals, *as* individuals. This thesis is essential to individualism, although it does not imply an atomistic view of man.[29] People may share values and cooperate in pursuing them. But it is important to distinguish in this regard between common and collective values. A collective value is a state of affairs considered as a single particular that a group seeks to achieve, through explicit cooperation or some other mechanism, with the intent of benefiting all members. A common value is a class of qualitatively similar values that different individuals seek to achieve for themselves. Many values are common to human beings as such, and thus to all members of a society: life and happiness, material wealth, love and friendship, truth and knowledge.

The teleological argument for regulation rests on two assumptions. The first is Mill's assumption that truth, and derivatively the marketplace of ideas, are collective values to society as a whole, properly pursued by society as a collective agent. "The First Amendment," says Bollinger, "both embodies and reflects a basic value of this society, namely, that we share a commitment to seeking truth and wisdom."[30] The second assumption is that the state has the ability to pursue this value morally and rationally.

There is no question that truth and other cognitive goods can be collective values for various groups, such as media firms or universities. As individualists, however, we would argue that such collective values are properly pursued through voluntary arrangements, and as a means to individual values, ultimately one's own happiness. Neither truth nor other primary goods should be pursued through the coercive apparatus of the state. Because these values must be pursued by rational action, our primary social need is the freedom to act on the basis of our judgment. As Ayn Rand put it:

> Since knowledge, thinking, and rational action are properties of the individual, since the choice to exercise his rational faculty or not depends on the individual, man's survival requires that those who think be free of the interference of those who don't. Since men are neither omniscient nor infallible, they must be free to agree or disagree, to cooperate or pursue their own independent course, each according to his own rational judgment. Freedom is the fundamental requirement of man's mind.[31]

Individual rights – to life, liberty, property, and the pursuit of happiness; to freedom of contract, privacy, freedom of speech – are principles defining that freedom. And the system of rights, embodied in a legal code, is a collective value to all members of a society. Rights can be secured only through a single joint agent, the government, with a monopoly on the use of coercion. If we had to protect our rights individually, neither our own nor those of other people would be secure. But the system of rights is the *only* value that must inherently be pursued as a collective value by society as a whole. The state may not look past this value, collectivizing the common values that underlie it and making them objects of its action. That would be like a corporation going beyond its role as a joint investment by shareholders to determine how the latter should spend their dividends. At the level of their common values, individuals differ in circumstances, in the way they seek to embody these values, in the way they rank them, in their judgments about the best means of pursuing them. It is precisely the function of rights to protect such differences. The diverse interests of individuals cannot be combined into a single object, "the public interest," for the state to pursue. The attempt to do so necessarily violates individual rights and creates an opportunity for some individuals to impose their values on others by force.

This philosophical argument has an economic corollary. The variations among people in specific values are one major basis of exchange. The millions of prices in an economy reflect a vast amount of information people have about their needs and preferences, local conditions, the possibilities of substituting one good for another, events that alter the supply of a good or the demand for it. As Friedrich von Hayek pointed out, this information is scattered among the millions of individuals in an economy and integrated automatically by the price system. For the government to pursue all these values as collective goods, it would have to assemble as much information, and respond to it as quickly, as the price system of a free market – an impossible task.[32] In addition, the information about relative valuations that government officials do manage to assemble is ineffective unless it is backed by the kinds of incentives they respond to – chiefly the prospect of maintaining and expanding their power. And the existence of an agency with power over some economic activity will not be a matter of indifference to the individuals affected. The more powerful among them, whether producers or consumers, will find ways to control the controllers.

As a result, government regulation typically fails to achieve its stated objective and often produces the opposite, as people use the information available to them to seize or circumvent the controls. Established firms and interest groups capture regulatory agencies, using that power to exclude competitors and maintain artificially high prices. Innovation is slowed, mistakes remain uncorrected, and economic activity becomes sclerotic, since the regulators' fortunes are not dependent on the effects of the regulations. They may even benefit from failure, if it generates a demand for new controls to correct problems created by previous ones.

These arguments challenge the modern liberal confidence in the efficacy and rationality of government action. And they are borne out by the history of media regulation. The FCC's allocation of the spectrum and assignment of TV licenses in the early 1950s was intended to promote localism: the idea that each broadcaster would tailor programming to the interests of the local community. In fact, the economic relationships between audience size and the costs of program production guaranteed that local stations could generate virtually no material of their own, and the result was the system of three national networks. The assignment of only thirteen channels in the VHF band, with a licensing system that eliminated any incentive to economize on bandwidths used to broadcast, excluded competition and allowed stations to earn extraordinary profits. The stations and networks acquired major power over FCC policy; they managed to stall domestic satellite communications for a decade, and cable television for fifteen years. The restrictions on multiple ownership of stations prevented the emergence of competition to the networks. The prohibition against owning more than one station in a single area guaranteed that separately owned stations would offer the same fare to compete for the same mass audience.[33]

An indication of the distortions caused by these controls is the torrent of innovation set free by deregulation. The relaxation of the multiple ownership rules in 1985 was quickly followed by Rupert Murdoch's attempt to create a fourth network. Cable television now offers, among its leading program services, an all-news channel, C-SPAN coverage of Congress and political events, channels devoted to black and Hispanic programming, and to arts, religion, and children's programs – a much wider range of diversity and public affairs material than anything the FCC ever accomplished with its program guidelines, which produced nothing more than superficial half-hour coverage on television and the "Sunday morning ghetto" on radio. These changes have occurred because producers and consumers have been freed to act on information they have about their own values – information that the market has released from regulatory bondage.

Knowledge, of course, is an epistemological as well as an economic good. The truth of an idea is determined by its relation to reality, not by the number of people who "buy" it. Its significance and fundamentality are determined by its relation to the wider body of knowledge, not by the degree of attention it attracts in the marketplace.[34] But this does not give proponents of regulation an escape from the problems just described, because Hayek's argument has an epistemological parallel.

Just as the economic critique of regulation begins by asking, of value to whom? the epistemological critique begins by asking, known by whom? Society as such is not a cognitive agent; knowledge consists ultimately in the grasp of facts by individuals. And knowledge is contextual. The content of an idea, and its relation to the facts that determine its truth or falsity, depend on the process by which it was acquired: a cognitive history of observation, comparison, concept-formation, searching for evidence, weighing the evidence, checking for consistency, distinguishing the essential from the nonessential. No matter how much we learn from one another, this process takes place in the individual mind, under the direction of one's interests and choices, and the conclusions we reach have no relation to reality except through that process.

This is why knowledge cannot be instilled by coercion. Even if those in power know that a certain proposition is true, compelling their subjects to assent will not produce knowledge, because it will not reproduce the process by which the proposition was verified. Nor can the government hope to reproduce that process by planning and regulating the cognitive lives of its subjects. The "knowledge czars" could not hope to assemble the information their subjects use in the self-directed process of thinking: information about their cognitive needs, skills, and style; the value to them of specific lines of inquiry, courses of study, books, or works of art; or, indeed, the value to them of knowledge as opposed to other goods that have a claim on their finite resources of time and effort.

The same principle applies when the government tries to promote diversity. It is the contextual character of knowledge that makes diversity of opinion a value. The effort to understand another point of view, to grasp an opposing line of argument or foreign conceptual framework, can serve as a check on the objectivity of the reasoning behind one's own view. But diversity is an instrumental good, not an end in itself. Indeed, it is a second-order instrument. The primary means of acquiring knowledge are the cognitive actions of observation and inference. Diversity provides no evidence that could not be acquired by those means directly; it serves only as an additional constraint against hasty or parochial conclusions. There is obviously no a priori or universal rule for deciding how much or what type of diversity is desirable. A theoretical physicist may reasonably forgo the exercise of debating a Flat Earther. There is a time to seek opposing views and a time to decide one has heard enough. Any such decision depends on the specific context of the individual, and no regulator could hope to assemble the relevant information about the contexts of millions of people.

Suppose the government attempts to increase diversity by granting subsidies to speakers. Whom will this benefit? Obviously, the speakers themselves. In the absence of a positive rights rationale, however, this is simply a transfer of money from one person to another. The teleological rationale must be that the subsidy will enrich the array of contents available to society as a whole. But enrichment requires that the subsidized ideas have some value as judged by the individual who receives them, and will advance his understanding in some area of inquiry. The subsidized ideas, moreover, must serve the individual's purpose better than the ideas he would otherwise have supported were he free to spend his money as he chose. Government regulators have no means of making rational judgments on these matters. They have no way to assess the cognitive contexts of the audience for ideas, nor any special competence in the subsidized fields of study. Instead, they turn to the establishment in such fields to review proposals and decide which will be funded. One result is to entrench established ideas and give their proponents political power over the field. Another and perhaps more deadening effect is that the government decides which opposing, nonestablishment ideas will be legitimated.

Or suppose the government regulates supply instead of demand. It may impose a contingent obligation such as the fairness doctrine – which requires that *if* a broadcaster takes a stand on a controversial issue of public importance, he must air opposing views. The effect will be to discourage the expression of opinion. There is a massive body of evidence that the fairness doctrine had this chilling effect.[35] Many stations refrained from editorializing, endorsing political candidates, or even covering controversial issues, in order to avoid the costs of fairness doctrine suits by disgruntled viewers. We see no reason to think the effect would be diminished if the doctrine were applied only at renewal time, as Henry Geller suggests.[36]

To solve this problem, some have suggested turning the doctrine into an affirmative obligation, requiring the media to cover some issues. To enforce such a rule, however, the government would have to decide what counts as an acceptable issue, and this raises a deeper problem with the idea of compelling diversity. Diversity cannot be measured in a vacuum. It means a range of answers to a specific question. But any question presupposes a conceptual framework and set of background assumptions. For anyone who lacks this cognitive context, or who rejects the framework and assumptions, diversity on that question is of no value. There is no neutral, canonical list of issues, and thus no way to regulate debate without joining it. In the attempt to enforce the fairness doctrine as a contingent obligation, as Geller observes,[37] the FCC has issued an arbitrary and inconsistent set of decisions about what constitutes "a controversial issue of public importance." In order to impose an affirmative obligation, and not simply deal ad hoc with topics broadcasters have already raised, it would have to accomplish the vastly more difficult task of originating a list of controversial issues on its own. This would involve massive intrusions into the realm of ideas – by government authorities or, more likely, by the pressure groups to whom they would abandon responsibility for the task. Since the government cannot possibly assemble information about the diverse cognitive contexts of all readers and viewers, the result would simply be that those with political power could impose their context by force.

A free marketplace of ideas has a self-righting tendency to correct errors and biases. In recent years, we have seen intensive criticism by private scholars and groups help decrease the superficiality and bias in the major media. The criticism has succeeded, to the extent that it has, because it leaves its targets free to weigh the merits of the charges; it appeals to their rationality and professional integrity. Government controls, on the other hand, appeal to fear. Even when regulations do not amount to overt censorship, they employ the chilling apparatus of arbitrary edicts, protracted litigation, bureaucratic procedures – all of them backed by the state's power of coercion. Questions of true or false, better or worse, are replaced with the question of legal or illegal. In a free marketplace, journalists and editors depend on their reputations. They have every incentive to avoid distortions that would subject them to legitimate criticism, and to correct such errors once made. Regulations like the fairness doctrine punish the best by treating everyone as equally suspect and by creating the illusion of government-ensured fairness.[38] As the state intrudes more deeply into matters of content, decisions about content become more cautious, less innovative. Independent minds are replaced by those willing to subject their judgment to the constellation of political pressures operating through Congress and the courts, above and below the table. No other consequence is possible when government attempts to collectivize a value and prohibit individuals from pursuing it freely.

THE ARGUMENT FROM DEMOCRACY

Truth is not the only value served by diversity or open and robust debate. The traditional case for free speech holds that these conditions are necessary as well for a democratic system of government. Freedom of speech ensures that opponents of the government can make their views known to the public, and thus provide the voters with a genuine choice in elections. The free flow of information and opinion from diverse and antagonistic sources is the best way to ensure that voters will learn what they need to know about the candidates and about government policies and public issues.

As in the teleological argument, proponents of regulation argue that these values may be served more effectively by positive government action than by the principle of noninterference. Virtually all cities now have a single daily newspaper, many of them owned by large chains and most linked by a few wire services. Three newsmagazines have the weekly market almost to themselves, and three networks provide the bulk of television news and commentary on public affairs. The argument is not that such concentration amounts to monopoly power in the economic sense; it may be that the prices of advertising and subscriptions are kept down by competition among rival firms. The argument, rather, is that because the major media *are* competing for a single mass audience, they tend to provide roughly the same kinds of information and range of views. The journalists and editors who decide on content share roughly the same worldview and interests. Nonestablishment views are thus excluded from public awareness and discussion. Some argue in addition that the major media have the power to impress on the public their own worldview, attitudes, and stereotypes by speaking with an authoritative voice of objectivity, an avuncular air of certainty about the world beyond the ken of the audience. Hence, the government must engage in a type of intellectual antitrust, breaking up these restraints on trade in ideas.

Proponents of regulation would probably put more weight on this argument than on the other arguments we have considered. Even the argument from truth appeals primarily to "truth regarding public matters," as Justice Frankfurter put it.[39] Should Unitarians come to predominate in the media, no one would urge government intervention on behalf of trinitarianism. Conversely, the danger feared from the alleged lack of diversity in the media today is not so much ignorance or error as excessive power over the public agenda on the part of the major media. Nor can we reject this branch of the teleological defense of regulation on the same fundamental grounds as we did the argument from truth. In the last section we attacked the idea that the government should promote truth as a collective value. But we observed that the system of rights *is* a collective value, necessarily pursued by society as a whole, and if democracy is a necessary means of preserving that system, then it too is properly considered a collective value. Nevertheless, we can be fairly brief in our reply to the argument, because the basic political philosophy we have outlined so far sets severe limits on what the government may do to enhance the democratic process. And it sets a much higher burden of proof for proposals to regulate the marketplace of ideas than the argument from democracy can hope to meet.

For classical liberalism, as we noted, democracy is a derivative political value. The purpose of government is to protect individual rights; democracy is only one among various means of achieving that end. To be sure, there is a natural link between individual rights and democracy. Both are based on the idea of man's independence and equality before the civil and natural law; both reflect the idea that government is a servant of its citizens, not their master. But the concept of rights is the primary expression of these ideas.

Democracy is only a means of protecting rights in practice. It is a risky means, given the propensity of majorities to violate the rights of minorities, and must be held in check by other instruments, primarily a constitution, with courts to enforce it against majority will. This view of the relationship between rights and democracy has three important implications.

1. Freedom of speech is an element in the natural right of liberty and thus helps to define the end that government serves. That it also plays a political role in the operation of the democratic means for controlling government, by fostering the exchange of information and ideas, is an important but derivative fact. The primary function of free speech is to protect individuals in seeking knowledge and enlightenment by their own rational action. To restrict that freedom for the purpose of enhancing democracy, therefore, is to foster the means of governing at the cost of the end. It would take overwhelming evidence of a problem to justify doing so.

The evidence of a problem is far from overwhelming. Indeed, we see no evidence whatever. The case for regulation outlined above contained two lines of argument. The "Citizen Kane" argument is that the concentration of the media, and their degree of penetration within a mass audience, restricts the range of information and ideas to which that audience is exposed. But what is the evidence for this factual claim? The diversity of information and ideas to which individuals have access cannot be measured in a vacuum, nor is there any a priori standard for deciding how much is required for a viable democracy. The argument must be a comparative one. And we see no evidence that the undeniable growth in the size and reach of major media firms has lessened the degree of diversity. The city that had three or four competing daily metropolitan newspapers at the turn of the century may now have only one. But it also has three or four television stations, ten or twenty radio stations, probably a cable system, and numerous urban, suburban, and regional weeklies and monthlies reporting on local affairs. The residents may also subscribe to the newsweeklies, as well as to dozens of opinion journals and special interest magazines.

By any reasonable standard, the diversity to which the individual has access has *increased* dramatically.

The second line of reasoning, which we might call the "Cronkite" argument, is that the voice of authority adopted by the media – as in Walter Cronkite's signature "and that's the way it is" – undercuts the critical capacities of its audience. "When there are great asymmetries of power to communicate," argues Onora O'Neill, "those who have the power easily come to write or speak or edit as if their own voices were true and authoritative." The methods of sensationalism and selective omission "can be used to sway public opinion while disabling public criticism," and the result may be a kind of "ideological domination." Therefore, "it is important to ask whether mass communication even in democratic societies may establish categories and modes of discourse which so dominate discussion and thought that they endanger the very formulation and communication of opposition."[40] In a similar vein, Judith Lichtenberg argues that because the mass media present themselves as neutral reporters of the facts, they have a special responsibility "for presenting all sides of an issue" – a responsibility that she feels may in principle be enforced.[41]

The Cronkite argument attributes to the mass audience a degree of credulity and passivity that we find implausible. During election campaigns, information about candidates is available in such profusion, and there is so strong an incentive for journalists to uncover flaws, that no organ of the press has anything like the power to put its candidate in office. On matters of policy, the content provided by the media *is* somewhat more restricted. It tends to emphasize debates among respectable, establishment opinions. Nevertheless, other views are available with modest effort in smaller organs of the press, and are covered periodically by the major media for novelty value. The vehement criticism of the media in recent years, moreover, has demonstrably affected its public credibility.[42] The Cronkite argument is also surprising, because it calls into question the very basis of democracy. Modern liberals began to support economic regulation when they expanded the concepts of interference, power, and coercion to include private influences as well as government force. But democracy remained among the liberal constellation of values in part because these concepts were not extended to matters of content and "the power to persuade." If independence of judgment on the part of a significant number of people cannot survive the charms of avuncular anchormen, it is difficult to see the rationale for giving people direct responsibility for judging the wisdom of government policy.

2. We have been speaking about the basic functions of the media in a democracy: coverage of political campaigns and public issues. At a deeper level, it is certainly true that the media rarely challenge the conceptual framework, the fundamental assumptions, that underlie establishment views and set the range of respectable opinion. But this is just what one would expect, given a second implication of our basic premises.

A government whose sole function is the protection of rights, and whose actions are constrained by a constitution, is a limited government. It is what the critics of classical liberalism have called the "night watchman state," offering defense against foreign aggression and domestic crime, providing a court system to adjudicate conflicts, and otherwise leaving its citizens to conduct their own affairs. The basic function of the state and the basic limits on its actions are not subject to democratic choice. The role of democracy is to choose the best policies for achieving the state's proper end, primarily by choosing government officials. Democracy in this setting tends naturally toward a two-party system, a party in power and a loyal opposition. The role of the press, at least its democratic function, is to provide information on the performance of the party in power and on the complaints and alternative policies put forward by the opposition. Broader and more fundamental questions of political philosophy would naturally be discussed in the universities and other cultural forums, but the daily political life of the nation would not raise these questions, because a set of answers would be embodied in the constitution, not subject to routine vote and thus not a topic for debate in ordinary democratic forums.

We do not live in such a society. The limits on government have attenuated. It is no longer a night watchman state; a much broader set of issues has been opened to democratic choice. Nevertheless, an attenuated version of the point still applies. At any moment, the range of open issues is not infinite. Settled public opinion, established institutions, expectations about benefits from the state and obligations toward it – these and other inertial forces restrict the kinds of candidates and policies that can expect to be taken seriously by the voters and the media. All of this operates within a wider set of assumptions about values, rights, human nature, and the role of government. This wider context is the object of discussion in intellectual forums, and it is subject to change over long periods of time. But it is unreasonable to expect that these issues would arise in the ordinary course of political life, or that alternative philosophical positions would be covered in the media. Any debate must take place within a context that is not itself subject to debate. Neither a left-wing critic of private property nor a right-wing critic of land-use regulation could expect much of a hearing at a town meeting debate on two- versus three-acre zoning.

Nor are these wider assumptions originated by the media. Journalists acquire their basic beliefs and values in the same way their audience does – from the education they received at the hands of parents, religious leaders, schoolteachers, and college professors. To provide more diversity at this level, the government would have to invade the schools, the universities, the intellectual journals. It would have to legislate on the most rarefied questions. Do Plato and Aristotle represent two fundamentally different outlooks or merely two sides of the same Western coin? Is the conventional political spectrum an accurate guide to possible views of man and state, or does it omit important alternatives? The list is endless. And the government would necessarily rely on the advice of leading intellectuals, granting them power to enforce their views.

In short, the media provide diversity in abundance at the level at which they operate: the coverage of contemporary issues in politics. They are not the source of the conceptual framework or basic assumptions within which they and their audience operate, nor can they reasonably be expected to serve as cultural critics. Of course, there is vast room for improvement in their performance of this limited role – improvement in accuracy, fairness, depth of analysis – and the democratic system would benefit from it. But for all the reasons we gave in the last section, it is not reasonable to seek improvement through the coercive power of the state. And the use of such power is exceptionally dangerous on issues pertaining to the conduct of the government – which brings us to the third implication.

3. We have distinguished two political roles of a free press in classical liberalism: the watchdog and the democratic functions. And we noted that for advocates of limited government, the first is by far the more important. It is set by the end of government, the protection of rights, and would be required regardless of whether or not such a government employed democratic means of operation. The implication of this priority is that even if, contrary to all the evidence we have cited, the government could use its power effectively to strengthen the democratic function, it would not be justified in doing so at the cost of the watchdog function.

And that is an unavoidable cost. A press that is licensed, franchised, or regulated is subject to political pressures, and it is most vulnerable to these pressures when it deals with issues affecting the interests of those in power. If a cable firm's franchise depends on the discretion of the city fathers, it is not likely to put its investment at risk by investigating municipal corruption. If a newspaper is subject to the fairness doctrine, it will err on the side of caution to avoid the legal costs and possible penalties of suits brought under the rule. Government regulations intended to enhance democracy routinely operate in practice to favor those in office. Campaign finance rules have made it more difficult to unseat incumbents. In the major court case involving a rule that broadcasters offer candidates political advertising time at their lowest rate, the FCC commissioners split along party lines in applying the rule; those appointed by the party in power naturally won.[43]

Thus, the burden of proof that advocates of regulation must carry, the limited nature of the media's democratic function, and the priority of the watchdog to the democratic function create too steep an obstacle for the argument to surmount without much more evidence of a problem than anyone has provided. In the end, the argument from democracy is no stronger than the arguments from positive rights and truth. Our critique of these arguments, of course, rests on assumptions that we have not defended fully in this essay. By the same token, the arguments for regulation rest on opposing assumptions that are not defended, and often not even identified, by their exponents. As we said at the outset, freedom of speech and press cannot be evaluated outside a system of rights, and ultimately an entire political philosophy.

NOTES

Some of the research for this article was drawn from our earlier work *Laissez Parler: Freedom in the Electronic Media* (New Brunswick, N.J.: Transaction Books, 1983), which was written for the Social Philosophy and Policy Center.

1 John Locke, *Two Treatises of Government*, ed. Peter Laslett (New York: New American Library, 1965), p. 311 [*Second Treatise*, sec. 6].

2 Ibid.

3 John Trenchard and Thomas Gordon, *Cato's Letters* (New York: Russell & Russell, 1969), vol. 3, p. 295.

4 Thus, freedom of speech was not an independent principle, in the sense defined by Frederick Schauer, *Free Speech: A Philosophi-*

cal Inquiry (Cambridge: Cambridge University Press, 1982), pp. 5–7. It did not set special restrictions on government action above and beyond the restrictions required by liberty in general.

5 John Locke, *Second Treatise of Civil Government*, sec. 222.

6 Martin Diamond, "The Declaration and the Constitution: Liberty, Democracy, and the Founders," in *The American Commonwealth – 1976*, ed. Nathan Glazer and Irving Kristol (New York: Basic, 1976). See also Forrest MacDonald, *Novus Ordo Seclorum: Intellectual Foundations of the Constitution* (Lawrence: University Press of Kansas, 1985), pp. 3–4. It is worth noting that of the passages on the political functions of the press cited by Stephen Holmes elsewhere in this volume ("Liberal Constraints on Private Power?: Reflections on the Origins and Rationale of Access Regulation"), more are concerned with the watchdog than with the democratic function.

7 John Austin's attack on individualism is typical: "To the ignorant and bawling fanatics who stun you with their pother about liberty, political or civil liberty seems to be the principal end for which government ought to exist. But the final cause or purpose for which government ought to exist, is the furtherance of the common weal, to the greatest possible extent." *Lectures on Jurisprudence*, 5th rev. ed. (London: John Murray, 1885), vol. 1, p. 274.

8 John Stuart Mill, *On Liberty*, ed. David Spitz (New York: Norton, 1975), p. 12 [chap. 1].

9 See especially John Dewey, *Liberalism and Social Action* (New York: Capricorn Books, 1963).

10 L. T. Hobhouse, *Liberalism* (London: Oxford University Press, 1964).

11 Benno C. Schmidt, Jr., *Freedom of the Press vs. Public Access* (New York: Praeger, 1976), p. 33.

12 Alexander Meiklejohn, *Political Freedom* (New York: Oxford University Press, 1965).

13 *Fairness Report*, 34 Fed. Reg., at 26383 (1974).

14 See, for example, testimony by Seattle Mayor Charles Royer and other municipal authorities in hearings before the Senate Committee on Commerce, Science, and Transportation, 97th Cong., 2nd sess., January 18, 1982, on cable television regulation (Washington, D.C.: U. S. Government Printing Office,

1982). See also Mark Nadel, "Editorial Freedom: Editors, Retailers, and Access to the Mass Media," *Comm/Ent: Hastings Journal of Communications and Entertainment Law* 9 (1987): 213–54.

15 *Red Lion Broadcasting v. FCC*, 395 U.S., at 390 (1969).

16 See, for example, Jerome Barron, "Access to the Press – A New First Amendment Right," *Harvard Law Review* 80 (1967): 1641–78; and David Selledy, "Access to the Press: A Teleological Analysis of a Constitutional Double Standard," *George Washington Law Review* 50 (1981–2): 430–64.

17 See Ford Rowan, *Broadcast Fairness: Doctrine, Practice, Prospects* (New York: Longman, 1984), for numerous examples.

18 *Mayflower Broadcasting Corp.*, 8 FCC 339 (1941).

19 For an example, see David Kelley and Roger Donway, "The Big Chill," *The Intellectual Activists* 3 (March 31, 1984).

20 This was the Court's argument in *National Broadcasting Company v. U.S.*, 319 U.S. at 213, 216, 226 (1943), and in *Red Lion*, cited in note 15.

21 We make this argument at greater length in *Laissez Parler*, pp. 8–14.

22 Judith Lichtenberg, "Foundations and Limits of Freedom of the Press," this volume.

23 Ayn Rand, "The Objectivist Ethics," in *The Virtue of Selfishness* (New York: New American Library, 1964), p. 26.

24 Lichtenberg, "Foundations and Limits."

25 See Jerome Barron, "Access to the Press," p. 1651, particularly the comment that positive rights of access apply "with greatest force to those media where the greatest public attention is focused."

26 Owen M. Fiss, "Why the State?" this volume.

27 Lee C. Bollinger, "The Rationale of Public Regulation of the Media," this volume.

28 An exception is Benjamin S. DuVal ("Free Communication of Ideas and the Quest for Truth," *George Washington Law Review* 41 [1972]: 161–259), who distinguishes the goal of truth (or "the possibility of correcting erroneous ideas") from the political functions of speech.

29 For that reason, the thesis cannot be dismissed by attacking atomism, as D. F. B. Tucker does in *Law, Liberalism and Free Speech* (Totowa, N.J.: Rowman & Allanheld, 1985), p. 32.

30 "Rationale of Public Regulation."

31 Ayn Rand, "What Is Capitalism?" in *Capitalism: The Unknown Ideal* (New York: New American Library, 1967), p. 17.

32 Friedrich von Hayek, "The Use of Knowledge in Society," *American Economic Review* 35 (1945): 519–30.

33 On these and other consequences of FCC regulation, see *Laissez Parler*, pp. 14–24, and sources cited there.

34 Thus, we do not "buy" Richard Posner's attempt to make epistemology a branch of economics: "When we say that an idea (the earth revolves around the sun) is correct we mean that all or most knowledgeable consumers have accepted ('bought') it." *Economic Analysis of Law* (Boston: Little, Brown, 1972), p. 308.

35 See *Laissez Parler*, chap. 3, and Ford Rowan, *Broadcast Fairness*. Fred Friendly, in *The Good Guys, the Bad Guys, and the First Amendment* (New York: Random House, 1977), describes the use of the fairness doctrine by the Democratic National Committee during the 1960s to intimidate right-wing radio broadcasters. Robert Corn, in "Broadcasters in Bondage," *Reason*, September 1985, describes similar efforts by conservative groups against the media.

36 Henry Geller, "Mass Communications Policy: Where We Are and Where We Should Be Going," this volume.

37 Ibid., note 10. See also Steven Simmons, *The Fairness Doctrine and the Media* (Berkeley: University of California Press, 1978), chap. 7.

38 Cf. Alan Greenspan, "The Assault on Integrity," in *Capitalism: The Unknown Ideal*.

39 Concurring opinion, *Associated Press v. U.S.* 326 U.S., at 28 (1945).

40 Onora O'Neill, "Practices of Toleration," this volume.

41 Lichtenberg, "Foundations and Limits," this volume.

42 For example, polls conducted for the American Society of Newspaper Editors in 1984–5 found that a bare majority of respondents (52% vs. 48%) felt that the media are careful to separate fact from opinion. Interestingly, 64 percent felt that "although there is some bias in the news media, the average person has enough sources of news to be able to sort out the facts." From William Schneider and I. A. Lewis, "Views on the News," *Public Opinion*, August–September 1985.

43 *CBS v. FCC*, 453 U.S. 367 (1981). See discussion of this case in *Laissez Parler*, pp. 36–7.

Chapter 3

Foundations and limits of freedom of the press

Judith Lichtenberg

> I confess that I do not entertain that firm and complete attachment to the liberty of the press which is wont to be excited by things that are supremely good in their very nature.
>
> Alexis de Tocqueville, *Democracy in America*[1]

> Freedom of the press is guaranteed only to those who own one.
>
> A. J. Liebling, *The Press*[2]

Tocqueville and Liebling notwithstanding, freedom of the press in democratic societies is a nearly unchallengeable dogma – essential, it is thought, to individual autonomy and self-expression, and an indispensable element in democracy and the attainment of truth. Both its eloquent theoreticians and its contemporary popular advocates defend freedom of speech and freedom of the press in the same stroke, with the implication that they are inseparable, probably equivalent, and equally fundamental.

At the same time, we know that the press in its most characteristic modern incarnation – mass media in mass society – works not only to enhance the flow of ideas and information but also to inhibit it. Nothing guarantees that all valuable information, ideas, theories, explanations, proposals, and points of view will find expression in the public forum.[3] Indeed, many factors lead us to expect that they will not. The most obvious is that "mass media space-time" is a scarce commodity: Only so much news, analysis, and editorial opinion can be aired in the major channels of mass communication.

Which views get covered, and in what way, depends mainly on the economic and political structure and context of press institutions, and on the characteristics of the media themselves.

These are some of the most important factors: (1) More often than not, contemporary news organizations belong to large corporations whose interests influence what gets covered (and, what is probably more central, what does not) and how.[4] (2) News organizations are driven economically to capture the largest possible audience, and thus not to turn it off with whatever does turn it off – coverage that is too controversial, too demanding, too disturbing.[5] (3) The media are easily manipulated by government officials (and others), for whom the press, by simply reporting press releases and official statements, can be a virtually unfiltered mouthpiece. (4) Characteristics of the media themselves constrain or influence coverage; thus, for example, television lends itself to an action-oriented, unanalytical treatment of events that can distort their meaning or importance.

It is not surprising, therefore, that a great range of opinion and analysis outside the narrow mainstream rarely sees the light of the mass media. This lack of diversity manifests itself in two ways. One is simply lack of adequate exposure to information and ideas that are true or interesting or useful, that help us to understand the world better or make life more satisfactory in one way or another. The range of views considered respectable enough to appear regularly in the American mass media is extraordinarily narrow.[6] As a result, we are more ignorant and more provincial than we could be, and we may be worse off in other ways as well.

The other consequence more directly concerns justice. The press, once thought of as an antidote to established power, is more likely to reinforce it, because access to the press – that is, the mass media – is distributed as unequally as are other forms of power. It is not, of course, that the less powerful never speak in the mass media or that their doings are never reported, or never sympathetically. But the deck is stacked against them, because the press is itself a formidable power in our society, allied intimately (although not simply) with other formidable powers. Displacing the attention of the media from the usual sources of news – the words and deeds of public officials and public figures – often demands nothing less than the politics of theater, for which those using such tactics may also be blamed.[7]

There are regulations meant to remedy these defects, to counteract the tendencies inhibiting diversity in the press.[8] Until recently, when the Federal Communications Commission under Ronald Reagan rescinded it, the fairness doctrine required broadcasters to devote a "reasonable percentage" of broadcast time to public issues in a way that presents contrasting viewpoints. Ownership of multiple media properties is limited (although rules limiting ownership were relaxed under Reagan's FCC). Cable television systems must dedicate some channels to public access. Nothing like the fairness doctrine ever applied to the print media, which, it is commonly thought, are rendered immune to such regulations in the United States by the First Amendment.[9] In any case, regulations mandating coverage of any kind, or enacting even limited rights of access to the press (whether print or electronic), are much in dispute today.[10] In part the dispute centers on the utility of such regulations – whether they produce or can be made to produce the intended effects. But at least as important in the current controversies is a central question of principle. Critics of regulation argue that freedom of the press, like freedom of speech, is at the core of what our society is about, and that commitment to it prohibits the policies in question: regulation of the press is incompatible with freedom of the press.

I believe that we have misunderstood what a modern democratic society's commitment to freedom of the press means and should be. Unlike freedom of speech, to certain aspects of which our commitment must be virtually unconditional, freedom of the press should be contingent on the degree to which it promotes certain values at the core of our interest in freedom of expression generally. Freedom of the press, in other words, is an instrumental good: It is good if it does certain things and not especially good (not good enough to justify special protections, anyway) otherwise. If, for example, the mass media tend to suppress diversity and impoverish public debate, the arguments meant to support freedom of the press turn against it, and we may rightly consider regulating the media to achieve the ultimate purposes of freedom of the press.

I

The press is often described as having a special "watchdog function" or as being a kind of "fourth branch of government." Some writers, noting the First Amendment's mention of freedom of the press in addition to freedom of speech (the only reference in the Constitution, they emphasize, to a specific commercial enterprise), argue that the press is entitled to special protections, beyond those accorded speech in general. Yet when we examine the most famous arguments for freedom of the press, we find nothing to distinguish them from those for freedom of speech or expression generally. Mill's discussion in *On Liberty* begins by asserting the need for "liberty of the press" and proceeds to enumerate arguments for freedom of expression in general. Similarly, in "What Is Enlightenment?" Kant defends freedom of the press with general arguments for the benefits of freedom of thought and discussion.[11] It is much the same with the other standard sources in the literature of freedom of the press: The press is treated as a voice, albeit a more powerful one, on a par with individual voices, and defending press freedom is then tantamount to a general defense of free speech.

In one way there is nothing wrong with this. The arguments for freedom of the press *are* arguments for a more general freedom of expression. But it does not follow that whatever supports freedom of speech also supports freedom of the press, for at least two related reasons, which are discussed in the sections that follow. First, considerations internal to the theory of free speech theory itself may provide reasons for limiting freedom of the press. That is what is at issue in the claim that the contemporary mass media may suppress information and stifle ideas rather than promote them.[12] Second, the modern press consists largely of vast and complex institutions that differ in essential respects both from individuals and from the early press, around which the concept of freedom of the press grew.[13] Arguments that support freedom of expression for individuals or for small publications do not necessarily support similar freedoms for the mass media. But contemporary defenders of freedom of the press commonly assimilate the new forms to the old.

It remains to be seen, then, to what extent the arguments for free speech support freedom of the press.

II

We want free speech for many reasons. Some involve essentially individual interests; others, the public interest or the common good. Some have to do with politics, or democratic politics in particular; others concern intellectual values like truth. Still others have to do with promoting certain virtues of character, such as tolerance.[14] Some involve the interests of speakers; others, the interests of listeners or society at large. Some arguments emphasize the disadvantages of suppressing speech rather than the advantages of allowing it. These considerations vary in strength and persuasive power, and not all support free speech in the same way. But one thing is clear: Any "monistic" theory of free speech, emphasizing only one of these values, will fail to do justice to the variety and richness of our interests in free speech.

But plurality is not miscellany. It is striking that these considerations do not stand to one another accidentally as distinct arguments for a single conclusion but are bound together in various ways. Each of the main arguments I shall consider shares assumptions with some of the others. (Together they stand as a fine example of Wittgensteinian family resemblances.) In some cases, this is not surprising; in others, the connections are less apparent. In the following pages, I hope to make some of these connections clear and so go some way toward explaining why the existence of a variety of arguments for free speech is not simply fortuitous.

Let us begin by imposing some order on these arguments, first, by asking what we want when we want free speech. I believe we have two main goals: (1) that people be able to communicate without interference and (2) that there be many people communicating, or at least many different ideas and points of view being communicated. These commitments can be described in terms of two basic principles. The first we may call the *noninterference* or *no censorship principle:* One should not be prevented from thinking, speaking, reading, writing, or listening as one sees fit. The other I call the *multiplicity of voices principle:* The purposes of freedom of speech are realized when expression and diversity of expression flourish. Although, as we shall see, the arguments for free speech demonstrate the importance of both principles, they seem capable of conflict. Indeed, their conjunction partly explains our dilemma about freedom of the press: Government intervention seems to intrude on the first principle, but it may advance the second.

In theory, and often in practice, the principles are compatible: My being free to speak without interference in no way inhibits others from expressing themselves. I can write in my diary and you can write in yours; I can distribute my propaganda in the airport and you can distribute yours. (Even here we can see the beginnings of strain: The airport will support only so many.) To the extent that the principles peacefully coexist – and assuming that communication is a natural human urge – we satisfy the multiplicity of voices principle, a "positive" principle requiring that something (talk, conversation, debate) happen, when we satisfy the "negative" noninterference principle, which requires that something (interference) not happen. Yet in fact the freedom of editors and publishers from outside control can inhibit the multiplication of voices in the public forum. A newspaper may not interfere with a person's right to speak or write, but it may very well prevent her from expressing her views in that newspaper, even if it is the only one in town, and even if she has a legitimate and significant grievance or point of view and no comparable opportunity to publicize it. Such decisions are simply exercises of the newspaper's editorial autonomy, which appears to fall neatly under the noninterference principle. It may seem just as obvious that when this principle clashes with the multiplicity of voices, it is the latter that must give way.

But things are not so simple; what seems obvious may be false. Our interests in free speech make it plausible to speak of a fundamental right or freedom to think and speak and write and listen and read without interference; but there is no "right to publish" or right to editorial autonomy in the same sense. No one – not even network presidents or newspaper publishers – possesses a fundamental right to editorial autonomy that is violated by regulation designed to enhance the multiplicity of voices.

To see why this is so, we must first examine the main arguments for free speech.

III

Among our deepest interests in free speech is a concern about individual autonomy and self-expression that cuts across any particular social or political ideal that is likely to divide us. Most basically, we take it to be of overriding importance that a person be able to think for himself, that whatever his "outer" condition he not be intellectually or psychologically subjugated to another's will.[15] Autonomy so understood requires freedom of speech because of the close connection between thought and language. A person cannot think freely if he cannot speak; and he cannot think freely if others cannot speak, for it is in hearing the thoughts of others and being able to communicate with them that we develop our thoughts. Thus, autonomy requires freedom to speak as well as freedom to hear. And it implies freedom of speech for others as well as for oneself – not simply on grounds of fairness but in order to attain one's own interests in freedom of speech.

To value autonomy is to value a certain intellectual or psychological condition, distinct from "outer" freedom – the ability to govern our actions. We want the latter as well, of course, but outer freedom is subject to all the limits that the rights and like freedom of others impose. An appeal to freedom-in-general will not, then, carve out special protections for speech. But autonomy, conceived as the ability to think for oneself, differs from this much broader freedom of action. And it is precisely because one person's autonomy does not limit another's that we can value autonomy in an unqualified, nearly absolute way.

Yet the focus on autonomy might seem to signal an exaggerated preoccupation with the inner life. Surely, it will be objected, our interest in freedom of speech does not derive only from our concern with freedom of thought; surely we want also to be able to express our thoughts "in the world." Our fundamental interest in freedom of expression is an interest not only in freedom to think for ourselves but also in communicating our thoughts to others, leaving a mark on the world, making outer what is inner.

As I have already acknowledged, the inner–outer distinction is overstated, because thinking requires language, and language requires communication – because often we do not know what we think or feel until we put our inchoate inner goings-on into words or discuss them with others. Yet there remains a distinction between autonomy, the ability to think for oneself, and self-expression, the communicating of one's thoughts to others. Both are important components of our interest in free speech.

Some critics resist the argument from self-expression, however, because they believe it proves too much. Because anything one might wish to do can be considered a mode of self-expression, the argument easily becomes an argument for liberty-in-general that again fails to make speech special.[16]

So we need a way of preventing self-expression from swallowing up the whole of action. We want to protect a person when she criticizes another but not when she punches him in the nose. I believe a relevant distinction can be drawn based on the notion of essentially symbolic expression. Freedom of speech protects expression that is essentially symbolic. Natural language is the obvious example but not the only one; painting and mathematics, for example, are also essentially symbolic. Punching someone in the nose, however, while expressive, is not essentially symbolic.

Why is symbolic expression special? It is definitively associated with human beings; it is the primary means by which we communicate beliefs, ideas, even feelings (its importance is not, then, tied exclusively to our rationality); its success requires distinctively human responses – understanding, and not mere reaction. Although some instances of speech (performatives) are rightly considered actions, and although all speech is action in a trivial sense, it is appropriate to distinguish speech from action insofar as speech possesses intentionality, insofar as it means something, insofar as what is expressed is "about" something.

So understood, self-expression is a legitimate and important ground for free speech.

IV

Very different from the arguments from autonomy and self-expression is the argument from democracy, usually credited to Alexander Meiklejohn.[17] Because democracy means popular sovereignty, Meiklejohn argues, the citizens in a democracy, as the ultimate decision makers, need full (or at least a lot of) information to make intelligent political choices. Meiklejohn's argument stresses two functions of freedom of speech and press in a democracy. One is the informative function: Free speech permits the flow of information necessary for citizens to make informed decisions and for leaders (public servants) to stay abreast of the interests of their constituents (the sovereign electorate). Second, and not easily separated from the first, is the critical function: The press, in particular, serves as the people's watchdog, ensuring independent criticism and evaluation of the established power of government and other institutions that may usurp democratic power.

But Meiklejohn's account ignores an essential feature of

democracy and an important function of free speech. Democracy means not only that "the people" are collectively self-governing, but also that they are equal in an important sense. The democratic equality of persons bears on free speech in two ways. First, democracy functions as it should only when each person's interests are represented in the political forum; freedom of speech and press enhances opportunities for representation. Second, we show the sort of respect for persons associated with democracy both by acknowledging that anyone (regardless of race or class or lack of company) may have a view worth expressing, and by assuming that people can be open-minded or intelligent enough to judge alien views on their merits. Only under these conditions can majority rule become morally respectable and not merely the best of a bad lot of decision procedures.[18]

The second point connects the democratic argument for free speech with the argument that freedom of speech is an indispensable means to the attainment of truth. The belief that anyone might make a valuable contribution to the search for truth or for better ways to do things does not mean that we think "anyone" is likely to. It means: (1) There is no way of telling in advance where a good idea will come from. (2) Valuable contributions to arriving at truth come in many forms, speaking the truth being only one of them. We arrive at truth or the best policy largely by indirection. (3) Thus, much of the value of a person's contribution to the "marketplace of ideas" is its role in stimulating others to defend or reformulate or refute, and that value may be quite independent of the merits of the original view. Even fallacy has its place in the search for truth. These are essentially Mill's points in Chapter 2 of *On Liberty.*

As I suggested earlier, the connection between the arguments from democracy and truth is not simply serendipitous. Most of us are democrats not only because we believe in an ultimate moral equality but in part because we believe that *things turn out better* in democracies. If this is not simply crude relativism (truth or goodness is whatever the majority thinks it is), then it must be rooted in the belief that the public exchange of ideas transforms popular decision making into something morally and epistemologically respectable. Moreover, egalitarianism, a linchpin of democracy, and fallibilism, a central assumption in the argument from truth, are mutually supportive: The first bids us attend to the views of the "lowly" and the second bids us question those of the expert and the elite.[19]

V

The interconnections among the various grounds for free speech help us understand another of its standard defenses. Both Kant and Mill stressed the role of freedom of expression in human self-realization or self-development. Although commentators usually cite Chapter 2 of *On Liberty* for the argument from truth, the whole work is an extended defense of the connection between freedom of expression and self-realization. Quoting Wilhelm von Humboldt, Mill proclaims that "the end of man . . . is the highest and most harmonious development of his powers to a complete and consistent whole," and that for this two conditions are requisite: "freedom, and variety of situations."[20] A variety of ideas is obviously both a precondition of and an essential ingredient in the latter. Kant argues that the "public use of man's reason," by which he means a person's ability to communicate ideas to the public at large, is essential to human enlightenment. On its face the argument from self-realization is vulnerable to the same kind of objection made against the argument from self-expression: All sorts of things (education and travel, for example) may enhance self-development, and nothing in the argument distinguishes speech. Self-development – making the most out of oneself, or making oneself as wise as possible – is surely an admirable goal, but one so broad and open-ended that it fails to mark out speech.

But this objection is not persuasive. One reason is that allowing people to speak and listen costs incomparably less than providing education and travel.[21] But there is another reason too. The foregoing objection conceives of self-realization or self-development as what we might call a "maximizing" concept: More is better, and nothing distinguishes the essential from the rest. Although for many purposes this is perfectly reasonable, I think self-development has a more circumscribed core that serves to bridge the arguments from autonomy and from truth. For a large area of human interests, the arguments for free speech from truth and from self-realization are so closely related as to be practically inseparable. The reason is that where "morals, religion, politics, social relations, and the business of life"[22] are concerned, truth, if we speak of truth at all, must be something inseparable from the process of arriving at it, and has therefore a great deal to do with the virtues of intellect and character central to self-development.[23] As Mill argues, "Truth, in the great practical concerns of life, is so much a question of the reconciling and combining of opposites that very few have minds sufficiently capacious and impartial to make the adjustment with an approach to correctness, and it has to be made by the rough process of a struggle between combatants fighting under hostile banners."[24] The nature of truth in these matters determines the nature of wisdom: "If the cultivation of the understanding consists in one thing more than in another, it is surely in learning the grounds of one's own opinions . . . on every subject on which difference of opinion is possible, the truth depends on a balance to be struck between two sets of conflicting reasons."[25] This is one essential element in enlightenment and self-development: not being everything you are capable of being, but understanding the bases and limitations of your views. So understood, self-development is very close to autonomy. Nor are the virtues here purely intellectual; the self-awareness Mill describes requires fairness and encourages tolerance. Moving from the individual to the society, an enlightened society is one in which, following on public dialogue and debate, a balance has been struck between conflicting interests. Enlightenment is thus inseparable from the democratic process.

All our interests in free speech have an important social and even a public component. To satisfy them, a certain quantity and diversity of speech must exist and be heard – a multiplicity of voices. That there must be a multiplicity of voices if free speech is to advance the causes of democracy and truth is obvious. But the same goes for autonomy and self-development, values that can seem purely private and isolated from the public world, and that may at first sight seem to support only the noninterference principle. This is not simply because all thinking involves language, which is public, but because thinking for oneself is a matter not of coming up with wholly original ideas but rather of subjecting one's ideas, which come largely from others, to certain tests.[26] Autonomy is not a matter of believing what you feel like believing, as freedom, on some accounts, is a matter of doing what you feel like doing and therefore tantamount to noninterference. Autonomy and self-development in an intellectual vacuum are impossible. Thus, a multiplicity of voices is central to achieving individual autonomy and not only to the more obviously social goods, democracy and truth. And, on the other hand, noninterference – the opportunity to express oneself and to hear others express themselves – is as essential to the attainment of the social values underlying free speech as to the individual.

VI

Taken together, these arguments support a strong free speech principle, one that enables individuals and groups to think, speak, write, listen, read, and publish freely.

Even under a strong free speech principle, however, all such activities take place under constraints. I may read what I like, but not without your permission if the only copy of my favorite book happens to be in your private library. I may orate on the evils of fluoridation, but not (unless she permits) in the dentist's waiting room. I may write what I think is a groundbreaking tract, but nothing guarantees its publication in the journal of my choice (or any, for that matter).

How do we account for these constraints? One way is to say that our commitment to free speech amounts only to prohibitions against restriction by *government*, leaving open restriction by private parties. But this is unsatisfactory, because insofar as we value free speech we will want to remove obstacles to it from whatever source, public or private. That we are morally barred from taking remedies when the obstacle is private must be demonstrated; it cannot simply be assumed.[27]

A related account of the constraints on free speech asserts that a person's freedom of speech is limited by the property rights of others.[28] But this is inadequate because it suggests both that property rights are ultimate, simple, and straightforward, marking a natural line between mine and thine, and that they always take priority, setting a rigid framework within which free speech (and other important moral and political principles) must maneuver a narrow course.

But the system of property relations, and its connection with other interests, is much more complicated than this account allows. Ownership rights over things (including everything from your toothbrush to the corner drugstore to General Motors) evolve in response to a variety of factors. Some are moral values, like privacy and equality. Some are pragmatic considerations: convenience, efficiency, and utility. Property rights are complex sets of relationships: With different kinds of property one can do different things; hardly ever can one do with one's property exactly what one pleases. Zoning laws; eminent domain; regulations concerning environmental protection, public utilities, health and safety – all attest to the qualified nature of property rights even in a system such as ours that accords great respect to private property.

If property relations did not have this character, the idea of a free speech principle (or anything rightly called a principle) would be very frail. However one thinks any specific free speech issue should be settled, a commitment to free speech of the kind embodied in the First Amendment means that when free speech clashes with other interests, the former has a pressing claim not automatically defeated by competing claims of property rights.

We can illustrate this point about the flexible and responsive character of property rights with an example from outside the area of free speech. On a simplistic view of property rights, a person who owns a restaurant ought to be able to exclude potential customers at will. But American law prohibits discrimination on the basis of race; one who opens a restaurant must serve anyone, assuming he is not rowdy, drunk, or inappropriately dressed, and that the restaurant is not full. Our law is founded on a strong commitment to equality, or the wrongness of racial discrimination. The law applies to "public accommodations," so called although restaurants and hotels are ordinarily considered private property. How do we justify this law?

In several ways. First, we distinguish between a restaurant and a person's dinner table. One is legally free to discriminate on the basis of race in choosing one's dinner guests. Although morally we may disapprove of all manifestations of racial discrimination, we hold that the value of privacy, of a sphere over which the individual is sovereign, is so important that it overrides or excludes the principle of equality. (A person's home is her castle; we do not say that a person's hotel is her castle.) Indeed, the near reverence with which we as a society regard private property derives in good part from thoughts of other people invading our homes or using our toothbrushes – from imagined violations of *personal* property. Such violations encroach on privacy, but not everything we call "private property" is private in this sense. Our acceptance of discrimination "within the home" also reflects the belief that in this sphere state coercion is not only wrong but largely ineffective, perhaps counterproductive: You can't legislate morality in *this* way.

But in opening a restaurant, which has an explicitly commercial purpose, one acknowledges the diminished importance in that realm of privacy; thus the assertion of privacy in defense of discrimination rings hollow. In addition, although a restaurant is privately owned, it depends on a variety of public benefits and privileges, the most obvious being a license to operate.[29] It therefore ceases to be a wholly private institution.

We can apply a similar analysis to the examples given at the beginning of this section. First, the case of my favorite book found only in your private library. Here my "right to read" does not include the right to enter your library without your permission. Two kinds of reasons support this conclusion. First, as in the case of choosing one's dinner guests, the value of privacy within a limited sphere is too important to sacrifice; and coercion in this sphere would probably be ineffective. At the same time, we acknowledge the importance of the ability to read freely through the institution of public libraries. It is rare for the book I want to be available only in one private place.[30] Public libraries are a means of fulfilling free speech values without having to invade other important interests.

The case of speechifying on fluoridation in the dentist's office can be understood in a similar way. Being able to orate on the subject of one's choice does not give one absolute discretion as to "time, place, and manner" (in the language of constitutional discussion), nor does it amount to the right to harangue a captive audience. Public space – streets and parks – is adequate to accommodate the interests at stake here.

We can sharpen our understanding of the relation between free speech and property values by examining a series of free speech cases on the right to speak or distribute literature on private property, and especially in shopping centers. Some of these cases do, and some do not, uphold the free speech claims in dispute. Taken together, they illuminate the subject at issue here.

In *Marsh v. Alabama* (1948), the first important case, the Supreme Court upheld the right of a Jehovah's Witness to distribute religious literature on a sidewalk in a company town – a town wholly owned by a shipbuilding company but otherwise indistinguishable from myriad other small southern towns.[31] In *NLRB v. Babcock & Wilcox* (1956), the Court ruled that a company could refuse to allow union organizers to distribute literature in the parking lot and on the walkway leading from it to the plant entrance, since alternative channels of communication with the workers existed.[32] Twelve years later, in *Amalgamated Food Employees v. Logan Valley Plaza,* the right of those involved in a labor dispute to picket a business within a shopping center complex was upheld.[33] *Central Hardware v. NLRB* (1972) also involved union organizers on company property, this time in the parking lot of the store.[34] The Court ruled that reasonable alternative means of reaching the employees were available, and thus that *Babcock* rather than *Logan Valley* controlled. Decided at the same time was *Lloyd v. Tanner,* upholding the right of a shopping center to exclude those distributing leaflets against the Vietnam War, on the grounds that the subject matter was unrelated to the purposes of the shopping center and so could be adequately "discussed" elsewhere.[35] Finally, in *PruneYard Shopping Center v. Robins* (1980), a case involving the distribution of handbills in opposition to a United Nations resolution against "Zionism," the Court upheld the California Supreme Court's ruling that access to shopping centers is protected by the California Constitution, and that such provisions do not violate the property rights of shopping center owners.[36]

At least two related principles emerge from these decisions. The first, articulated in *Marsh,* is that insofar as a private corporation adopts the functions of a municipality, it assumes the obligations with respect to free speech that fall to public bodies. Gulf Shipbuilding owned the streets and sidewalks in Chickasaw, Alabama; it provided police protection, sewerage, and other services. It was therefore required to permit First Amendment freedoms to be exercised in the usual manner, on streets and sidewalks.

Part of the rationale for this principle leads to the other important principle implicit in these decisions. Chickasaw had no public streets and sidewalks; thus no comparable alternatives existed for the exercise of free speech rights. How heavily free speech weighs against property rights – and it is clear from these decisions that this is a question of degree varying from case to case – depends on the availability of reasonable alternative means of communicating. What constitutes a reasonable alternative, in turn, depends on physical facts, on the nature of the message to be communicated, and (relatedly) on the intended or appropriate audience. What distinguishes *Logan Valley* from *Babcock* and *Central Hardware* is the physical layout – the existence of a genuine shopping center and not simply a private business with a parking lot – which made other means of communicating with workers ineffective. What distinguishes *Lloyd* from all three is that the speakers' message – concerning the Vietnam War – bore no special relation to the business of the shopping center, so that leafleting could reasonably take place elsewhere.

This last argument might be disputed on grounds that return us to the first principle. If shopping centers have become our modern Main Streets – if they have replaced downtown business districts as the hub of commercial and social life – then to that extent the principles implicit in *Marsh* ought to apply. The shopping center in *Lloyd* employed a security force with police powers within the center; it had an auditorium used by various groups (most fee-paying), including presidential candidates, and walkways where the Salvation Army and similar charitable groups were permitted to solicit donations. In the suburbs where shopping centers reign, there may be nowhere else to find large numbers of people not locked in their cars. The California Supreme Court's construal of its constitution's free speech provision to permit individuals access to shopping centers, which was upheld in *PruneYard*, rests on precisely this kind of reasoning.[37]

VII

The case of publishing, central to our discussion of freedom of the press, raises further complications. What is obvious is that no one has a right to publish, if that means a right to succeed in publishing where one chooses. I may send off my writings to any number of book or journal publishers – that is to say, I have the right to *try* to publish – but whether I succeed typically depends on choices that they are entitled to make.[38]

This is just to acknowledge that the ability to publish is

embedded in a system of property relations. But this is the beginning, not the end, of inquiry. For, as I have argued, property rights are not the simple and ultimate given from which all policy choices must begin; they themselves result from the interplay of a variety of considerations moral and pragmatic. And exactly what rights and duties follow upon property ownership in a particular kind of case depends on the interests at stake there.

It does not suffice, then, simply to assert the property rights of publishers and editors against all claims to regulate the press. The publisher may say, "It's my newspaper and I can print what I want," but the question remains why we should accept the absolutist conception of property rights lurking in that statement as defining the publisher's role. The appeal to property rights may explain why it is the publisher – rather than the reporter or the printer or the janitor – in whom editorial authority is invested, but it does not explain why newspapers and other media organizations should be immune from regulation when other businesses are not.

The answer cannot be that editorial autonomy is implicit in the commitment to free speech, for, as we have seen, the free speech principle does not imply a right to publish where one chooses. And that is as true for newspaper owners and network presidents as for anyone else. This point undercuts a great deal of the moral suasion that is supposed to attach to the assertion of editorial autonomy; editorial autonomy – unlike the kind of individual autonomy discussed earlier – is not a fundamental human right, and defending it requires more than the appeal to the nobility of free speech values.

We can now see that the typical claim of editorial autonomy by publishers and editors is really a disguised property claim – it is the assertion of a property right in the guise of a free speech right. Because, as we have seen, property claims are not always decisive, and because the "right" to free speech does not equal the right to editorial autonomy, the defense of editorial autonomy requires something more. If, even where there are serious costs to diversity and public debate, we grant publishers or editors the right of editorial autonomy, that is because on the whole doing so is the best way to advance free speech values. The question, discussed in the following section, is whether a policy of nonregulation of the press is good for the values underlying free speech.[39]

Let me put these conclusions in terms of the two basic principles described earlier as characterizing our interests in free speech: *noninterference* and the *multiplicity of voices*. Obviously, our worry about editorial autonomy is that it can inhibit the multiplicity of voices. But does the noninterference principle not support editorial autonomy? And how do we arrive at the judgment (which may seem to conflict with a standard liberal presumption in favor of noninterference as definitive of liberty) that multiplicity of voices takes priority over noninterference?

The answer has two parts. First, while the term "noninterference" covers some crucial free speech values, it is made to carry more weight than it can bear. Its essential core is autonomy: What we fear most when we fear interference with freedom of expression is mind control, Big Brother style, being thrown into prison for opposing the government, and generally the extreme suppression we find in totalitarian regimes. Everyone can agree that these form the core of our concern with free speech – it is the freedoms at stake here that must be protected first and foremost. As soon as we get beyond these fundamental freedoms, however – as soon as the question is not whether one may speak, but where and in what form – the ability to express oneself becomes entangled with questions of property. It is not that at that point noninterference ceases to matter, but that its value is spread so thin as to make it a useless guide to action: The question is whether to interfere with my freedom to orate in the dentist's office or with her freedom to exclude trespassers from her property. The fact that here the dentist's claim wins hands down shows that noninterference-in-matters-of-speech is not the knockdown argument it sometimes seems. "Time, place, and manner" restrictions – often added as if they were minor qualifications – lie at the heart of the matter.

While the first part of the answer shrinks the scope and

power of the noninterference principle, the second enhances the multiplicity of voices. All the arguments for freedom of expression, with the possible exception of the argument from self-expression, demonstrate the centrality not of speech simply but of discussion, debate, diversity of ideas and sources of information. They point to the multiplicity of voices as their central and unifying theme. Noninterference is sovereign in its place – but its place is much smaller.

VIII

Doctrines do not become dogmas for nothing. Considering the press in all its variations over the last several hundred years, we may be satisfied that overall freedom of the press does work to advance the values of free speech. Ever since colonial times, the United States has seen a great abundance of publications of every description: pamphlets, newsletters, magazines, newspapers, and journals spanning the whole spectrum of social and political thought.

What, then, is the complaint? It is that the cornucopia has less and less to do with the spread of information and the formation of public opinion in our society. Most people get the vast majority of their news from the mass media – from the three commercial networks, *Time* and *Newsweek*, the wire services and daily newspapers. The *New York Times* and the *Washington Post* are the essential sources for those who hope to understand economic or political affairs in American society. It is not simply that each person learns mostly from one source but that we all learn from the same few sources. Moreover, the mass media do more than provide the news. They are instrumental in shaping our worldview, and so play a role in our society much greater than that of their forerunners.

Several things account for the special role of the mass media. None is individually sufficient to distinguish them or to justify special treatment, but together they add up to a compelling set of reasons. One simple fact is the increasing extent and power of media corporations, which are often part of and interlocked with other large corporations. It would be naive to think that the economic and political interests of these institutions do not get reflected in their informational "products."[40] To the extent that they do get reflected, less powerful interests and perspectives get less than a fair hearing in the political forum.

But this is only the most obvious source of the problem. Partly the mass media are mass in virtue of the size of their audiences and the extent of their penetration within a population. In some cases, a mass medium may function as a monopoly, and this is a powerful argument for ensuring diversity. More and more cities and towns in the United States, for example, are served by only one newspaper. But most mass media institutions are not monopolies: There are, after all, three commercial networks, and they do compete. Yet the economics of the mass media, in which profit is the uppermost consideration, makes it virtually impossible for any to provide programming that differs significantly from the others. In this respect the nonmass media are different. Economically, their aim is often more modest: to survive. Their primary purpose often lies in advancing a point of view, or promoting discussion of certain issues.

Out of the differences between the mass media and the ordinary press emerges a difference in role, a role both defined by the mass media themselves and assumed by others. Precisely because the mass media do not present themselves as having a distinctive point of view but rather as describing the world "as it is," and because people take them to be engaged primarily in this descriptive enterprise, they bear a kind of responsibility for presenting many sides of an issue that the nonmass media do not. The smaller publications (on the order of *The National Review, The New Republic,* and *The Nation*) do not in general purport to be engaged in this purely descriptive activity. They would, I think, be more likely to characterize what they do as analysis or interpretation of events – or opinion – rather than pure reportage.[41] As such they function as elements in the public forum. But in a crucial sense the *New York Times* and the *Washington Post* constitute the forum itself.

We should perhaps always view with suspicion proposals to tamper with deeply entrenched practices, and freedom of the press is no exception. But the change in practice, if there is to be one, would reflect not a new attitude toward "the press" but rather the rise of a new institution, the mass media. The concept of freedom of the press developed in the seventeenth and eighteenth centuries. The mass media began to emerge only in the 1830s, with the penny press. Before this, political newspapers made no pretense of objectivity or neutrality, and were marked by a degree of vitriol and bias unmatched today.[42] They were financed by political parties, candidates for office, or political factions, who were directly responsible for editorial policy.[43] But this was common knowledge, and it is safe to assume that readers did not view these publications as sources of "the truth" about the world as we regard the mass media today.[44]

IX

Our earlier discussion of speech in shopping centers bears directly on the mass media, and it is appropriate here to draw the lessons from it. There are obvious analogies between the modern American shopping center and the mass media. Both mass media organizations and shopping centers consist of large private organizations that serve (one as an essential part of its role, the other accidentally) as forums for discussion and debate; both have largely driven out smaller competitors. Each has assumed an essentially different function from those of the institutions out of which it has evolved. The shopping center is more than a collection of private stores; it includes the spaces between and around them, and so replicates not just the businesses of Main Street but the municipality as well. Analogously, the mass news organization is not simply a larger version of its predecessor; for all the reasons described in the last section, it has become not only an actor but the stage as well. Alternative channels of communication to the mass media are not comparable to it, and so not satisfactory: They cannot possibly reach the same or equivalent audiences. Thus the principle that emerges from the shopping center cases – that the weight of arguments for access depends on the availability of reasonable alternative channels of communication – suggests the appropriateness of regulating the media.[45]

Some will resist the analogy between shopping centers and mass media, for at least two reasons. In the first place, the shopping center cases produce a mixed bag of results and hardly provide resounding support for the rights of free speech. Second, the analogy ignores an important difference between shopping centers and the mass media: The opposing interests of the mass media are themselves free speech interests, while those of shopping centers are merely property interests. Once this difference is taken into account, it may be argued, the interests of those who desire access to the mass media pale to insignificance.

In response to the first objection, we should remember that the principle in the shopping center cases takes the form of a hypothetical: *if*, or *to the extent that*, reasonable alternative channels of communication do not exist, to that extent the claims of free speech weigh more heavily. The Court's view that in many cases reasonable alternatives to the shopping center do exist does not affect the principle. I believe it is clear that the antecedent is fulfilled in the case of the mass media: Small journals and pamphlets are not reasonable alternatives to CBS and the *New York Times*.

How important, then, is the fact that the interests not only of those desiring access but also of their opponents are free speech interests? (Partly free speech interests, anyway; like shopping centers, mass media organizations are also commercial enterprises.) Journalists and media executives imagine that granting access rights must entail censorship of their own views, or, what may seem worse, coercion to publish something against their will. But we need to examine such fears more carefully. One concern is that in being forced to publish an opinion, a person or an organization will be identified with a view it does not hold, and this is very troubling. But a "contingent" right of access, say, to respond to an attack in a newspaper does not have this character; no one wants to prevent the publisher from disowning the view. The other fear rests on the belief that having to publish one thing means the inability to publish something else, and so in effect amounts to censorship. In the real world, however, not every inability to publish because of having to publish something else can be seriously regarded as censorship. If a network cancels *Wheel of Fortune* to carry a political debate, censorship is not at issue. Moreover, publishing is not always a zero-sum game: It is sometimes possible just to publish more.[46]

It does not follow, then, that because news organizations, unlike shopping centers, possess significant free speech interests and not merely property interests, access claims are stripped of their legitimacy or their power. What follows is just that we may sometimes have to weigh one free speech interest against another.

X

No one likes to have his freedom curtailed, and so it is not surprising that journalists and media professionals find the foregoing arguments extremely distasteful. I have been trying to show why some of the most important weapons in journalists' defense of freedom of the press do not find their mark, and in the process to explode some of the rhetoric surrounding the role of the press in our society, by analyzing the idea of a "right" to editorial autonomy and the interconnections and confusions between speech and property interests. Still, it may be argued, I have neglected an argument against government regulation just as fundamental as those I have rejected. This is the simple idea that the press must be free of government interference just because, whatever the defects or corruptions of the press, government can never be trusted to correct them. The prospect of regulators regulating their own potential critics appears to involve a basic conflict of interest. The principle implicit here, that the state should not interfere in the workings of the press, is as fundamental as any.

The appropriate response is not that we can trust government more than opponents of regulation believe, but that we can trust others less. Regulation is needed just because private power poses a grave threat to the independence and integrity of the press. Reasonable people will disagree, of course, about whether the dangers to the press posed by enormous concentrations of private power are so great that we must risk government regulation, or whether the state is so untrustworthy, its motives so compromised by conflict of interest, that we must take our chances and leave the mass media entirely in the hands of corporations.

Against the latter view – that here government cannot be trusted, period – several things can be said. First, anyone who suspects government so unrelentingly needs to justify his (relative) trust of corporations. Both, after all, are made up of human beings with (we may assume) similar psychologies and motivational structures. Second, the state is not a monolithic force but a collection of varied agencies, some of which can be more insulated from partisan politics than others. Third, support of government regulation of the press is compatible with strict opposition to censorship. The point is not to prevent news organizations from expressing their views but to ensure the expression of other views; and, as I argued earlier, the latter does not entail the former. Finally, only some forms of regulation involve the kind of intrusion that is so worrisome. Two broad approaches to regulation of the media are usually distinguished. *Content regulation* makes specific demands of press institutions to cover certain kinds of issues, to cover them in a certain way, or to provide access to certain points of view. (The fairness doctrine is the most prominent example.) *Structural regulation* instead builds rules and constraints into the structure and organization of the media taken as a whole. Structural regulation includes a variety of approaches. Certain rules prohibit multiple ownership of news organizations, and others designate a number of cable channels for public access. Economic incentives can be offered to news organizations to promote diversity or provide services that are unlikely to be provided in the unrestricted marketplace. Subsidies can be given to public media institutions. Government currently subsidizes public broadcasting with tax dollars, but other approaches are possible. One attractive proposal is to exact a "spectrum fee" from broadcasters for the privilege (now granted free) of being able to broadcast,[47] and to use the funds to finance public broadcasting or to subsidize groups lacking the resources to penetrate the major avenues of mass communication.

Structural approaches to regulation considerably weaken the objection that in principle government is in no position to regulate the press; they demonstrate that how intrusive regulation is depends on the form it takes, something over which we have a great deal of control. Structural approaches also counter the argument that regulation is counterproductive – that it causes "chilling effects" because news organizations, fearing, for example, that controversial programming will trigger fairness doctrine complaints, will simply avoid conflict by airing innocuous or frivolous programs. These objections still hold for content regulation, but even there their validity and force are still very much under debate.

I do not mean by the brevity of this discussion to suggest that these objections have been overcome. On the contrary, they require more discussion than is possible here. My point is, rather, to relocate the focus of debate about freedom of the press, and the justifiability of its regulation, from the realm of rights and principles to that of practical possibility and utility – to questions about what works to produce more diversity, and whether regulation does more harm than good. The debate needs to be relocated not, of course, because rights and principles have no place in the discussion of these issues or in the formation of public policy, but because the press appears to be claiming special rights not possessed by the rest of us, and these require special justification. If press institutions or their agents have special rights, it is because the people as a whole have granted them; if the people have granted them, it is because doing so is to the benefit of us all. It is the unthinking assumption that we are all better off if the mass media are left to their own devices that is challenged by the character of the mass media and their role in the structure of contemporary society.

NOTES

This essay was written under a grant from the Markle Foundation, whose generous support I gratefully acknowledge. A slightly different version appeared in *Philosophy & Public Affairs* 16, no. 4 (Fall 1987). Copyright © 1987 by Princeton University Press. Reprinted with permission. I have benefited from discussion with the Institute for Philosophy and Public Policy's Working Group on News, the Mass Media, and Democratic Values, and with the New York Society for Philosophy and Public Affairs. Among the many people who commented on earlier versions of this essay, I especially want to thank Lee Bollinger, Owen Fiss, Robert Fullinwider, David Luban, Claudia Mills, Richard Mohr, Thomas Scanlon, and Michael Schudson.

1 Vol. 1, chap. 11.
2 (New York: Ballantine Books, 1964), pp. 30–1.
3 This formulation is neat but misleading. Viewed in purely quantitative terms, information is plentiful; indeed, the problem is that we are flooded with it and must take measures to stem the tide. When we talk about enhancing or inhibiting the flow of ideas and information, then, we are thinking about quality and diversity, not mere quantity. Our concern is that we find less diversity in the mass media than we could and should, and than we would in the absence of *mass* media altogether.
4 See, e.g., Ben Bagdikian, *The Media Monopoly* (Boston: Beacon, 1983), esp. chap. 3; Tom Goldstein, *The News at Any Cost* (New York: Simon & Schuster, 1985), chap. 5; Peter Dreier and Steve Weinberg, "Interlocking Directorates," *Columbia Journalism Review* (November–December 1979).
5 For an extensively illustrated discussion of this and the third factor, see Jeffrey Abramson, "Four Criticisms of Press Ethics," this volume.
6 As compared, for example, with the European press. I mean to include here not just pure opinion (in the sense used by journalists) – what is found on the editorial and op-ed pages –

but explanatory journalism and news analysis as well as straight news. The narrowness is evident, for example, in the debate about providing military aid to the Nicaraguan Contras – no one argues that we ought to support the Sandinistas ("opinion"); in analysis of the arms race and arms control, where American government allegations that apparent moves by the Soviets toward arms reduction are merely public relations ploys are rarely questioned (news analysis); and in coverage of events – compare, for example, the amount of coverage allocated to the murder of Alex Odeh, Los Angeles regional director of the American-Arab Anti-Discrimination Committee, during the *Achille Lauro* crisis, with that allocated to the murder of Leon Klinghoffer. For a critical analysis of American media coverage of terrorism and related phenomena, see Edward S. Herman, *The Real Terror Network: Terrorism in Fact and Propaganda* (Boston: South End Press, 1982). Views out of the mainstream do occasionally appear, but not often or prominently enough to engage public debate.

7 Especially for a nonjournalist, specifying what of importance is not reported is fraught with paradox because it requires independent access to news sources. How do you know what is news except by following the usual sources? But see, e.g., Jerry Kammer, "The Navajos, the Hopis, and the U.S. Press," *Columbia Journalism Review* (July–August 1986), on the media's neglect of the federal government's largest forcible relocation since the internment of Japanese-Americans in World War II: the relocation of Navajo Indians as part of an attempt to resolve a historic feud between the Navajos and the Hopis. Unlike Wounded Knee, this story has not (yet) become theater.

8 See Henry Geller, "Mass Communications Policy: Where We Are and Where We Should Be Going," this volume, for a detailed discussion of actual and possible regulations.

9 The crucial case is *Miami Herald v. Tornillo*, 418 U.S. 241 (1974), where the Supreme Court held that a newspaper was not required to print a reply by a candidate attacked in editorials. The case contrasts sharply with *Red Lion Broadcasting v. FCC*, 395 U.S. 367 (1969), in which the Court upheld the FCC's requirements that radio and television stations provide free reply time to those attacked in station broadcasts.

10 By limited rights of access I mean so-called contingent access rights, those triggered by actions of a news organization –

such as editorials attacking a candidate of the kind involved in *Miami Herald*.

11 "The *public* use of man's reason must always be free, and it alone can bring about enlightenment among men . . . by the public use of one's own reason I mean that use which anyone may make of it *as a man of learning* addressing the entire *reading public*" (*Kant's Political Writings*, ed. Hans Reiss [Cambridge: Cambridge University Press, 1970], p. 55).

12 Such "internal" arguments are also made to restrict nonpress speech – to justify not tolerating the intolerant, or silencing the heckler, for example. The success of such arguments rests largely on their internal character, especially since the First Amendment (or, more generally, a serious commitment to free speech) means that a much stronger justification is required to restrict speech than to restrict most other activities. Thus, the argument that the values of free speech themselves justify restriction has a persuasive force that most other arguments for restriction lack. See Owen Fiss, "Why the State?," this volume.

13 For a related argument see Owen Fiss, "Free Speech and Social Structure," *Iowa Law Review* 71 (1986): 1408–10.

14 For the argument from tolerance, see Lee C. Bollinger, *The Tolerant Society: Freedom of Speech and Extremist Speech in America* (Oxford: Clarendon Press, 1986).

15 For a view of autonomy as the preeminent value in freedom of expression, see Thomas Scanlon, "A Theory of Freedom of Expression," *Philosophy & Public Affairs* 1 (1972). The emphasis on inner freedom goes back at least to Epictetus and Socrates.

16 See Frederick Schauer, *Free Speech: A Philosophical Inquiry* (Cambridge: Cambridge University Press, 1982), chap. 4, for this kind of objection.

17 Meiklejohn, *Political Freedom: The Constitutional Powers of the People* (New York: Harper, 1960), pp. 8–28.

18 Some democrats (and others) would emphasize another value bearing on free speech that Meiklejohn ignores: political participation. If, as Aristotle and Hannah Arendt believed, the good life includes public activity and the good society supports a high degree of civic participation, then the political value of free speech will not be exhausted by its informational, critical, or even representational functions. But although participation is a value, I do not believe it is an indispensable precondition

of democracy, as equality is. At most, the more participation the better. But even this is not obvious, since political involvement precludes other valuable commitments for which many people would choose to sacrifice it. (Participation might still be better for the society, even if not for all participating members.) In any case, the value of civic participation is a further argument for the worth of freedom of speech.

19 It does not follow that there is a strict deductive relation (in either direction) between the argument from truth and the argument from democracy. Socrates was certainly a fallibilist and an eloquent defender of the argument from truth but was no democrat, precisely because he doubted that people in general could put aside their passions and prejudices long enough to hear a case on its merits. It is much more difficult to imagine a democrat not committed to the argument from truth, however. (That is partly because of the complex nature of truth in "the great practical concerns of life," in Mill's words. See the next section.) But it may be possible. My claim is just that these arguments have a natural affinity; and especially that a democrat is almost certain to subscribe to the argument from truth.

20 *On Liberty* (Indianapolis: Bobbs-Merrill, 1956), pp. 69–70.

21 It does, of course, cost something to protect free speech and to keep order in the face of occasional violent outbreaks. Sometimes, traditions may even die and governments fall partly as a result of free speech. But education also creates these risks (if they are risks), in addition to its enormous monetary costs.

22 Mill, *On Liberty*, p. 44.

23 For a general view of truth as inseparable from the criteria for settling truth claims – a consensus theory of truth – see Jurgen Habermas, "A Postscript to *Knowledge and Human Interests*," *Philosophy of the Social Sciences* 3 (1973): 166–72; and Thomas McCarthy, *The Critical Theory of Jurgen Habermas* (Cambridge, Mass.: MIT Press, 1978), pp. 299–307.

24 Mill, *On Liberty*, p. 58.

25 Ibid., p. 44.

26 See Karl Popper, *Conjectures and Refutations: The Growth of Scientific Knowledge* (New York: Harper Torchbooks, 1968), esp. p. 352.

27 For a defense of the view that early liberal theorists were just as concerned to prevent concentrations and abuses of private as of state power, see Stephen Holmes, "Liberal Constraints

on Private Power?" this volume; for the idea of the state as a countervailing power to private powers heavily imprinted with "social structure," see Owen Fiss, "Why the State?," this volume.

28 See David Kelley and Roger Donway, "Liberalism and Free Speech," this volume.

29 It might be argued that this begs the question, since opponents of antidiscrimination laws may also object to the entire system of public accommodations licensing as an illegitimate encroachment on their rights. I strongly suspect, however, that few who opposed the civil rights laws took this principled stand. They did not object to health and other regulations governing their restaurants, but insisted only that it was their (God-given) right to exclude blacks.

30 Perhaps I want to read your rare edition, though. Tough luck: The values of free speech support access to the content of books, not their form.

31 326 U.S. 501.

32 351 U.S. 105.

33 391 U.S. 308.

34 407 U.S. 539.

35 407 U.S. 551.

36 447 U.S. 74.

37 *Robins v. PruneYard Shopping Center*, 23 Cal. 3d 899, 907.

38 If these attempts fail, I may choose to publish my essay "privately" (as we say): I may engage a printer, or have my essay duplicated, or perhaps find a "vanity" press. Here, too, I am dependent on others who own things that I need; like the ordinary book or journal publisher, they are at liberty to refuse to handle my work (although they are much less likely to). The argument that follows supports the conclusion that if *everyone* whose cooperation was necessary for me to publish my essay refused to cooperate (i.e., if no one would sell me access to a copy machine, and no one would sell me a copy machine, and no one would sell me paper for it), the state ought to help me get my essay published in some form.

39 For a similar argument concerning the press's "right" to maintain confidentiality of sources, see Ronald Dworkin, "The Farber Case: Reporters and Informers," in *A Matter of Principle* (Cambridge, Mass.: Harvard University Press, 1985), pp. 373–80.

40 See note 5, above. It does not follow that the news is crassly ideological; indeed, news organizations' need for a mass audience may dictate that news *not* be ideological in the usual sense, for this might turn off large numbers of people. The bias in the news toward official statements as against those of critical outsiders is a built-in advantage for officials that implies no explicit ideological message. See Gaye Tuchman, "Objectivity as Strategic Ritual: An Examination of Newsmen's Notions of Objectivity," *American Journal of Sociology* 77 (1972). The economic and political interests of news organizations manifest themselves most clearly in what does *not* make its way into the news, and in how stories relevant to the organizations' interests are reported.

41 I am opening a large can of worms here. The critique of the mass media rests partly on the claim that no sharp line can be drawn between "news" and "editorial" (and in turn between fact and value), that much of what is presented as news involves judgments of value and other controversial judgments. A better understanding of such complications by members of the press and the public might help to put the mass media's role in perspective.

42 The alternative was commercial newspapers, which consisted mainly of advertising and shipping news. See Michael Schudson, *Discovering the News: A Social History of American Newspapers* (New York: Basic, 1978), pp. 14–15.

43 Ibid.

44 See Anthony Smith, *Goodbye Gutenberg: The Newspaper Revolution of the 1980s* (London: Oxford University Press, 1980), chap. 1 (esp. p. 30), for the view that readers now look to newspapers for "facts" rather than for an overall ideological picture of the world, as they did in the seventeenth and eighteenth centuries.

45 We might put this in terms of Habermas's notion of an "ideal speech situation." The aim of regulation would be to approach (although never, realistically, to achieve) an ideal speech situation: to equalize the chances of all participants or points of view to speak – to speak, that is, approximately as often and as loudly as others. Only in such circumstances, according to Habermas, can the quest for truth be free of distorting influences such as explicit or implicit relations of domination. Habermas's concern here is with truth, but the point applies to the other arguments for free speech as well. See Habermas,

"Towards a Theory of Communicative Competence," *Inquiry* 13 (1970): 371–4; and McCarthy, *The Critical Theory of Jurgen Habermas*, pp. 307–10.

46 This would be true if newspapers were granted subsidies to cover costs of expanded op-ed pages and the like. Ironically, this argument makes the case for access to print stronger than for access to broadcast media, because the latter, as time-based rather than space-based, contain an inherent limit that the former does not. This conflicts with the standard view (rooted in First Amendment tradition) of the print media as more resistant to regulation than broadcasting.

47 For a defense of the spectrum fee idea, see Geller, "Mass Communications Policy."

Chapter 4

Why the state?

Owen M. Fiss

Americans are distrustful of the state. There have been occasional reversals of this attitude, for example, during the two world wars, the New Deal, and the civil rights era. But for the most part we have looked upon the state with great distrust, and for almost two decades now an attack on "big government" has been the organizing principle of American politics. It has provided the energy behind the demand for "deregulation," "privatization," a "balanced budget," and the "new federalism." No one has been more successful in conducting this war on the activist state than Ronald Reagan, and for this purpose he drew upon the classical liberal tradition of the United States.

For many, the First Amendment is seen as the apotheosis of this tradition. It is read as a bar to state action and given an almost absolutist quality. Exceptions are now and then permitted, when the stakes get high enough and urgent enough, as in the case of national security, but at its core the amendment is generally read as creating a strong presumption against state interferences with almost any form of speech. This reading of the First Amendment has been sustained and nurtured by the more general distrust of the state that is associated with classical liberalism and that was given such forceful expression by the Reagan administration. The amendment has returned the favor and has served as an important breeding ground of libertarian sentiment. Indeed, advocates of economic laissez-faire have often used the First Amendment to remind New Deal liberals of the virtues of limited government.[1]

It is within this context that recent debates about the media have proceeded, and thus it is not surprising that representatives of the media have added a constitutional dimension to their plea for deregulation. They have insisted that any government regulation of the media would contravene the First Amendment. Laws protecting against libel and obscenity have generally withstood this attack, but other forms of state intervention have not fared as well. A case in point is the FCC's fairness doctrine, which figures so prominently in the discussions in this volume and which is the focus of great political and legal controversy today. The fairness doctrine – a body of government regulations that has evolved through agency action, case law, and congressional legislation – consists first of a requirement that broadcasters cover issues of great public importance. The second and more frequently litigated part of the doctrine requires that the coverage of such public issues be balanced.[2]

In a 1969 decision, *Red Lion Broadcasting v. FCC*,[3] the Supreme Court upheld the fairness doctrine as consistent with the First Amendment. That decision was not adequately rationalized and for the most part has been an embattled precedent. It has been thoroughly criticized by commentators[4] and limited by the Court itself. During the seventies the Court held that it would be unconstitutional for a state to attempt similar regulation of newspapers,[5] and that even with respect to the electronic media, the fairness doctrine was a wholly discretionary matter. The Court held that there was no judicial warrant for requiring the FCC to apply the doctrine in such a way as to require a network to carry a paid editorial advertisement critical of American involvement in the Vietnam War.[6] Some justices expressed the view that *Red Lion* was a mistake and should be overruled.[7] In the 1980s, during the Reagan years, the attack against the fairness doctrine took on increasing energy and intensity.

A turning point came in 1985, when the FCC, filled with

Reagan appointees, formally took the position that the fairness doctrine was inconsistent with the First Amendment.[8] But out of a deference to what it perceived to be Congressional will, the FCC refused to renounce the doctrine altogether, although the prospect of enforcement appeared dim indeed. In the spring of 1987, Congress responded to these developments by passing a statute that purported to give the fairness doctrine a more secure statutory basis.[9] This action, however, failed to stabilize the situation, because, as anticipated, President Reagan vetoed the measure on First Amendment grounds,[10] and Congress was unable to overcome the veto.[11] Then on August 4, 1987, in the *Syracuse Peace Council* case, the Reagan FCC finally took that additional step and voted to abolish the fairness doctrine.[12] A fairly straightforward reading of the FCC's opinion suggests that its action was an exercise in constitutional theory and that its judgment was based on the view that the fairness doctrine violated broadcast journalists' constitutional free speech rights: The conditions that allowed the Supreme Court to uphold the doctrine in *Red Lion* – above all, spectrum scarcity – were, according to the FCC, no longer applicable given certain technological changes. But in February 1989 the Court of Appeals upheld the action of the FCC, not as a repudiation of *Red Lion* and the constitutional principles upon which it rested, but as a public policy choice.[13] The Court of Appeals found that choice to be within the prerogative of the agency, at least within the present statutory framework.

In terms of the long run and the larger issues, the particular battles being fought over the fairness doctrine, which are far from over, have only a representative significance. The fight has an intensity that far transcends any plausible account of the concrete benefits or burdens that might be attributed to this body of regulation. The struggle is not so much over the doctrine as over the role of the state. Some have used the *Syracuse Peace Council* decision to reaffirm that reading of the First Amendment which puts it at war with the activist state.[14] Those who defend the fairness doctrine, on the other hand, see it as the embodiment of a more welcoming attitude toward the state: Their claim is not simply that state regulation of the media is constitutionally permissible, but that state regulation is required to further the democratic values that lie at the heart of the First Amendment. Far from mandating a system of laissez-faire, the First Amendment offers a constitutional basis for state activism and for reopening questions long foreclosed by classical liberalism.

I

The Constitution is not a testamentary document that distributes to future generations pieces of property in the form of rights. Rather, it is a charter of governance that establishes the institutions of government and the norms, standards, and principles that are to control those institutions. The Bill of Rights assumes that the institutions of government have already been established and proceeds to make authoritative a set of social ideals or values. Adjudication is one process by which these abstract ideals are given concrete meaning and expression and are thereby translated into rights.

For some seventy years, the courts have been systematically engaged in the process of interpreting and enforcing the First Amendment and the values it embodies. As a result of this process, a near consensus has developed that the First Amendment's aim is political and social – that it seeks to further democracy by protecting collective self-determination, the capacity of a people to exercise its sovereign prerogative and to decide what kind of life it wishes to live. There is, however, disagreement over the particular principles or rules that should be applied to realize this ideal. One is couched in terms of autonomy, another in terms of public debate. Each principle is offered as a way of understanding and furthering the democratic purposes of the First Amendment, but the distinction between the public-debate and autonomy principles is crucial in clarifying the role the state might play in furthering free speech values.

Those who reduce the First Amendment to a limit on state action and fight the fairness doctrine on constitutional grounds tend to regard the First Amendment as a protection of autonomy. The individual is allowed to say what he or she wishes, free from interference from the state. It is as though the First Amendment placed a zone of noninterference around each individual, and the state – and the state alone – were prohibited from crossing that boundary. Even in this account, however, autonomy is not viewed as good in itself, or as means of individual self-actualization.[15] Rather, it is seen as a way of furthering the larger political purposes attributed to the amendment. It is assumed that the protection of autonomy will produce a debate on issues of public importance that is, to use Justice Brennan's now classic formula, "uninhibited, robust, and wide-open."[16] Of course, rich public debate will not itself ensure self-governance, because the electorate must still listen to what is said and act on the basis of what it learns, but free debate remains an essential precondition for democratic government, and autonomy is seen as the method of bringing that debate into being.

Philosophers tend to doubt this instrumental view of autonomy, but it has been embraced by lawyers as far apart on the political spectrum as Harry Kalven and Robert Bork, and it now dominates our thinking about the First Amendment. It is rooted in the fact that the free speech guarantee appears as part of a legal instrument, the Constitution, which is for the most part concerned with establishing the structure of government. The instrumental theory also explains why speech, among the many forms of self-expression, is singled out by the Constitution,[17] why the autonomy protected under the First Amendment can belong to institutions (CBS or the NAACP) as well as to individuals, and why speech can be preferred even when it harms someone else and thus infringes on that person's efforts at self-actualization.[18] The link between autonomy and democracy also accounts for the favored position in First Amendment jurisprudence of the presumption against content regulation. It is assumed that a rule denying the state power to silence speech on the basis of content will produce the broadest possible debate.

In some social settings, the instrumental assumption underlying the protection of autonomy may be well founded. In a Jeffersonian democracy, for example, where the dominant social unit is the individual and power is distributed equally among the citizens, autonomy might well enhance public debate and thus promote collective self-determination. But in a society characterized by grossly unequal distributions of power and a limited capacity of people to learn all that they must to function effectively as citizens, this assumption appears more problematic. Placing a zone of noninterference around the individual or around certain institutions, and in that way protecting autonomy, is likely to produce a public debate that is not "uninhibited, robust and wide-open" but, rather, dominated, and thus constrained, by the same forces that dominate the social structure.

The public-debate principle, in contrast, recognizes the problematic character of the instrumental assumption underlying the protection of autonomy and seeks to provide a foundation for the necessary corrective action. The general purpose of the First Amendment remains what it was under autonomy – to protect the ability of people, as a collectivity, to decide their own fate. Rich public debate also continues to appear as an essential precondition for the exercise of that sovereign prerogative. But now action is judged by its impact on public debate, rather than in terms of whether it constrains or otherwise interferes with the autonomy of some individual or institution. The concern is not with the frustration of would-be speakers but with the quality of public discourse; as Meiklejohn put it, what is important is not that everyone speak, but that everything worth saying shall be said.[19] Autonomy may be protected, but only when it enriches public debate, and it might well have to be sacrificed when, for example, the speech of some drowns out the voices of others or systematically distorts the public agenda.

Disfavoring state action is not the same as precluding such action altogether. Even those who read the First Amendment as part of the classical liberal tradition are not necessarily committed to the absolutist position identified with Justice Black.[20] They sometimes allow the state to cross the boundary and interfere with autonomy in order to serve other social interests; speakers may, for example, be silenced to preserve national security or to protect interests in reputation. What they insist on, however, and what the autonomy principle provides, is a very strong presumption against state interference with speech. Under the public-debate principle, there is no such presumption. The state stands on an equal footing with other institutions and is allowed, encouraged, and sometimes required to enact measures or issue decrees designed to enrich public debate, even if that action entails an interference with the speech of some and thus a denial of individual or institutional autonomy.

Of course, the state might act wrongfully and thereby restrict or impoverish rather than enhance public debate. We must always stand on guard against this danger, but we should do so mindful that this same danger is presented by all social institutions, private or public, and that there is no reason for *presuming* that the state will be more likely than any other institution to exercise its power to distort public debate. It has no special incentive to do so; government officials like to preserve their positions and the system that brought them to power, but the same can be said of the owners and managers of the media, who might well use their power to protect themselves and those government officials and entrepreneurs who serve their interests.

Admittedly, the state does have some unique resources at its disposal, including a monopoly over the lawful means of violence, but once we cease to think of the state as a monolith (the Leviathian) and realize that it is a network of competing and overlapping agencies, one checking another, and all being checked by private institutions, that power will appear less remarkable and less fearsome. We will come to see that the state's monopoly over the lawful infliction of violence is not a true measure of the power of any agency and that the power of the FCC is no greater than that of CBS. Terror comes in many forms. The powers of the FCC and CBS differ – one regulates whereas the other edits – but there is no reason to assume that one kind of power will be more inhibiting or limiting of public debate than the other. A state agency, like any other institution, can act as either a friend or an enemy of speech, and we must learn to recognize when it is acting in one capacity rather than another.

II

Today, public debate is dominated by the television networks and a number of large newspapers and magazines. The competition among these institutions is far from perfect, and some might argue for state intervention on a theory of market failure: The state is needed to perfect the market or to compensate for its deficiencies. The fairness doctrine could then be depicted as a species of antitrust analogous to regulatory regimes imposed on public utilities. There is a great deal of force to those arguments, but they obscure a deeper truth, namely, that a market, even one working perfectly, is itself a structure of constraint. A fully competitive market might produce a diversity of programs, formats, and reportage, but, to borrow an image from Renata Adler, it will be the diversity of "a pack going essentially in one direction."[21]

The market constrains the presentation of matters of public interest and importance in two ways. First, the market privileges select groups, by making programs, journals, and newspapers especially responsive to their needs and desires. One such group consists of those who have the capital to acquire or own a television station, newspaper, or journal; another consists of those who control the advertising budgets of various businesses; and still another consists of those who are most able and most likely to respond enthusiastically to advertising. The number in the last group is no doubt quite large (it probably includes every nine-year-old who can bully his or her parents into purchasing one thing or another), but it is not coextensive with the electorate. To be a consumer, even a sovereign one, is not to be a citizen.

Second, the market brings to bear on editorial and programming decisions factors that might have a great deal to do with profitability or allocative efficiency, but little to do with the democratic needs of the electorate. For a businessman, the costs of production and the revenue likely to be generated are highly pertinent factors in determining what shows to run and when, or what to feature in a newspaper; a perfectly competitive market will produce shows or publications whose marginal cost equals marginal revenue. Reruns of *I Love Lucy* are profitable and an efficient use of resources. So is MTV. But there is no necessary, or even probabilistic, relationship between making a profit or allocating resources efficiently and supplying the electorate with the information they need to make free and intelligent choices about government policy, the structure of government, or the nature of society. This point was well understood when we freed our educational systems and our universities from the grasp of the market. It applies with equal force to the media.

None of this is meant to denigrate the market. It is only to recognize its limitations. For me the issue is not market failure but market reach. The market might be splendid for some purposes but not for others. It might be an effective institution for producing cheap and varied consumer goods and for providing essential services (including entertainment), but not for producing the kind of debate that constantly renews the capacity of a people for self-determination. The state should act as a much needed countervailing power, to counteract the skew of public debate attributable to the market and thus preserve the essential conditions of democracy. The purpose of the state is not to supplant the market (as it would under a socialist theory) or to perfect the market (as it would under a theory of market failure) but, rather, to supplement it. The state must act as the corrective for the market. The state must put on the agenda issues that are systematically ignored and slighted and allow us to hear voices and viewpoints that would otherwise be silenced or muffled.

To turn to the state for these reasons does not presuppose that the people who staff a government agency are different in moral quality or in personality from those who control or manage the so-called private media. The state has no corner on virtue. What the theory of countervailing power does presuppose, however, is that, simply because of their position, government employees are subject to a different set of constraints than are those who run the media. They are public officials. We know that sometimes the word "public" becomes hollow and empty, a mere cover for the advancement of private interests, and that systems of public accountability are not perfect. But that is not to deny the force of these systems of accountability altogether. They may be imperfect but nonetheless of some effect. There is also an important difference of aspiration. It is one thing to empower someone called a public official and to worry whether the power entrusted is being used for public ends; it is another simply to leave that power in the hands of those who openly and unabashedly serve institutions that rest on private capital and are subject to market pressures.

In recent years, there has been increasing talk among journalists about professionalism, and it has been suggested that a new professional ethos exists today that will temper the influence of the market on journalists, editors, and program managers and strengthen their democratic resolve. This theme is emphasized elsewhere in this volume.[22] Such a development is, of course, salutary, but it does not render state intervention unnecessary. Indeed, the growth of professional norms emphasizing democratic values rather than the economic imperatives of the media might well be traced in part to various state interventions, such as the fairness doctrine. Whatever the cause, the fact remains that these norms must continuously be reinforced by state intervention or other forms of institutionalized power if they are to be capable of resisting the pressures of the marketplace. As we know from *Brown v. Board of Education*[23] and the civil rights movement of the sixties, the structure of our values and the patterns of our behavior can be influenced and changed by strong exercises of state power.

Drawing on its power to tax and its organizational advantages, the state can discharge its corrective or countervailing function through the provision of subsidies. Examples of this form of state intervention include aid to public libraries, public schools, private and state universities, and public broadcasting. These subsidies make an enormous contribution to public discourse and further First Amendment values, although we would never know it from the Reagan years or a reading of the First Amendment that emphasizes the protection of autonomy. Autonomy does not create a bar to such state activities, but it does produce a constitutional indifference, leaving these activities to suffer the vicissitudes of a politics itself dominated by the market. Under the public-debate principle, state subsidies to such forms of speech are favored, and when inaction becomes a form of action, such subsidies may also be required, although the remedial problems of implementing such an affirmative duty are acute and well known.[24]

With respect to the form of state intervention represented by the fairness doctrine – state action of a regulatory nature – the autonomy principle does have strong legal implications. It does something more than invite a certain politics. The autonomy principle has placed a constitutional cloud over the fairness doctrine, first precluding the extension of that doctrine to the print media, then enfeebling its enforcement, and now calling into question its very existence. The autonomy principle insulates institutions and individuals (whether they be reporters, editors, broadcasters, station managers, or the owners of the media) from governmental interferences with what they see fit to do, what issues are to be covered and how; from this perspective, the fairness doctrine is seen as a forbidden intrusion. The public-debate principle does not immunize the fairness doctrine or any other regulatory measure from a First Amendment attack; such measures might well be challenged on the theory that they impoverish rather than enrich public debate. The shift of principles from autonomy to public debate does, however, change the nature of the objection and thus the issue to be resolved.

For one thing, the shift of principles requires the attack to proceed without the aid of the presumption against state regulation that is derived from the autonomy principle. It also places the First Amendment, so to speak, on both sides of the issue. Those who defend the fairness doctrine can invoke the First Amendment just as passionately as those who challenge it, for the doctrine seeks to further First Amendment values by ensuring a debate that is "uninhibited, robust and wide-open." The fairness doctrine might fall under the public-debate principle, but only if it were proved to be counterproductive – far from established in the *Syracuse Peace Council* case and, in any event, a less threatening and less startling claim than one founded on the notion that through the very adoption of the fairness doctrine the state had entered a sacred and inviolable sphere.

III

The right currently dominates American politics and has done so for the last twenty years, and it is the right that has commandeered the assault on the activist state and the fairness doctrine in particular. By the "right" I mean those who are prepared to accept as just or even natural the distribution of wealth and power produced by the market and who seek to curb the state because of its reconstructive capacity and propensity. It is the right whom I have in mind when I speak of the Reagan administration. There are others, however, who are critical of the present distribution of wealth and power and thus might be seen as on the left, but who are also wary of the state, particularly the one headquartered in Washington now, and maybe forever. They, too, have denounced the activist state, not because it interferes with the market but rather because of the threat they believe it poses to our political freedom.

I began with the claim that, left to itself, public debate will not be "uninhibited, robust, and wide-open" but instead will be skewed by the forces that dominate society. The state should be allowed to intervene, and sometimes even required to do so, I argued, to correct for the market. In saying this, I assumed that the state would act as a countervailing power, but there is a danger, so the leftist critic of state activism insists, that it will not act in this way but will instead become the victim of the same forces that dominate public debate. There is a risk that the state will reinforce rather than counteract the skew of the market, because it is as much an object of social forces as it is an agent of change. The state might do some good, but the prospect of its doing so is so slim, and the danger of its doing just the opposite is so great, that it would be best, the leftist critic concludes, to bar state intervention altogether, or at least to create a strong presumption against it – now not to secure autonomy, which the left agrees is a false principle, but rather to ensure the richness of public debate.

In the late 1970s, Charles Lindblom published an important book, *Politics and Markets,* which described with great force and clarity the so-called danger of "circularity."[25] The state was supposed to govern business, but there was good reason to believe that the system of control largely worked the other way around. The picture that Lindblom painted was a sobering one – the danger of circularity is indeed real – but my own view of the facts and, more particularly, of our historical experience with the activist state in the early sixties, leads me to believe that the elements of independence possessed by the state are real and substantial. This independence is not complete, but it is nonetheless sufficient to make the theory of countervailing power viable. I also believe that we might cope with the danger of circularity in ways other than by creating the strong presumption against state action urged by the leftist critic. To begin with, we might recognize that some state agencies are more independent of market forces than others and accordingly allocate more power to them.

In the past, First Amendment jurisprudence has allowed the courts to play an important role in evaluating the intervention of various political agencies, in order to avoid the tyranny of the majority. I would continue that practice, but now as a way of gaining some measure of protection against circularity. The courts are part of the state and obviously are not wholly independent from the same forces that shape and dominate our social life, but they are likely to achieve a greater measure of independence from particularized political pressure or social demands than the legislature or administrative agencies. The independence of the judiciary stems from the fact that judges have long and sometimes even life tenure, are subject to well-established professional norms that require them to respond to grievances they might prefer to ignore, and must justify their decisions publicly on the basis of principle.

The danger of circularity also might be reduced by changes in the design of particular institutions. The aim is not to free the various agencies of the state from the dominant social forces and institutions (surely an impossible task), but only to make it more likely that they will exert a countervailing force. This goal might be achieved by creating within state agencies certain processes or mechanisms that would enhance the power of the weaker elements in society (for example, creating in administrative agencies offices of public advocacy) and that would lessen the power of those who already dominate the social structure (for example, establishing open-hearing requirements). In this way, Naderism might have a First Amendment basis because, in fighting "agency capture," we might be increasing the independence of the state from the market and thus enhancing its capacity to correct for the constraints that social structure imposes on public debate.

None of these ameliorative measures will eliminate the danger of circularity altogether. We should recognize their imperfect character and act with caution. But to do more, as leftist critics insist, and join in the attack on the activist state, would expose us to an even greater danger: politics dominated by the market. We would be left without a remedy. Circularity is typically raised as an objection to regulatory action by the state, when, for example, a prohibition backed by a criminal or civil sanction is enforced against an individual or some institutional speaker. It is hard to understand, however, why the same objection does not extend to the subsidy programs of the state as well. Some may favor these programs over regulatory measures on the theory that they do not violate autonomy, but since rich public debate rather than autonomy is for me and the leftist critic the key First Amendment value, it is hard to transform that preference into a constitutional rule. Under the public-debate principle, the fairness doctrine and public television stand on the same constitutional plane. If one fails because of circularity, so must the other.

Circularity, then, would infect all forms of state intervention, but leftists are not without hope. They might turn their backs on such regulatory measures of the activist state as the fairness doctrine, and might even denounce state subsidies, but they, too, are determined to free democracy from the grasp of market forces and, in pursuit of that end, emphasize self-organizational activities and modes of expression such as picketing and parading. Such activities, of course, have an important role to play in any account of the First Amendment and indeed are essential for a true and effective democracy. The civil rights marches of the sixties, the protests against the Vietnam War, the shanties that have recently been raised on our campuses, and the historic movement in Poland known as Solidarity bear ample and glorious witness to this fact. The issue is not, however, whether self-organization and demonstration are necessary, but whether they are sufficient, at least to the point of justifying the attack on the activist state. This they surely are not. Such activities are an important part of any First Amendment theory, but they are not adequate substitutes for the fairness doctrine or other forms of state regulation and state subsidization of the media for the purpose of enhancing the quality of public discourse.

In assessing the affirmative program of the left, one should begin with the simple observation that the expressive activities they favor do not eliminate the problem of circularity altogether. The state is often needed to legitimate and protect those activities, and there is no reason to be more suspicious of the state when it, for example, grants subsidies or regulates the media than when it regulates access to the shopping centers, silences hecklers, or legitimates and protects union activity.[26] Moreover, to rely exclusively, or even primarily, on parading or picketing (referred to by one of my colleagues, not a radical, as "cheap speech") would leave to the less powerful elements in society only the least effective modes of political persuasion. Compare one day's work of distributing pamphlets at a local shopping center with a half hour on TV. Effective speech in the modern age is not cheap.

Things needn't be so. I can imagine a social setting in which the expressive activities celebrated by the left would be sufficient. They might work in the polis of ancient Greece or in an America divided, as Jefferson proposed, into a multitude of little wards.[27] Then we would have a social, as well as a political, decentralization, a setting in which parading or picketing could make an effective contribution toward both informing and educating the public, and developing the talents and fixing the character and identity of those individuals who take part in such activities. The attack on the activist state and the emphasis on cheap speech would not then be based just on a fear, the danger of circularity, but could also make plausible claim to a theory of participatory democracy. Such a theory would give the First Amendment program of the left its greatest appeal, but, alas, like the now forsaken autonomy principle, it rests on an impossible dream. It entails a division and reorganization of American society that is unlikely ever to materialize. It presupposes a localism that is barely imaginable.

The left is wary of the activist state, and may have good reasons for that wariness, but in resurrecting the presumption against the state, and joining the attack on the activist state, they offer no plausible alternative to a politics dominated by the market. They emphasize self-organization and direct action, like parading and picketing, rather than state regulation or subsidization, but under the forms of social life we know, or are ever likely to know, such forms of expression would be insufficient to protect democratic self-governance. Something would be missing. The citizen would be little more than an athlete (or, to use Hannah Arendt's metaphor, a flute player).[28] Politics would become a species of performance. Those who happened to be engaged in the demonstration would be ennobled and would feel the special pleasures of struggle and contest, but for the most part the public – the voters – would sit by, unengaged and unmoved by the spectacle, anxious to get on with the business of the day.

In another world things might be different, but in this one we need the state. With forms of state intervention like the fairness doctrine, we risk a number of dangers, including circularity, but only to save our democracy. We turn to the state because it is the most public of all our institutions and because only it has the power to resist the pressures of the market and thus to enlarge and invigorate our politics.

NOTES

1 See, e.g., R. H. Coase, "The Market for Goods and the Market for Ideas," *American Economic Review Proceedings* 64 (May 1974): 384–91; Aaron Director, "The Parity of the Economic Market Place," *Journal of Law and Economics* 7 (October 1964): 1–10.

2 47 C.F.R. § 73.1910 (1988). See also Henry Geller, "Mass Communications Policy: Where We Are and Where We Should Be Going," this volume. Two additional aspects of the fairness doctrine were codified in 1967. The personal-attack rule gives an individual an opportunity to respond when he or she is attacked in the course of a broadcast concerning a controversial issue of public importance (47 C.F.R. § 73.1920 [1988]). The political editorial rule provides that when a broadcaster has editorially endorsed a candidate, opposition candidates must be offered a reasonable opportunity to respond (47 C.F.R. § 73.1930 [1988]).

3 395 U.S. 367 (1969).

4 See, e.g., Lee C. Bollinger, Jr., "Freedom of the Press and Public Access: Toward a Theory of Partial Regulation of the Mass Media," *Michigan Law Review* 75 (November 1976): 1–42; Thomas G. Krattenmaker and L. A. Powe, Jr., "The Fairness Doctrine Today: A Constitutional Curiosity and an Impossible Dream," *Duke Law Journal* (1985): 151–76; L. A. Powe, Jr., *American Broadcasting and the First Amendment* (Berkeley: University of California Press, 1987).

5 *Miami Herald v. Tornillo*, 418 U.S. 241 (1974).

6 *Columbia Broadcasting System v. Democratic National Committee*, 412 U.S. 94 (1973).

7 412 U.S. at 154 (Douglas, J., concurring in judgment). Justice Stewart, also concurring, expressed sympathy for Douglas's position, but stopped short of declaring the *Red Lion* decision a mistake that should be overruled (412 U.S. at 146 [Stewart, J., concurring]).

8 See *In re Inquiry into Section 73.1910 of the Commission's Rules and Regulations Concerning the General Fairness Doctrine Obligations of Broadcast Licensees*, 102 FCC 2d 143 (1985).

9 H.R. 1934, 100th Cong., 1st sess., 133 Cong. Rec. H4139–60 (daily ed. June 3, 1987); S. 742, 100th Cong., 1st sess., 133 Cong. Rec. S5218–32 (daily ed. April 21, 1987).

10 *Veto of the Fairness in Broadcasting Act of 1987*, 23 Weekly Comp. Pres. Doc. 715–716 (June 19, 1987); see also 133 Cong. Rec. S8438, S8453–4 (daily ed. June 23, 1987).

11 133 Cong. Rec. S8438–50 (daily ed. June 23, 1987) (motion to refer to Committee on Commerce).

12 *Syracuse Peace Council*, 2 FCC Rcd. 5043 (1987). The FCC vote to abolish the fairness doctrine did not address the personal attack or political editorial rules described in note 2, above. Proposals, however, to modify or eliminate these rules are currently under agency consideration. See *Notice of Proposed Rule Making*, Docket 83–484, 48 Fed. Reg. 28,295 (1983); see also *In re Inquiry into Section 73.1910 of the Commissions's Rules and Regulations Concerning Alternatives to the General Fairness Doctrine Obligations of Broadcast Licensees*, 2 FCC Rcd. 5272, 5284–5 (1987).

13 *Syracuse Peace Council v. FCC*, 867 F.2d 654 (D.C. Cir. 1989).

14 An example is the concurring opinion of Judge Starr, a Reagan appointee, in the Court of Appeals. See *Syracuse Peace Council v. FCC*, 867 F.2d at 673–88 (Starr, J., concurring).

15 See Judith Lichtenberg, "Foundations and Limits of Freedom of the Press," this volume.

16 *New York Times v. Sullivan*, 376 U.S. 254, 270 (1964).

17 See Robert H. Bork, "Neutral Principles and Some First Amendment Problems," *Indiana Law Journal* 47 (Fall 1971): 26.

18 See Frederick F. Schauer, *Free Speech: A Philosophical Enquiry* (Cambridge: Cambridge University Press, 1982), pp. 11–12.

19 Alexander Meiklejohn, *Political Freedom: The Constitutional Powers of the People* (New York: Harper, 1960), p. 26.

20 See, e.g., *New York Times v. United States*, 403 U.S. 713, 717–18 (1971) (Black, J., concurring).

21 Renata Adler, *Reckless Disregard* (New York: Knopf, 1986), p. 17.

22 See Carl Sessions Stepp, "Access in a Post–Social Responsibility Age," this volume.

23 347 U.S. 483 (1954); 349 U.S. 294 (1955).

24 See, e.g., Seth F. Kreimer, "Allocational Sanctions: The Problem of Negative Rights in a Positive State," *University of Pennsylvania Law Review* 132 (July 1984): 1297.

25 Charles E. Lindblom, *Politics and Markets: The World's Political-Economic Systems* (New York: Basic, 1977), pp. 201–21.

26 See, e.g., Karl E. Klare, "Judicial Deradicalization of the Wagner Act and the Origins of Modern Legal Consciousness, 1937–1941," *Minnesota Law Review* 62 (March 1978): 265–339.

27 See Letter to Samuel Kercheval, 5 September 1816, *The Political Writings of Thomas Jefferson: Representative Selections*, ed. Edward Dumbauld (New York: Liberal Arts Press, 1955), pp. 97–8.

28 See Hannah Arendt, "What Is Freedom?" in *Between Past and Future: Eight Exercises in Political Thought*, expanded ed. (New York: Viking, 1968), pp. 143, 153. See generally Hannah Arendt, *The Human Condition* (Chicago: University of Chicago Press, 1958); Hannah Arendt, *On Revolution* (New York: Viking, 1963).

Chapter 5

Practices of toleration

Onora O'Neill

ORIENTATION

Ethical discussion of the media often centers on various freedoms, including freedom of expression, freedom of speech, freedom of the press, and freedom of information. These freedoms are seen as *rights* that protect speech, publication, and other sorts of representation from varied interferences. The grounds, the boundaries, and the implementation of these rights are controversial. Should the line between protected and unprotected speech be drawn at the same place for print and for broadcasting? What is that place? Can government interference with speech and publication be prevented without risking interferences by "private" powers?[1] Can "private" powers be prevented from dominating the media except by government action? How, if at all, may or must these freedoms be curtailed for the sake of other objectives? Are these rights held only by individuals, or do they also belong to institutions, publishers, and editors? These questions are interesting, important, and unsettled.

Such topics are reached quite naturally if we begin by asking, How are we entitled to express ourselves? and if we worry that others may prevent us from doing so. Advocates of rights-based thinking see the First Amendment to the U.S. Constitution and John Stuart Mill's *On Liberty* as canonical texts and think interference with speech, publication, and other sorts of representation can only be justified when needed to protect other important rights.

At present rights-based thinking, whose central concern is the treatment to which people are entitled, is often taken as constitutive of deontological liberal thinking. This essay takes a broader view of deontological liberalism. It begins not from the *recipient's* question, How are we entitled to express ourselves? but from the *agent's* question, How ought we to express ourselves? and its more specific version: How ought we to communicate? Neither the First Amendment of the Constitution nor *On Liberty* addresses this last question directly. They are concerned, in the first instance, with the protection that communicators should be accorded, with the ways in which they should be *treated,* rather than with how they should *act.* (Of course, rights to be treated in certain ways entail obligations; but the line of thought begins with rights and argues to obligations.)

Some rights-based thinking construes all communication that does not violate rights as acceptable. Others who make rights ethically fundamental take it that communicative acts that violate no rights could be wrong. However, it is difficult to show within rights-based thinking what can make a rights-respecting communicative or expressive act wrong. Many modern liberals insist that they neither offer nor assume any account of the good for man; they see rights not only as ethically basic but as the sole ethical constraints on the pursuit of personal preference.

I shall dispute the coherence and adequacy of liberalism that is agnostic about the good for man, by sketching some of its implications for the ethics of communication. In particular, I shall argue that when others' rights are seen as the *sole* ethical constraints on permissible action, including permissible communication, we lack sufficient basis for judging which communicative practices must be tolerated in democratic societies. My aim is not to show that the rights on which discussions of toleration and the media so often center are bogus; rather, I shall argue that rights to speak and communicate are better justified by deriving them from an ethical theory that takes obligations rather than rights as basic. This approach takes rights entirely seriously; but it does not take them as the basic ethical category.

The ethical landscape looks different when we begin from the agent's perspective of a theory of obligations. The difference is not just one of perspective: rights-based deontological liberalism, I shall argue, is both *narrower* than and *derivative* from obligation-based liberal thinking. Deontological thinking that tries to make the category of rights *fundamental* falls into incoherence because thought about rights constitutes a proper part of thought about obligations, and cannot be vindicated in abstraction from the wider, agent-centered mode of thought. Far from requiring agnosticism about the good for man, deontological liberalism is made incoherent by such agnosticism. (Hence, liberals who reject utilitarian foundations have reason to include Kant's writing as well as Mill's among their canonical texts: Kantian thought – unlike that of many modern self-styled Kantians – makes the category of obligation more basic than the category of rights.)[2]

However, liberalism is now often construed as at bottom a theory of freedoms or rights, both by libertarians and by liberal advocates of "welfare"[3] rights, as well as by many nonliberals. The only remnants of an account of the good that survives in much contemporary liberal thinking (whether deontological or utilitarian) is concern to allow agents to pursue their (subjective) "conceptions of the good": a rhetorical gesture that bestows a scanty ethical respectability on the pursuit of individual preferences.

We can only meet those who see liberalism as rights-based and agnostic about the good by starting out on their chosen terrain. Hence, the arguments presented here begin from premises that would be accepted by those who take rights as fundamental to liberalism. These very premises lead, I shall argue, to an older and wider view of the liberal tradition, in which rights are not fundamental. This wider, Kantian form of liberalism claims not that rights are unimportant or dispensable but, rather, that any coherent theory of rights must be embedded in the broader perspective of obligations, within which rights have a place – but not the whole place.[4] The perspective of rights is not *suppressed* but *aufgehoben* in the perspective of obligations.

I shall skirt two better-known revisionary approaches to rights that are current in liberal political debates. The first of these rejects specifically deontological liberalism and tries to embed rights in consequentialist thinking. This is a fairly popular undertaking – after all, it has Mill's authority behind it and can lead in interesting directions. If liberty and rights are justified only as means to (subjectively) good results, they lack justification when they don't lead to such results. Despite Mill's eloquence, it is unlikely that freedom of the press and freedom of expression always produce optimal results. If we are utilitarians before we are liberals, we are likely to find many cases where speech and expression should *not* be protected.[5] In a way it is a curiosity of our intellectual history that Mill was so firmly convinced that utilitarian arguments would yield liberal conclusions. If the facts fall out in ways that are not ruled out, utilitarian reasoning will endorse forms of paternalism, restraint, and censorship. This well-known consequentialist critique of rights, however, is neither interesting nor decisive for those liberal advocates of rights who reject its starting point.

Liberals who shun consequentialism have more reason to take seriously a second revisionist program that is advocated in great variety by proponents of "welfare" rights. "Welfare" liberals think that some human rights are rights to assistance, subsidy, or "access" rather than liberties not to be interfered with. Freedom itself, they hold, cannot be sustained just by "noninterference" (and its enforcement); rather, "positive" action (and its enforcement) may be needed to secure freedom. Free speech is inadequately realized unless there is guaranteed (if necessary, subsidized) access to the media for a range of viewpoints (alternatively for the viewpoints of a range of people), which ensures participation for a "multiplicity of voices." More generally a serious account of toleration cannot equate it with noninterference – with doing nothing.

Libertarians have responded to these revisionist claims by

arguing that the "welfare" account of human rights is incoherent. The persistent disputes between "welfare" and libertarian liberals over many issues have produced doubt and uncertainty about what rights there are. Both sorts of deontological liberals try to make rights basic, and both are led to a difficulty that can be sketched in the following terms: In taking rights as fundamental we commit ourselves to constructing an account of how people ought to be treated without drawing on an objective theory of the good. Such constructions are often seen as elaborating what respect for persons, their autonomy, and their liberty amounts to. To move from such general notions to a determinate account of human rights we have to work out which set of mutually consistent equal rights is the maximal one.[6] Libertarian rights theorists correctly point out that advocates of "welfare" rights introduce rights inconsistent with rights libertarians favor. Subsidized public access to the media is inconsistent with a libertarian conception of property rights. Equally, "welfare" rights theorists correctly point out that libertarians advocate property rights that are incompatible with central "welfare" rights. Full capitalist property rights are incompatible with rights to be published by presses others own. These disputes could be settled by picking out a unique consistent set of rights as maximal, or at least a unique "core" set of rights that any maximal set of rights must contain. There are good reasons to believe that this cannot be done. If there is no metric for rights, comparing the "size" of different sets of rights that can be universally held is a futile exercise.[7]

If rights theorists cannot (without recourse to other, e.g., consequentialist, foundations) show one rather than another set of consistent rights maximal or optimal, disputes about freedom of expression and free speech that take rights as ethically basic will be inconclusive and irresolvable. This is one good reason not to take rights as fundamental. However, the indeterminacy of rights-based approaches is not a reason for rejecting deontological liberalism. Rather, it provides a reason for looking at obligation-based theories, for asking in the first place not how people ought to be treated, but what they ought to do. Rather than asking what it would be for everyone to have the same rights, we may ask what it would be for everyone to have the same obligations. I shall explore this approach and bracket both consequentialist critiques of rights to freedom of expression and publication, and the disputes between those who agree in thinking rights ethically fundamental but cannot settle what rights there are. This essay, however, does not present a full array of arguments to show that a theory of obligations escapes the radical indeterminacy of nonteleological theories that make rights fundamental. Its strategy is to offer a range of reasons for those who are committed to rights and do not accept consequentialism to shift to the perspective of obligations, and in particular to argue for communicative rights via a theory of communicative obligations. In particular, a shift to an obligation-based starting point allows for communication that is wrong although it violates no rights.[8]

REORIENTATION

Why should those who are committed to rights treat the perspective of obligations as basic? It is easy enough to see why those who are committed to rights must allow for the perspective of obligations. Rights are no more than the rhetoric of charters and manifestos unless there are correlative obligations to respect those rights.[9] If nobody has corresponding obligations, human (moral, natural) rights are shams, just as positive rights are shams when nobody has corresponding positive (legal, institutional) obligations. The vocabulary of obligations offers *at least* an alternative and indispensable perspective on the very ethical or legal relationships that a theory of rights depicts. The perspective of rights looks at these relationships from the position of those on the receiving end of treatment, whose first concern may be to claim their rights. The perspective of obligations looks at these relationships from an agent's perspective, where the first concern is to work out what to do and, more generally, how to live. Even the reasons commonly given for thinking that human beings have rights point to their capacities to reason and act. These considerations provide one rather general reason for thinking that the perspective of agency may be suitable for articulating the full structure of thought about rights; but they do not show why obligations rather than rights should be treated as basic.

However, consider which perspective offers the *wider* view. Anything we can say about A's rights can be spelled out in terms of others' obligations to A. The converse is false. Not everything that can be said about obligation can be stated in terms of rights. For there may be some obligations to which no rights correspond. Traditional ethical theory allowed for these and called them *imperfect* obligations.

Imperfect obligations have been demarcated in various ways. Sometimes they are said to be more indeterminate than perfect obligations; sometimes they are said to be obligations that cannot justly be enforced by law. These points may be correct, but I shall rest nothing on them. Rather, I shall reserve the term "imperfect obligation" simply for those obligations (if there are any) that cannot have correlative rights *because no determinate right-holders are identified,* since the allocation of the performance of the obligation is left to the discretion of its bearer.[10] If there are any such obligations, there is no way for individual claimants to demand performance as a matter of right, or to waive performance as a matter of grace: for there are no right holders. It is no category mistake when we read (for example) of "duties to help" or "duties of sympathy," which are owed neither to all nor to any specified individuals. In the natural law tradition (of which theories that make rights fundamental are one, but only one, development) only some obligations had correlative rights. Whether or not we are convinced that there are imperfect obligations, the wider scope of theories of obligations is a powerful reason for *beginning* a discussion of ethically required action in terms of obligations.

A shift from looking at ethical relations in terms of rights to doing so in terms of obligations need not deny the importance of rights. All beliefs about rights can be expressed in terms of correlative (perfect) obligations. The alternative perspective, however, may reveal other (imperfect) obligations that lack correlative rights, whose fulfillment limits and in part determines what rights there can be.

This thought will seem contentious to those who believe they have unequivocally identified what rights there are – for example, by showing how the idea of the largest liberty compatible with like liberty for all is to be constructed. In particular those who believe that these rights include a liberty of the person, which "fills" any "space" remaining when other rights have been specified, will deny that there can be imperfect obligations, because these would be inconsistent with such a liberty of the person.

The belief that there can be no imperfect obligations can be held by "welfare" as well as by libertarian rights theorists. Although "welfare" liberals argue for a different composition of human rights, they also may think that a (less extensive) liberty of the person preempts imperfect obligations. (This belief helps explain both their eagerness to show that the values they believe libertarians neglect are *rights*, and the libertarians' conviction that advocates of "welfare" rights confuse optional matters of personal preference with obligations.) However, if we do not know what rights there are, and do not posit a liberty of the person that requires us to classify all acts exhaustively either as violations of others' rights or as permitted uses of our own, we cannot simply assert that there are no imperfect obligations. Prima facie they are just obligations that specify no individual right-holders who can claim performance of the obligation. It is open to debate what such obligations there may be, how they may constrain the set of rights that can consistently be held, and whether any of them may or must be legally enforced.

A switch to the perspective of agency and obligations has the advantage that *if* we conclude there are no imperfect obligations, the conclusion will not have been reached merely by relying on a perspective from which they are guaranteed to be invisible (and if a suitable liberty of the person is assumed impossible). Advocates of rights should then welcome the shift of perspective. However, it is apparent that some will not welcome it at all. There are those (mainly libertarian rights theorists) who *prefer* to neglect the whole ethical agenda that is made invisible by taking rights as fundamental. By restricting their vision to rights, so to those obligations traditionally called "perfect," some libertarians have managed to dismiss topics traditionally thought matters of imperfect obligation as ethically insignificant. The trivializing terms used in some discussions are revealing: We are asked to think of matters such as help and sympathy for the vulnerable and needy, or providing access to the media and employment, not as matters of right but as optional, even as "matters of decency" or as reflections of individual style and preference. This is entirely reasonable: What can those who try to base everything on rights do but classify all action that violates no others' rights as permitted uses of one's own rights? They have to see such action as permissible. If rights preempt all other ethical considerations, the only way to do wrong is to violate a right.

Advocates of "welfare" rights take another tack. Rather than dismiss the traditional imperfect obligations as matters for personal preference they try to show that these obligations too are perfect. Yet in following this program, they need to show which obligation bearers are obliged to which right holders. This raises difficulties with obligations whose performance demands not noninterference (which can be offered to all others) but positive action (which can at most be offered to some others). The "promotion" of imperfect to perfect obligations is unconvincing unless it can be shown against whom the supposed rights can be claimed. But if the promotion could be vindicated by showing how the allocation is to be made, rights would once again preempt all other ethical considerations.

RIGHTS, OBLIGATIONS, AND MEDIATED COMMUNICATION

A choice between rights-based and obligations-based thinking has interesting implications for our views of the media. Rights-based thinking approaches issues of toleration in terms of rights to expression and corresponding obligations not to censor but to protect expression. Our concern then centers on determining which sorts of representations and publications are protected, what it takes to protect and what constitutes censorship. Our account of the limits of rights of expression and publication will depend on showing which sorts of acts of expression would violate (other) rights, so should not be protected. Perhaps we will hold slander, libel, and clear-and-present-endangering wrong because they violate what we take to be other rights. Yet we need not even *ask* how freedom of expression should be used when respect for others' rights is no constraint.

If rights preempt other ethical categories, there will be nothing we can say about many sorts of expression that we find alarming. We do not have to be enemies of free speech to find a lot alarming that is not usually thought to violate rights. Anybody who has read critiques of race and gender stereotyping[11] must be bothered by the claim that certain sorts of portrayals of others are just permissible uses of rights to self-expression. Anybody who has thought about the mindless drivel flavored with commercials and violence that is offered to children on some TV channels must be bothered by the thought that such programming is just a permissible use of the freedom defined by whatever meager regulations govern children's television in a given jurisdiction.

If we raise these questions with somebody who is thinking solely from the perspective of rights, and thus lacks an account of imperfect obligations, we are quite likely to get a response of the following sort: Forbidding speech acts, publications, and programs on grounds of content (where not required to protect other rights) amounts to censorship and violates rights. There are no objective standards to discriminate stereotyping from journalism or literature, or good from bad children's programs. Censorship of stereotyping would license purging our theater and literature; content control of portrayals of violence to children would banish the story of the crucifixion in Sunday schools. From the perspective that makes rights fundamental the issue must be seen in this way.

Either there is nothing wrong with a speech act, and preventing it or its publication amounts to censorship – or it violates rights and can justly be forbidden.

Within the perspective of obligation, neither speech nor publishing nor programming is shown permissible merely by demonstrating that it violates no rights. Acts that violate no rights may yet be wrong. The danger of starting a discussion of speech and publication from the perspective of recipience, which is taken as basic in rights-based approaches, is that we then ask only one basic question, "How may we express ourselves?" whose political corollary is the question, "What may we silence?" If we approach matters from the perspective of obligation, we can still ask this question, but we can also ask more broadly how we ought to speak, publish, and program, and what sorts of practices of representation and communication ought to be be prized and fostered.

TOLERATION, EXPRESSION, AND COMMUNICATION

These reasons for starting from the perspective of obligations rather than of rights can be put in a rather more specific light by asking what the proper object of toleration is. A standard answer, which fits well into the perspective of rights, classifies speech acts as "self-regarding" acts and sees *expressions of opinion* rather than *communicative acts* as the proper objects of toleration. Rights approaches to speech and expression insist on rights to express opinions, but deny that there are rights to communicate. This is because advocates of freedom of expression doubt whether anyone has rights to have an audience or to be understood, or to be published by presses others own. Both libertarian and "welfare" rights theorists repudiate "rights" to be heard or "rights" to be published because these would violate others' rights (e.g., to privacy, to freedom of association). Libertarians also claim more specifically that "rights" of access to privately owned organs of communication would violate others' property rights. Freedom of expression is not violated just because nobody hears, nobody understands, nobody listens; it isn't violated even if nobody can hear, understand, or listen. Self-expression can be solitary, and freedom of association entails no right to have associates, let alone associates who listen.

This is, at the least, a one-sided perspective on speech acts, publication, and programming. It is hardly appropriate for a consideration of the *political* importance of speech. The media are important, especially in democracies, not simply because they are organs for self-expression (for most they are no such thing), but mainly because they are organs of communication. A view that makes self-expression the proper object of toleration is ill-suited for discussing the regulation of the media in democratic societies. In democratic life we need to ask not only, How may we express ourselves? but also, How ought we communicate? Communication is not a solitary act. Even a communication that fails and finds no audience must use socially established modes of communication. Unless a use of language (in the broadest sense of the term) can in principle be interpreted by others, it is not even a case of attempted communication. We are more likely to attend to the full range of democratic values that are important to the media if we view communication, not self-expression, as the proper object of toleration.[12]

If communication is the proper object of toleration, then part of an answer to "How may we communicate?" is that at the least we may not do so in ways that destroy the possibility of communicating for all or for some. The Kantian source of this answer is plain: If it is wrong to conduct our communicating on principles that cannot be shared by all, then we may not base our communicating on principles that if universally acted on would make communication impossible for some or for all. Because communication always requires communicators, some shared and interpretable languages, and mediated communication must use some form of technology, it is wrong to communicate in ways that destroy or threaten communicators, or destroy and do not replace languages and technologies and so make acts or practices of communication, or specifically of mediated communication, impossible for some or for all. Orwell's Newspeak is an image of vile intolerance because it destroys the very possibility of communication: It damages not merely particular communicators and communications but whole practices of communication. In the end it destroys not just freedom of public speech but freedom of thought.[13]

Those who view speech primarily as *self-expression* may think that their speaking is not obliged to take account of social context, that their speech acts ought only to refrain from violating others' rights, including rights of self-expression. Those who aim to *communicate,* and who do not preempt others' acting on like principles, must do more than refrain from violating others' rights. They must also communicate in ways that do not destroy or erode linguistic, social, and technical conditions of communication. Toleration of *expression* may need only noninterference; toleration of *communication* must also sustain conditions of communication.

More specific points can be made about communicative obligations in democratic societies. Those who are committed to democracy must see communication between citizens as important. A conception of toleration will be inadequate to democratic life if it demands only noninterference with acts of expression. An adequate view would have to identify practices of toleration that sustain the presuppositions of public communication, in forms from which nobody is excluded.[14]

CONTEXTS OF COMMUNICATION

Practices of toleration demand not merely that communicators neither coerce nor destroy one another, but more specifically that they act to institute and sustain practices of communication that exclude nobody. Such practices must be adjusted to actual linguistic, social, and technical conditions. Communicative obligations therefore cannot be fully specified in abstraction from circumstance; they can only be illustrated for one or another context of communication. It is therefore relevant to rehearse briefly some of the typical features of modern contexts of communication.

Our earliest paradigm of communication is a speech act in which a speaker conveys a message to a hearer. To interpret this message, speaker and hearer must share a language, and the hearer must grasp not only propositional content but the force of the speech act (e.g., statement, command, warning). Of course, these formulations are highly simplified. A shared language is not just a matter of shared vocabulary and generative grammar; it is a matter of sharing an amazing and extendable range of strategies of interpretation. These, in turn, depend on considerable sharing of a "world." Quite ordinary conversations rely on spectacular abilities to coordinate shifts in temporal, spatial, and personal perspective: Consider the shifts of frames of reference needed to interpret tenses and pronouns. When, and only when, speaker and hearer share enough and the hearer can form some view of the content and claims of the speaker's message can there be (some) communication.[15]

The specific form in which these conditions are met can vary greatly. The shift from oral to literate communication demanded a revolution in capacities to interpret. Writers and their readers are often neither present nor known to one another, and clues to interpretation that speech gains from gesture, expression, and shared and simultaneous perception of the world are erased. When we write, communication is more often one way, and risks of noncommunication are transformed. To cover these risks, writing relies on a wide range of substitutes for the constraints of speech context. Above all, it relies on the durability of the written trace, which allows readers to backtrack and try out multiple interpretations. This hearers cannot do, since (unmediated) speech is heard and gone. Literary form and hermeneutic strategies, in the widest senses of the terms, provide alternative clues by which readers interpret texts. We can be wholly at sea when unsure about the literary form of a text. (The same sentences can have quite different import in a play, a court transcript, a personal letter.) It is easy to see (also, perhaps, easy to forget) why writing made Socrates so uneasy that he didn't do it.

When communication is mediated the requirements for intepretation are again transformed. Mediated communication in modern, mass democracies is often intended for an audience that is not merely distant from the communicator but diverse and dispersed; and modern mediated communication can, of course, be spoken or pictorial rather than written. This only complicates the range of interpretive skills, technical devices, and social structures that various sorts of communication presuppose. The "immediacy" of broadcasting is illusory: It relies on capacities to interpret as complex as those needed by readers. When we listen to the radio we have to work out who speaks to us, from what context, or with what purpose (if we can) from information that may be conveyed only by the frame and format of the program: Once again communication is largely one-way. Television uses some of what we rely on face-to-face – gesture, expression, a shared view of a setting – but redeploys these to present us with interpretive problems that are far less like those of face-to-face speech acts than we may imagine. To interpret what we see on the screen we rely on complex and distinctive conventions.

In answering the question, How may we communicate? the varying presuppositions of face-to-face and distance communication, of personal and mass communication, are crucial. We cannot know what it takes to preserve and sustain the presuppositions of communication until we know what they are in a particular context, how far they can be varied, and what might damage any of them irrevocably. The only general point we can make is that these presuppositions are highly complex and vary for different sorts of mediated communication and different audiences. We can, perhaps, suggest some principles of communicative obligations and illustrate them for some of the contexts just sketched. These illustrations neither are nor could be a complete answer to the question "How ought we communicate?" But they suggest why we should expect communicative obligations in democratic societies to demand more than respect for others' rights.

COMMUNICATIVE OBLIGATIONS

Let us start with the thought that democracy requires the possibility of public communication. We need not assume that much public communication takes place, let alone that all communication is public.[16] If citizens are to conduct their communicating on principles that could (not "would": we are considering only universalizability, not uniformity) be shared by all, then their communicating must conform to fundamental principles that do not undermine but, rather, preserve, conditions of public communication.

To get a feel for the "shape" of some of the communicative obligations in a democracy we should consider a few ways in which public communication can be undermined.[17] Communicative obligations will demand not only that citizens, officials, and institutions do not silence communicators or restrain and disperse audiences but also that they maintain the possibility of public communication. Because public communication in mass, indirect democracies must be mediated communication, democratic communicative obligations will include obligations not to destroy but rather to preserve and maintain some technological as well as linguistic and social conditions for public communication.

The communicative obligations of any democratic society will always include some perfect obligations. For example, those who silence other voices, whether by physical destruction or gagging or by threatened violence, act on principles that cannot be universalized. Noncoercion is a perfect obligation in communicating, as in other matters.[18] Equally, here as elsewhere, deception is parasitic on a trust that would be destroyed if deceiving were universally practiced, hence is nonuniversalizable. Nondeception, too, then, is a principle of perfect obligation.

Rights to self-expression are corollaries of these perfect obligations. Imperfect obligations not to destroy or erode means of communication lack counterpart individual rights. The means of communicating can also be irreparably damaged by acts that do not deceive or coerce individual communicators.

Languages can be debased and killed; cultural traditions, dispersed and vulgarized; technologies can be introduced and others displaced in ways that destroy possibilities of communication without coercing or deceiving individuals. Modernization and market relations can transform communicative possibilities without violating rights to free expression. They do so by shifting the background conditions that enable communication. Sometimes these shifts may erode or reduce possibilities for communication. Here the value of starting from the perspective of obligations is clear: It allows for imperfect communicative obligations, which are not owed to specified others so have no correlative rights, yet must be met if public communication in a democracy is to be possible. Much that these imperfect obligations require is part and parcel of wider obligations to preserve civil and democratic society; some specific implications for communicative obligations are of interest.

Consider, for example, the implications of the thought that communication is potentially a *reciprocal* process, and in democratic life must at times actually be two-way. By its very structure mediated communication obscures this. Much mediated communication is one-way mass communication. Only a few modes allow audience response; those that do generally subject the response of a necessarily fragmented audience to severe editorial control and formatting. However, if communicators view communication as (potentially) a two-way process, they must adopt and reveal a certain view both of their own communicating and of their audience. In particular they must treat their own communication, as well as the communications of others whom they report as *particular voices among many,* as voices that are subject to challenge and error and not as the oracles of truth or authorities beyond question. Second, they must *respect the voices of their audiences.* They must be committed to communicating only in ways that neither *mislead* by assuming bogus authority nor *silence* others by undermining their standing and capacities to respond. Neither obligation is easily met: Each can be fulfilled only by developing and sustaining complex networks of conventions and standards, as well as modes of self-discipline, professional regulation, and accountability, for those who address wide audiences.

Consider first the requirement that those who communicate do so as one voice among others rather than with assumed authority. When there are great asymmetries of power to communicate, those who have the power easily come to write or speak or edit as if their own voices were true and authoritative. They may suppress qualifications and disclaimers and obscure clues and conventions that are vital for interpreting and so for checking and challenging their own communication. All this is easily done even in communicating that is informal and chatty in tone. There can be many reasons, ranging from political interest to mere laziness, for shunning the hard and often boring task of writing, speaking, or editing for a heterogeneous audience in a way that is open to challenge and shows that and how it is open. Editorial combination of a number of competing viewpoints is meant to help audiences judge and challenge what they read and hear, yet can be done in ways that reduce public communication to goodies on an opinion smorgasbord. A large range of techniques can disguise communicators' fallibility and their latent agenda, and reflect principles that, if universally acted on, would mislead and ultimately destroy the very possibility of communication. Straightforward lying is, of course, a tried and tested way of misleading; but disinformation is continuous with misinformation, as well as simpler techniques of sensationalism, selective omission, noncoverage, and neglect of views that lie beyond the assumed limits of "acceptable" opinion. All these methods can be used to sway public opinion while disabling public criticism. The terms of discourse established in the public life of a society and its mass media may mask and obscure injustices and interests that affect citizens vitally. We have only to consider how critical history can revise our views of past complacencies to become uneasy about our own. Without a vantage point that offers a distanced eye on our own present, we can specify what is needed for communication that fosters rather than damages possibilities of communication only in rather general, sometimes procedural, terms. We can insist that it should aim to be interpretable and judgeable by its audience; that communicators should assume and reveal their own fallibility; that they stress rather than suppress the difficulties of their own viewpoint.[19]

This insistence may seem no more than a demand for responsible journalism. I doubt, however, that such a demand goes far to secure the practices of toleration needed for democracy. We have plenty of evidence of the power of established and establishment modes of thought, and of ways in which these are used to set the terms of debate, to co-opt criticism and to marginalize dissent. A more specific account of how communicative obligations could be secured in a modern society probably requires a theory of ideology and of the critique of ideology: These are further and enormous topics.

The communicative practices important for democracy require communicators not only to avoid presenting their own voices as authoritative but also to respect the voices of their audiences. This obligation is taken too lightly if it is seen only as a matter of providing a limited "right to reply" such as letters to the editor, op-ed pages, and phone-in programs. Given what we know about the power of dominant ideologies to structure our thinking, these arrangements go only a little way to secure a hearing for other positions. A deep commitment to respecting and hearing other voices must always take seriously the thought that other voices have been smothered and silenced, so that mere opportunity to speak may not enable them to become audible. The commitment may have to be expressed by developing and sustaining institutions that foster diversity of communication and protect positions and voices that are in danger of being silenced or marginalized.

Feminist discussions provide a good illustration of this theme. In most developed democratic countries women have had the central rights of citizenship for two generations, yet their participation in "public" life remains low.[20] Many analyses of this phenomenon conclude that the very categories of established political life and public communication marginalize women and devalue their standing and their understanding. Those whose persons and voices are standardly devalued in communication ranging from certain sorts of pornography through ordinary gender stereotyping to daily gossip understandably say less than those whose standing the status quo secures and enhances. Generalizing from these points suggests that democratic *public* communication must take *all* other voices seriously, that it must treat others and their categories of discourse with respect. This is never easy. It can demand effort to follow and respect unfamiliar categories of discourse rather than put words into others' mouths, or impose established categories of discourse on those who do not share them, or assume that those who are silent have nothing to say.[21] It may demand that we stop labeling others in wounding and belittling ways, and refrain from ways of speech that are common coin yet damage or silence others. We are all, I expect, aware of the difference between success and failure in this area when we contrast respectful, nonintrusive interviewing techniques with dominating and intrusive techniques. It is harder to be aware of analogous phenomena where cultural practice is more uniform (e.g., racism and gender stereotyping). There are Oldspeaks as well as Newspeaks that marginalize and silence voices.

Still, thinking about Newspeaks is instructive because we are less likely to dismiss as trivial the intrusion of an ideology that is not already dominant and thus taken for granted. Orwell's Newspeak is a paradigm of a mode of discourse that neither acknowledges that the communicator's is only one of many voices nor respects other voices, and so can be used both to mislead and to silence. A Newspeak can lead rapidly from literary barbarism through political domination to thought control. Communication in such Newspeaks violates democratic communicative obligations, for it is communication on principles that ultimately both mislead and silence, so cannot be universally shared. Democracies need oppositions: Newspeaks undercut them.

It is perhaps surprising that a right-based approach (whether libertarian or "welfare") need discern nothing wrong with Newspeak as such. A Newspeak may be seen as just one more mode of self-expression that (unless used to defame or deceive or the like) need violate no rights.[22] It is only wrong to establish a Newspeak by violating rights (on standard accounts of rights it would be wrong to establish a Newspeak, as in *1984*, by central control of the media and silencing of nonofficial voices). A Newspeak established without these would violate no standardly accepted rights; yet it would flout other communicative obligations. Hence it is important to ask whether mass communication *even in democratic societies* may establish categories and modes of discourses that so dominate discussion and thought that they endanger the very formulation and communication of opposition. Ideological domination is perhaps not solely a problem of *un*democratic political life. Wherever people find it hard to formulate or discuss the thoughts of opposition (whether antisocialist or anticapitalist, anti-Islamic or antinationalist), we may suspect that established ideology *whether or not imposed by overt exercises of state power* threatens democratic communication. This suspicion extends not only to what is seen as Newspeak: Oldspeaks too may silence and the tyranny of majorities may be an ideological tyranny.[23]

If we approach these dangers from the perspective of rights, our main focus must be on providing (some) protection for right holders' speech. Typically, coercion and silencing of individuals will be ruled out, and (some form of) press freedom will be enforced to provide some protection for fundamental rights. Rights-based theories insist that rights be respected, in other words, that perfect obligations be met; but imperfect obligations to secure the conditions of public communication in a democracy cannot be grounded in a rights-based theory.

A more adequate picture can be reached by considering the full range of communicative obligations, including specific "practices of toleration" that go beyond respect for individual rights and may be needed in a particular linguistic, social, and technological context. We need to ask not only what freedom of speech and expression requires, but which other practices of protecting and regulating communication may be important to prevent the emergence and domination of ideologies that (even without violence or threat to communicators) exclude or silence communicators or types of communication and damage languages or communication technologies irreparably and without replacement. Whenever noninterference is likely to produce ideological uniformity rather than a debate with many voices, democratic communication needs more than noninterference with others' speech. To take the communicative obligations of democratic life seriously we need to think more broadly about ways in which we can discipline and regulate our uses of language, of communication technologies, and of editorial power. Communicative obligations may require us to strive for communication that displays its allegiances and the principles of its own construction and hence for its interpretation, evaluation, (and even deconstruction), and so takes seriously communication with others whose allegiances and principles of communication may differ.

CENSORSHIP AND THE REGULATION OF DISCOURSE

I have left till last some questions that I find hard. Suppose we acknowledge that communication in democracies imposes obligations that run wider than those demanded merely by respect for others' rights, however these may be construed. We can then ask whether obligations that lack corresponding rights should be enforced, by legal or other sanctions. (I deliberately avoided "settling" this issue by building into the definition of imperfect obligations that they ought not to be legally enforced.) Some rights theorists will deny that the question arises, because their supposed principle for constructing human rights divides acts exclusively into violations of others' rights and permitted uses of their own right to liberty, and thus leaves no room for other, imperfect obligations; here no question arises about the enforcement of imperfect obligations since there are none. Others, who allow for imperfect obligations, for whom the question arises, may think that only perfect obligations (and perhaps not all of these) and their correlative rights may or can be legally enforced. They may hold that *enforcement* of other communicative obligations would always be unjust and would often interfere with acts of self-expression or with other rights.

Those who take obligations as fundamental, like those who take rights as basic, will find serious reasons for legal sanctions against destruction or threats to communicators on account of the form or content of their speech acts. Such action may harm and intimidate individuals; when done systematically it may damage not only particular attempts at communication but the security and so possibility of communication as well. No "laundry list" of forbidden topics, words, or languages can be enforced without coercing communicators. The perspective of obligations offers as much reason as that of rights to use sanctions, including those backed by state power, to prevent these sorts of interference with communication.

However, control of communicative content need not be done by coercing communicators. Such censorship is only one, rather limited, mode of regulating discourse. Even societies that eschew control of communication by coercion of communicators regulate communication in myriad ways. Legal, economic, and social structures and traditions as well as conversational and literary forms and conventions regulate who communicates with whom, and the topics and occasions on which they communicate. Nor is regulation avoidable, for it not only restricts but enables communication, which always depends on determinate social and linguistic structures and traditions.

Particular ways of regulating discourse are, however, open to change. A democratic society might vary the extent to which it permits commercial or sectarian interests to form and regulate public discourse and communication, or the extent to which it uses political and legal modes of regulation to prevent its public discourse being dominated by those interest groups. But no society can institutionalize zero-regulation of public discourse. The choice can only be between differing patterns of regulation. Modes of regulation are preferable if (in a given context) they secure a relatively ample fulfillment of communicative obligations. No society can guarantee that all communicators will be able to express every possible content in every possible context. Supposed attempts to do this by laissez-faire communications policies merely assign the regulation of communication to nonstate powers. They secure a particular configuration of freedom of expression, which may leave some unable to find their voices and does not guarantee the expression of diverse views. A better and less abstract aim for a democratic society is a set of practices that enables a wide range of communication, especially of public communication, for all.

Modern democracies are not *and cannot be* neutral or unconcerned about the regulation of mediated communication. Complete noninterference with communication is impossible, and minimal *legal* regulation of communication may not constitute minimal interference. In any case, it may not be *minimal* interference (whatever that might be) that best secures the sustained possibility of communication. Under modern conditions communicative obligations demand complex institutions. It is unlikely that complex institutions will arise and thrive in modern states without some political and legal regulation. A simple contrast between legal and political regulation of public communication (labeled "interference") and commercial, educational, or, indeed, media regulation of communication (labeled "noninterference") misleads. Commercial and sectoral groups and institutions themselves are in part legally and politically constituted and regulated. By rejecting direct political or legal regulation of communication and the media we may fail to advance practices of toleration and may even create additional demands for political and legal regulation of other institutions.

There is then little prospect of discovering how the media ought *generally* be regulated by appealing to a supposed ideal of noninterference. Some may, however, claim that in some specific situations legal and political regulation should not be extended. They may think that, as things are, at least in some societies, a minimal legal regulation plus traditional, nonlegal modes of regulating communication are adequate or perhaps optimal for sustaining democratic life. They may hold that at least some fortunate societies inherit so tolerant and robust a public culture that the conditions of public communication can best be sustained without adding political guarantees or legal enforcement. Two comments are in order. First, a robust public culture of this sort is not likely to be independent of legal regulation, even if the laws that sustain it do not always bear directly on the regulation of communication. Second, those who inherit a fortunate moral and cultural legacy, which does not depend heavily on legal regulation of communication, may wonder whether it is a vulnerable or depleting legacy and what must be done to preserve or renew it.[24] If it cannot be renewed without (additional) legislation and enforcement, there are good reasons to use state power to establish, regulate, and enforce whatever practices of toleration democratic modes of life need in a given time and place.

Worries about censorship are not groundless, but they are typically focused only on part of what we need to worry about if we take communicative obligations seriously. If toleration cannot be identified with a policy of noninterference, there will be no unique set of policies that counts as censorship in all contexts. No doubt, we would retain the term "censorship" for the harshest, most coercive, and least justifiable ways of regulating discourse. No doubt we will usually include the prevention of speech and publication by exercise of state power under the heading of censorship, since it is generally an unjustifiable way of regulating communication. It *both* coerces individuals *and* damages communicative practices. On occasion we may think other ways of regulating discourse also deserve this harsh label – for example, preventing people from speaking their vernacular in schools or in public life, mocking and ignoring communication attempted by those whose standing or identity is vulnerable or fragile. The assumption that *only* legal regulation constitutes interference or censorship trades on a specific and highly contentious use of a public–private distinction.

SELF-REFLECTION

The strategy of argument of this essay may have seemed unnecessarily strenuous. I have spent as much time commenting on the perspective of recipience, and particularly on the implications of treating rights as fundamental, as I have spent in exploring the perspective of agency and the implications of making obligations fundamental. I hope that the point of this perversity is now clearer. To speak in voices that communicate, we must neither assume bogus authority nor mislead; we must take the categories of discourse of our audiences seriously. This I have tried to do. I made the prevailing discourse of rights my point of departure. I then tried to show how that discourse draws its coherence from a wider mode of thought that centers on agency and obligations, allows for imperfect obligations, and thus can offer an account of wrongdoing that goes beyond nonviolation of rights. I sketched some of the advantages for nonutilitarian liberals of grounding rights by way of a broader constructivist account of human obligations. I suggested how the wider mode of discourse offered by an agent's perspective dissolves the supposedly simple antithesis between state censorship and individual freedom of expression, and requires us to consider the whole range of institutions and practices that regulate public communication. Of course, all regulation restricts; but in a world of interdependent and mutually vulnerable agents it also enables. Toleration in democratic polities requires us to identify modes of regulation that best enable communication, especially public communication, for all. We institute such practices of toleration not by aiming for a mythical situation of noninterference in communication, but by seeking, instituting, and supporting modes of regulation that best enable and least restrict communication between all potential communicators in the actual situations in which we find ourselves. Practices of toleration must protect not only communicators and communicative acts but practices of communication; the practices of communication that ought to be protected are not those that happen to prevail here or there, now or once before, but those that themselves best enable and least obstruct communication here and now.

NOTES

I have been given a lot of help in reaching and expressing these thoughts. Special thanks to Jay Blumler, Lee Bollinger, Owen Fiss, Keith Graham, Andrew Harrison, Stephen Holmes, Sheldon Leader, Judith Lichtenberg, Lawrence Lustgarten, Susan Mendus, Alan Montefiore, Tim Scanlon, and Anthony Smith.

1 Why the scare quotes? Because the view that major corporations and market forces are *private* powers is ideologically contentious.

2 Kant sees the category of obligation as itself partially constitutive of the good: Duty is defined as action out of good will by rational beings whose spontaneous action need not exemplify good will; good willing is defined as the only unconditional good. Kant's constructivism is deployed in showing why good willing is a matter of the form rather than content of an agent's maxim, and hence a matter of acting out of universalizable maxims. Needless to say, the relation between obligatory action and good will is not the instrumental relation between right action and good results familiar in utilitarian thought. Cf. particularly Chapter 1 of his *Groundwork of the Metaphysic of Morals*.

3 Again the scare quotes to remind us that labeling certain rights "welfare rights" is ideologically contentious, particularly since there are milieux in which rights and welfare are taken to be antithetical. Oddly, the term is often (if riskily) used by those who *favor* such rights.

4 I have argued more systematically for the view that theories of rights *taken in isolation* are indeterminate in "The Most Extensive Liberty," *Proceedings of the Aristotelian Society* (1979–80); "Rights, Obligations and Needs," *Logos* (1985); and in *Faces of*

Hunger: An Essay on Poverty, Development and Justice (London: Allen & Unwin, 1986), chap. 6.

5 Cf. T. Scanlon, "A Theory of Freedom of Expression," *Philosophy and Public Affairs* 1 (1972): 204–26; John Horton, "Toleration, Morality and Harm," in *Aspects of Toleration*, ed. John Horton and Susan Mendus (London: Methuen, 1985).

6 For constructivist approaches to deontological liberalism that make rights fundamental, see, e.g., John Rawls, "Kantian Constructivism and Moral Theory," *Journal of Philosophy* 77 (1980): 515–72; Alan Gewirth, *Human Rights: Essays on Justification and Applications* (Chicago: University of Chicago Press, 1980).

7 For discussions of the idea of a metric of rights and some associated difficulties, see Hillel Steiner, "Individual Liberty," *Proceedings of the Aristotelian Society* 75 (1974–5): 33–50; Charles Taylor, "What's Wrong with Negative Liberty," in his *Philosophy and the Human Sciences"* (Cambridge: Cambridge University Press, 1982), vol. 2 of *Philosophical Papers*, 211–29; Onora O'Neill, "The Most Extensive Liberty," *Proceedings of the Aristotelian Society* 80 (1979–80): 45–59, and "Children's Rights and Children's Lives," *Ethics* 98 (1988): 445–63.

8 This starting point is chosen as one that all modern "deontological" liberals will accept. The theoretical position to be sketched can also be reached without using this starting point by constructing an account of the principles of action that can be shared by a plurality of rational but finite beings. If the argument is developed from that starting point, claims about rights drop out as one corollary of a theory of obligations rather than forming the starting point.

9 The only "rights" that can be coherently thought of as lacking correlative obligations are Hobbesian natural rights (Hohfeldian liberties). These "rights" are no more than an absence of obligation to refrain and are no sort of entitlement. If there were only such rights, there would indeed be no obligations; but there would also be no entitlements, hence little that rights theorists are interested in asserting.

10 This point may be disputed because *institutionalized* imperfect obligations are often specified in ways that identify the holders of counterpart *institutionalized* rights. To make a "welfare" right (e.g., a right to food, a right to care) justiciable, right holders as well as obligations bearers must be specified. However, this point about institutionalized obligations does not hold for fun-

damental (natural, moral, human) obligations: Where these obligations are not owed to *all* others (as perfect fundamental obligations are) they may be owed to *unspecified* others. In that case *nobody* holds rights corresponding to them.

11 See, e.g., Susan Griffin, *Pornography and Silence* (New York: Harper & Row, 1981); Susan Mendus, "Harm, Offence and Censorship," in *Aspects of Toleration*, ed. Horton and Mendus; Susanne Kappeler, *The Pornography of Representation* (Cambridge: Polity Press, 1986).

12 There are good reasons to doubt whether even self-expression can go far without depending on shared standards. This is an important topic raised both by discussions of the Private Language Argument and by consideration of the degree to which human agency is socially formed. Both topics must be bracketed here. On many views of the matter, modes of self-expression, and thus acts of self-expression, also presuppose a social context and capacities for communication, and hence permissible (universalizable) self-expression too must depend on, and not destroy, the means of communication.

13 Again, an intimation that expression, even thinking, is parasitic on communication. Cf. Kant's essay "What Is Orientation in Thinking?" in *Immanuel Kant: Critique of Practical Reason and Other Writings in Moral Philosophy*, trans. L. W. Beck (Chicago: University of Chicago Press, 1949), pp. 295–305.

14 The account of democratic toleration that I sketch in part here is unlike Marcuse's concept of liberating, selective (as opposed to abstract, repressive) toleration except in negative ways. I accept that noninterference provides an inadequate basis for the practices of toleration needed for democracy. However, the conclusions I gesture toward are more Orwellian than Marcusan in spirit, and more Kantian than Orwellian.

15 The echo of Habermas's universal pragmatics will be evident here. But the argument does not assume that Habermas's account of the types of claims that must be discursively redeemable is correct or the whole story. I learned a great deal from various quarters: The debts to Kant's political writings, and to Wittgenstein and Foucault, will be obvious; there are others to Walter Ong. I try here only to make minimal assumptions: In particular I do not assume that language mastery has to be total, or that communicators are unable to master more than one language. Even if we take account of the resilience of

communication in the face of imperfect mastery of language and communications technology, there are still bounds below which the possibility of communication fades and is damaged.

16 I leave untouched the complicated question of how the public–private distinction should be interpreted in this context.

17 This particular articulation of communicative obligations can be derived from the Categorical Imperative and is articulated in some of Kant's more political writings as well as in the First and Third Critiques. I have discussed these texts and Kant's views on communicative obligations in "The Public Use of Reason," *Political Theory* 14 (1986): 523–51. It is sometimes suggested that communicators have obligations to tell the truth. This seems to me to require too much: Often the truth is obscure; sometimes communication of true propositions misleads. It is sometimes suggested that they ought merely to avoid lying. This seems to me to demand too little: An audience can be greatly misled even when told no lies. I have settled on a no doubt insufficiently articulated view that the crucial thing if the conditions of communication are to be preserved is not to communicate in ways likely to mislead. Misleading communications standardly produce mistrust; only communication based on principles of not misleading is universalizable. This has the corollary that permissible communication must be adjusted to meet actual and possible audiences.

18 It is no defense of coercion of communication that a few writers succeed – maybe even brilliantly – in outwitting the censorship, whether by irony, esotericism, or *samizdat*. Censorship detroys communicative powers and possibilities even when not 100 percent effective. Cf. Leo Strauss, *Persecution and the Art of Writing* (Glencoe, Ill., Free Press, 1952).

19 Refusal to mislead is compatible with advocacy: Often the most convincing advocacy does not mislead and even displays its own limitations. Of course, the situation is more complex when advocacy is undertaken under the surveillance of censors, or in the face of an opposition that deploys misleading modes of communication. As often, an account of what is permissible when others are complying imperfectly will be highly complex.

20 Why the scare quotes? Because standard versions of a public–private distinction are disputed by feminists. Some relevant works are: Janet Silatianen and Michelle Stanworth, *Women and*

the Public Sphere (London: Hutchinson, 1984); Jean Bethke Elshtain, *Public Man, Private Woman* (Princeton, N.J.: Princeton University Press 1981); also Carol Gilligan, *In a Different Voice* (Cambridge, Mass.: Harvard University Press, 1982).

21 Of course, some others may have nothing or nothing coherent to say. The point is not to take drivel or babel more seriously than they deserve, but to refrain from misclassifying others' discourse as drivel or babel – for example, by strategies that silence others.

22 The insidious evil of a Newspeak is underestimated if it is supposed that all that is wrong is that lies are told. That can be done in any language. What is more serious is that certain thoughts may become unthinkable, that certain modes of expression and practices of communication that are vital to people may become obsolete and unavailable.

23 Here Foucault's work is clearly of immense importance.

24 This phrase comes from F. Hirsch, *The Social Limits of Growth* (Cambridge, Mass.: Harvard University Press, 1976); the thought that our public culture is fragile and that "the barbarians" are within is more widespread. See, e.g., Alasdair MacIntyre, *After Virtue* (London: Duckworth, 1981); J. M. Coetzee, *Waiting for the Barbarians* (Harmondsworth: Penguin, 1982).

Chapter 6

Access in a post–social responsibility age

CARL SESSIONS STEPP

Nearly thirty-five years after the landmark report by Robert Hutchins and his Commission on Freedom of the Press, Barbara W. Hartung published in the *Journalism Quarterly* an article examining the "Attitudes Toward the Applicability of the Hutchins Report." She concluded, "It is somewhat startling to find how contemporary the directives of the Commission are and how unchanging the problems of the press in America appear to be."[1]

Hartung's observations remain applicable to this day. In her Introduction to this volume, Judith Lichtenberg identifies central issues in contention today as those that "have to do with diversity in and access to the press." They include "the availability of the press to diverse points of view, to perspectives other than those of a privileged and powerful minority," and "a lack of significant diversity of opinion and points of view represented in the news and public affairs coverage of the mass media."[2]

As Hartung might note, this complaint is strikingly similar to the classic statement drafted in the mid-1940s by the thirteen-member commission headed by Hutchins, who was then chancellor of the University of Chicago. The commission's report, on its first page, went straight to the issue of access. It charged that the press is "available to a small minority of the people only" and that "the few who are able to use the machinery of the press as an instrument of mass communication have not provided a service adequate to the needs of society."[3]

This thought was not new to the commission. Similar complaints have recurred throughout the century, both before and after the Hutchins period. Will Irwin, in an ambitious fifteen-part series in *Collier's* magazine in 1911, lamented the control of the press by the business class, the resulting suppression of unpopular opinions and news, and the difficulty that unmoneyed individuals encounter in asserting their voice. "The youth with a free message has no million dollars" to begin a paper, Irwin wrote. "If he manages to borrow it, he must go, usually, to the very institutions which pull the wires on his contemporaries."[4]

Critic A. J. Liebling followed his often quoted maxim "Freedom of the press is guaranteed only to those who own one" with the observation that "anybody who owns the price of a newspaper nowadays must be a businessman."[5] More recently, Ben Bagdikian reported that fifty conglomerates control more than half the American media and seldom hesitate to stifle voices that threaten their interest. He added, "The small voices, as always, are important, a saving remnant of diversity. But their diminutive sounds tend to be drowned by the controlled thunder of half the media power of a great society."[6]

Although the Hutchins Commission was hardly unique in identifying the persistent access problem in the media, it proved more potent than other complainants in promoting a manifesto for reform. Its recommendations – in particular, its call that "the agencies of mass communication accept the responsibilities of common carriers of information and discussion"[7] and provide the diversity, criticism, and interchange necessary for society to thrive – became the building blocks of a "social responsibility" doctrine. Although they incurred early criticism from publishers and media managers, they sank roots and were in effect anointed and codified by Theodore Peterson, who concluded in *Four Theories of the Press* that pure libertarian theory was "obsolescent" and that "taking its place is an emerging theory which puts increasing emphasis on the responsibilities of the press."[8]

For the next several decades, the words of social responsibility effectively lubricated the debate about journalistic ethics: They echoed through the professional press, in articles such as Norman E. Isaacs's "A Small Town Paper Has One Supreme Ethical Duty – to Print the News." Writing in *Quill* in 1953, Isaacs proclaimed, "I cannot tolerate a newspaper operated like a factory, or a mine, or a garage. The newspaper is a community's soul – not a market place."[9]

They echoed through professional codes of conduct. One, issued in 1973, begins, "The Society of Professional Journalists, Sigma Delta Chi, believes the duty of journalists is to serve the truth. We believe the agencies of mass communication are carriers of public discussion and information. . . . The purpose of distributing news and enlightened opinion is to serve the general welfare."[10]

They echoed in the critical literature. In *The Media Monopoly,* Bagdikian asserted that "there are conventions that often protect the journalist. They hold that news should be produced fearlessly and fairly by professional journalists working without coercion. . . . The force of the conventions is not supported by law or contract but by a general ethic in the trade."[11]

And the doctrine's underpinnings stuck firm: As Hartung discovered in her 1981 study, "Editors and publishers and journalism educators generally agreed on the Hutchins Commission's directives of what is responsible reporting and what the newspaper ought to do to protect freedom of the press."[12]

Yet still the access issue lingered, unresolved, as it lingers today. It now seems appropriate, therefore, to ask whether the press has entered a post–social responsibility era, in which the doctrine midwifed by the Hutchins Commission has taken hold as much as it is going to, without remedying the entrenched, reform-resistant problems of access and diversity. It is the purpose of this essay to examine the fate of the social responsibility doctrine in the present day, in view of questions such as: Has the Hutchins prescription been rendered toothless, obsolete, or impractical by the realities of contemporary media and society? Should it be abandoned or modified or fortified in philosophy or operation? If so, what new legal, political, or social controls over the press are required, and how should they be enforced?

DEVELOPMENTS SINCE HUTCHINS

The Hutchins report provided an influential ideological guide for the development of postwar journalism, but one that was critically grounded in the voluntary enforcement of the social responsibility contract by the media themselves. Thus, the doctrine is vulnerable. It can be undermined by conditions that induce publishers and media managers to seek to exempt themselves from the onus of self-enforcement. It is possible to identify several contemporary conditions that can provide such incentive for the media managers.

1. *Intensified concentration:* The Hutchins report stated that "the outstanding fact about the communications industry today is that the number of its units has declined. . . . Throughout the communications industry the little fellow exists on very narrow margins, and the opportunities for initiating new ventures are strictly limited."[13] Since then, concentration has increased even more dramatically. According to Bagdikian:

> By the beginning of the 1980s most major American media – newspapers, magazines, radio, television, books, and movies – were controlled by fifty corporations. Twenty corporations control more than half the 61 million daily newspapers sold every day; twenty corporations control more than half the revenues of the country's 11,000 magazines; three corporations control most of the revenues and audience in television; ten corporations in radio; eleven corporations in all kinds of books; and four corporations in the motion pictures.[14]

The consequence is to raise, as Bagdikian does, "the questions whether our mass media are free to exercise their traditional role of mediating among the forces of society at a time when they have become an integral part of one of those forces."[15]

Continuing concentration has the potential of reducing the incentive for social responsibility by taking decision makers farther from local affairs, elevating business considerations over social and journalistic values, and further aligning media managers with the power-class institutions of business and government.

2. *The increasing intrusion of nonnews corporations into the news enterprise:* If colonial American journalism was the age of the printer and the nineteenth century the age of the editor, then the twentieth century is the age of the manager. The press is part of big business, and, increasingly, it is owned and operated by big business corporations that may have only incidental interest in journalism and that may be controlled by individuals without grounding in journalistic principles. Bagdikian notes that the fifty corporations controlling most of the media are partners in agribusiness, timber, banking, insurance, electronics, weapons production, religious instruction, utilities, pipelines, construction, tobacco, computers, plastics, microprocessing, chemicals, and space flight engineering. They have a vested stake in legislation, regulations, taxes, trade policy, foreign investments, and broad domestic and foreign policy. Further, "conflicts of interest, real and potential, are infinitely greater because the large media companies exchange directors, and therefore have common policy views, with nonmedia corporations."[16]

An obvious danger of such intermingling is the submergence of press operations into an overall strategy in which they become simply one more profit venture. Within such an environment, the press risks being stripped of its special status as, in Liebling's words, "a privately owned public utility"[17] and may find itself less able to sustain socially responsible behavior that may not jibe with a conglomerate's profit goals. In 1985, two press giants – CBS and Time Inc. – instituted financial cutbacks in their news operations, following feared or actual attempts by outsiders to take over the companies. *New York* magazine reported that CBS chairman

Thomas "Wyman has made it clear within CBS . . . that he does not see the news division as substantially different from any other unit."[18]

3. *The rise of broadcasting:* Television was an infant when the Hutchins Commission deliberated during the 1940s. Since then, it has risen to media dominance, along the way blurring news and entertainment functions into what is now sometimes derided as "infotainment." Broadcast news has encountered greater government regulation than print news (thereby arguably weakening the incentive for voluntary industry accountability); has been excluded from certain First Amendment protection; and has evolved more or less outside the tradition of social responsibility widely accepted in the print media. Yet since 1963, according to periodic studies by the Roper Organization, Americans have cited television over newspapers as their primary source of "most" of their news.[19]

Many newspapers have responded to the economic, professional, and cultural pressures from broadcasting by increasing their emphasis on entertainment, visual quality, and dramatic presentation, sometimes at the expense of more serious, but supposedly less exciting, national and international news coverage. They have sometimes defended decreases in "news of record" coverage by pointing to the proliferation of broadcast outlets as evidence of alternative sources now available to consumers.[20] Carried just a bit farther, this argument can encourage a mind-set in which social responsibility is so diffused among the many media that no one paper or station feels an ongoing individual duty to serve the public interest regularly. The result is still further potential for subordinating long-term social responsibility.

4. *A perceived economic and social squeeze on the news media:* The decades since Hutchins have seen an explosion in media usage, a technological revolution that has delivered to millions of doorsteps not just radio and television but cable, teletext, computerization, stereo and video recording, satellite reception, and much more. Today, the image of consumers reading the evening paper as they listen to the radio news

is a quaint, bygone memory. Media and submedia compete incessantly for consumer time: not just the daily paper but also specialty publications, newsletters, direct mailings, computer mail exchanges; not just a local television channel but also cable choices ranging from all news to all music to all weather to all sports; not just the neighborhood cinema but also Home Box Office, adult channels, and thousands of cassettes readily available for the home video recorder. An important result of this explosion is this: Although the profitability of media *in general* may rise, *each media unit* feels more besieged and vulnerable than ever. The number of newspapers declines; fewer cities have competitive papers; time spent with media is spread over far more choices, reducing loyalty and attention spans; advertisers, also given more choices, spread their spending thinner; media managers hesitate to risk stodginess or extravagance. Once again, the danger seems clear: The abstract goal of social responsibility can come to be viewed as an outdated, impractical luxury that must yield in the face of contemporary corporate insecurities.

Compounding the economic equation is the press perception that it faces substantial public hostility. Many studies in recent years have provided evidence on this point: Confidence in the press, as measured by the Harris Survey, dropped from 29 percent in 1966 to 14 percent in 1982;[21] in a 1984 study by Clark, Martire & Bartolomeo, commissioned by the American Society of Newspaper Editors (ASNE), 50 percent of 1,202 respondents disagreed that "newspapers are usually fair, they bend over backwards to tell both sides of the story," and 63 percent disagreed that television is fair;[22] in a 1985 study by MORI Research Inc., also commissioned by ASNE, 42 percent of 1,002 respondents agreed that "sometimes there's too much freedom of the press";[23] in a 1985 Gallup study for *Times-Mirror,* 73 percent felt the media "invade people's privacy," 53 percent said media "favor one side," and 45 percent said they are "politically biased in their reporting."[24] The accumulated impact of such data has engendered nervousness and defensiveness throughout the profession; the result is an added pressure to cater to consumer "wants" (such as entertainment) as opposed to editorially determined consumer "needs" (such as watchdog investigations or unpopular presentations that may invite reader criticism, legal trouble, and political or economic repercussions).

In summary, it can be argued that the press commitment to social responsibility, which deepened following Hutchins and became entrenched in the language of journalistic ethics, may stand on increasingly unsteady pillars. In the modern marketplace, journalism becomes more like a conventional enterprise and less like a quasi-public social franchise. It becomes bigger and riskier business, blended increasingly into corporate America and more subject to control by managers schooled in profit making than by editors passionate for fierce journalism.

These developments, coupled with the chronic and continuing problems of access and diversity, strongly suggest that a post–social responsibility era is at hand. They suggest the need for a muscular redefinition of the social contract that takes into account contemporary economic, political, and professional reality and that builds on the social responsibility notion in ways more likely to produce action. At the same time, it remains important that proposed remedies stop short of undermining inherent and enduring strengths of the American press.

THE CHALLENGE NOW

As noted earlier, the problems of access, diversity, and service are abiding ones. Only two major options appear to exist for addressing them: through government, political, and legal pressures and mandates, or through institutional self-regulation of some sort.

Government's role

It is possible to envision many roles for government in reforming the media: mandating access and fairness, enforcing an official ethics code, creating an information ministry, linking postal subsidies to quotas of public service content, and so on. Although the issue is admittedly arguable, I take as my point of departure that government regulation and control are not the appropriate avenues. Without belaboring the point, I will summarize why I believe the government-regulatory model is neither desirable nor achievable.

Although direct government control of media content seems to have few supporters, two lesser steps are often mentioned: first, that government can be insulated and restrained to the point that some benevolent "regulation" would not be tantamount to "control"; and second, that "structural" regulation can be applied without necessarily leading to "content" control. However, I maintain, these arguments, as well as other recommendations that government be relied on for redressing problems of access, diversity, and service, will inevitably fail, individually and collectively, on several grounds:

1. *Constitutionally:* Government control of the press content is, simply put, unconstitutional on its face, short of extreme cases of directly demonstrated clear and present danger. I cannot envision any kind of content regulation, however indirect, that wouldn't project government into the position of favoring or disfavoring some views and information over others. Even so-called structural steps aimed at opening channels for freer expression would post government in the intolerable role of super-gatekeeper.

2. *Politically:* If one defines the problem of access and diversity as Judith Lichtenberg does (in seeking voice for "perspectives other than those of a privileged and powerful minority"),[25] then government seems an ironic place to turn for help. Government is by definition integrated with the power class in American society, and it is axiomatic that the press already gives greater voice to the "outs" than the government does or is likely to. De Tocqueville recognized this reality in calling the press "the chief democratic instrument of freedom."[26] Part of the problem at hand is that the institutional press is already too much in alliance with the power classes; turning to government hardly alleviates the situation.

3. *Pragmatically:* The essays in this book originated, in part,

from a perception that government regulation of broadcasting has failed. Such experimental remedies as the fairness doctrine and equal time provisions have not served to maximize social responsibility within broadcasting; by contrast, they have helped to shield broadcasters from a full and willful embracing of the social contract with consumers. Some might argue that the solution is stronger regulation. But far from bolstering this conclusion, the record of government intervention so far undermines it.

4. *Professionally:* To impose government regulation, even with the most benign intent, on the American press would risk wrecking a fragile system that is arguably the most responsible and effective in the world, even given its imperfections. The system is animated by the ideal of First Amendment freedom from government interference; government intrusion would necessarily subvert that ideal and demolish the fundamental assumption on which the press operates. It is hard to imagine that the ensuing system would be an improvement.

If government fails as a reliable source of reform, then the only alternative seems to be reform within the press. Yet this is the same avenue recommended by the Hutchins Commission and depended on throughout history. If it hasn't succeeded so far, why should it now?

There are two possible answers. The first is that internal reform is logically the only alternative that stands a chance of working; thus, it is the place to concentrate the effort, for better or worse. The second, more important response is that journalism is a craft peculiarly suited to internal reform, if critics and would-be reformers study the system and locate the suitable levers for producing change.

Individual journalists (in contrast to journalistic institutions) are by nature independent and self-critical; that they voluntarily express and accept the social responsibility doctrine is itself an indication of goodwill that can be turned to powerful advantage. Journalists are propelled by a First Amendment syndrome, a set of beliefs (perhaps a mythology, but powerful nevertheless) that, via broad acceptance, assumes a self-fulfilling power that can drive the profession. It holds that journalists are free, responsible, and accountable. Journalists may not be "professionals" in the formal sense (under which licenses are required, for instance), but they tend to accept that their field operates under social and professional standards extending beyond immediate profit and self-interest. Journalists believe this, and in their belief resides the power to impose and sustain change.

This power can be employed effectively inside the newsroom. The news-craft sociology was described by Warren Breed, who identified six factors for achieving "social control in the newsroom." They included the power of institutional authority and sanctions; feelings of obligation and esteem for superiors; mobility aspirations; the absence of competing group allegiance; the pleasant nature of the activity; and the fact that news becomes a value and a continuing challenge for workers. Of the six, Breed wrote, the most powerful is the journalist's esteem for superiors; "the newsman's source of rewards is located not among the readers, who are manifestly his clients, but among his colleagues and superiors." Breed concluded: "Any important change toward a more 'free and responsible press' must stem from various possible pressures on the publisher, who epitomizes the policy making and coordinating role."[27]

More recently, Ed Lambeth listed influences that shape journalists' ethics as (in order) day-to-day newsroom learning, family upbringing, senior editors, peers, journalism professors, and senior reporters.[28] Like Breed's, his list supports the argument that internal newsroom influences serve as leading motivating forces for individual journalists. It therefore seems quite practical to move toward a strategy that utilizes this understanding of journalists and their workplaces to derive the greatest benefit for the social contract.

NEW DIRECTIONS

If problems of access and diversity have persisted for decades and remain chronic today, perhaps it is in part because reformers have failed to heed adequately the sociology of the newsplace. Journalists are driven by an abstract but powerful and self-regulating ideology that idealizes the First Amendment; publishers, managers, and line journalists exert fundamental mutual influences that profoundly affect their work. These two concepts can provide the posts for a post–social responsibility strategy directed at bringing professional influences onto the media's managerial class.

Given the proliferation of media outlets, there is, strictly speaking, no problem of access for proponents of practically any idea; the range of specialty channels and publications has become dazzling. Instead, the heart of the problem lies in acquiring not mere access at the fringe, but effective access to the mass audience – that is, in obtaining access to the dominant media in a given market. Steps such as mandating public use of obscure cable channels or financing small newsletters or offering cheap radio time at 5:00 A.M. on Sundays, as commendable as they may be, fail to address the larger problem: penetrating the central media. Such a goal entails negotiating a commitment from the major outlets to regularly devote a fair percentage of their prime space and time to matters of public interest and to offer views far removed from their own. Success requires converting publishers and managers to a steadfast social responsibility in the face of the current drift toward self-exemption from such abstract social duties.

In devising their strategy, advocates of a reinvigorated social contract might consider a modified model, one that could be called a "professional responsibility model." In this model, the notion of social responsibility would be instilled and enforced at the professional (as opposed to the institutional) level. This model would acknowledge the continuing viability of the social responsibility goal and would formulate a new strategy for enforcing it, based on a maturing understanding of contemporary journalism. The strategy could incorporate objectives such as the following:

1. *Co-opting the professional ideology and building on journalists' image of themselves as independent, accountable professionals:* To achieve this goal requires distinguishing between institu-

tional reform (via the corporation) and professional reform (via the work force). Although corporate structures may be resistant to change and unable (or unwilling) to self-mandate social responsibility, the work force is less so. As Breed, Lambeth, Bagdikian, and others note, journalists tend to be deeply influenced by other journalists and by newsroom conditions; in a real sense, journalism is a profession that runs itself. For all their administrative authority, publishers and managers remain fundamentally dependent on their news forces. In part because of the frantic and relentless nature of the work, managers cede much of their operational authority to the newsroom. There, individual journalists have power to forge the content and to influence the role a medium plays. Those professional conventions and convictions that root deeply enough in the newsroom, therefore, have strong likelihood of prevailing.

Journalism has no formal, universally accepted ideology, but its ethical standards travel powerfully and informally through the professional network. That network can be tapped at many points to promote a unified and revivified notion of social responsibility: through journalism schools, professional associations, and convention programs; in trade, critical, and academic literature; and via the formidable career-training apparatus (including facilities such as the American Press Institute, the Poynter Institute for Media Studies, the ongoing fellowship programs for journalists, etc.) that is a hallmark of journalists' desire for continuing education and self-criticism.

What is needed is not new institutions or agencies to propagate a professional responsibility doctrine, but the use of existing institutions and associations to trigger debate and action in much the same manner as the Hutchins report penetrated the field. With the notion of social responsibility already having taken root, the next step is a modern reaffirmation that the social contract overrides changing economic, cultural, and professional conditions and that the responsibility of enforcing and applying it rests with each individual journalist. If the body of practicing journalists adopted this precept as a working part of their First Amendment understanding – much as professionals such as doctors and clerics insist on working within certain social parameters regardless of their corporate affiliations – it would go a long way toward converting their institutions.

2. *Broadening public exposure to education about journalism and its social role:* This involves, in effect, acting to influence institutions and journalists from the outside, by changing their expectations through changing public expectations. A public educated in the need for a socially responsible press becomes one capable of pressuring the press to fulfill its obligations. Journalism education for the consumer is inexcusably neglected within public schools and universities. A serious effort to remedy this deficiency could produce healthy new demand for more responsive media. Here, too, the organizational structure is in place to accomplish this objective; what is needed is unified action on the part of associations of administrators, faculty, professional journalists, and educators at large. The existing cultural and educational system can be used to inculcate an understanding of press responsibility regarding access and diversity (including views however unpopular) and to make such a social tenet as acceptable as the idea that lawyers have a duty to give the most obviously guilty heinous criminals the best possible defense.

3. *Encouraging government to eschew an overregulatory role and limit itself to benign assistance to public affairs communication:* Although government should have no role in applying professional press responsibility, there is no reason to forbid its acting in a manner generally supportive of free speech. This could take any number of forms: lower postal rates to promote the free flow of ideas; the financial underwriting of media, like National Public Radio, that offer alternative programming; the reinforcement by political leaders, at every level, of the transcendent importance of the press's social role and the commitment of government to promote and not impede it. Individually, these steps would produce minimal results; in the aggregate, they could help signal the determination of all segments of society to nurture the social contract.

In a world that is coming to call itself an information society, no one can logically doubt the paramount importance of institutions that traffic in facts and ideas. They fuel the social machinery. They exist of necessity. Historically, society has depended on their willingness to balance economic and sociopolitical objectives responsibly, in exchange for the freedom of the First Amendment. Yet that dependence has yielded chronic problems of access and diversity that stand in danger of worsening in the face of growing concentration, corporate diversification, and social, political, and economic uncertainties. In searching for solutions, we might well draw on an ongoing understanding of the field to advance a model that places more responsibility where the power is: in the body of professional journalists.

NOTES

1 Barbara W. Hartung, "Attitudes Toward the Applicability of the Hutchins Report on Press Responsibility," *Journalism Quarterly* (Autumn 1981): 428–33.
2 Judith Lichtenberg, "Foundations and Limits of Freedom of the Press," this volume.
3 Commission on Freedom of the Press, *A Free and Responsible Press* (Chicago: University of Chicago Press, 1947), p. 1.
4 Will Irwin, "The American Newspaper: The Voice of a Generation," *Collier's*, July 29, 1911, 23.
5 A. J. Liebling, *The Press* (New York: Ballantine, 1964), pp. 30–1.
6 Ben H. Bagdikian, *The Media Monopoly* (Boston: Beacon, 1983), p. xv.
7 *A Free and Responsible Press*, p. 92.
8 Theodore Peterson, "The Social Responsibility Theory," in F. Siebert, T. Peterson, and W. Schramm, *Four Theories of the Press* (Chicago: University of Illinois Press, 1969), p. 103.
9 Norman E. Isaacs, "A Small Town Paper Has One Supreme Ethical Duty – to Print the News," *Quill*, December, 1953, 8.
10 "Code of Ethics," Society of Professional Journalists, in Dennis Ismach, *Reporting Processes and Practices* (Belmont, Calif: Wadsworth, 1981), p. 370.
11 Bagdikian, *The Media Monopoly*, pp. 223–4.

12 Hartung, "Attitudes," p. 433.
13 *A Free and Responsible Press*, p. 37.
14 Bagdikian, *The Media Monopoly*, p. 4.
15 Ibid., p. 153.
16 Ibid., pp. 4–5.
17 Liebling, *The Press*, p. 31.
18 Tony Schwartz, "Inside CBS," *New York*, November 4, 1985, 38.
19 Roper Organization, *Public Attitudes Toward Television and Other Media in a Time of Change* (1985), pp. 2–3.
20 See "Gannett's Neuharth: Eliminate Broadcast Regulations," *Editor & Publisher* (November 16, 1985): 41.
21 *The Public Perception of Newspapers: Examining Credibility* (Reston, Va.: American Press Institute, 1984), p. 2.
22 *Relating to Readers in the '80s* (American Society of Newspaper Editors, 1984), p. 27.
23 *Newspaper Credibility: Building Reader Trust* (American Society of Newspaper Editors, 1985), p. 51.
24 "The People and The Press," *Times Mirror*, 1986, 28–30.
25 Lichtenberg, "Foundations and Limits," this volume.
26 Alexis de Tocqueville, *Democracy in America* (New York: Random House, Vintage, 1945), p. 343.
27 Warren Breed, "Social Control in the Newsroom: A Functional Analysis," *Social Forces*, 33 (May 1955): 326–35.
28 *The Public Perception of Newspapers*, p. 7.

Chapter 7

Who decides?

FREDERICK SCHAUER

The First Amendment is not so much about truth as about power. To all but the most resolute moral or epistemological skeptic, many determinations made pursuant to First Amendment law or free speech principles involve the protection of ideas or arguments we commonly take to be false or invalid. We conscript young men and sacrifice their lives not because we believe the Nazis different but because we believe them wrong. We outlaw slavery and discrimination on the basis of race and gender because we think those activities morally reprehensible, and our reaction to those who assert the healthfulness of cigarettes or the safety of Pintos is something other than the ambivalence we reflect when as eaters of strawberry ice cream we encounter someone who prefers butter pecan.

Thinking about questions such as these, in which our actions and our discourse belie a moral or epistemological skepticism, prompts us to consider the close relationship, perhaps even the identity, between a theory of free speech and a theory of comparative personal and institutional competence. If we can with so little difficulty locate many instances in which our ability to distinguish the true from the false is not a sufficient justification for government to entrench the true and suppress the false, then we must search for reasons of institutional design and allocation of power that would disable an institution from acting on a correct decision about factual, scientific, or moral truth. As we pursue this theme, we discover that the limitation on authority imposed by a free speech principle is something other than withdrawal of authority in an area of incompetence, but may involve instead a withdrawal of authority *despite* the competence of the disabled institution. Any theory of free speech that transcends an implausible moral or epistemological skepticism is likely to be a theory that divorces the *ability* on some occasions to identify truth from the *authority* on any occasion to do so.

Locating a theory of free speech in institutional and power-allocating concerns, however, generates a series of further complications. Questions about institutional design and decision-making competence not only undergird the principle of free speech but also surround the application of that principle. What does a theory of free speech tell us, therefore, about *who* should make free speech decisions? Does a strong theory of free speech compel, as Ronald Dworkin argues, the establishment of a countermajoritarian judiciary to enforce that theory?[1] And if that is so, does the necessity of countermajoritarian institutions to enforce the principle of free speech entail the necessity of similar institutions to delineate the contours of the principle itself? And if, in turn, such a conclusion about the disability of popularly responsive and accountable decision-making institutions does follow from the principles of freedom of speech, does this conclusion then apply only when free speech is in tension with public interest values, or also when free speech is in tension, as it so often is, with other individual rights? Finally, who is to make the decision when free speech principles can be deployed on both sides of the question, as when we think about rights of access to the mass media, or restrictions on inflammatory or misleading speech in the name of improving the quality and therefore the utility of public discourse? Indeed, many concrete questions about the law and the mass media, questions commonly discussed in free speech and free press terms, can usefully be viewed as questions about second-order decision-making authority. At one level we are concerned with who should make decisions about the content of, say, the electronic media, with some arguing that these decisions should be made by networks (or producers or directors or individual stations), and others maintaining that regulatory agencies such as the Federal Communications Commission have a role to play as well. But the *second*-order question asks who should make the decision about who should make the decision. Who should decide, in this example, between the FCC and the networks? Or who should decide whether restricting the advertisement of cigarettes is justifiable? When engaging in philosophical exploration, the question is rarely addressed, because implicit in the philosophical enterprise is that *we*, the philosophers, are deciding. But when these questions arise in the world, the decisions are not left to philosophers but are resolved by one of any number of institutions, such as the courts, legislatures, popular referenda, or the competition of the economic market. My claim is that questions about which among these institutions should resolve the first-order questions is itself a question worthy of philosophical exploration.

These second-order questions about the allocation of decision-making authority are not easy ones to answer. But what is most interesting is that they are rarely even asked. Because of this, I want to focus less on answers and more on the questions, an approach necessitated by the extent to which the search for high theory rarely stops to pause over questions of role allocation and institutional design. This is a problem for any theory of anything, but it may be a special problem for free speech, for the questions we ignore are as much a part of the theory as they are part of its implementation. Consequently, I want to bring some of these questions to the surface for examination, believing that the process of raising questions about free speech and institutional design will itself advance thinking about free speech as much as if not more than venturing answers to those questions.

I

Let us consider the problem with the assistance of a concrete example. Start with the proposition that Nazism as a viewpoint, as a practice, and as a program is morally inferior to almost any non-Nazi political program imaginable. To make the claim even more precise, start with the proposition that Nazism as promoted and practiced in Germany from 1933 to 1945 is morally inferior as a theory of political organization to the theory of political organization (whatever it is) promoted and practiced in the United States of America in 1988.

This example is not intended to be controversial. Indeed, that is exactly why I picked it. I want to locate what I have to say in a moral (or epistemological, for that matter) metatheory that is objectivist at least insofar as it accepts that a moral proposition (and, a fortiori, a fact) can be true independent of the fact that some culture at some time subscribes to it (and thus false independent of the fact that some culture rejects it), and independent of the fact that some speaker at some time articulates it. I consequently reject relativism insofar as it says that we cannot evaluate Nazism independent of the fact that it was subscribed to by the bulk of a given population at a given time. Even were the Germany of 1933–45 a discrete political and social culture, and even if every German during that time believed in Nazism, Nazism would still then have been wrong, and would still be wrong now.[2] Similarly, I reject subjectivism insofar as it reduces statements of right and wrong (at least in the realm of the moral) to reports of the beliefs of the speaker.[3] A person who condemns Nazism as wrong is not merely reporting his beliefs. He is making a statement both externally justifiable and externally justified.

I want to make the same kinds of objectivist claims in the realm of fact and not of value, but here the issue tends to be less controversial.[4] The seller of beef who maintains that his product contains no cholesterol is wrong, and so is the person who maintains that George Bush is not old enough to be president, that Michael Dukakis has been convicted of a felony, that Virgos make better civil servants than Capricorns, that the earth is flat, or that Elvis Presley is alive and living with Amelia Earhart in Newark.[5]

It is perhaps more controversial, although I believe no less true, that the propagation of many of these plainly false views may under some conditions increase the likelihood for a particular listener (or the incidence for a population of listeners) of acceptance of those views by other than those who have propagated them. In short, false speech may be persuasive despite and sometimes because of its falsity.[6] Although it is possible that the propagation of false views will be ineffective by virtue of the falsity of the views propagated, the rejection of falsity on account of its falsity by any given listener or population of listeners is far from inevitable, the ideals of the Enlightenment notwithstanding. Recognizing that these are unavoidably empirical questions, involving issues of great psychological and sociological complexity, I still want to venture an answer to them. I thus take the truth or falsity (or correctness or incorrectness, or validity or invalidity, and so on) of an assertion to be only one factor, and not always the dispositive factor, in explaining which assertions are accepted and which are rejected. And if truth has only a limited role to play in explaining for the population at large which moral and factual propositions are accepted and which are rejected, then it follows that under some circumstances more people will believe certain false propositions, such as the scientific propositions of astrology and the moral propositions of Nazism, when those propositions are propagated, especially by persuasive or authoritative propagators (e.g., the *Washington Post* and Adolf Hitler, respectively), than would have been the case had that persuasive propagation not existed. Our experience with, and research on, television and in the advertising industry makes it seem romantically naive to conclude that the truth of a proposition has significantly more explanatory power than who says it, how it is said, and how much money is spent in its saying in determining which propositions are accepted and which are not.

We must add a third assumption. To the assumption that there is truth and falsity in the realm of the factual and the moral, and to the assumption that that truth and falsity have only limited explanatory power in determining which ideas will be accepted and which will be rejected in the population at large, we must add the equally plausible assumption that under some circumstances individuals will be worse off for holding false beliefs and societies will be worse off if their members hold false beliefs. Although it is not necessarily the case that in every circumstance it is better to have a true belief than a false one, it still seems safe to assume that societies would be better in some objective sense if people did not believe in Nazism, in astrology, in the flatness of the earth, or in the fact that all women secretly desire to be raped.

In order to pursue the implications of these assumptions in thinking about freedom of speech and the press, I rely on two commonplace distinctions between political theories, distinctions that are fully applicable to questions about the justifiability of an occasion of government control over some act. First, political theories may be consequentialist or deontological. If they are the former, then control over an act (speech or otherwise) is justifiable under the theory depending on the consequences of that act. If the latter, then control over an act may be a function of the nature of the act rather than its consequences, and control over some acts may be impermissible even if controlling those acts will, all things considered, have beneficial consequences. Second, political theories may be act-based or rule-based. If they are act-based, the permissibility of an occasion of government control is a function of the features of *that* occasion. If they are rule-based, the permissibility of an occasion of government control is determined by whether that occasion falls within some *type* whose control is impermissible or permissible.

These two distinctions cut across each other. It is easy to see how theories may be consequentialist and act-based (as with traditional act-utilitarianism) or consequentialist and rule-based (as with traditional rule-utilitarianism). But although not so obvious, deontological theories may also be act- or rule-based, depending on whether the deontologically relevant feature of an act must be present in every case or only be present as a tendency of a class of which particular acts are members.

Thus, a theory of free speech can initially be characterized as falling within one of these four compartments of political theory: act-based consequentialist; rule-based consequentialist; act-based deontological; or rule-based deontological. Let us examine each of them in light of our assumptions about the nature of communication. Looking first at act-based consequentialism, if a particular act of communication of a false factual or moral proposition can (as we have quite plausibly assumed) cause consequences that are on balance harmful, an act-based consequentialist political theory allowing the state to regulate whenever that regulation would decrease the amount of harm appears to permit the regulation of some false speech on account of its falsity. Yet this is precisely what almost any theory of free speech says that government may not do. To allow the harmful falsity of speech to be a sufficient condition for its lack of (comparative) immunity from official control is to deny the existence of a principle of free speech.[7]

Thus, harmful falsity, although not a sufficient condition for regulation under the minimum conditions necessary for the existence of a free speech principle, appears to be a sufficient condition for regulation if freedom of speech is taken to be both act-based and consequentialist.[8] Consequently, it appears that a principle of free speech cannot be both consequentialist and act-based. Under an act-based consequentialist political theory, various speeches might go uncontrolled, but no principle would say that the presence of an act of speech would change the method of analysis.

But perhaps our difficulty in explaining the protection of harmful falsity lies in our characterization of free speech in consequentialist terms. One way of explaining why harmful falsity is not a sufficient condition for regulation is to maintain that a theory of free speech is necessarily nonconsequentialist, even though it might still be act-based. But such an act-based nonconsequentialist theory of free speech seems implausible, for it would necessarily have to hold that particular harm-producing acts, independent of the tendencies of any category of acts of which they are a member, are to be immune from governmental limitation despite the harm they may cause. In order to hold such a theory, we would have to believe that an individual's particular act of self-expression or exercise of autonomy, when manifested in speech, is necessarily nonconsequentially morally superior to the rights of those individuals who would be involuntarily harmed by the activity. Such a view may be correct, but I will take the emptiness of the set of adherents to that position as strong support for my assertion of its implausibility.[9]

If neither an act-based consequentialist nor an act-based nonconsequentialist explanation of the way in which freedom of speech operates can be supported, then government's disability from prohibiting the propagation of the false views I have just delineated must be a function not of a nonconsequentialist rather than a consequentialist approach within an act-oriented decision procedure, but instead of a rule-based rather than an act-based approach to the question of government regulation of communicative activity.[10] Government disability with respect to restricting other-regarding communicative acts is thus not a function of the properties of any one such act, but is a disability imposed with respect to a *type* of act, independent of whether the properties and tendencies generally characteristic of the type are present in any particular communicative act. We protect the harmful speech of Nazis, for example, because we believe that unrestricted political speech serves valuable ends, and because we believe that the speech of Nazis is an instance of the type that is political speech. Insofar as this is so, we do not inquire whether this token of the type possesses the properties that led to the protection of political speech in the first instance. Similarly, the widespread endorsement of astrology by major American newspapers may impede rather than foster the search for truth, but it still falls within the category of information published in a newspaper that we take to constitute a class of instances that, as a class, does foster the search for truth. That one member of the class does not serve this end is immaterial, for the same reasons that any rule-based decision procedure will treat the fact of an event's falling under the rule as a reason for action even in those cases in which the result indicated by the rule would not have been indicated by direct application to the event of the justification undergirding the rule.

Hence, it seems that any free speech principle, whether consequentialist or deontological, will be rule-based, derived from a perception about categories of communicative acts, perceptions that, as with the perceptions that provide the foundation for any rule, may still be false in particular cases. Thus, even if the inability of government to deal with particular harm-producing false statements cannot rationally be justified in an act-based way, it may be justified by reference to a rule disabling government from dealing with cases *of this kind,* where "of this kind" refers not to a maximally precise rule but instead to a necessarily crude rule of limited specificity embracing a category of communicative acts some of which, if evaluated in isolation, would be subject to regulation.[11]

Thus, it appears that our understanding of freedom of speech is necessarily rule-based, and the only way we have of explaining a government disability in dealing with harm-producing false statements is to treat such statements as examples of types rather than self-contained particulars. But what, then, might be the justification for such a rule, and what would a rule premised on that justification look like? Put somewhat differently, what would lead a society to want to disable the *institution* of government truth determination, even in the face of particular examples in which such a determination would be both correct and desirable?

II

Rules (as well as institutions) are devices for the allocation of power. A rule-based decision procedure is distinguished from one that is act-based, or maximally particularistic, just by the way that rules render irrelevant what would otherwise be decisionally relevant facts or reasons.[12] Rules, by declaring out of bounds considerations that would otherwise lie within the decisional playing field, have the effect of empowering some decision makers and disabling others. They determine who can determine what, and, conversely, who is disabled from determining what. Rules thus determine roles as much if not more than they determine specific substantive results.

The conclusion of the previous section was that any plausible free speech principle, whether consequentialist or deontological, will necessarily be rule-based. As a result, we must think about the falsity and harmfulness of a proposition as among the otherwise relevant properties of an act that are rendered (at least presumptively) irrelevant under a free speech principle. This means, in turn, that we should consider why the institution of government should be disabled by rule from taking these otherwise relevant reasons for government action into account.

Two different types of concerns may inform the decision to disable an institution from engaging in a particular task. One is a concern with comparative competence, where "competence" refers simply to the ability to engage in a particular task. I am competent in one sense to be a carpenter if I have the ability to work with wood, regardless of any other considerations. When this conception of competence is applied to the task of determining truth, the only question is how good some institution is at determining truth. Suppose we stipulate that this is the only variety of competence that concerns us, and that as a result we want truth determined by the body that is best at doing it, just as we want our furniture built by the best carpenter.

Under this stipulation, a society might conclude that institutions other than government are better than government at determining truth. Worried about government biases, about the self justifying tendencies of government (and other) bureaucracies, about the potentially skewed inefficiencies of complex political organizations, and about myriad other factors,[13] we may conclude that allocating truth-determining power to the sociology of the marketplace is likely to be a better procedure for determining truth than allocating that power to some government agency.[14] "Better," of course, is complex when we are considering any institution that makes multiple decisions, for "better" decision making is then a function not only of the proportion of correct decisions but also of the consequences of incorrect ones. We want the greatest number of correct decisions, but we want other things that are inconsistent with this goal. If we have determined, for example, that the consequences of a mistaken suppression of truth are more serious than the consequences of a mistaken acceptance of error, then the determination of which institution will make more correct decisions is only part of the inquiry. Another part involves an evaluation of the consequences of an incorrect decision, and here a conclusion of greater comparative competence on the part of the sociology of the marketplace appears especially plausible. Although J. S. Mill was surely right in identifying the ways in which the sociology of the marketplace as well as government could suppress truth, it may still be that government, with the power to imprison as well as to condemn, has the capacity to suppress with particular efficiency. As a result, the marketplace's inefficient and leaky methods of suppression may minimize the consequences of erroneous suppression more than government's, and that very inefficiency would give the marketplace a comparative advantage if we thought an error of this kind to be more serious than the kind of error to which marketplaces are perhaps particularly susceptible, the erroneous acceptance of mistake.

All of this, however, addresses only the first of our two concerns, the concern with truth-determining *ability*. The foregoing discussion presupposed it to be preferable to allocate truth-determining responsibilities to the institution best able to perform that task, where "best" is a task-specific dimension. It is not necessarily the case, however, that tasks should always be performed by the institutions best suited to those tasks, for values other than a narrow conception of competency may intrude.[15] It may be, therefore, that values external to the process of truth determination are such that we would want to allocate truth-determination responsibilities to an institution other than the one best able to perform that task. Consider, for example, the question of determining moral truth, for the purpose of, say, settling American responsibilities to support or resist certain foreign governments. Consider further two alternative decision-making mechanisms: (1) the American practice of representative government as presently constituted and (2) entrusting the making of those decisions to the assembled past presidents of the three divisions of the American Philosophical Association. Now even if the latter decision-making body produced better decisions (a not implausible hypothesis, although not necessarily a correct one), arguments from democracy and representative government might still militate in favor of the former. That is, some decision-making institutions might be preferred to others for reasons independent of the ability to make better decisions within the areas of competence of the decision-making institution.

We thus have two types of arguments for allowing the sociology of the market rather than government to identify harmful falsity, or, for that matter, to determine whether a particular presentation is "fair" or "balanced." The first asserts simply that the sociology of the market is better able to perform the task than government. The second treats the question of ability as secondary, relying instead on certain powers that a conception of democratic theory might grant to the people, regardless of their ability to use those powers effectively, even in a comparative sense. Evaluating the first of these arguments is an unavoidably empirical task, and I want to avoid that here. Moreover, it is likely that the standard platitudes about free speech vastly overstate the inability of the government to engage in this task, taking some number of notorious mistakes as sufficient evidence to prove the intrinsic inability of government as truth determiner, without considering equally notorious mistakes by the sociology of the market. As a result, I want to focus on the latter approach to institutional responsibilities, the one holding that certain principles of governmental organization, principles *other than* comparative truth-determining ability, argue for governmental disability with respect to the truth-determination function. Under this view, a free speech principle emerges from a theory of democracy, and is a product of the conclusion that the determination of political (and possibly other) truth is to be made by the people. According to this argument, allocating the determination of political truth to the sociology of the marketplace is, if not definitional of democracy, at least a necessary condition of its existence.[16]

What is most interesting, and at the same time paradoxical, about this view is that questions *about free speech* are themselves questions about political truth. If it is central to any plausible conception of democracy that popular decision making of one kind or another will determine questions of political truth, wisdom, and policy, do these include the determinations of political truth, wisdom, and policy about the process of determining political truth, wisdom, and policy?[17] At the greatest extreme, and reminiscent of many of the traditional paradoxes of democracy and sovereignty,[18] we can thus observe that the conclusion that the people should have the ability to determine political truth is itself a question of political truth. But I make no claims to have solved the paradox of democracy, and thus will conclude, nonoriginally, that we might hold the public determination of political truth to be so definitional of democracy, and thus constitute such an antecedent conception of democracy, that it ought to be considered impermissible for a people to alienate its right to determine political truth, just as it would be similarly inconceivable for it to alienate its right to vote. But even if this conclusion about the nonalienability of the ability to determine political truth is valid, what follows from that conclusion?

III

Let me be more specific about the question with which I concluded the foregoing section. The question I want to ask is: What does the antecedent (with respect to a theory of democracy) nature of the right to determine political truth and the consequent inability of a population to alienate its right to determine political truth tell us about decision making *about* that right, given that questions about that right are themselves questions about political truth?

We commonly take the right of the people to determine political truth to be a disempowerment of government, even when that government is specifically empowered by the people themselves. That is, if the antecedent nature of the people's right to have questions of political truth determined by the sociology of the market is such that that right may not be alienated to a monarch or to a foreign government, then so, too, according to the traditional argument, may it not be alienated (or, less pejoratively, delegated) to a governor.[19] But this suggests that our previous conception of the extent of the antecedent conception of democracy was too thin. Just as the people may not alienate to a monarch or to a foreign government their right and power to determine political truth, then so, too, may they not alienate it to governors who will almost invariably share some attributes of nonresponsive sovereigns. And if governors are consequently antecedently disempowered from determining political truth even when a sovereign people would have them do so, this disempowerment would seem, based on the same theory, to apply as well to the application of free speech and free press principles. If our worries about governmental determination of truth and falsity relate to the ways in which governors have interests divergent from those they purport to represent, then it may be similarly within an antecedent conception of democracy that the people may no more alienate their right to determine political truth to governors than they may alienate that right to foreign states.

But suppose there is no question of alienation of decision-making responsibility to others, with its consequent risks. Suppose instead that the people themselves simply make, by referendum, for example, the decision that propagation of Nazism shall be forbidden because of its conjoined falsity and danger. Or suppose the people determine that the content of the electronic media should be regulated in the service of fairness, or accuracy, or even decency. Or that the people decide that defamation laws should be stricter, so that newspapers are less likely to publish information that turns out to be false. Although the referendum is the purest manifestation of direct democracy in a system too large for a town meeting, these possibilities may arise with any other method, such as jury determination or legislative action plainly responsive to popular desires.[20] For *if* we now assume that it is a substantive theory of democracy that reserves to the people the right to determine political truth, it now appears that there are political truths – that the espousal of Nazi views should not be restricted, that the content of the electronic media should not be controlled, and that newspapers should not be chilled in reporting on the activities of public officials and public figures – that the people under one conception of freedom of speech and press are not to be permitted to make. If this is true, then it seems that it is also part of an antecedent conception of democracy that political truths *about* the espousal of ideas are beyond the power of popular determination. But why would this be?

It appears that the removal of questions about freedom of speech from popular decision making is based on the view that the availability to the public of a wide range of ideas, expressed in a wide variety of ways, is a necessary condition for democratic decision making. Here the argument is not directed so much to what democracy is about as to what, instrumentally, is necessary to foster the conditions of democratic decision making. Yet this more instrumental view is in turn based on the assumption that the maximum availabilty of ideas will in fact improve the quality of public decision making. At this point, however, opposing views seem, at the very least, not implausible.[21] Consider, for example, the view that limitations on the power of certain wealthy and influential speakers, such as corporations, political action committees, television stations, newspaper conglomerates, televangelists, labor unions, and the government, would balance the sociology of the market, or would clear the channels of communication of certain sources of noise, the result being the improved ability of the people to make determinations of political truth. Or consider the view that the distortions caused by the use of certain styles of discourse (racial epithets, cross burnings, vulgar language, negligently erroneous factual statements about public figures) impede the process of public discourse more than does the risk of mistaken application of sanctions in these areas.

These examples point up the central issue. Classical free speech theory assumes that the greatest danger to freedom of speech comes from governmental or even majoritarian suppression of ideas that might be true, or at least valuable to the pursuit of truth. Indeed, some conceptions of freedom of speech even *define* it in terms of the dangers of governmental regulation, for ultimately any successful theory of free speech must explain why the state is more disabled from controlling speech than it is from controlling other activities with commensurate consequences. Thus, a successful theory of free speech that does not collapse into a theory of general liberty must explain either why speech is special or why its regulation is especially dangerous.[22] Modern challenges to that view are legion. Consider, for example, the views of Owen Fiss, both in this volume and elsewhere.[23] And consider as well the presuppositions about the source of the greatest danger embodied in laws regulating campaign communication, or in laws guaranteeing rights of reply and imposing obligations of fairness and balance with respect to large and dominant communicators. Consider also the assumptions behind the view that certain abusive, offensive, false, or misleading forms of discourse impede the best consideration of the respective merits of various ideas. What all of these laws and proposals share in common is the desire to promote the fullest and fairest consideration of ideas. They are arguments for fostering the process of public deliberation, and thus they are arguments in furtherance of a conception of free speech, rather than arguments whose conclusions are in tension to freedom of speech. In this respect proposals of this variety differ from those seeking to promote countervailing values, such as preservation of order, protection of reputation, protection of privacy, maintenance of national security, and promotion of the dignity of women and members of racial, religious, and ethnic minorities. Unlike this latter group, the former category of proposals – those that would regulate campaign advertising, or mandate access to the mass media, or control the content of the electronic media in the name of balance or fairness – does not argue for limiting the extent of freedom of speech but pits free speech against itself. The arguments, entirely instrumental on both sides, are about which method of regulation (including the method of nonregulation) will best serve a shared goal, optimizing the conditions under which the people can best deliberate about and then determine questions of political truth. And when the disagreements are of this quite special but increasingly common variety, how should they be settled? In other words, who should decide what free speech requires when free speech inspires the arguments on both sides?

IV

Our paradox is thus complete. Although much of the principle of free speech itself can be understood in terms of an allocation to the people of the power to determine political truth, it appears as if that power does not include the power to determine contested issues of political truth about free speech, *even* when there is no question of alienation of the power itself, *even* when the contested questions are only ones of how best to foster free speech, and *even* when the resolution of those contested questions turns on empirical rather than conceptual determinations.

Even though this issue, as so clarified, is a difficult one to resolve as a matter of political theory, that difficulty is not reflected in contemporary American First Amendment doctrine. The conjunction of a textually entrenched protection for freedom of speech and press with the power of judicial review has yielded, for American courts, the conclusion that free speech determinations, including determinations where free speech arguments can plausibly be marshaled on both sides of the issue, are for the courts and not for the people.[24] Were this conclusion a product of a deontological rather than a consequentialist theory of free speech, or of a Millian commitment to the theory of the marketplace of ideas independent of any political component, this conclusion would follow easily. If freedom of speech protects individual rights in a strong sense, or if it serves instrumental goals having nothing to do with any conception of democracy, then there is no reason to be concerned with deference to popular decision making when nonpopular institutions such as courts preserve free speech values. Moreover, in addition to there being no reason to defer under such understandings of freedom of speech, there may be strong reasons not to defer. Ronald Dworkin and others have argued persuasively that if we have a nonconsequentialist rights-based theory of free speech, then it is either logically anomalous or practically treacherous to have determinations of what are intrinsically rights against the public decided by that public.[25]

Recently, however, American courts have shown an increased willingness to treat the First Amendment's protection of political speech as primary[26] (although not, as Judge Bork and others would have it, exclusive)[27] and to do so for reasons that resemble the consequentialist arguments from democratic theory that I have been discussing. Yet this theoretical and doctrinal shift has not been accompanied by a commensurate shift away from the view that all free speech decisions should be made by the judiciary, a view more compatible with increasingly unimportant individual-rights or search-for-truth rationales than it is with increasingly important rationales that focus on the democratic process. As a result, the reflexive assumption that *under an argument from democracy* popular decision making has no more a role to play than it does under a deontological argument from self-expression would seem in need of at least some doctrinal reexamination.

Doctrine aside, however, the theoretical question remains. *If* popular determination of questions of political truth and political policy is central to what any conception of democracy must include, then what justifies removing questions about free speech from the scope of the consequent free speech principle? I have tried to suggest that simple answers to this question may just be too simple. An answer to this question in terms of free speech being part of an antecedent conception of democracy, not changeable by democratic processes themselves, explains why the determination of truth can no more be alienated to governors than it can be alienated to tyrants. Such an answer in terms of an antecedent conception of democracy, however, does not explain why the impermissibility of total alienation entails the impermissibility of popular determination of nonfoundational instrumental questions about the contours of free speech, and about the ways in which it might be fostered. Where free speech arguments can be made on both sides of a question, and where free speech is itself taken to be instrumental to or a component of popular decision making, then there is something compelling about the argument that resolving these contested questions of free speech strategy ought to be for that decision-making institution that it is the very idea of free speech to promote.

These questions are not limited to free speech issues, for there is a large range of political, philosophical, and empirical issues that relate to the "mechanisms of democracy" but are not narrowly about freedom of speech or freedom of the press. Assuming again an argument for free speech that relates free speech to a theory of political organization, and consequently to a theory of democracy (none of which entails the view that only political speech is to be protected), then the same considerations arise with respect to other specifications of a theory of democracy in the broadest sense. Take voting, for example. Let us assume again that, for reasons well rehearsed in the literature, it would be impermissible for a polity, even by democratic processes, to alienate its right to vote.[28] The reign of a tyrant does not become permissible just because that tyrant was elected. But from this does it follow that popular decision making about the subject of voting in general is similarly invalid? Think of the numerous difficult questions that might arise with respect to the details of the right to vote. Should ballots be secret or public? Should elections be on Tuesdays or Sundays? Should elections be scheduled so that polls open and close at uniform times throughout the country, with differences in time zones no longer being a factor? Should voting be compulsory or optional? Should election campaigns be publicly funded? Should representatives be elected every year, every two years, every four years, or some other number? Should elections be partisan or nonpartisan? Should representatives be elected by district or at large? And what of proportional representation?

All of these questions can be considered constitutional ones, but constitutional with a small *c*. Declaring the issues to be constitutional, however, shifts only the locus of the issues and not the issues themselves. For now, we can recast the question as: Who in a democracy should determine constitutional questions, especially constitutional questions not involving individual rights in any strong sense? Designating the issues as antecedent does not answer the questions about who should resolve them, and when and how they should be resolved. Similarly, the fact that some of these issues happen to be decided by the courts in some countries, such as the United States, is far from a conclusive argument that that is how they *ought* to be decided.

The free speech question can be seen, therefore, to be just one of a panoply of constitutional questions, questions involving the resolution of clashing understandings of democracy itself, and mutually exclusive strategies of how best to serve even agreed-upon understandings of democracy. These questions are arising with increasing frequency, and involve issues of pervasive importance, but they still have received little attention in the literature. This lack of attention might be explainable in part by the way in which the subject has been dominated by questions about American constitutional interpretation, but that causes many of the questions to turn on textual fortuity. We take for granted popular sovereignty with respect to constitutional questions, such as the time and style of elections, that are not textually enshrined, and we conversely take for granted the lack of popular sovereignty with respect to those constitutional questions, such as the terms of representatives and the contours of a politically derived right to freedom of the press, that *are* textually enshrined. The result has been that in the United States these questions have been reduced to ones about judicial review of certain canonically inscribed features of democracy, but rarely are the issues debated in any meaningful pretextual way.

Contributing to the problem is the fact that once we leave questions of American constitutional theory and focus instead on larger questions of political theory, the issues become largely ones of non-ideal theory. In most of the cases I am discussing, non-ideal psychological and sociological concerns, or disagreement about theoretically resolvable questions, convert what without these factors would be easy issues into hard ones. But the fact that the hardness is created at the non-ideal level does not make the issues less interesting or less important. To believe otherwise is quite simply a mistake. Questions of decisional authority and role allocation in a non-ideal world are central questions that can and should be analyzed with philosophical rigor. When we consider them we may better understand, as I have attempted to show in the earlier parts of this essay, the roots of the free speech principle. And we may also, as I have then tried to show, better understand how to think about the application of that principle. But most interesting is the range of questions larger than free speech itself. Only when we can think about questions of role allocation can we think about how a democracy can determine what kind of democracy it wants to be.

NOTES

1 See Ronald Dworkin, *Taking Rights Seriously* (Cambridge, Mass.: Harvard University Press, 1977), pp. 142–4, 188–205.

2 On relativism, see John Mackie, *Ethics: Inventing Right and*

Wrong (Harmondsworth: Penguin, 1977), pp. 36–42; Mary Warnock, *Ethics Since 1900*, 3rd ed. (Oxford: Oxford University Press, 1978), pp. 142–4; Bernard Williams, *Morality: An Introduction to Ethics* (Cambridge: Cambridge University Press, 1972), pp. 34–9. Although the sentence in the text may be a caricature, it is a caricature resembling the metaethical views of an enormous number of undergraduates and a surprising number of social scientists.

3 Again, my one-sentence summary of the position is a bit of a caricature, conflating, for example, crude emotivism with a more sophisticated prescriptivism. Still, there is something that all such views share in common, and that something is something I reject, for it makes it difficult if not impossible to say why a speaker who agrees with the position of the Ku Klux Klan is morally *wrong* to do so. See Ted Honderich, ed., *Morality and Objectivity: A Tribute to J. L. Mackie* (London: Routledge & Kegan Paul, 1985); J. D. Mabbott, *An Introduction to Ethics* (London: Hutchinson, 1966), pp. 92–108; J. J. C. Smart, *Ethics, Persuasion and Truth* (London: Routledge & Kegan Paul, 1984); G. J. Warnock, *Contemporary Moral Philosophy* (London: Macmillan, 1967), pp. 18–47.

4 Which is not to say it is totally without detractors, particularly from the vantage point of a modernist epistemology. But the valuable contributions of modernism in exposing the contingent choices built into many of our assertions of truth and falsity do not, in my view, render the notions of truth and falsity empty or reduce them to the perceptions of the perceiver. For present purposes I will stand on the assertions that the earth is not flat, spiders are not mammals, and Grant's Tomb is not in New Mexico.

5 On the relationship of moral and epistemological skepticism to a theory of free speech, see also Steven Smith, "Skepticism, Tolerance, and Truth in the Theory of Free Expression," *Southern California Law Review* 60 (1987): 649–731.

6 I define "persuasive" in terms of acceptance of a proposition, regardless of the truth of that proposition.

7 The parenthetical is intended to signal the way in which the statement in the text is a necessary oversimplification. A theory of free speech need not protect speech absolutely, even within the area (likely a subset of the universe of speech acts) of greatest stringency of the principle generated by the theory. But a

theory of free speech, to be anything other than a platitude, must protect at least some communicative acts under circumstances in which those acts cause consequences that would otherwise be sufficient to justify regulation. See my *Free Speech: A Philosophical Enquiry* (Cambridge: Cambridge University Press, 1982), pp. 3–86, and Thomas Scanlon, "A Theory of Freedom of Expression," *Philosophy & Public Affairs* 1 (1971): 213–28. Thus, a nonempty principle of free speech must provide at least comparative immunity, although it need not provide absolute immunity. A principle providing that speech covered by the principle may justifiably be regulated if the justification for its regulation is better than is otherwise sufficient to justify regulation meets the standard I describe here.

8 I recognize that a complex and sophisticated act-consequentialism could hold that in our evaluation of the consequences of limiting a particular act of communication, it will almost always turn out that the consequences, taking into account the effect of that act of limitation on future cases, will not be sufficient to justify limitation. Insofar as this conclusion requires that in almost every case the spillover effect into other acts be dispositive, however, it begins to resemble, in practice if not in theory, the kind of rule-based consequentialism I address presently.

9 This is not to say that there are no adherents to a nonconsequentialist theory of free speech. Among those holding such a view are Ronald Dworkin, *Taking Rights Seriously*, pp. 188–205; Dworkin, *A Matter of Principle* (Cambridge, Mass.: Harvard University Press, 1985), pp. 196–7; Martin Redish, *Freedom of Expression: A Critical Analysis* (Charlottesville, Va.: Michie, 1984); C. Edwin Baker, "Realizing Self-Realization: Corporate Political Expenditures and Redish's The Value of Free Speech," *University of Pennsylvania Law Review* 130 (1982): 646–85; C. Edwin Baker, "Commercial Speech: A Problem in the Theory of Freedom," *Iowa Law Review* 62 (1976): 1–45; David A. J. Richards, "Free Speech and Obscenity Law: Toward a Moral Theory of the First Amendment," *University of Pennsylvania Law Review* 123 (1974): 45–103. All of these positions, however, and many others, still have a more or less categorical view about a class of communicative acts, and do not hold it necessarily to be the case that the intrinsic wrongness of regulating a particular communicative act is morally superior to the harm

the act may cause, especially where the harm is a harm to an individual, as in cases of injury to reputation, invasion of privacy, public humiliation, and assault by racial epithet.

10 I take pains to show why a principle of free speech, or just free speech *simpliciter,* cannot be act-based in large part because there are indeed scholars who appear to think otherwise. The claim is rarely put in exactly these terms but instead is couched in terms of "particularism," or a "practical reason" that places a primacy in reaching the best result in individual cases. See, for example, Daniel Farber and Philip Frickey, "Practical Reason and the First Amendment," *UCLA Law Review* 34 (1987): 1615–56.

11 It should be obvious that I reject the idea that a rule can be of unlimited specificity and still be a rule in any interesting sense. Thus, my conception of a rule differs from, for example, that of David Lyons in *Forms and Limits of Utilitarianism* (Oxford: Clarendon Press, 1965), and Donald Regan in *Utilitarianism and Co-operation* (Oxford: Clarendon Press, 1980). Rather, I align myself with those who see limited specificity as verging on an essential property of ruleness. R. M. Hare, *Moral Thinking: Its Levels, Method and Point* (Oxford: Clarendon Press, 1981); Larry Alexander, "Pursuing the Good – Indirectly," *Ethics* 95 (1985): 315–24; Richard Brandt, "Fairness to Indirect Optimific Theories in Ethics," *Ethics* 98 (1988): 341–60.

12 On roles as second-order reasons that exclude certain otherwise relevant first-order reasons, the work of Joseph Raz is especially germane. See Joseph Raz, *Practical Reason and Norms* (London: Hutchinson, 1975); Raz, *The Morality of Freedom* (Oxford: Clarendon Press, 1986), pp. 23–69; Raz, "Introduction," in Joseph Raz, ed., *Practical Reasoning* (Oxford: Oxford University Press, 1978), pp. 1–17.

13 I do not want here to go into detail about the reasons why a society might think that government is worse as a truth determiner than other institutions. For a more extensive discussion, see my *Free Speech: A Philosophical Enquiry,* pp. 15–34, 73–86. There I maintain that governmental officials might, in part to preserve their own power and prerogatives, be more susceptible to overregulate communication than to overregulate noncommunicative activities. If that is so, then a principle of free speech may serve to counterbalance these overregulatory tendencies.

14 I use the term "sociology of the marketplace" to designate an enormously complex array of forces that determine which propositions a society will accept and which it will reject. The very notion of a society's accepting or rejecting a proposition is itself problematic, for propositions are almost always accepted by some members of a society and rejected by others. Is it clear, for example, that the marketplace of ideas has accepted the falsity of astrology or the truth of evolution? Even if we pass over these issues and assume that some propositions are accepted and others rejected, the process by which this happens is multifactored, involving the influence of the mass media (itself highly complex), the power of certain authoritative transmitters of ideas, the extent of a population's predisposition toward some ideas and hostility to others, and much, much more. Sorting all of this out is far beyond the scope of this essay, so I submerge all of these issues beneath the simple phrase "sociology of the marketplace."

15 Perhaps we could call this, after Nozick, a "side constraint" view of competency.

16 I take such a view to be central to the views of, for example, Alexander Meiklejohn, *Political Freedom: The Constitutional Powers of the People* (New York: Oxford University Press, 1965). My thinking about these issues has also been assisted by an unpublished paper by Dr. Carlos Santiago Nino entitled "The Epistemological Value of Democracy."

17 In what follows I will use the phrase "political truth" as shorthand for determinations of political truth, wisdom, morality, or policy.

18 See Karl Popper, *The Open Society and Its Enemies*, 5th ed. (London: Routledge & Kegan Paul, 1965).

19 Of interest in this connection is Hume's unfortunately neglected essay on freedom of the press. David Hume, "Of the Liberty of the Press," in *Essays: Moral, Political and Literary* (Oxford: Oxford University Press, 1963). In this essay Hume argues that freedom of the press is superfluous or internally inconsistent in pure monarchies or in pure democracies. In a pure monarchy the monarch need not tolerate criticism, and in a pure democracy the people need not be limited in the decision they could make about anything, including the press. Only in a mixed government, where elected representatives have some of the attributes of delegates and some of mon-

archs, is freedom of the press necessary to prevent these hybrid creatures from turning into pure monarchs. Following this lesson from Hume, we would seem justified in concluding that modern-day governors share some attributes of sovereigns and some of servants, such that the theoretical permissibility of popular delegation of certain functions to the people's servants collides with the way in which those servants are also likely to act as sovereigns, and consequently interfere with rather than serve the popular determination of questions of political truth and political policy.

20 I discuss this issue at length, with particular reference to defamation, in Frederick Schauer, "The Role of the People in First Amendment Theory," *California Law Review* 74 (1986): 761–88.

21 I have benefited here from Stephen Holmes's "Gag Rules or the Politics of Omission" in *Constitutionalism and Democracy,* eds. Jon Elster and Rune Slagstad (Cambridge: Cambridge University Press, 1988).

22 My own thinking about the subject has often tended toward the view that the only way to explain the principle of free speech is in terms of the special dangers of government regulation of communication. See *Free Speech: A Philosophical Enquiry,* chap. 6; "Slippery Slopes," *Harvard Law Review* 99 (1985): 361–83; "Public Figures," *William and Mary Law Review* 25 (1984): 905–32.

23 Owen M. Fiss, "Why the State?" this volume; Fiss, "Free Speech and Social Structure," *Iowa Law Review* 71 (1986): 1405–25.

24 Among the prominent cases supporting this conclusion are *Buckley v. Valeo,* 424 U.S. 1 (1976), striking down restrictions on campaign expenditures; *First National Bank of Boston v. Bellotti,* 435 U.S. 765 (1978), holding unconstitutional a limitation on corporate influence in referenda; *Citizens Against Rent Control v. Berkeley,* 454 U.S. 290 (1981), invalidating a limitation on large contributions to ballot initiative campaigns; *Brown v. Hartlage,* 456 U.S. 45 (1982), rejecting a Kentucky law designed to prevent misstatements in political campaigns; and *Miami Herald v. Tornillo,* 418 U.S. 241 (1974), finding constitutionally impermissible a mandated right of reply to criticism published in major newspapers.

25 Dworkin, *Taking Rights Seriously,* pp. 140–7. See also Robert Ladenson, *A Philosophy of Free Expression and Its Constitutional*

Applications (Totowa, N.J.: Rowman & Littlefield, 1983); David A. J. Richards, *The Moral Criticism of Law* (Encino, Calif.: Dickenson, 1977).

26 See *Connick v. Meyers*, 461 U.S. 138 (1983), providing special protection for public employee speech at the workplace, but only if the speech relates to matters of public concern; *NAACP v. Clairborne Hardware*, 458 U.S. 886 (1982), protecting incitements to politically inspired consumer boycott; *Dun & Bradstreet v. Greenmoss Builders*, 472 U.S. 749 (1985), giving commercial defamation less First Amendment protection than defamatory statements that either are about public figures or relate to matters of public concern.

27 Robert Bork, "Neutral Principles and Some First Amendment Problems," *Indiana Law Journal* 47 (1971): 1–43.

28 In large part, the impermissibility is a product of the conclusion that there is much more to democracy than popular sovereignty. See J. Roland Pennock, *Democratic Political Theory* (Princeton, N.J.: Princeton University Press, 1979), pp. 376–8; K Popper, *The Open Society and Its Enemies*, chap. 7.

Chapter 8

Four criticisms of press ethics

JEFFREY B. ABRAMSON

In this essay, I discuss four criticisms of press ethics. I do not claim to know how prevalent these criticisms are, but I think they will be familiar enough to readers from the popular debates of the day.

I. THE PRESS AS JACKALS

Here is how some people talk about the press: "The press are a pack of jackals. They are so hungry and greedy for a story – any story – that whenever they smell one, they go after it without restraint or respect for privacy, rummaging everywhere, hounding anyone, and all without considering whether the story is worth all the poking and rooting." Reporters, so these critics would have it, are professional vultures preying on the unfortunate. A plane crashes and a microphone is thrust into the grieving widow's face; a hostage sends a video message from Lebanon and a camera crew is dispatched to televise the family's tearful reaction.

But merely to express a distaste for the nerve of some reporters does not take us very far. Left unanswered is the question of what distinguishes legitimate from illegitimate press hounding. Most journalists would try to answer that question, I believe, by invoking some version of the "public–private" distinction. In this view, certain matters are unambiguously private (the widow's grief, for example) and others are just as clearly public (the president's campaign promises). The good journalist pesters the president but leaves the widow alone.

This rough-and-ready distinction between the personal and the political is sufficient in many cases to answer the question of which stories are worth pursuing. It has the considerable merit of announcing that some "human interest" stories that no doubt would sell the news are nonetheless beyond the pursuit of responsible journalism. The standard fails the journalist, however, when an event does not fall neatly on one side of the public–private line. This was the problem raised during the 1988 presidential campaign by press coverage of candidate Gary Hart's private relations with women other than his wife. Because Hart was an announced candidate for the presidency, his public record was fair game for the press. But was it legitimate for the press to hound him about his private life, about matters that were ostensibly nonpolitical? The quick statement of the public–private ethic provides reporters with no guidance on this difficult middle ground.

Before further examining this middle ground, however, it may be well to discuss two stories where the public–private distinction does provide guidance about the proper reach of a reporter's curiosity. The first example shows the bad jackal making news out of private life; the second has the good jackal hounding government on a matter of secrecy.

The bad jackal

In December 1985, *Boston Magazine,* a monthly publication, ran a story under the headline "The Boogeyman Comes Home." The subject of the story was thirty-year-old Albert Thompson, who, after many years of absence, had returned to his hometown to assume the post of director of the town housing authority. In 1967, then twelve years old, Thompson and a friend had walked into the woods to flip knives in the ground. One of Thompson's flips struck the friend in the chest. The playmate screamed, and a frightened Thompson stabbed him twenty-five more times in the face, hands, and stomach. Thompson was sent to a juvenile detention facility until the age of seventeen. For the next decade, he drifted through odd jobs until enrolling in a government training program and landing a job as a counselor at a New Hampshire prison in 1983. In 1985 he returned to his hometown and assumed the housing authority post.

By state law, juvenile records are sealed in Massachusetts, but older residents remembered the lurid incident. A *Boston Magazine* reporter picked up on the town stir, pursued a reluctant Thompson for an interview, and finally persuaded him to do the interview, since "we are going to do the article with or without [you]." "The Boogeyman Comes Home" article thus appeared, provoking an avalanche of stories in the local paper and editorials calling for Thompson's dismissal from the housing authority. In June 1986, Thompson's contract with the housing authority was not renewed, and in November, Thompson committed suicide by hanging.[1]

Because Thompson held a government position, there was some attempt after the fact to justify the magazine article as a public service, as a valid exposé of the character of the town housing authority director. But this was a transparent rationalization. The article as written made no attempt to show the relevance of Thompson's past to his performance of housing authority duties. Instead, the gory details of that day in the woods eighteen years previously were dwelt upon for their own sensational effect, all as advertised under the screaming "boogeyman" headline. The story was not one whit about Thompson's public life as a housing authority official; it was entirely a story about a tragedy in the past that had ceased to be news until the magazine resurrected it in order to serve its own circulation, not the community. It cannot be called journalism to expose a person's past personal life for no public purpose at all.

The good jackal

Press hounding of the likes of a Thompson so poisons the public image of reporters that even the good in the press hound suffers. Consider, for instance, the Reagan administration's attempts in 1986 to quash press investigations of whether the administration was trading arms to Iran in exchange for the release of American hostages held in Lebanon by pro-Iranian groups. In late 1986, recently released hostage David Jacobsen appeared with President Reagan on the White House lawn and warned the assembled throng of reporters that the administration's secret negotiations for the release of the hostages were none of their business, that "unreasonable" or "unwarranted" speculations as to whether these negotiations involved arms sales to Iran might jeopardize the hostages' release or lives. When reporters continued peppering the president with questions, Jacobsen further took it upon himself to scold the press corps as if they were a gallery of rogues, warning the hounds to "back off."[2]

What was Jacobsen accusing the press of doing wrong? The explicit comment was both lame and misleading: In their hunger for a scoop, the jackals were accused of being misled by mad rumors and wild speculations. To such a complaint, the press could and did rightly respond that it was not speculating but publishing on the basis of credible, substantiated sources from within the administration itself. The subsequent unwinding of the "Iran-Contra" story bore out this press defense.

But although the Reagan administration publicly scolded the press only for being a rumor mill, it now seems clear that those officials responsible for the arms-for-hostages idea were bothered by the press hounding precisely because they knew the hounds were on the trail of the truth. A responsible press, they intimated, would not dig up the truth if this meant revealing state secrets that might jeopardize the safety or the release of the hostages. Their claim, in essence, was that the public had no more right to know about the administration's private contacts with Iran than about a widow's private grief. In the case of the widow, the reporter invades personal privacy and betrays remarkable indifference toward the woman's suffering. In the hostage case, the reporter invades the state's privacy and betrays remarkable indifference to the hostages' welfare.

These were serious charges. But surely there is all the difference in the world between hounding the President of the United States on a crucial foreign policy issue and hounding one widow into displaying her grief on television. The difference is that in one case reporters serve the needs of democratic citizenship and in the other they do not. The issue of whether the United States was trading arms for hostages was one of paramount importance to the republic. It was also, of course, a story that was individually important to the hostages and their families. That left reporters and editors to make difficult and stressful choices, because there very well could have been harmful consequences from exposing the administration's dealings with Iran. My personal view is that the administration vastly exaggerated the potential harm of press coverage and was moved more by fear of political embarrassment than by fear for the hostages' safety. In my judgment, therefore, the press made the right decision in pursuing the story. But there is certainly legitimate room for disagreement here. What was alarming about the administration's press bashing was the refusal to acknowledge the difference between hounding the grieving widow and hounding the president over his foreign policy. The ease with which the administration thought it could appeal to popular distaste for the jackal press should alert the press to a characteristic danger in the present. By now we are so on the lookout for the bad jackal rooting in our private affairs that we sometimes forget there is also good in the jackal, in the hound on the trail of issues vital to the republic.

The Gary Hart affair: good or bad jackal?

In recent years, criticism of the jackal press reached its high-water mark over coverage of the private sexual life of presidential candidate Gary Hart. As noted earlier, this case raised the difficult question of whether the press is serving a legitimate public purpose when it reports on the private life of a public figure. According to an older press ethic, the personal affairs of a public official were not themselves newsworthy; indiscretions were to be revealed "only if germane to another patently newsworthy story."[3] One prominent example of this older ethic was the press's treatment of Senator Edward Kennedy's womanizing – a matter considered newsworthy only *after* Chappaquidick. Similarly, the Washington press corps considered former Representative Robert Bauman's homosexuality to be a nonstory *until* he was arrested for soliciting sex from a minor.[4] There was also the nonreporting of the love lives of Lloyd George, Franklin Roosevelt, Dwight Eisenhower, John Kennedy, and Martin Luther King, Jr.[5]

Gary Hart was clearly the recipient of a more inquisitive and aggressive press ethic. Even before he announced his candidacy in April 1987 for the 1988 Democratic presidential nomination, *Newsweek* featured a profile that had the early Democratic front-runner "haunted by rumors of womanizing." The article quoted the quip of a former Hart adviser that "he's always in jeopardy of having the sex issue raised if he can't keep his pants on."[6] On May 3, E. J. Dionne, Jr., chief political correspondent for the *New York Times,* similarly reported in a feature article for its Sunday magazine that "no candidate suffers as much from scurrilous talk as Hart – about his relation with his wife and other women." Dionne then quoted this unprophetic challenge of Hart's: "Follow me around. I don't care . . . about the womanizing question. I'm serious. If anybody wants to put a tail on me, go ahead. They'd be very bored."[7]

Unbeknownst to Hart, the *Miami Herald* had already put him under just this kind of sexual surveillance. Acting on a tip, the *Herald* dispatched a team of reporters to sit in a parked van and observe the comings and goings of twenty-nine-year-old model and actress Donna Rice from Hart's Washington town house. On May 3, the same day Hart's challenge to reporters was ironically appearing in the *Times,* the *Herald* reported that "Gary Hart, the Democratic presidential candidate who has dismissed allegations of womanizing, spent Friday night and most of Saturday in his Capitol Hill townhouse with a young woman who flew from Miami and met him."

The story caused an immediate flap. Hart denied he had spent the night with Rice and asserted she had left the town house by a back door that the *Herald* reporters, amateur sleuths that they were, neglected to cover. But such a defense, even if true, seemed beside the point, and soon details about former meetings between Hart and Rice at an Aspen party or aboard a yacht in Bimini flooded the news. With the water "chummed and bloodied," columnist Tom Wicker wrote, the press corps surrounded Hart like "sharks . . . closing in for the kill."[8]

The kill began during a May 6 press conference in New Hampshire, when a *Washington Post* reporter virtually obliterated the distinction between public and private in the life of Gary Hart by point-blank asking the candidate whether he had "ever committed adultery." Hart invoked privacy as a shield ("I don't have to answer that question"), but the fact that a *Post* reporter felt entitled to probe Hart on such a matter showed just how untenable his presidential candidacy had become.

The *Post* reporter's question about adultery was not entirely the shot in the dark it appeared to be. In fact, the same reporter contacted Hart's press secretary the night after the press conference to inform him that the *Post* had "documented evidence" of a long-standing relationship between Hart and a prominent Washington social figure. The press secretary relayed the report to Hart, together with his impression that the *Post* intended to run the story unless Hart bowed out of the race. Hart replied, with words to the effect that "this thing is never going to end, is it? Look, let's just go home."[9]

On May 8, a scant five days after the *Herald* story hit the stands, the erstwhile leading candidate for the Democratic presidential nomination withdrew from the race. The *Post* chose not to publish its documented evidence about Hart's alleged affair but reported only that it had informed Hart the paper was in possession of such evidence. In announcing his withdrawal, Hart angrily pinned the blame on the jackal press:

> We're all going to have to seriously question the system for selecting our national leaders for it reduces the press of this nation to hunters and Presidential candidates to being hunted. That has reporters in the bushes; false and inaccurate stories being printed; photographers peeking in our windows; swarms of helicopters hovering over our roof, and my very strong wife close to tears because she cannot even get in her own house at night without being harassed.[10]

Holding the press responsible for the tears of his wife was unseemly on Hart's part. But the overall charge – that press scrutiny of the private lives of presidential candidates had gone too far – was a serious one that provoked lively debate among journalists themselves. Those who felt the press had hounded Hart unfairly tended to direct their outrage initially at the *manner* in which the *Miami Herald* carried out its investigation – the infamous "stakeout" of Hart's residence. Tom Wicker called the press's adoption of such police tactics "deplorable" and wondered "who will be staked out next?"[11] *Times* columnist Anthony Lewis agreed: "When I read about the *Miami Herald* story on Gary Hart, I felt degraded in my profession. Is that what journalism is about, hiding in a van outside a politician's home?"[12] And former *Times* executive editor A. M. Rosenthal added that, as a reporter, he would have refused such a surveillance assignment; as an editor, he would not have given such an assignment or permitted one to be carried out.[13] It damages "journalistic self-respect," Rosenthal lamented, to picture reporters "skulking around Mr. Hart's house all night, hiding in the bushes."

But this condemnation of the stakeout as inherently unethical seems overblown. Surely *some* press stakeouts of *some* politicians – for instance, those taking bribes – would meet with universal approval. Ultimately the outrage was not with *how* the *Herald* obtained its story but with *what* the story was. The Wicker–Lewis–Rosenthal thesis was that a candidate's sex life is private, not public, business. To treat Hart's tryst with Donna Rice as "news" relevant to the presidential campaign was to trivialize that campaign by subordinating questions of public policy to personal matters. "Judging from history," Lewis wrote, "the correlation between puritan sexual behavior and wise political leadership is zero."[14] Or, as a columnist for the *Los Angeles Times* more graphically put it:

> It doesn't necessarily follow that a man who can't keep his fly zipped can't govern the country. I don't recall anyone charging that Roosevelt's liaison with Lucy Mercer Rutherford raised serious questions about his ability to lead the United States through the Depression and World War II. Or that Eisenhower's relationship with Kay Summersby rendered him unfit to lead Allied forces in the D-Day invasion.[15]

On the other side of the debate were those who thought the revelations were indeed relevant to Hart's presidential timber. There were strong and weak versions of the relevance defense. The strong version came from those such as Ellen Goodman, who argued that Hart's womanizing was in itself a relevant issue. Womanizing was said to reveal "something about a man's capacity for deception, vulnerability to exposure, fascination with risk-taking."[16] Few journalists followed Goodman in making this direct link between Hart's sex life and his presidential qualifications. Instead, those establishment newspapers that editorially defended the *Herald* – including the *New York Times* and the *Los Angeles Times* – disclaimed making any moral judgment about Hart's *sexual* conduct. Rather, what was important and relevant in the Donna Rice affair was that it showed "poor judgment" on Hart's part, an "insensitivity to appearances," a "recklessness and lack of discipline," a candidate "indifferent to trust" who "courted danger" and believed he did not have to play "the normal political game."[17] This weaker or indirect version of the relevancy of the Hart affair ("the issue is judgment, not sex") was as close as the press came to an official defense of the *Herald* story.

But it is a response that does not take us very far. The editors of two of the nation's leading papers were willing to say only that *Gary Hart* got the press coverage he deserved, that there were special factors that made *his* private sex life relevant to the presidential campaign. The question of what we might learn about the quality of other candidates' judgment by investigating their personal lives was ducked. Almost nothing was offered by way of general standards for distinguishing what was private from what was public in the lives of presidential candidates.

Moreover, the relevant-to-his-judgment argument may work as a defense of the *Herald*'s story about Donna Rice, but it falls flat as a defense of the *Post*'s threatened disclosures. After all, what were we supposed to learn about the quality of Hart's judgment, as opposed to the quality of his marriage, from the fact that he may have had a long-standing and discreet relationship with a Washington woman? Few, if any, of the phrases used to condemn Hart's conduct with a young model (womanizing, reckless, insensitive to appearances, courting danger) appeared to apply to this part of Hart's private life.

There is a saying in law that hard cases make bad law. This may be true of journalism too, hard cases making bad ethics. It is tempting, therefore, to follow the lead of the *New York Times* and the *Los Angeles Times* and refuse to treat the Hart case as a precedent for investigating the private life of any future presidential candidate. But the issue is unlikely to go away. As political scientist Nelson Polsby perceptively commented, cases like Gary Hart's are bound to recur, given the job we ask the press to do in modern campaigns. It used to be, Polsby writes, that party bosses and other power brokers actually knew the character of the candidates and could engage in some kind of intelligent peer review. Now, in mass-based primaries, the people must make the same character judgments about persons they know only from the press.

Thus it is that the press inherits responsibility for being the "character cop" in campaigns.[18]

I think Polsby has located the issue correctly. In the end, the issue is not an isolated one about the propriety of press behavior; it is about the propriety of our entire electoral process. And the press cannot be asked to shoulder the blame for turning American presidential elections into an ever more searching but empty referendum on character and personality. After all, the post-1968 reforms in the presidential selection process were designed precisely to let the people-at-large, rather than party bosses and party regulars, nominate candidates for president. Those reforms obliterated the old system of peer review and gave us primary elections where millions of persons normally inattentive to politics are suddenly enlisted to make their party's choice of candidates. It is not surprising that the campaign for their vote should center on selling the candidate as a person of character, as someone at least to trust, perhaps to like. Given the rise of this modern personality-centered campaign, it would be hypocritical to charge the press with having crossed some imaginary line into taboo or irrelevant areas of a potential president's character. For there do not appear to be any such areas anymore. Perhaps the old party bosses could be expected to know whether a candidate's womanizing was relevant to his presidential fiber and to keep mum about it if they thought it irrelevant. But the press cannot be expected to make these kinds of decisions on its own, nor would we like it if it did. The peer review is now ours, and this inevitably puts the press in the position of passing on whatever it knows.

II. THE PRESS: POWERFUL OR WEAK?

Popular criticism of the press waffles between fearing its power and bemoaning its impotence. Sometimes we hear that the problem with the press is that it controls what we think, or at least what we think about. The press, so the argument goes, controls the agenda of public discussion, decides whose views get aired or printed, manipulates candidates for election, changes votes, and even tilts the outcome of close elections.[19] But often we hear just the opposite – that it is the candidate or elected official who manipulates the press, feeding an all too hungry and passive press corps a steady diet of prepackaged images, staged events, and sound bites. In this view, the press is the captive, even the dupe, of crafty media advisers who dress their political clients in the fashions of the latest poll.[20]

Criticisms of the press as too powerful and as too weak may seem contradictory, but together they capture our intuitive sense that the problem in American politics is no longer who is manipulating whom; it is the paradox of how politicians and the press manipulate each other. At the root of the paradox is the way elected officials and candidates alike have come to rely on the press, rather than the political party, to communicate their views directly to voters. Especially at the level of presidential elections, candidates behave as if the only campaign that matters is the press campaign. Television in particular is singled out as "the force that shapes the process through which voters select their Presidents."[21] "The next president will have been chosen in a campaign dominated as never before by television," the *New York Times* announced the week before the 1988 election.[22] This dominance of television is so complete, the *Times* found, that it is no longer a question of ethics but simply a "matter of survival" for candidates to tailor their messages to television.[23]

When a candidate and his media advisers prove good at the television game – as with George Bush in 1988 – we hear complaints about the weak and manipulated press. When a candidate fumbles on television, as Michael Dukakis is widely thought to have fumbled during the second of his televised debates with Bush in 1988, we hear complaints that television cost him the election. But even those candidates who succeed in manipulating media coverage are manipulated by that coverage in turn. Fixation on how their messages play on television causes politicians to participate all too willingly in their own degradation, in the selling of themselves as if they were a soap powder, in tailoring their media messages according to the results of the latest poll, in reducing their stands on issues to the size of a thirty-second advertisement or sound bite for the network news. In short, the only answer to the riddle of whether candidates manipulate the media or the media manipulate candidates is that the manipulation is mutual.

I want to discuss whether the popular wisdom about the 1988 election – that Bush owed his victory to the influence of television news and advertising on voters – is accurate. But first we may be able to gain some perspective on the current anxiety about television's power or impotence in elections by looking back at the role of the press and television in previous campaigns.

1960–1984: the cycle of press criticism

In the era before television, political scientists were almost unanimous in finding that the influence of the press on voters was vastly exaggerated. Not surprisingly, the primary effect of press coverage on voters with a preexisting preference among candidates was to reinforce the preference, rarely to convert it. Press accounts had only minimal effect on undecided voters as well, since these voters were the least likely to read or listen to political news at all. At best, press accounts trickled down to the undecideds, filtered through the opinions of community leaders.[24]

In the 1950s, the first studies of television's impact on elections showed that it too had only minimal impact on voter choice, even on voter turnout.[25] But, of course, television was still in its political infancy during the Eisenhower years. It was not until the 1960 Kennedy–Nixon election campaign and the famous first televised debate that anxiety about television's power really gained momentum. Those who *watched* the debate on television thought Kennedy the winner, whereas the radio audience heard Nixon do better. Such a finding seemed to support the theories of Marshall McLuhan and others who argued that on television the "medium was the message." It was as if how Kennedy and Nixon *looked* in delivering their views was more important than *what* they actually said. Given Kennedy's razor-thin margin of victory in the election, the popular view of television as a decisive new political force was launched.

As the sixties progressed and television brought us pictures of the Kennedy assassination and funeral, the civil rights movement, the war in Vietnam, urban riots, and the student revolution, a mass of anecdotal evidence piled up for television's imperial power. How many millions of Americans saw the fire hoses blasting civil rights marchers against a wall or George Wallace blocking the entrance to the University of Alabama or the Buddhist monk setting fire to himself or the point-blank execution of a Vietcong suspect? In an influential revisionist article in the *American Political Science Review,* Michael Robinson coined the term "videomalaise" to summarize the distinct and powerful effects television journalism in the sixties and early seventies was credited with having on viewers.[26] Those who depended on television as their prime source of news (in 1972, nearly two-thirds of those polled listed television as their principal source of information about politics) exhibited a greater sense of cynicism and distrust about politics than did people with some alternative news source. Robinson saw such "network induced videomalaise" as reaching its high-water mark in 1968, translating directly into protest votes for Nixon and third-party votes for Wallace. The reason television viewing tended to make viewers cynical about politics, Robinson argued, was that television news exhibited a "negative bias." Time pressures alone condemned the network news programs to ignore policy issues and to reduce politics to banal, even disrespectful, terms. Ratings pressures and the need to hook and sustain the interest of a mass audience led to overconcentration on violence, conflict, scandal, and wrongdoing. Although concentrating on the bad over the good might be characteristic of the press in general, Robinson concluded it was even more characteristic of news as filtered through the medium of television.

The series of failed presidencies from Johnson's to Carter's (none finished two full terms) lent further anecdotal support to the videomalaise thesis and to the popular view that television tarnished the popular image of politicians. Critics talked about the "overexposure" of presidents on television, the way in which television had destroyed the president's charisma by making him such a familiar visitor in our living rooms. As one widely read book put it, television news was so "compulsively" interested in a politician's personality that all our public officials were constantly being set up for a downfall. In the TV version of "personality politics," a "flaw in one sphere is taken to mean the whole person was no good."[27]

In the era of Ronald Reagan and George Bush, one does not hear much anymore about "overexposure" or "videomalaise." The anxiety about television's political influence is still there – but it has shifted to a concern for how politicians have learned to capture the power of the press and to manipulate it for their own propaganda purposes. The complaint is that the media have fallen prey to the media handlers and spin doctors who form the modern president's entourage. As deputy chief of staff during Reagan's first term, Michael Deaver was the first and greatest target of this new wave of press criticism. Deaver turned the staging of "media events" – what historian Daniel Boorstin referred to as "pseudo-events" planned only for the purpose of being reported[28] – into a virtual form of governance. The press was fed a daily "photo opportunity" of the president, selected to communicate the "theme of the day." In addition press conferences were avoided wherever possible, reporters were kept at a distance (behind so-called shout lines) or bypassed altogether, and the president spoke for the cameras directly, "without intervention by such troublesome middlemen as the Lesley Stahls and Sam Donaldsons."[29]

The Reagan White House proved remarkably successful in performing its bypass surgery on the press. Over and over again, the networks' need for good visuals made them unable to resist the prefabricated video performances being served up, no matter how painfully obvious it was that the performance was for the sake of the cameras alone. But in the end there remains the paradox of how the manipulator is also the manipulated. Nothing mattered more than how "'the nets' portrayed the president and his policies," former Reagan budget director David Stockman noted. Special remote-control television was installed in Chief of Staff James Baker's office, and all activity was suspended for monitoring of the nightly news. The Reagan "theory and practice of governance" assigned such "supreme importance . . . to network television news," Stockman recalls, that basic policy decisions were made according to what played best on television.[30] In this way, the supposed adversaries, press and White House, came to be, in media critic Edwin Diamond's phrase, "secret sharers."

The 1988 campaign: How important was television?

How well did television perform in the latest presidential campaign? Criticisms of both television's power and its weakness were again heard, but the predominant criticism certainly concerned weakness and the alleged ability of the Bush campaign to manipulate both television news and television advertising. In fact, many attribute Bush's victory to his victory in the battle for control of television. "The difference in this election," the *New York Times* quoted political experts as saying the week before voting actually took place, "is that Vice President Bush outmanuevered Governor . . . Dukakis . . . on television."[31] Added pollster Lou Harris: "The simple story of this election is that the Bush commercials have worked and the Dukakis commercials have not."[32]

Of course, the story was more complicated than that. Bush had substantial advantages apart from the success of his media campaign – principally peace, prosperity, and Ronald Reagan. "It's never easy to throw a party out of the White House when you've got a world more or less at peace and 3% growth in the economy," noted political scientist Walter Dean Burnham.[33] And exit polls showed the single greatest factor influencing the election was Reagan's popularity. Of the voters who went to the polls, 56 percent approved of

Reagan's performance as president – roughly the same percentage as voted for Bush.[34]

But despite the favorable conditions, Bush support remained weak and vulnerable throughout the campaign. "Dukakis probably should have won," Republican strategist Kevin Phillips has written, citing both Dukakis's eighteen-point lead in the June and July 1988 polls and the eventual Democratic tide in the November election that led to unprecedented gains in the Senate, House, and governorships. Dukakis was bound to lose a substantial portion of his early lead to the peace, prosperity, and Reagan factors, Phillips acknowledged, but his further decline to an eight-point loss is attributable to an "inept" media campaign and to the success of Bush in using television to turn the election into a referendum on the conservative agenda of social and patriotic issues.[35]

For our purposes, it is not necessary to resolve the issue of whether Dukakis could have won the election, given the peace/prosperity/Reagan popularity effect. What seems beyond dispute is that Dukakis could have made it at least a close race to the finish, and that his failure to do so has much to do with the adroit uses the Bush campaign made of television. Let me attend first to the influence of television advertising on voters. The centerpiece of the Bush ad campaign was negative, anti-Dukakis attacks that portrayed Dukakis as soft on crime and soft on national defense. These ads allowed Bush, with surprisingly little resistance from either his opponent or the press, to select what issues the campaign would be about – crime, patriotism, the death penalty, furloughs for convicted murderers, and national defense. These were the gut emotional issues where the Bush campaign thought it was strongest – and by all accounts, the ads were highly successful in getting voters both to focus on these issues and to accept the advertised view of Dukakis as unacceptably liberal. One voter in four admitted to relying on candidate advertisements to make his or her presidential choice in 1988 – twice as many as acknowledged relying on advertisements in 1984.[36] Pollster Lou Harris thought the evidence was clear that "doubts about Dukakis grew as the Bush commercials were shown." In particular, Harris attributed the substantial 8 percent decline during the fall of 1988 in Dukakis's rating as a leader to the "continuous pounding" he was taking at the time on television commercials.[37]

Many of the Bush ads – the furlough ones especially – raised issues over which a president has little control. Some ads contained outright distortions: for instance, the Bush advertisement denouncing Dukakis for failing to end pollution of Boston Harbor showed a dirty pool with a sign saying, "Danger/Radiation Hazard/No Swimming." In fact, the picture was taken not in Boston Harbor but at a nuclear submarine repair facility.[38] Still other ads were at least designed to mislead – the furlough ads implied that Dukakis had initiated the Massachusetts furlough program, although in fact he had inherited it from a previous Republican governor. Worst of all, the deliberate choice to focus the furlough ad campaign on Willie Horton (a black man who had raped a white woman after escaping when on furlough) added an unfortunate racial element to the campaign. The Bush commercials themselves did not include a picture of Horton or otherwise specify his race, but the campaign did not put an early foot down on the independent political action committee that did feature Horton's picture in its own cable television advertising against Dukakis. And as early as the summer of 1988, Bush campaign manager Lee Atwater had flagged for reporters his intention to hammer away at the Willie Horton case, particularly for its resonance in the South.[39]

Part of the blame for not setting the record straight no doubt rests with the strange inability of the Dukakis campaign to respond – what Kevin Phillips ridiculed as the Dukakis summer "nerd out."[40] Still, there is a limit to how much one should blame the victim and the Bush ad campaign raised anew old questions about the power of television advertising over voters. Previous studies of television ads during a presidential campaign showed that their influence on the vote was more mythic than real. In a leading study of television advertisements during the 1972 campaign, political scientists Thomas

Patterson and Robert McClure concluded that spot ads devoted to pure "image-making" were a "wasted effort."[41] The study found voters remarkably resistant to the typical flag-waving, family-togetherness portrait, but it reached far more tentative conclusions about the power of "issue" advertisements. For undecided voters, the authors found that television advertisements were a principal source of information about where the candidates stood on the issues. In fact, such voters tended to get more issue information from the simple, repeated thirty-second ad message than they gleaned from television news. This reliance on ads by a sizable portion of the electorate meant that "the potential for manipulation was there." By a crafty selection of which issues to advertise, a candidate could select and limit the "issue domain" of the campaign.[42]

Bush ads showed just such an ability to craft and control the campaign agenda. Moreover, the negative information in the ads about Dukakis's positions meant that the Bush campaign achieved the remarkable coup of being a principal source of information about the opponent's views – at least when Dukakis proved strangely unable to respond. Negative ads had, of course, been used in the past. But even one of the most famous negative ads – the "daisy" commercial suggesting that Barry Goldwater as president might mean nuclear holocaust – was aired only once by the Johnson campaign in 1964. By contrast, at least half of the Bush ads in 1988 were negative attacks on Dukakis.[43]

In an October 27 *New York Times* column, Anthony Lewis lamented that the facts about crime and furloughs in Massachusetts "have been overwhelmed by the Mephistophelian skill of Messrs. Baker, Atwater and Ailes in playing on emotions in their advertising."[44] "The question this election raises with me," noted media expert and political scientist Kathleen Hall Jamieson, "is whether it is now possible to misstate one's record and misstate one's opponent's record and get by with it."[45] The *New York Times*–CBS exit poll after the general election showed that the early issues upon which Dukakis had been staked to his eighteen-point lead – the

Iran-Contra affair, the Meese and Deaver ethics problems, administration support for Panama dictator and drug runner General Noriega – had ceased to be major campaign issues. Instead, the Bush campaign was successful in getting one-fifth of those who voted to consider punishment of criminals a key consideration. These voters went 71 percent to 28 percent for Bush.[46]

Where was television news while Bush was picking and choosing what issues the campaign would be about? When it came to raising issues beyond those Bush had made his own, or exploring the accuracy of the advertised versions of the Bush and Dukakis records, the networks were largely passive. As a reviewer for the *Columbia Journalism Review* put it, the networks understood themselves as "the playing field" on which the candidates contended and thus they could hardly abrogate to themselves a more active role in redrawing the proper boundaries of the field in midgame.[47] The result was that Bush media adviser Roger Ailes carried forward the Deaver strategy for capturing the network news with a vengeance. "Television covers three things – visuals, attacks, and mistakes," Ailes noted, in explaining why the daily Bush stump speech was typically a video attack on Dukakis. The secret of the good media campaign was to maintain control of the news by staying on the offensive and avoiding mistakes by avoiding reporters.

Each day the Bush campaign therefore settled on a message of the day – a sound bite – to feed to television, and more often than not television accommodated. The network news programs dutifully reported as news the "L" word attacks; the news that Dukakis was a "card-carrying" member of the American Civil Liberties Union (ACLU); the news that Bush was attacking Dukakis for vetoing, some years previously, a Massachusetts law requiring teachers to recite the pledge of allegiance in public school classrooms; the news that Bush was ridiculing Dukakis's lack of foreign policy experience with the remark that Dukakis "thinks a naval exercise is something Jane Fonda does." Not seeing themselves as accuracy cops, the networks therefore ignored the fact that

Dukakis had spoken of being a member of the ACLU only during a far-ranging disagreement with the ACLU position on pornography and obscenity. Not being arbiters of fairness, the networks obliged Bush by treating the flap over flag salutes as lead news, despite the obvious slur on Dukakis's patriotism. And even when the staging of an event for television coverage was abundantly clear – as it was with Bush's trip to Boston to accept the endorsement of a Boston police union in Dukakis's own backyard – the networks still could not resist the story.

Criticizing the easy prey that television news was for the Bush campaign, a lead article in the *Columbia Journalism Review* satirized the Deaver–Ailes approach to television news as follows:

> "Read my lips. No access. Daily visuals. Simple message." Adhering religiously to that credo, Bush's handlers kept reporters at such a distance that some resorted to binoculars and megaphones. And at least once a day they cast their bait – carefully staged visuals concocted to exploit TV's hunger for lively pictures. With the bait came the hook, the so-called message of the day, usually a barbed one-liner about Dukakis. With astonishing frequency, the networks bit, the hook was set, and TV was running with the Republican message.[48]

Why just the *Republican* message – where was Dukakis in all of this? Certainly he was playing the same media game, surrounded by his own host of media types and spin doctors, delivering his own sound bites, and spending tens of millions of dollars on paid advertising. It would be entirely misleading to portray Dukakis as somehow above the fray or as having some kind of moral objection to mixing it up with Bush. It would be misleading also to portray the networks as partisans of Bush or as giving him more airtime. The networks were scrupulously nonpartisan in giving each candidate equal opportunity to play for the cameras. But the "one crucial thing television demands of modern campaigning – an absolute focus on clear and powerful messages" – was not coming from the Dukakis camp.[49] Dukakis had started the campaign with the media slogan that the election would be about "competence, not ideology." When Bush insisted nevertheless on making the campaign a nasty referendum on "liberal" ideology, Dukakis had no coherent response. Reports from within the Dukakis camp showed that they were surprised by the success of the negative attacks on the governor, that it wasn't until the last weeks of the campaign that they settled on a populist theme to summarize the Dukakis message.[50] The belated response was, of course, Dukakis's fault, not the media's and it cost him dearly. "One senses that fewer voters would have seized upon Mr. Dukakis's problems with furloughed prisoners or with Boston Harbor as reasons to oppose his candidacy . . . had they been more impressed with his vision for the country's future," *New York Times* correspondent R. W. Apple offered by way of election postmortem.[51]

It may be true, therefore, as the *Times* reported, that television came "of age in the [1988] Presidential election."[52] But it is still a television journalism that remains paradoxically weak and powerful at the same time, the manipulator of candidates and the manipulated. In 1988, the candidates – or at least one of them – seemed to have the upper hand. Television news played a primarily passive role in the campaign, deferring to the Bush campaign's skewed and self-serving selection of issues, cooperative in its own co-optation by all those good photo opportunities and sound bites. For all the talk over the years about the power of television news to control the agenda of public debate,[53] that power was little in evidence in 1988. Indeed, the decision of the press to put the "womanizing issue" on the campaign agenda for Gary Hart now seems aberrational, nowhere matched by equally aggressive oversight of the campaign morality of Bush and Dukakis. Given the amount of distortion that was occurring, this default was substantial.

But in the end it is important not to exaggerate the media's default, for it was decidedly secondary to Dukakis's own default. Perhaps on advice of his own media handlers and pollsters, perhaps frightened by Bush's bullying of him on the liberal issue, Dukakis spent most of the campaign running away from the heritage of the Democratic Party as the home of labor, the less well off, minorities, immigrants, and ethnic Americans. At times, it was almost as if he were a Democrat trying to masquerade as a Republican. When Bush seized the opportunity to paint Dukakis into a liberal corner on such issues as the death penalty or abortion, Dukakis's responses were muted and hardly the ringing affirmation of an alternative vision that it would have taken to rally his natural constituents and to appeal to undecideds in search of a man with a message and a vision. Most of the time Dukakis simply fell into the Bush trap by denying he was a liberal. This became the only story there was to the campaign, and the media had little choice but to center their coverage on it. It was a silly script, no doubt written for the media but not by the media.

III. OBJECTIVITY AND THE PRESS

I turn now to a discussion of objectivity and its critics. By "objectivity," I mean simply a commitment to telling the truth. This commitment is the journalist's sovereign value. It is the end that guides and justifies the standard journalistic practices of the day – the obligations of nonpartisanship, of neutrality and impartiality, of balanced presentations of opposing points of view. Indeed, the very existence of journalism as a specialized profession rests on the view that we cannot depend on government and others with a vested interest in the news to tell us the truth.

Of course, objective journalism is a myth if it requires editors and reporters to do the impossible – to report the facts wholly uninfluenced by values. At least since Walter Lippmann, reflective journalists have acknowledged the influence of values on which stories they choose to cover, as well as on which facts they choose to include in a story. All reports of reality are subjective reports, and for that reason philosophers continue to debate – rightly so – the issue of whether there is any such thing as "objective" reality "out there." Fortunately, journalists can for the most part put aside such philosophical questions and carry on their profession. Notwithstanding Bishop Berkeley, no one seriously disputes that "the Yankees won on a certain day or they did not and by a certain score."[54]

It is surprising to learn how recent is the hold of objectivity over American journalism. Throughout much of the nineteenth century, "objectivity was not an issue," as newspapers were typically funded by political parties and existed precisely to trumpet the party line.[55] In such a scheme of things, there was only a rough balance among competitors and no obligation imposed on any one competitor to present a neutral, balanced account of the news. Still, with different papers reporting from different political viewpoints, an informal system of checks and balances emerged. For partisanship itself gave a newspaper the motive to "uncover a truth that papers loyal to other party lines . . . simply did [not] pursue."[56]

But the ethic of a partisan press seems fit only for combat between small journals, none of whose decisions about what is newsworthy effectively controls what news reaches a local population. With the birth of the telegraph, and then the telephone and radio and television, the era of the small press passed from history. In its place came mass media giants whose size and reach gave rise to fears of news monopolies and management of the news for partisan purposes. In the case of radio and television, this fear proved great enough to support a whole set of legal regulations premised on the ideal of objectivity. Broadcast news organizations were licensed as public trustees and placed under general obligations of nonpartisanship, of equal treatment of opposing candidates, and of balanced presentations of opposing views.[57] Some of these legal pillars of the ethic of objectivity – notably the fairness doctrine – have now been repealed.[58] And the ideal of balanced news has never been legislated for the print press. But I think it is fair to say that from the journalist's own point of view, neither the repeal of the fairness doctrine nor the remaining legal distinctions between the electronic and print press is of any ethical import. With or without a fairness doctrine, all reporters today understand themselves as bound by the ethic of objective reporting – by the obligations to report the truth, not the party line.

Some critics object to press objectivity as a flawed ideal. They see it as deterring journalists from covering controversial issues out of fear of being accused of being one-sided. They credit it only with encouraging safe, middle-of-the-road journalism, bland and homogeneous accounts robbed of the rich texture provided by a point of view. But I think it is dead wrong to equate objectivity with blandness in this way. A commitment to publishing the truth makes journalism an inherently risky profession, obliged to be the adversary of powerful institutions with a vested interest in suppressing the news.

Some critics accept objectivity as an ideal but find it too little practiced. The problem, it is said, is bias, not blandness. It used to be common, for instance, to accuse the networks in particular of explicit "liberal bias." But the Reagan–Bush era has put a damper on such criticism and we now hear quite the opposite complaint, about how the press loves a winner and has fallen in step with the conservative mood of the country. The very fact that opposing sides so often tend to see the press as biased in their opponent's favor shows most complaints about press bias to be nothing more than sour grapes. Every study of network coverage of elections, for instance, has shown a remarkable absence of partisan remarks or tone and a scrupulous division of time among major candidates.[59] And when the content of television coverage is compared with the content of newspaper coverage, the evidence shows that the stories covered and the themes presented are virtually the same.[60] Thus, unless one is prepared to accuse the entire press of biased election coverage, there is no empirical basis for singling out either television or the newspapers as the culprit.

Beyond the issue of blandness versus bias, there is a particular problem with press objectivity that I wish to focus on. Journalists often behave as if the best, or at least safest, way to be objective is to lead with official statements by government officials and the like. The prevailing norm seems to be that official statements are more reliable simply by virtue of being official statements. Within the category of official government statements, the norm seems also to dictate that in case of a dispute between our country and another over what happened, one should lead with our own government's account. The opposing account is usually presented but either buried or phrased in a way that undercuts it.

Now, there is nothing all that alarming in these practices, so long as those using them understand that reliance on statements by government officials *is not itself* objectivity. How could it be when all governments, even our own, have a vested interest in presenting their side of the story and not necessarily the truth? Surely objectivity, understood as a commitment to truth, requires a reporter to be an agnostic about official statements – to accept them or expose them as the case may require. I. F. Stone's credo (that "every government is run by liars and nothing they say should be believed") may be overstated, but it has the merit of making clear once and for all that only a press ready to be an adversary of government (and other powerful actors with an interest in managing the news) is a press ready to be an advocate of the truth. In other words, we need to recover our sense that objective reporting and adversarial reporting go together.

I believe many reporters have trouble with this juxtaposition of the values of objectivity and adversariness. They see the adversary posture as a *departure* from objectivity, the assumption of a partisan mission on the part of a press corps out "to get" the government. By contrast, reliance on official statements seems so much more neutral. But reliance, or overreliance on official statements, is not neutral; it is only noncontroversial. When that reliance becomes exclusive, the ethic of objectivity is perverted into an ideology through which the government controls the press. Let me give two examples of how government can abuse the ethic of objectivity as a way of managing the news.

The most famous one is still the early free ride Senator

Joseph McCarthy got from some segments of the press for his rampage of charges about Communists in the United States government. Reviewing wire service stories about McCarthy, one former stringer noted in hindsight that "the objective reporting standards of the day held that if a Senator was going to make charges of treason, espionage and communism in high places, that in itself was news."[61] The wire services thus sent out entirely accurate stories reciting and repeating McCarthy's charges. But the stringers did not see it as their job to interpret or investigate the charges. Instead, "we had to take what McCarthy said at face value."[62] But surely this is a perverse understanding of objective reporting, one that twists an obligation to report the truth into its exact opposite. Apparently the wire services did not adequately appreciate that sometimes objective reporting requires them to be the adversary of a senator, and not just his megaphone.

The second example is the happier one set by the *New York Times* during the Vietnam War. By 1966 the United States had begun the aerial bombing of Hanoi; press accounts of the bombing depended primarily on Pentagon briefings and these briefings portrayed it as strictly limited to military targets. Contrary reports from Hanoi (and from American antiwar activists who had visited Hanoi) insisted that the civilian population was being subjected to massive bombardment. A debate ensued among *Times* editors about how to be objective in this situation. To their credit, they refused to think the *Times* had sufficiently discharged its obligation to the truth once the Pentagon's version of the war had been passed on to readers. On the other hand, it would be no small step to send a reporter during time of war to the capital city of the enemy. Such a step hardly seemed impartial or neutral, betraying as it did an extraordinary distrust of one's own government. Nonetheless, the *Times*'s editors concluded that their obligation to the truth required them to send their own reporter, Harrison Salisbury, to Hanoi in December 1966. The dispatches Salisbury sent back included eyewitness accounts of hospitals and other civilian installations as targets of massive and repeated bombings. Publishing these dispatches certainly put the *Times* in the position of being an adversary of the Pentagon, but the ethic of objectivity required no less of the nation's leading paper of record.

I. F. Stone once remarked that the philosophy of journalism is "the philosophy of risk."[63] The particular risk he had in mind was the one taken in 1971 by the *New York Times* (and subsequently the *Washington Post*) in publishing top-secret Pentagon documents about the origins of U.S. involvement in Vietnam (the "Pentagon Papers"). These documents had been stolen from the Pentagon and given to the newspapers. The *Times*'s lawyers strenuously advised it not to publish the secret material, warning the editors that it was a criminal violation even to be in possession of stolen government documents. Worse, the lawyers warned that it would be a form of espionage to publish government secrets during wartime, since publication effectively meant passing the secrets on to North Vietnam. The editors at the *Times*, and later at the *Post*, appreciated the gravity of the risk, but they concluded that a commitment to reporting the truth required them to go forward with publication. This was an extraordinarily unconventional editorial decision. Not only did it understand the ethic of objectivity as outweighing the normal ethic against receiving stolen property; more important, it understood the people's right to know as outweighing the government's interest in secrecy. More conventional editors might have refused to second-guess the government's classification of the Pentagon study as top secret. But that kind of deference would allow the government to abuse the classification system at will, stamping embarrassing political decisions as "state secrets" and fobbing off the secrets as about national security matters. Editors at the *Times* and at the *Post* ran the Pentagon Papers story only after concluding that just such an abuse had occurred in classifying as top secret what was essentially a work of history.

It could not, certainly should not, have been easy for the editors to substitute their judgments about the parameters of national security for the government's judgment. The circumstances that bring editors to this point must be rare indeed. But in such circumstances a commitment to objective reporting requires a conscientious journalist to display the full adversary power implicit in the obligation to publish the truth.

IV. TELEVISION NEWS AND THE RATINGS GAME

"The dictates of advertising and the ratings game make television news more a matter of entertainment than journalism. A bad situation is getting worse." Of all the complaints that single out television news for special condemnation, this one seems to me the most prevalent and yet the most difficult to assess. On the one hand, the criticism exaggerates the tension between news values and advertising revenues – a tension, after all, that is characteristic of newspapers as well as television in the United States. On the other hand, the criticism is alive to very recent changes at the television networks that threaten the traditional autonomy of the news divisions within the corporate structure.

Let me attend first to the problems with scapegoating advertisers for all the woes of television journalism. The argument is usually expressed as follows:

> The economics of television . . . is based not on the providing of programs to audiences but rather on the selling of audiences to advertisers. The profitability of television is a direct mathematical function of the number of heads in front of television sets as measured by the Nielsen and Arbitron audience ratings. Television news is not exempted from Nielsen economics.[64]

Thus, the more eyeballs a program delivers to an advertiser, the more the advertiser is willing to pay the network or the station for commercial time. In this way, all networks and all stations are seen as condemned to program only for the tastes of the mass audience. With few exceptions, public affairs programs cannot compete in the mass ratings sweepstakes and thus they are aired only out of prime time or on time preempted from advertisers by reasons of law, request of the president, or by the networks' own occasional concern with their public image. Television news itself competes better for ratings than other public affairs programs, but only to the extent that the broadcast is kept short and breezy, with plenty of video footage narrated lightly by handsome anchors.

The basic problem with this argument is that it conveniently forgets that newspapers are as dependent as the networks are on advertiser financing. Newspapers derive 90 percent of their income from advertising, with subscription revenues barely paying for the paper and the ink.[65] Magazines generate a somewhat greater percentage of their revenues from subscriptions but "few mass circulation magazines would be economically viable without advertising support."[66] These figures indicate that if there is some inherent conflict between quality journalism and dependence on advertising revenues, that conflict would apply just as much to newspapers and newsmagazines as to television. There is no reason to single out network journalism for special trashing, simply on account of its commercial nature.

If network news were somehow more the prostitute of its sponsors than newspapers were of theirs, we should expect the content of television news to differ noticeably from the newspapers' content. But this turns out not to be the case. Comparative studies of newspaper versus network television coverage of the 1968, 1972, and 1976 presidential elections all showed "the consistency of coverage by the various news outlets."[67] And it is apparently standard practice among the staff for all three network programs to rely heavily on the morning newspapers for their selection of lead stories for the evening news.

Moreover, the popular view that newspapers are different from television in being primarily a medium for news rather than for entertainment is also incorrect. To begin with, 60 percent of newspaper content is given over to advertisers. The remaining content is not primarily hard-news stories but, rather, circulation boosters such as horoscopes, comics, sport scores, movie and television listings, and recipes. Indeed, it has been estimated that only 4 percent of the total newspaper content is devoted to national and international news – roughly the same percent of television programming devoted to news.[68]

My purpose in stressing that newspapers are as dependent on advertising revenues as are the television networks is to drive home one major point. In the case of newspapers, American journalism since the days of the penny press has had a long and successful history of accommodating basic news values with the desire of advertisers for mass circulation figures. That is not to deny that circulation wars sometimes triggered excesses of sensationalism, but on the whole the print press has found in advertiser financing a way of ensuring its economic and therefore editorial independence from government. Indeed, when one compares the experience of a commercial press in the United States with that of a government-financed press in a nation such as France, there is much to support the argument that commercial financing has been a friend, not foe, to the ideal of an independent and adversarial press.

There is thus no a priori reason to believe that television journalists cannot achieve the same accommodation with pressure from advertisers for ratings that their print counterparts have achieved with pressure from advertisers for circulation. But have they? It gives one pause when a reflective television journalist such as former CBS special correspondent Bill Moyers argues that the accommodation, though once there, has recently collapsed. "Television news," Moyers remarks, "has never been pure. It has always been an alloy of journalism and show business." But, at least at CBS, the alloy once worked: "The line between news and show business has traditionally been there and the people in charge have tried to protect news against the intrusion of entertainment values."[69] Moyers's recollection of the tradition of journalistic integrity at CBS is similar to a former NBC News vice-president's memories of his network's early days:

> The Huntley–Brinkley Report started on October 20, 1956. . . . The ratings were terrible for almost a year. . . . I believe that for

> most of the summer of 1957 we did not have one commercial spot on that show. . . . Chet, David and I used to talk about it. And what we decided was that we weren't going to do anything about it. Granted, there was a certain amount of learning to be done, but we were doing the show the way we wanted to do it. It was not a matter of celebrity. We never thought of it in those terms.[70]

Clearly, no one today could offer a similar view about the insulation of television news from ratings pressure. Moyers himself left CBS in 1986 after concluding that traditional ways of accommodating news and entertainment values had collapsed. He connects the collapse to anxiety in the boardroom over attempts at an outside takeover of CBS. Having successfully defended CBS from Ted Turner's takeover bid in 1984, CBS executives became ever more conscious of the need to please shareholders and to hold up profit lines. The new view was that the corporation could no longer afford the luxury of exempting its news division from general corporate economics. The result was pressure on the news division for staff cutbacks and for better ratings. Moyers found that the

> center of gravity shifted from the standards and practices of the news business to show business. In meeting after meeting, "Entertainment Tonight" was touted as the model – breezy, entertaining and undemanding. In meeting after meeting, the discussion was about "moments" – visual images containing a high emotional quotient that are passed on to the viewer unfiltered and unexamined.[71]

These meetings took place at a time when the CBS Evening News had slipped from first place in the ratings and when the CBS Morning News was an also-ran. One prominent sign of the new ratings pressure was the transfer of the Morning News out of the news division altogether, its conversion to a much softer sell of the news, then finally threats of cancellation when ratings did not improve. Then president of CBS News, Van Gordon Sauter took the position that "Americans were tired of government, tired of bureaucracy, tired of politics, even." When it was a question of airing a story on the evening news about the latest vote in Ways and Means or about a strike by government workers in Spain, Sauter would ask, "Why should any American care about that?"[72] What he was looking for was the "gripping story," the "story that seems to touch an incredibly responsive chord in people," the "human drama" without which "the facts get lost."

One particular story that filled the bill for Sauter was the tragic story of Jeremy Ghiloni from Ohio. On December 18, 1985, both NBC and ABC led their nightly news with the top story out of Washington – the progress of the Reagan tax reform bill. But before CBS turned to politics that night, they opened with footage of schoolchildren in Ohio preparing get-well cards for critically ill classmate Jeremy, who had been rescued and resuscitated the day before after falling through the ice on a pond and spending forty-five minutes underwater. CBS followed this story all that week, until it ended in Jeremy's death. To find CBS functioning as a national tabloid service shows that complaints such as Moyers's have to be taken seriously. Whatever one thinks of the newsworthiness of the story at all, the decision to lead with it as the principal piece of national news of the day was a transparent ploy to hook, not educate, viewers.

What accounts for the increased anxiety at the networks about the ratings of the nightly news? One factor is the networks' overall concern about potential loss of advertising revenue as they continue to lose portions of the television audience to cable television, videocassettes, independent stations, and fourth-network attempts such as Fox Broadcasting. In 1989, the networks' combined shared of the prime-time audience stood at 66 percent of all television households, down from 73 percent as recently as 1986 and 86 percent in 1980.[73] In this new competitive environment, there is a growing impatience at the head of the corporation with the old-order notion that the news divisions should be insulated from traditional cost-benefit economics.

Another factor is that news itself has surprisingly emerged as a marketable commodity. The fact of the matter is that *60*

Minutes "has made more money for CBS than any other show at the network ever has."[74] Local news has emerged as a particularly successful kind of programming for local stations, causing many to devote one hour to the evening news. Some affiliates are even talking about dropping the network news entirely and doing the national and international news themselves, with help from modern satellite technology.[75] For the networks, already losing market share to new media competitors, this threat of defections by their own affiliates must seem like the final straw. As sober a newsman as former CBS News president Fred Friendly has issued the doomsday warning that "unless the networks make their product appreciably and dramatically superior, I doubt there's much of a future for network news."[76] There seems little doubt that the networks have heard the warning and that some wish to heed it by converting the network news to the tabloid look that has brought the local news its popularity.

It is high time to ask what is so bad, after all, about ratings. Here is a voice raised in their defense: "Ratings are the democratic way; the Nielsen or Arbitron services are but polls of the people to find out what they want from television. In fact, ratings are a way of empowering the people to have the final say on television programming. The networks seek to do nothing other than accurately mirror the state of popular tastes."

But this defense is too cunning about democracy. First, it makes it seem as if the only news democratic citizens need is news that pleases them – news that they watch for the same reasons they watch a situation comedy. But this is to treat viewers not as democratic citizens but as consumers tuning in to be amused and flattered. Once the news is produced to hook and please the largest possible audience, it is demeaned, as Moyers states so eloquently, from the "conversation of democracy" to "the small talk of diversion." The news begins "to win viewers the same way Ronald Reagan won voters: by making them feel good."[77] But "feel good" news has to be in principle superficial, episodic, unengaging, and undemanding. It can flatter the culture but not examine it; it can please viewers but not make them think.

The defense of ratings is too cunning about democracy in a second sense as well. The PBS television documentary on the history of the civil rights movement (*Eyes on the Prize*) held an audience of 5.9 million persons per segment.[78] By the standards of any communication medium other than television, this is a colossal audience. But by Nielsen standards, it is a mediocre showing, one that would get a prime-time, commercial network series promptly canceled. The result is the familiar homogeneity of television programming: each of the Big Three pushing the same mass audience fare. Left unserved are the democratic ideals we commonly associate with diversity in programming or with access to the marketplace of ideas for the widest possible array of tastes and views. As has been so often said, the nation gets to conduct its democratic business on television only on borrowed or preempted time.

Where are we then? Moyers framed the issue nicely when he prefaced his criticism with the remark that no one expects television news to be kept "pure" of ratings pressure. Whether we are talking about television or newspapers, journalism is a business – big business – and that inevitably means accommodating news values to the needs of commercial success. To say anything else would be pie-in-the-sky nonsense that did not relate to a this-worldly ethic for journalists. But even in this world it is possible to come to a better or worse accommodation. For reasons I have tried to review in this section, the better accommodation that the networks once achieved between news business and show business has been replaced by a more sinister insistence that the news business is a business like any other. In retreat is any sense that the media corporation is also performing a public service, for which it receives such long-range assets as a good name and the public's trust. As the networks themselves get swallowed up by nonmedia corporations (RCA, parent company of NBC, was recently taken over by General Electric), we can only expect the notion of being a public trust to have less of a hold on network executives. That is why it is important for television journalists to follow the lead of Moyers in bearing witness to what is happening, and to remember that the television medium that once brought us the likes of an Edward R. Murrow or documentaries such as CBS's *Selling of the Pentagon* has a long and proud journalistic tradition to which it should return, one hopes one day soon.

CONCLUSION

A commitment to the truth provides journalism with its ethical center of gravity. This is not an easy commitment to carry out. It asks reporters – I have asked them in this essay – to pester the powerful, betray state secrets, and corroborate the enemy's version of wartime events. I have also asked reporters not to be swayed by the pressures of ratings or to be fooled by the machinations of candidates. All this might sound utopian, except that real-life reporters keep on getting the truth to us, out of prisons and refugee camps, during wars and famines, from closed boardrooms and corrupt police precincts. For all the grousing we do about the press, we still marvel that reporters uncover the truth as often as they do, especially given the vested interest so many powerful institutions have in public ignorance.

I have emphasized that a commitment to truth requires journalists to become at times the adversary of their own government. But not just government. Other institutions – be they corporations, universities, or religions – have the power to, and sometimes an interest in, managing the news. And the news they seek to manage is often, by anyone's definition, crucial to informed democratic debate. The debate might be about dumping of toxic wastes, for instance, or spray cans and the ozone layer, or overcharging by a defense contractor, or university research on "star wars," or the extent of insider trading on Wall Street. For the truth in so many of these areas of public debate, we are dependent on a press that understands itself to be an adversary of power everywhere, private as well as public.

The adversarial posture is not an end in itself; it is a way of getting at the truth. Sometimes muckrackers and gadflies forget this and get carried away with their own power. Then we hear the familiar litany of complaints about reporters making nuisances of themselves. But democracy can survive the excesses of muckracking. What it cannot survive is its absence.

NOTES

1 John Strahinich, "The Boogeyman Comes Home," *Boston Magazine*, December 1985, 12; Peter S. Canellos, "Would You Have Run This Piece?" *Columbia Journalism Review* (May–June 1987): 18; Suzanne Wetlaufer, "A Wayland Man Finds Hostility, Compassion 18 Years After Crime," *Boston Globe*, February 9, 1986, p. 29; Peter B. Sleeper, "He Found His Pain, Past Were Inescapable," *Boston Globe*, November 22, 1986, p. 1.

2 Bernard Weinraub, "Pleas for Silence on Mideast Deals," *New York Times*, November 8, 1986, p. A1.

3 John B. Judis, "Comment: the Hart Affair," *Columbia Journalism Review* (July–August 1987): 21.

4 Ibid.

5 Anthony Lewis, "Degrading the Press," *New York Times*, May 5, 1987, p. A35.

6 H. Fineman, "Gary Hart: A Candidate in Search of Himself," *Newsweek*, vol. 109, April 13, 1987, 25–7.

7 E. J. Dionne, Jr., "Gary Hart: The Elusive Front Runner," *New York Times*, May 3, 1987, sec. 6, p. 38.

8 Tom Wicker, "Much to Regret," *New York Times*, May 9, 1987, p. A31.

9 Judis, "Comments," p. 27.

10 "Transcript of Hart Statement Withdrawing His Candidacy," *New York Times*, May 9, 1987, p. A9.

11 Wicker, "Much to Regret," p. A31.

12 Lewis, "Degrading the Press," p. A35.

13 A. M. Rosenthal, "The Tears of Mr. Hart," *New York Times*, May 10, 1987, sec. E., p. 25.

14 Lewis, "Degrading the Press," p. A35.

15 David Shaw, "Have Hart, Miami Herald Really Behaved Themselves?," *Los Angeles Times,* May 6, 1987, p. 5.
16 Quoted in Judis, "Comments," p. 22.
17 "Gary Hart's Judgment," *New York Times,* May 5, 1987, p. A34; E. J. Dionne, Jr., et al., "Courting Danger: The Fall of Gary Hart," *New York Times,* May 9, p. A1; "Hart and Danger," *Los Angeles Times,* May 6, 1987, p. 4.
18 Nelson Polsby, "The Public Interest Outweighs Privacy," *New York Times,* May 6, 1987, p. A35.
19 See, e.g., Michael Robinson, "Public Affairs Television and the Growth of Political Malaise: The Case of 'The Selling of the Pentagon,' " *American Political Science Review* 70 (1976): 409–22.
20 See, e.g., Michael Oreskes, "Talking Heads: Weighing Imagery in a Campaign Made for Television," *New York Times,* October 2, 1988, sec. 4, p. 1.
21 Ibid.
22 Michael Oreskes, "TV's Role in '88: The Medium is the Election," *New York Times,* October 30, 1988, p. A1.
23 Oreskes, "Talking Heads," sec. 4, p.1
24 Paul Lazarsfeld et al., *The People's Choice: How the Voter Makes Up His Mind in a Presidential Campaign* (New York: Columbia University Press, 1984); W. Russell Neuman, *The Paradox of Mass Politics* (Cambridge, Mass.: Harvard University Press, 1986), pp. 133–4; David Blomquist, *Elections and the Mass Media* (Washington, D.C.: American Political Science Association, 1982), pp. 4–8.
25 Joseph T. Klapper, *The Effects of Mass Communication* (New York: Free Press, 1960); Blomquist, *Elections and the Mass Media,* pp. 4–8.
26 Robinson, "Public Affairs Television," pp. 409–22.
27 Richard Sennett, *The Fall of Public Man* (New York: Knopf, 1977), pp. 284, 286, 292–3.
28 Daniel Boorstin, "From News-Gathering to News-Making: A Flood of Pseudo-Events," in *The Process and Effects of Mass Communications,* ed. William Schram and Donald Roberts (Urbana: University of Illinois Press, 1971), p. 120.
29 Edwin Diamond and Stephen Bates, "30-Second Elections," *New York,* vol. 17, October 1, 1984, 46.
30 David Stockman, *The Triumph of Politics: How the Reagan Revolution Failed* (New York, Harper & Row, 1986), pp. 5, 7, 12.
31 Oreskes, "TV's Role in '88," p. A1.
32 Ibid.

33 R. W. Apple, Jr., "Early Euphoria in Texas Turns Sour for Dukakis," *New York Times*, October 17, 1988, pp. A1, 17.
34 E. J. Dionne, Jr., "Voters Delay Republican Hopes of Dominance in Post Reagan Era," *New York Times*, November 10, 1988, pp. A1, B6.
35 Kevin Phillips, "The Election and the Bush Future," *New York Review of Books* 25 (December 22, 1988): 16–18.
36 Oreskes, "TV's Role in '88," p. A1.
37 Ibid.
38 Anthony Lewis, "Who Is George Bush," *New York Times*, November 6, 1988, p. E25.
39 Andrew Rosenthal, "Foes Accuse Bush Campaign of Inflaming Racial Tension," *New York Times*, October 24, 1988, pp. A1, B5.
40 Phillips, "The Election and the Bush Future," p. 16.
41 Thomas Patterson and Robert McClure, *The Unseeing Eye: The Myth of Television Power in National Politics* (New York: Putnam, 1976), p. 111.
42 Ibid., pp. 116, 129.
43 Oreskes, "TV's Role in '88," p. A1.
44 Anthony Lewis, "What Is a Man Profited," *New York Times*, October 27, 1988, p. A27.
45 Oreskes, "TV's Role in '88," p. A1.
46 E. J. Dionne, Jr., "Voters Delay Republican Hopes of Dominance in Post Reagan Era," pp. A1, B6.
47 William Boot, "Campaign '88: TV Overdoses on the Inside Dope," *Columbia Journalism Review* (January–February 1989): 24.
48 Ibid.
49 Oreskes, "TV's Role in '88," p. A1.
50 Michael Oreskes, "Dukakis Ads: Blurred Signs, Uncertain Path," *New York Times*, October 19, 1988, p. A1.
51 R. W. Apple, Jr., "People Are Yearning for a Leader but Expecting Much Less," *New York Times*, November 6, 1988, sec. 4, p. 1.
52 Oreskes, "Talking Heads," sec. 4, p. 1.
53 See, e.g., Bernard Cohen, *The Press and Foreign Policy* (Princeton, N.J.: Princeton University Press, 1963).
54 Renata Adler, "Annals of Law (Libel Trials – Part I)," *New Yorker*, June 16, 1983, p. 50.
55 Michael Schudson, *Discovering the News: A Social History of American Newspapers* (New York: Basic, 1978), p. 41.
56 Adler, "Annals," p. 50.

57 See 47 U.S.C., secs. 301, 312(a)(7), 315(a).
58 Robert D. Hershey, Jr., "F.C.C. Votes Down Fairness Doctrine in a 4–0 Decision," *New York Times,* August 5, 1987, p. A1.
59 See, e.g., Patterson and McClure, *The Unseeing Eye,* chaps. 1–3.
60 See, e.g., Neuman, *The Paradox of Mass Politics,* pp. 140–2.
61 The remark was made by George Reedy, former press secretary to President Lyndon Johnson, and is quoted in *Columbia Journalism Review* (March–April 1985): 36.
62 Ibid., p. 38.
63 Neil Middleton, ed., *The I. F. Stone Weekly Reader* (New York: Random House, Vintage, 1974), p. 15.
64 I have taken this compact statement of the argument from Neuman, *Paradox,* p. 135. It is important to note, however, that Neuman himself does not agree with this position and derives it from such sources as Erik Barnouw, *The Sponsor* (New York: Oxford University Press, 1978), and Bruce Owen, Jack H. Beebee, and William G. Manning, Jr., *Television Economics* (Lexington, Mass.: Lexington Books, 1975).
65 Ibid., p. 135.
66 Ibid.
67 Ibid., p. 140.
68 Ibid., p. 138.
69 Quoted in Jonathan Alter, "Taking CBS to Task," *Newsweek,* September 15, 1986, 53.
70 "Seven Voices: Journalists Talk About Their Lives – and How the World in Which They Work Has Been Transformed," *Columbia Journalism Review* (May–June, 1986): 48.
71 Quoted in Alter, "Taking CBS to Task," p. 53.
72 Quoted in Michael Massing, "CBS: Sauterizing the News," *Columbia Journalism Review* (March–April, 1986): 27, 30.
73 Jeremy Gerard, "Television: A Season the Networks Would Rather Not Repeat," *New York Times,* January 16, 1989, p. D8.
74 Peter J. Boyer, " '60 Minutes': A Hit Confronts the Odds," *New York Times,* September 13, 1987, sec. 2, p. 1.
75 William J. Drummond, "Is Time Running Out for Network News?" *Columbia Journalism Review* (March–April 1986): 52.
76 Quoted in ibid.
77 Alter, "Taking CBS to Task," p. 53.
78 *Report on the National Broadcast: Eyes on the Prize, America's Civil Rights Years, 1954–1965* (Boston: WGBH National Productions Department, 1987).

Chapter 9

Political communication systems and democratic values

MICHAEL GUREVITCH and JAY G. BLUMLER

The American media system is presumably animated by certain democratic principles. Some of these concern the relationship of the mass media to government – for example, the proposition that, acting on behalf of the citizenry, the media should guard against abuses of power by officeholders. Others concern the relationship of the mass media to diverse opinion sources – for example, the proposition that the media should provide a robust, uninhibited, and wide-open marketplace of ideas, in which opposing views may meet, contend, and take each other's measure. Yet others concern the relationship of the mass media to the public at large – for example, the propositions that they should serve the public's "right to know" and offer options for meaningful political choices and nourishment for effective participation in civic affairs.

Yet, a glance at the world of the American media today reveals a landscape dominated by a few giant media corporations. These enterprises may be as remote from the people as are other powerful and dominant institutions in society. Their inner workings are rarely opened to voluntary outside scrutiny. And they seem committed to the presentation, not of a broad spectrum of ideas but of mainstream opinion currents, whose flows are bounded politically by the two-party system, economically by the imperatives of private enterprise capitalism, and culturally by the values of a consumer society.

This essay deals with the tensions and disparities between the ostensibly democratic ideals that the mass media are supposed to serve and the communication structures and practices that actually prevail. We argue that such disparities undermine the capacity of the system to serve these democratic ideals. Our diagnosis rests on some broad assumptions that are stated, elaborated, and illustrated in the following sections.

DEMOCRATIC EXPECTATIONS OF MEDIA PERFORMANCE

Democracy is a highly exacting creed in its expectations of the mass media. It requires that the media perform and provide a number of functions and services for the political system. Among the more significant are:

1. Surveillance of the sociopolitical environment, reporting developments likely to impinge, positively or negatively, on the welfare of citizens
2. Meaningful agenda-setting, identifying the key issues of the day, including the forces that have formed and may resolve them
3. Platforms for an intelligible and illuminating advocacy by politicians and spokespersons of other causes and interest groups
4. Dialogue across a diverse range of views, as well as between power holders (actual and prospective) and mass publics
5. Mechanisms for holding officials to account for how they have exercised power
6. Incentives for citizens to learn, choose, and become involved, rather than merely to follow and kibitz over the political process
7. A principled resistance to the efforts of forces outside the media to subvert their independence, integrity, and ability to serve the audience
8. A sense of respect for the audience member, as potentially concerned and able to make sense of his or her political environment

But it is no easy matter to achieve and serve these goals. At least four kinds of obstacles hinder their attainment.

First, conflicts among democratic values themselves may

necessitate trade-offs and compromises in the organization and performance of the media. There are tensions, for example, between the principle of editorial autonomy and the ideal of offering individuals and groups wide-ranging access to the media. The aim of serving the public by catering to its immediate tastes and interests is likely to conflict with the aim of providing what the public *needs* to know. Media organizations are also confronted by the conflict between a majoritarian concentration on mainstream opinions and interests and the rights of dissident and marginal views to be heard.

Second, authoritative political communicators often appear to exist in an elite world of their own, distanced from the circumstances and perspectives of ordinary people. In fact, political communication could virtually be defined as the transmission of messages and pressures to and from individuals who are demonstrably unequal: the highly informed and the abysmally ignorant, the highly powerful and the pitifully powerless, the highly involved and the blissfully indifferent. Thus, the very structure of political communication involves a division between movers and shakers at the top and bystanders below, imposing limits on the participatory energy the system can generate.

Third, not everyone in the audience for political communication is a political animal, nor is obliged to be. On the one hand, a viable democracy presupposes an engaged citizenry; on the other hand, one of the freedoms the members of a liberal society enjoy is the freedom to define for themselves their stance toward the political system, including the right to be politically apathetic. As a result, political messages are doubly vulnerable. For one thing, they must jostle and compete for limited time and space with other, often more entertaining and beguiling, kinds of messages. They are not guaranteed a favored share of our attention. For another, their ultimate dependence on winning and holding the attention of a heterogeneous audience can inhibit the media from committing themselves wholeheartedly to the democratic task.

Fourth, the media can pursue democratic values only in ways that are compatible with the sociopolitical and economic environment in which they operate. Political communication arrangements follow the contours of and derive their resources from the society of which they are a part. Even when formally autonomous and sheltered by sacrosanct constitutional guarantees of a free press, they are part and parcel of the larger social system, performing functions for it and impelled to respond to predominant drives within it. In the United States, for example, media organizations are large business enterprises and first and foremost must survive (and if possible prosper) in a highly competitive marketplace. Their pursuit of their democratic role is inexorably shaped by that overriding economic goal. Politically, too, media institutions are linked inextricably to the governing institutions of society, not least because of their mutual dependence as suppliers of raw materials (government to media) and channels of publicity (media to government). In fact, a central issue in current research on the "agenda setting" role of the mass media is the degree to which they exercise a discretionary power to highlight certain issues for public attention, as against the degree to which they depend on the policy initiatives of the big power battalions whose activities and statements they report.[1]

SOME REDEEMING FEATURES

However constraining such pressures and problems, symbolically at least, journalism in the Western liberal democracies does reflect the influence of democratic values.

For example, the news media provide a daily parade of political disagreement and conflict. In that way what appears regularly in the news is a standing refutation of the antidemocratic notion that there is some single valid social purpose for pursuit through politics and some single group that is entitled to monopolize power because it alone knows what that purpose is and how best to realize it. In addition, the existence of a free press enshrines the democratic concept of the political accountability of power holders to ordinary citizens. Much of what the press reports in political affairs can be thought of as designed to encourage audience members to judge how what the government has been doing relates to their interests, problems, and concerns. Similarly, a free press can be said to embody the notion of citizen autonomy. It implicitly stands for the assumption that readers, viewers, and listeners are offered material on the basis of which they can make up their own minds about who the "good guys" and the "bad guys" in politics are.

Beyond what it represents symbolically, the press in a democratic society can be seen as performing an indispensable bridging function in democratic politics. Inevitably, an enormous gulf stretches between the political world and ordinary people's perceptions of it. Although political decisions may affect people's lives in many ways, from *their* perspective the political world often seems remote, confusing, and boring. What the press does, it might be argued, is to bring developments in this distant and difficult arena within the reach of the average person in terms that he or she can understand. Viewed in this light, certain features of political reporting may be regarded as enticements to become involved in political questions, ways of interesting the public in affairs for which they might feel little prior enthusiasm. So the crowd-pulling appeal of journalism, the tendency to dramatize, the projection of hard-hitting conflict, the use of sporting analogies to awaken a horse race–like excitement, are, in this view, inducements to become interested in and aware of political matters. Even the media's proclivity toward the dramatic may be applauded in this spirit. A dramatic story can be treated as a peg for more information about the wider political context in which it occurred.

Even the much criticized tendency of the press to trade in simple stereotypes can be viewed in this light. As Winfried Schulz has put it, "In order to make politics comprehensible to the citizen, it must first be reduced by journalists to a few simple structural patterns."[2] This, of course, echoes Walter Lippmann's classic observation on the role of the press as constructors of "pictures in our minds."[3] Personalization, the penchant for clear-cut issues, the tendency to reduce most political conflicts to only two sides of the argument – all might be thought of as aids to popular understanding.

Yet such a positive evaluation ignores three problems. First, surveys of what audience members actually glean from the news demonstrate that it is a highly inefficient mechanism for conveying information.[4] Second, there are few signs that media personnel seriously try to verify for themselves how much information and insight their audiences get out of news reports, with a prospect of changing their news-telling ways accordingly. Third, with many journalistic practices the means seem to have become the end. An election campaign is predominantly treated *as* (not like) a horse race.[5] Journalists and their audiences are more often stalled on the bridge than transported to a more enlightened land beyond it.

SYSTEMIC CONSTRAINTS

Allegations that news organizations fail to serve democracy well are not unique to the United States. Even in democracies whose structures and institutions appear to be less dominated by capitalist spirit, and where large and impressive public service broadcasting organizations have long existed and enjoyed much esteem, similar complaints have been voiced by academics and pressure groups alike.[6] In our view, the incidence and the obduracy of these problems can be traced to the fact that in large, complex, industrialized societies, political messages emanate from more or less rigidly structured and enduring political communication systems.

The notion of a political communication *system*[7] is intended to highlight the interdependence of key communicators within it, the reciprocal nature of their relationship with each other and with the audience, and a crystallization of communication norms, roles, genres, formats, traditions, and practices that tend to persist over time. Presumably the "system" character of political communication arrangements confers predictability and familiarity on the otherwise hectic, volatile, and uncertain climate of the modern publicity process. Officials, opinion leaders, and journalists can form some sense of the ground rules and behaviors they can count on their counterparts to observe. Audience members also learn what to expect and how to respond accordingly. Nevertheless, built-in system constraints tend to block and thwart the realization of democratic values. To structure the discussion, we will consider the role of such constraints at four different levels of the political communication system: the societal level, the inter-institutional level, the intra-institutional level, and the audience level.

The societal level

We have already suggested that the production and dissemination of political messages occur within a web of economic, political, and cultural subsystems, which exert "pressure" on the media to select certain issues rather than others as subjects for public attention; to frame their stories according to favored scenarios; and to give the views of certain groups and individuals privileged treatment and heightened exposure. Such pressures need not be applied overtly or deliberately. Indeed, our emphasis on political communication as a systemic product reflects our view that the reciprocal flow of influence between the media and other social institutions is a more or less "natural" and mutually accepted phenomenon, tending to reproduce the power relations and reciprocal dependencies that obtain between them. And it is the varying linkages between such institutions, including closer relations and more powerful dependencies in some cases and more remote links and lesser dependencies in others, that may result in various constraints on "communications for democracy."

We can examine media linkages to the *economic* environment via the structure of ownership and control and via the dynamics of supply and demand in a commercial marketplace. Researchers have paid some attention to the former, where current trends point to an increased concentration of ownership in fewer hands, as well as a process of conglomeration, placing media organizations within larger corporate structures controlled by nonmedia interests.[8] The implications of such ownership patterns for media "bias" toward certain opinions and interests are not clear-cut. Owners of media outlets may leave editors free to follow their own political and professional leanings; yet the potential for influencing editorial policy is clearly present. The Conservative bias of the Fleet Street press in Britain is now blatant and open, while Rupert Murdoch has exercised control with a vengeance over the editorial policies of certain newspapers he has acquired. In American television the recent wave of mergers and takeovers is bringing new actors – such as Capital Cities and General Electric – into the media arena, and potentially giving even greater weight to financial "bottom line" considerations.

Market mechanisms may threaten democratic aspirations when two or more media organizations compete for a large and heterogeneous mass audience. Such circumstances are likely to generate pressures to:

1. *Limit the amount of public affairs coverage, and shift its style from the serious and extended to the entertaining and arresting:* There is simply no way in which an hour-long news show could be ventured on American commercial network television, although local stations do offer such programs. These, however, constitute a mixture of "hard" and "soft" local news, sometimes bordering on "infotainment."
2. *Impose format rigidities on public affairs coverage:* Even in election campaigns, the nightly news shows on American network television cannot be extended beyond their twenty-two-minute ration; nor can their commercials be retimed to create room for longer and more coherent reports.
3. *Deal blandly with social issues in non-news programming:* Many advertisers have guidelines on acceptable and unacceptable program features for their commercials, enforced through a prescreening of episodes to be aired.

Of course, *political* constraints on the media can take different forms, ranging from direct political controls, through overt political pressures to promote or suppress specific contents, to strategies for steering journalists toward favored stories and away from less favored ones, to a more subtle reliance on informal channels and contacts. Much has been said and written about this area,[9] and it requires little further elaboration, except to point out that ultimately the media's ability to withstand such pressures turns on their credibility for doing the sort of job they claim to be undertaking and for serving the audience properly.

Another form of political "control," however, is less often noticed. Powerful institutions in society *are* powerful at least in part because they can plausibly claim authority over the definition of the issues falling in their spheres. This is to imply not that critics are silenced but that they often have to make their case on grounds not of their own choosing. Thus, the police are perceived to be the authority on issues of law and order;[10] the Treasury and the Federal Reserve Bank, on the state of the economy; the Pentagon, on defense and military matters; and the President of the United States is the "primary definer" of what constitutes the "national interest." Not surprisingly, when journalists seek an authoritative perspective on a certain field of issues, they turn to those officials who are defined by their positions as authoritative sources.[11] Media professionals do not see this practice as a violation of the canon of objectivity, since the sources are consulted precisely for their presumed expertise and not merely as proponents of a certain point of view. Alternative definitions of social issues are then disadvantaged – either not represented at all, given short shrift, or labeled as "interested" and "biased."

Social systems also structure a pecking order of status and prestige, giving those higher up the ladder a better chance of having their affairs reported in line with their own perspectives. Thus, certain institutions are commonly accorded respect, even reverence, in the news – for example, the institutions of the presidency and the Supreme Court (though not necessarily the incumbents in these positions), and the British royal family. Some enjoy a benign neglect. Some evoke a mixture of symbolic deference and pragmatic exploitation (for example, the British Parliament).[12] Some mainly suffer the slings and arrows of straight news-values fortunes (often trade unions). Some can get attention only if they stir up trouble (e.g., political "terrorists"). Elsewhere, we have outlined a conceptual framework for analyzing news personnel's orientations toward social institutions, based on a continuum between more sacerdotal and more pragmatic approaches to institutional reporting.[13] We argued that social institutions that are regarded as the symbolic embodiment of the core values of their society tend to elicit portrayals of their activities as if "through their own eyes." Conversely, the treatment of institutions, groups, and individuals that represent less central values, or dissident and deviant values, is likely to be guided more strictly by journalists' news values.

The inter-institutional level

In modern political communication systems mediated political messages are a subtly composite product, reflecting the contributions and interactions of two different types of communicators: advocates and journalists. Each side is striving to realize different goals vis-à-vis the audience; yet it cannot normally pursue these without securing the cooperation of the other side. Politicians need access to the communication channels operated by media organizations; and they must adjust their messages to the demands of formats and genres that have been devised inside such organizations. Nor can journalists perform their task of political reporting without access to politicians for interviews, news, and comment. Thus, the practice of addressing citizens is something of a compromise for both groups of communicators. It is not merely that they have different goals. It is also that in order to proceed at all, they must work through and with the other side. And from this interwoven process three problems of democratic communication arise.

First, there is a potential for blurring institutional functions that ideally ought to be kept distinct. For their part, politicians start to think, speak, and behave like journalists – a tendency epitomized by presidential statements couched in one-liners designed to guide and ease the work of newspaper headline writers and to give television reporters pithy ten-second sound bites. For their part, journalists, despite their professional values, may be reduced to virtual channels of propaganda. This poses a dilemma for the media. When politicians can predict confidently which events and comments will ring reportorial bells, media professionals are deprived of opportunities to exercise their own judgment. (This line of self-criticism became especially visible in postmortem analyses of the media's role in the 1988 presidential campaign.) Yet the routines that open the media to such manipulation cannot be discarded or overhauled without much disruption and cost. Thus, reform of the political communication process is seriously hampered by professionally rooted inertia in the media and by the coziness of the relationship between journalists and politicians, which appears to accommodate both sides, notwithstanding its occasional rough edges and adversarial explosions. This problem, too, is increasingly recognized and discussed by journalists.

Second, striking strategic developments have occurred in recent years on the advocates' side of the political communication process. Because politicians and other would-be opinion molders are competing fiercely for access to exposure in the media; because in order to achieve this they must tailor their messages to the requirements of journalists' formats, news values, and work habits; and because this is thought to demand anticipatory planning, fast footwork, and a range of specialist skills – for all these reasons, a significant degree of "source professionalization" has emerged. By this we mean the ever deeper and more extensive involvement in political message making of publicity advisers, public relations experts, campaign management consultants, and the like.

Such "source professionals" are not only farsighted, assiduous, and gifted at fashioning messages for media consumption. They immerse journalists in what appears to be an increasingly manipulative opinion environment. Perceiving themselves to be "professionals" rather than "advocates," source professionals regard newsmaking as a power struggle rather than a process of issue clarification. Consequently, they introduce into the political communication process a potentially corrosive and disturbing set of assumptions. For example, many of them tend to be skeptical about such notions as:

1. *The free marketplace of ideas:* According to an assistant attorney general in the Reagan administration, "Freedom of information is not cost free; it is not an absolute good."
2. *The social responsibility theory of the press:* According to a publicity adviser of the Reagan administration, to govern successfully the government must set the agenda; it cannot allow the press to set the agenda for it; it is therefore involved in a battle with the news media over what version of political reality will be communicated to the public.
3. *Any obligation to cater to the conscientious, information-seeking citizen:* Such a person is thought to be a fiction, since most people's responses to politics are said to stem from a medley of emotions, impressions, sentiments, wishful feelings, valued symbols, hopes and fears, plus a lacing of direct personal experience.

Third, faced with such developments, journalists become uneasy and concerned to reassert the significance of their own contribution. In fact, during an observation study we conducted at the headquarters of NBC News during the 1984 presidential election campaign, producers and correspondents talked to us about their awareness of this problem and their efforts to resolve the dilemma of reporting the activities of candidates without becoming extensions of their propaganda machines.[14] One device they have developed for this purpose has been termed "disdaining the news."[15] This involves attempts by reporters to distance themselves from the propagandistic features of an event by suggesting that it has been contrived and should be taken with a grain of salt. As one interviewee told us:

> There is a naiveté of people out there. They see a one-minute to two-minute story, cutting from one election scene to another and can be taken in by them. . . . Many television news stories can give a false sense of what the event is like. So if viewers are helped to recognize by a story of this kind that they're being manipulated, they can then analyze the situation and understand it even better. If that is the way politicians want to run their campaign, then that is also the way in which we should report it.

Clearly such an approach has a potential for cultivating political cynicism and mistrust among viewers and further undermining the contributions of the media to the democratic process.

The intra-organizational level

Significant constraints on the portrayal of social and political issues in the media also stem from factors internal to the organization of journalism, including relations between news media outlets and the values and ideologies that guide media professionals in their work.

In liberal-democratic societies, the relationship between media organizations is characterized primarily by competition – to maximize audiences, to be first with the news, or to scoop one's rivals in other ways. Thus, although competition for audience patronage is related directly to the media's economic goals, it is also rooted deeply in the professional culture of Western journalism. This diverts attention away from the aim of serving the audience toward the democratically irrelevant goal of beating the competition. One example in recent years is the competitive zeal that fueled the coverage by the television networks and CNN of the highjacked TWA plane in Beirut in 1985. Nationally that competition was geared to serve a news-hungry public, eager for information about the crisis. It soon became apparent, however, that when the reporting from Beirut ceased to carry any "news" or to have any significant informational value, it was motivated primarily by inter-network competition for the highest journalistic profile. Whether the country, the audience, or, indeed, the hostages were best served by this rivalry remained moot points.

Competition is only one force shaping the behavior of journalists. Professional values, such as objectivity, impartiality, fairness, and an ability to recognize the newsworthiness of an event, also serve as influential guidelines when framing stories. At one level, such norms provide safeguards essential to a democratic media system. They prescribe that reporters should stand above the political battle, serve the audience rather than politicians with partisan axes to grind, and do so with due regard for all the interests at stake in an issue. But at another level, the routinized application of such values can have distorting consequences. Many writers have pointed out, for example, that the neutral stance enjoined by the values of objectivity and impartiality can lend implicit support to the more powerful institutions and groups in society and for the social order from which they benefit.[16] Instead of promoting a "marketplace of ideas," in which all viewpoints are given adequate play, media neutrality can tend to privilege dominant, mainstream positions.

Adherence to professional definitions of news values may also act as a powerful force for conformity, for arriving, that is, at a common answer, across an otherwise diverse set of news outlets, to the question, What is the most significant news today?[17] Widely shared and professionally endorsed definitions of news values may force journalists' hand in other ways. For example, during our election observation study at NBC, one reporter, assigned to cover Geraldine Ferraro, described to us how within thirty seconds of her selection by Mondale as his running mate she was typecast by news editors and producers as the "first woman Vice-Presidential candidate."[18] His own wish to report her in terms, say, of the compatibility of her campaign utterances with her voting record in the House of Representatives, was rejected by editors as not part of "the Ferraro story," and a later attempt to place the same item ran into the obstacle that by then the dominant theme of "the Ferraro story" had become her response to the issue of her family finances. Revealed here is how widely shared news values can severely constrain the range of options within which reporters themselves can deal with political issues and leaders. Clearly, such tendencies constrict the potential of the media to serve as a genuine "marketplace of ideas" or to transcend the boundaries of the social and political mainstream.

Thus, the principal mass media openings for political information are molded into standardized formats and conventions, which control what journalists can do in conveying ideas to the audience, while at the same time reflecting how much time and space media organizations consider they can afford to devote to the examination of social and political issues. Although they are the major channels of political communication, the mass media dance to other tunes than those of democratic communication alone. Through their acceptance of the imperatives of competition, and in their adherence to a self-generated and self-imposed set of professional standards, they shape their contributions to the political process in ways that may well fall short of the democratic ideals they claim to serve.

The audience level

What role does the audience play in a democratic media system? Ideally, its needs and interests should be uppermost. In practice, the media promptly heed any sign of decided audience dislike or rejection of certain ways of addressing it – if, that is, the media's competitive goals are perceived to be at risk as a result. In that sense, the audience holds a sort of reserve veto power.

Such sensitivity to audience attitudes may be interpreted as reflecting the media's democratic impulses. Nevertheless, there are systemic reasons why the audience for political communication is vulnerable to neglect and misrepresentation. Of the three main elements in a political communication system – politicians, journalists, and audience members – it is the audience that, though most numerous, is least powerful, because least organized. Amid their preoccupations with the intricacies, problems, calculations, and subtleties of coping with one another, politicians and journalists are liable to lose sight of the ordinary voter's concerns and instead attempt to accommodate one another. Thus, audiences are "known" to the media primarily as statistical aggregates produced by ratings services and market researchers, and the media's orientation to their audiences is dominated by numbers. Three problems arise from these circumstances.

First, research suggests strongly that if useful information is to be effectively conveyed to people through the mass media, a sine qua non is sensitivity to what the audience wants or needs to know.[19] The system does not foster such sensitivity.

Second, an audience known mainly through numbers is open to oversimplification, stereotyping, even contempt. This is illustrated by the comment of a news executive we interviewed during our observation study at NBC in 1984, who said: "The only thing that viewers want to know about this election is who is going to win."

Third, this statement (taken in conjunction with other similarly pithy maxims about audience propensities that gain currency in the lore of media executives) illustrates a feature of widely held audience images that contributes to the entrenchment of the system: Authoritative communicators tend to dismiss the audience *as if it were capable only of absorbing what the system supplies.* A deeply conservative view of the audience is thus propagated, one that reinforces the communicators' own identities and interests, and preserves the communication status quo.

OPPORTUNITIES FOR REFORM

System-based constraints on the workings of the mass media, such as those highlighted here, must be sobering to democrats because they are so resistant to change; yet within current political communication arrangements there are certain "chinks," which may open up some opportunities for reform.

First, it should be asked whether there are any advocates for democratic political communication. A first look suggests not. Instead (as we have already suggested), when preparing speeches, media events, and political stories, major political communicators (whether journalists or politicians) are not normally moved by abstractly conceived principles, such as the promotion of an informed citizenry. Rather, they are constrained by more or less abiding pressures, traditions, and relationships, embedded in the fabric of the system in which they are placed, to communicate in ways that do not necessarily promote democratic goals. Nevertheless, the elements of an advocacy group for democratic political communication can be found among some academics concerned with democratic policy issues, media critics, foundations and various civic groups, plus a handful of media professionals who occasionally rise above the daily pressures of their job to consider its broader issues and consequences. Yet such a constituency cannot claim to have any organized support at present. Our own experience in Britain suggests that academic advocacy for change, even when it is welcomed and supported in principle, can quickly wither on the vine (or gather dust on the shelf), when entrusted to politicians and media organizations for implementation.[20]

The constituency needs, then, to be expanded and bolstered. Where might such support come from? In our view, the most important source could be journalists themselves. Western journalism is experiencing a crisis of legitimacy at present. In part this springs from the increasing inability of many groups with a stake in civic affairs to recognize themselves in the stereotyped portraits of their activities in the major media; in part, from a sense that the authority and veracity of media coverage are questioned by many ordinary audience members. And in part it stems from the academic critique of the conventional journalistic view of the nature of news. Rather than regarding news (as journalists typically do) as a selection of the significant and interesting happenings of the day, these critics have depicted news personnel as active constructors of social reality,[21] with the resulting implication that it might be permissible after all to blame the messenger for the message. This crisis may be resolved only by defining certain purposes for media organizations, above and beyond their survival, which the media are expected to serve and which do not entail their subordination to dominant particular interests. Notice how this conclusion points to a need to formulate notions of democratic media purposes, from which fresh statements of the purposes and standards of journalism could be drawn. For journalists themselves, then, a way out of the toils could be a stronger and deeper commitment to democratic service.

In addition, pressures for change may come from the present inadequacy of political journalism. If journalism-steered-by-news-values converts so readily into news-management-for-politicians, something will have to be done from within to put this right. Again a need to rethink the journalistic role arises. Too often the alternative to the conventional journalistic role of "gatekeeper" has been posited as one of an "advocate" on behalf of deprived groups and neglected issues.[22] Other possibilities exist and should be explored, including the role of "democratic midwife."

Additional pressures for reform may come from outside the media as well. Evidence suggests that various groups in society are targeting the media as sources of distorted portrayals of their aims and activities. Although some of these complaints are *parti pris,* the media may be obliged to respond in a self-critical but principled spirit. After all, they are notorious for their sensitivity to shifting public currents and moods: This too is part of the climate of democracy.

A final chink may be found in the largely ignored potential among audience orientations to political communication. Research into the ways in which audience members "use" and relate to political content in the media reveals a rich mixture of varying expectations, needs, concerns, and resistances.[23] This is not to claim that the average audience member is a highly politicized person constantly longing for reasoned political argument and enlightenment on complex issues. But more serious forms of political discourse and coverage could strike neglected chords and find an audience ready and willing to attend to them. In the long run such coverage might even awaken dormant interests in some audience members and, hence, expand the circle of politically aware citizens.

NOTES

1 Phillip Tichenor, "Agenda-Setting: Media as Political Kingmakers?" *Journalism Quarterly* 59, no. 3 (1982); Michael Gurevitch and Jay G. Blumler, "Sources of Cross-national Differences in the Discretionary Power of the Mass Media: A Conceptual Introduction," in Holli Semetko et al., *The Formation of Campaign Agendas: A Comparative Analysis of Party and Media Roles in Recent American and British Elections* (Hillside, N.J.: Erlbaum, in press).

2 Winfried Schulz, "One Campaign or Nine?" in *Communicating to Voters: The Role of Television in the First European Parliamentary Elections*, ed. Jay G. Blumler (Beverly Hills, Calif.: Sage, 1983).

3 Walter Lippmann, *Public Opinion* (New York: Harcourt Brace, 1922).

4 E.g., John Robinson and Mark R. Levy, *The Main Source* (Beverly Hills, Calif.: Sage, 1986).

5 Jay G. Blumler and Michael Gurevitch, "The Election Agenda-setting Rules of Television Journalists: Comparative Observation at the BBC and NBC," in Semetko et al., *The Formation of Campaign Agendas*.

6 E.g., Michael Tracy, *The Production of Political Television* (London: Routledge & Kegan Paul, 1978); John Westergaard, "Power, Class and the Media," in *Mass Communication and Society*, ed. James Curran, Michael Gurevitch, and Janet Woollacott (London: Edward Arnold, 1977).

7 See, e.g., Michael Gurevitch and Jay G. Blumler, "Linkages Between the Mass Media and Politics: A Model for the Analysis of Political Communication Systems," in *Mass Communication and Society*, ed. Curran, Gurevitch, and Woollacott; Jack M. McLeod and Jay G. Blumler, "The Macrosocial Level of Communication Science," in *Handbook of Communication Science*, ed.

Charles Berger and Steven Chaffee (Newbury Park, Calif.: Sage, 1987).

8 E.g., Graham Murdock, "Large Corporations and the Control of the Communication Industries," in *Culture, Society and the Media,* ed. Michael Gurevitch et al. (London: Methuen, 1982); Ben Bagdikian, *The Media Monopoly,* 2nd ed. (Boston: Beacon, 1987).

9 See, e.g., Colin Seymour-Ure, *The Political Impact of Mass Media* (London: Constable, 1974); Jay G. Blumler and Michael Gurevitch, "Towards a Comparative Framework for Political Communication Research," in *Political Communication: Issues and Strategies for Research,* ed. Steven Chaffee (Beverly Hills, Calif.: Sage, 1975); Anthony Smith, ed., *Television and Political Life: Studies in Six European Countries* (London: Macmillan, 1979).

10 Steve Chibnall, *Law-and-Order-News* (London: Tavistock, 1974).

11 S. Hall et al., *Policing the Crisis* (London: Macmillan, 1978); Gaye Tuchman, *Making News: A Study in the Construction of Reality* (New York: Free Press, 1978); Mark Fishman, *Manufacturing the News* (Austin: University of Texas Press, 1980); Herbert Gans, *Deciding What's News* (New York: Pantheon, 1979).

12 See Jay G. Blumler and Michael Gurevitch, "Journalists' Orientations to Political Institutions: The Case of Parliamentary Broadcasting," in *Communicating Politics,* ed. Peter Golding et al. (Leicester: Leicester University Press, 1986).

13 Ibid.

14 See note 5, above.

15 Mark R. Levy, "Disdaining the News," *Journal of Communication* 31 (1981).

16 Hall et al., *Policing the Crisis.*

17 Leon V. Sigal, *Reporters and Officials* (Lexington, Mass.: Lexington Books, 1973); Timothy Crouse, *The Boys on the Bus* (New York: Random House, 1973).

18 See note 5.

19 Kjell Nowak, "From Information Gaps to Communication Potential," in *Current Theories in Scandinavian Mass Communication,* ed. M. Berg et al. (Grenaa, Denmark: GMT, 1977); Robinson and Levy, *The Main Source.*

20 Jay G. Blumler, Michael Gurevitch, and Julian Ives, *The Challenge of Election Broadcasting* (Leeds: Leeds University Press, 1978).

21 See, e.g., Hall et al., *Policing the Crisis;* Tony Bennett, "Media,

Signification, 'Reality,' " in *Culture, Society and the Media*, ed. Gurevitch et al.

22 Morris Janowitz, "Professional Roles in Journalism: The Gatekeeper and Advocate," *Journalism Quarterly*, 52 (4), 1975.

23 Jay G. Blumler and Denis McQuail, *Television in Politics: Its Uses and Influence* (London: Faber & Faber, 1968); Jack M. McLeod and Lee B. Becker, "The Uses and Gratifications Approach," in *Handbook of Political Communication*, ed. Dan Nimmo and Keith R. Sanders (Beverly Hills, Calif.: Sage, 1981).

Chapter 10

Mass communications policy: where we are and where we should be going

HENRY GELLER

INTRODUCTION

This essay discusses the current state of government policy concerning mass communications, with particular reference to news and public affairs: Does the policy promote democratic values or work against them, and, if the latter, what would constitute a different, better policy?

There are two initial caveats. First, it will be necessary to oversimplify in light of the enormous scope of the topic. And second, I shall oversimplify with respect to the definition of the key goal here: promotion of democratic values. I recognize that there can be heated argument concerning the term "democratic values." I intend to finesse this important area by focusing on a "motherhood" approach. We can all agree that, in the words of Learned Hand and Hugo Black, the United States has committed itself to a marketplace of ideas – to robust, wide-open debate; that, although others may regard this as folly, we have staked our all on this approach. A democracy – in our case, a republic depending on representative government – critically depends on an informed electorate and, therefore, on a free and unfettered press bringing to it all worthwhile ideas and views.

A further corollary of this First Amendment goal of robust, wide-open debate is that the American people should receive information from as diverse and antagonistic sources as possible (the so-called *Associated Press* principle set out in *Associated Press v. United States*).[1] And obviously it is desirable that the citizens themselves have access to the media to bring to the fore their notions of issues or views. So the key questions that I shall be asking concerning government policy are, Does it promote or inhibit robust, wide-open debate? Does it promote or inhibit the press in discharging its important role of contributing to an informed electorate? Does the policy do all it can to promote access by the citizenry?

As a final initial matter, I also note the obvious: that First Amendment values, however vital to us, are not absolutes (Justices Black and Douglas to the contrary). Frequently they must be balanced against other, equally important values in a democracy, and a compromise struck.

I shall discuss the three main regulatory models that are important here and address the policy issues in the electronic arena and finally in the print arena.

THE THREE REGULATORY MODELS

It is not possible to pigeonhole each new mass medium under a particular regulatory regime. Hybrid technologies like cable TV appear to cut across several models (television, print, common carrier). Nevertheless, I think it is helpful to keep in mind those three main models – broadcasting, print, and common carrier – because often "law is determined by a choice between competing analogies."[2]

In *broadcasting,* there is government licensing to avoid engineering chaos and scarcity (defined as more people wanting to broadcast than there are channels available). The government bestows the scarce licenses on a short-term renewable basis in exchange for a commitment by the private licensee to serve the public interest. This public-trustee concept necessarily carries with it government supervision of overall programming, including an equal opportunities provision for candidates and, until recently, a fairness doctrine for the coverage of controversial issues of public importance.[3]

In *print,* licensing is unthinkable under the First Amendment, and so also there can be no overall government supervision of the operation – no public-trustee concept, with its equal time and fairness aspects.[4] And this is so even if there is economic scarcity – a monopoly resulting from the marketplace.[5] Government intrusion is strictly limited to narrow areas like obscenity or libel, although the latter is proving particularly troublesome, as we shall see in a subsequent section.

Finally, in the *common carrier* area, there is an indifferent holding out of service to the public at large; the information supplied by the customer will be transmitted for a price on a nondiscriminatory, first-come, first-served basis to the points specified by the customer.[6] From a First Amendment point of view, this separation of content and conduit has well served the nation in the print field (i.e., the use of the U.S. Postal Service by thousands of publications). It obviously would be the optimal model in the electronic publishing field – namely, a common carrier reaching into every home and delivering electronic intelligence. Indeed, a model exists for narrowband distribution of electronic material – the ubiquitous telephone line (93 percent penetration in the United States). No comparable model exists today for broadband wire distribution. Although this will undoubtedly change in the next century with fiber in every home (perhaps with the so-called broadband integrated service digital network [ISDN]), policy for the next decade must be made without this highly desirable technological breakthrough.

Based on experience with these three models, I would derive the following principles:

1. If the regulation – whether it be structural (access or common carrier) or behavioral (fairness doctrine) – interferes with editorial autonomy (e.g., by requiring the operator to give up control of some of its "publication" or to present some additional speech), there must be the "hook" of government bestowing a scarce license or privilege of operation. Thus, the government has no such "hook" with videocassettes or disks and thus no ability to impose access or fairness requirements on these media. On the other hand, the government can properly insist, when franchising a tele-

phone operation, that it be conducted essentially on a common carrier basis.

2. The reason for the regulation is generally the diversification principle – the notion that the diversity of sources of information is paramount. The First Amendment "rests on the assumption that the widest possible dissemination of information from diverse and antagonistic sources is essential to the welfare of the public, that a free press is a condition of a free society."[7]

3. As a constitutional matter, the approach taken to achieve the diversification principle must be the least intrusive – interfering least with daily editorial operation.[8]

As a policy matter, wherever feasible, the scheme to promote diversification should opt for structural (content-neutral) approaches rather than behavioral ones where the content of what is transmitted becomes the critical focus.

4. Regulation to promote diversification or robust debate in some other fashion should be clearly called for in the circumstances. Regulation serving no clear or solid diversity purpose is simply unwarranted government intrusion, even if it is structural in nature.

With the foregoing as background, I turn now to government policy as it affects *broadcast* journalism.

GOVERNMENT POLICY AFFECTING BROADCAST JOURNALISM

The equal opportunity provisions of Section 315

Broadcasting, especially television, is *the* most powerful mass medium. A majority of people rely primarily on television for news.[9] And candidates for important offices also place tremendous reliance on this medium. There are thus two ways in which broadcasting contributes to the informed electorate – a goal stressed at the outset of this discussion: broadcast journalism and the electronic soapbox. The first involves the broadcasters' own coverage of the political news – in newscasts, documentaries, interviews, special events such as staging a debate or covering a convention, and so forth. The second is the presentation of issues by the candidates themselves – directly rather than through the editorial selectivity of the broadcast journalist. The equal opportunity provision of Section 315 works against the full use of broadcasting in both respects.

Because the broadcaster is a public trustee, Congress decreed in the Communications Act that if the broadcaster allows one candidate for office to use its facilities, it must afford equal opportunities to all other qualified candidates for that office. The difficulty arises because of the fringe party candidates – Socialist, Socialist Labor, Vegetarian, Prohibition, and so forth (e.g., in the 1960 presidential election, there were fourteen candidates on the ballot in the several states). If then the broadcaster presented a clip of one of the major party candidates in the evening news, it would have to afford precisely equal time to these other candidates. Because a 1959 FCC ruling so required, Congress amended Section 315 to exempt appearances of candidates on four news-type programs: (1) bona fide newscasts, (2) bona fide news interview shows, (3) bona fide news documentaries (if the appearance of the candidate is incidental to presentation of the subjects covered), and (4) on-the-spot coverage of bona fide news events (e.g., the political conventions).

The exemptions have certainly helped; indeed, recent FCC constructions of the fourth exemption have made possible coverage of the presidential debates and press conferences. A recent Court ruling has opened the possibility of one or all three networks presenting the two major party presidential candidates in a series of back-to-back speeches on the great issues (e.g., one session on the economy; another on social issues; another on foreign policy; still another on defense).[10] But if the broadcast activity does not fit within an exemption, it can be blocked by the Section 315 requirement that equal hours of prime time be afforded the fringe party candidates – and many worthwhile programs do not fit. For example, the following types of broadcast journalism are blocked: in-depth interviews with the major candidates, documentaries delving into their positions and backgrounds with extensive use of interviews or clips (thus not falling within the present exemption with its emphasis on *incidental* appearance), or the appearance of a candidate on an *Advocates*-type program. The list could be extended greatly because it is not possible to forecast all the formats to which broadcast journalism might turn.

It is important to bear in mind that in these circumstances the Section 315 requirement accomplishes nothing: The program is not presented, so the fringe party candidates receive no time, and the public is simply deprived of many informational programs about candidates in whom it is really interested.

There are a number of good and readily apparent solutions to this problem. Congress could amend the law to make the equal opportunities requirement applicable only to paid broadcasts by candidates. This would maintain substantial protection against abuse and at the same time completely free broadcasters to make a maximum contribution to political discussion. As to the claim that they might abuse this freedom, the short answer is that we trust the broadcasters to act appropriately in the newscast area where they must make innumerable editorial judgments every day, so why shouldn't we trust them in the area of special events, where there is much more of a spotlight?

Or Section 315 could be amended to limit to major party candidates the applicability of the equal time provision in partisan general election campaigns. The term "major party" would be defined liberally to include all significant candidates (e.g., the candidate's party garnered 2 percent of the vote in the state in the last election or, if a new party, had petitions signed by 1 percent of the number of voters in the last election).[11] But so defined, it would eliminate the fringe party candidates who now block the presentation of so much worthwhile informational programming.

There are other approaches: Additional exemptions to 315(a) could be added to cover *any* bona fide journalistic effort that is under the licensee's control and not designed to advance a particular candidacy.[12] Or the equal opportunities provision could be made inapplicable to the presidential and vice-presidential races. After all, there is a spotlight on these races, and the 1960 suspension worked well in the general election: More than thirty-nine hours of free time were afforded the candidates (as contrasted with only about four hours four years later, when there was no suspension), with no abuses.

I have been making some obvious and quite pragmatic suggestions to improve the present situation markedly. There are other approaches that are more "blue sky" but would result in an *ideal* situation. There is, for example, the Voters Time proposal, put forth by the Twentieth Century Fund's Commission on Campaign Costs in the Electronic Era, which called for Congress to create a new form of nationwide television and radio campaign broadcasts for presidential candidates.[13] These programs would be presented in prime time simultaneously over every broadcast and cable TV facility in the United States during the thirty-five days before the election. Six 30-minute broadcasts would be allotted to candidates of major parties which had placed first or second in two of the three preceding elections. Candidates of parties on the ballot in three-quarters of the states accounting for a majority of electoral votes, which had won one-eighth of the votes in the preceding election, would receive two 30-minute program slots. And the candidate of a party meeting the three-quarters rule but not having obtained sufficient votes previously would be allowed one broadcast.

Other sweeping reforms could be examined in this field – for example, the British political broadcast election process of allocating set blocks of free television time to the parties to be used as they wish. I will not dwell on these far-ranging proposals because they have little chance of serious consideration, let alone enactment. The present major parties do not want them, and the electronic industries would strongly oppose them. Indeed, the bottom line here is that we cannot even take the easy and clearly called for modest reforms I have listed above, so as to allow our most powerful medium, broadcasting, to make its full contribution to robust debate and an informed electorate.

The fairness doctrine

The fairness doctrine, as described in the 1959 Amendments to the Communications Act – see Section 315(a) – requires broadcasters to afford reasonable opportunity for the discussion of conflicting views on issues of public importance. As the Supreme Court has stated in the seminal 1969 *Red Lion* case, this imposes a twofold duty: (1) to devote a reasonable amount of time to the coverage of controversial issues of public importance; and (2) to do so fairly. The first duty has never been effectively implemented by the FCC and will be discussed later in this essay. I treat here the second duty, about which so much has been written.[14]

First, however, I must note the present controversy and uncertainty concerning the doctrine's validity. The court of appeals has held that the fairness doctrine is not statutorily mandated.[15] The FCC, relying heavily upon the 1985 report,[16] declared in a 1987 report that "the fairness doctrine chills speech and is not narrowly tailored to achieve a substantial government interest," and that therefore "the fairness doctrine contravenes the First Amendment and thereby disserves the public interest."[17] The FCC also eliminated the first duty as no longer needed.[18]

Upon appeal, the court affirmed the FCC upon statutory – that is, nonconstitutional – grounds.[19] The petitioners have filed a petition for certiorari in the Supreme Court. Congress is considering legislation to require the doctrine and will probably pass such legislation in this Congress (the 101st). What is not certain is whether President Bush will sign the legislation or, like President Reagan, veto it; and if the latter, whether this Congress will override the veto. If the legislation were to become law, there would undoubtedly be a new suit brought by a broadcaster like Meredith Corp. to test its constitutionality.[20]

In these circumstances, I put aside the litigation and legislative activities and will simply give my own views of how I believe this important issue should be treated.

First, the charge that there is no longer any scarcity justifying a fairness doctrine ignores the basis for the unique broadcast regulatory approach. In the 1920s, there was no effective licensing of radio stations. Many more people wanted to broadcast than there were frequencies available. Engineering chaos resulted: Without government licensing, no one could be heard.

But the government did not pass out the licenses by auctioning them to the highest bidder as in the case of other scarce, valuable privileges like offshore oil or mineral drilling rights. The licenses are bestowed free as a public trust. To promote diversification, the government could have given each frequency or channel to several licensees, dividing the broadcast day or week. That would be constitutional but poor policy. So the government chooses one licensee and enjoins everyone else from using the frequency. But it insists that this short-term licensee – which acknowledges it has no property right in the frequency – act as a fiduciary for all those kept off by the government. The broadcaster thus volunteers for this public trust accountable to the government both initially and at renewal of the short-term license.[21]

Thus, the key issue of scarcity was not a relative one (e.g., the number of broadcast outlets as against newspapers). At the time of the 1969 *Red Lion* decision, there were 45 radio stations in New York City, all under the fairness doctrine, and only three daily newspapers. Nationwide, there were about 7,000 radio stations and only 1,700 daily newspapers. Rather, the scarcity turned on the need to license, *and that more people want to obtain such licenses than there are channels available.* That is still true today: There are no frequencies available in the top fifty markets where close to 70 percent of the population resides, and if a frequency opened in, say, Washington, there would be a dozen applicants for it.

That brings me to the second key issue – whether the fairness doctrine has chilling effects. In *Red Lion* the Court held that there was no showing of chilling effects on robust debate and that even if there were such effects, the commission could take action to compel coverage of issues.[22] From the point of view of our study, resolution of this issue of chilling effects is the critical one. Does the fairness doctrine simply add more speech and thus contribute to robust debate and an informed electorate, or does governmental intrusion to ensure fairness add such costs and possible penalties that it results in less coverage of issues or a skewing of the coverage to "safe" topics?

The studies of the FCC on this issue are in conflict. In 1974 the commission, under a Republican chairman (Richard E. Wiley), concluded that there was "no credible evidence of a chilling effect."[23] In 1985, under Republican chairman Mark Fowler, the commission reached the opposite conclusion.[24] The FCC relied heavily upon the showing of broadcast commentators like the National Association of Broadcasters (NAB) (which cited forty-five examples of chilling effects in its comments). These examples were extensively criticized by proponents of the doctrine.[25] Proponents argue that the doctrine works well on an informal negotiating basis[26] and does not interfere unduly with editorial operations, because the licensee is afforded so much discretion under the doctrine, with commission interference only in the few cases where the broadcaster's action can be said to be arbitrary.[27] As noted, the court affirmed the FCC's holding as not arbitrary, while itself observing "some perplexity" at the commission's insistence that "the doctrine's overall net effect was to reduce the coverage of controversial issues."[28] It pointed out the great difficulty of evaluating the "quality" of coverage.[29]

In my view, resolution of this issue results in a mixed verdict. The networks and large broadcasters are not chilled; they are "big boys" with adequate resources to defend themselves against any fairness complaint. They follow practices of fairness going far beyond the governmental requirements. Thus, the doctrine does not call for balance in every program – yet in all network documentaries, there is a strong effort to achieve balance in *that* program, so that the same audience hears both sides. I would thus tend to agree that the fairness doctrine has not caused the large broadcaster "to treat issues in any manner other than it would have done based on reasons of good journalistic practice."[30]

On the other hand, the smaller station might be adversely affected by the existence of the fairness doctrine. Such stations already tend to avoid controversy because it is not attractive to advertisers. The expense involved with the doctrine can reinforce this tendency, although it is thus not the major or controlling factor in why such stations avoid controversy (and why implementation of the first duty under the doctrine is so necessary).

Consider just one routine case, *Complaint of Sherwyn H. Hecht.*[31] The case was picked up in a Rand study of all fairness rulings in a six-month period.[32] The routine case seems at first blush to support the commission. The complaint was resolved in favor of the licensee. But the resolution took two and a half years, and the station's license was held up during the resolution process; it involved 480 man-hours of the station personnel's time and a legal bill of $20,000 (with station profits probably in the $50,000 range). This raises the question, What effect – perhaps even unconscious – does this have on the manager or news director the next time he is considering an editorial campaign on some contested local issue? What may be crucially important here is not the number of fairness rulings like *Hecht*, even if favorable.

Further, the government has a most difficult time in its effort to determine fairness or unfairness. Thus, the commission's practice of ad hoc fairness rulings has led it ever deeper into the journalistic process and has raised several serious problems:

1. *Defining issue or personal attack:* What is a controversial issue of public importance or a personal attack can be extremely difficult to judge; indeed, it is only after a commission ruling and court review that the matter can be definitively settled.[33]

2. *Defining balance or reasonable opportunity:* The doctrine

requires that *reasonable* opportunity be afforded the contrasting viewpoints on an issue. Lurking in the doctrine's administration is a very difficult question – namely, at what ratio of overall time (e.g., 2 to 1, 3 to 1, etc.) would the FCC say that the opportunity for presenting opposing viewpoints has not been reasonable? Even more difficult, how does frequency (e.g., imbalance of 5 or 8 or 12 to 1) or choice of time (e.g., prime or non-prime time) affect this evaluation? I refer here to one example, the *Public Media Center* case.[34] It establishes conclusively that there is no way for the FCC to determine rationally fairness in the complex situations of amount, frequency, and different time periods (e.g., side A got 4 to 1 in amount, but 1 to 8 in frequency, and its times were two-thirds prime whereas side B was all prime – and so on). A broadcaster can know whether it has been fair or not only when the FCC by fiat so declares.

3. *The "stopwatch" problem:* In order to determine whether there has been reasonable balance, the FCC literally has used a stopwatch to time the presentations made on both sides of an issue.[35] Even more difficult can be the problem of judging whether a particular program segment is for, against, or neutral in regard to a particular issue. In the gray areas that are bound to arise in this respect, it is not appropriate for a government agency to make such sensitive programming judgments.

4. *The "stop-time" problem:* An associated problem arises from the fact that during and after the period in which the FCC makes a decision on a fairness complaint, a broadcaster often continues its coverage of an issue for a number of reasons, such as new developments. The commission then finds that the circumstances on which it made its decision have changed significantly.[36]

There are solutions to these problems, but the commission has refused to adopt them. In my view, it is not legally feasible for the commission to eliminate the doctrine. As long as the licensee remains a public trustee, the doctrine is called for. A public trustee cannot act as the station in Jackson, Mississippi, did in the late 1950s and the 1960s: WLBT-TV was run by a racist who presented only the segregationist point of view; such a station is not acting consistently with the role of public fiduciary.[37] But that is what the commission should focus on: complying with the public-trustee obligation rather than trying to ensure fairness on every issue. The latter leads the commission to interfere deeply with daily broadcast journalism.

Thus, I suggest that the commission consider fairness matters only at renewal (or anytime it decides to revoke a license) and only under a *New York Times v. Sullivan* standard[38] – namely, whether there is a malicious pattern of unfairness inconsistent with the notion of a public fiduciary. If there is malice (i.e., operation deliberately violative of the doctrine or a pattern showing reckless disregard of the doctrine), the licensee lacks the requisite qualifications. It is the character of the licensee – whether it is a responsible public fiduciary – that is critical here, and not whether the licensee has achieved fairness on some particular issue. Good-faith mistakes should be tolerated, in order to allow breathing space for robust, wide-open debate. Thus, while appropriate complaints would be referred to licensees as received, they would not be considered at renewal (or revocation) absent a pattern of malice. And the FCC has the power to adopt this approach: It did not consider fairness complaints except at renewal until 1962, when it adopted the present ad hoc procedure over the protest of Congress.[39] Significantly, when the fairness doctrine was codified into law in 1959, it was applied at renewal on an overall basis.

The commission should also eliminate its personal attack and political editorializing rules. The FCC now does not apply the personal attack rule to most news-type situations (i.e., newscasts, interviews, on-the-spot coverage of news events). If those large-scale exemptions have proved satisfactory (as they have), why keep the rule for documentaries, and so forth? General fairness affords more flexibility to the licensee and suffices.

Similarly, the political editorializing rule makes no sense and is chilling. If the licensee has hours of programming on both sides of a ballot issue and then adds its editorial voice, it need do nothing; general fairness has been served. But in the same situation, if its editorial endorses a candidate, it must notify all the rivals and afford them opportunity to respond. Why, if fairness has been achieved in the station's programming?

Finally, the FCC should consider promoting voluntary access schemes instead of dumping cold water on them.[40] Indeed, Congress should consider requiring such access schemes (e.g., setting aside one hour per week for spot announcements and lengthier programming, like the "op-ed" approach that has worked so well for newspapers).[41] Access has the following advantages over fairness:

1. With access, a broader range of controversial issues will receive airtime. The licensee will be presenting issues on which it believes the public should be informed. But now there will be a valuable supplement: Persons granted access will be free to introduce significant issues that the licensee ignores.

2. The access scheme will render the great majority of fairness complaints nugatory. Only in the most egregious cases would the FCC have to resort to action. A substantial portion of complaints that reach the FCC come from disgruntled viewers with no other recourse. An access scheme thus provides an effective alternative to government intervention.

3. Access allows prompt response to controversial issues. Under the FCC's present complaint-oriented approach, it takes months and often years to resolve a fairness dispute.[42] By that time the issue may be moot or of much reduced importance.

4. Views aired during access time will come from partisan spokesmen, a factor both the Supreme Court and the FCC have considered important, but which the commission has never enforced.[43]

Efficacy of public trustee scheme with respect to informational programming

The Communications Act requires the broadcaster to devote a reasonable amount of time to informational programming so that broadcasting will make its contribution to an informed electorate.[44] Although the FCC has stressed the importance of this duty since 1949,[45] it has failed miserably in its implementation of the policy. Thus, it has authorized operation with 0/0 percent in news and public affairs, and less than 1 percent informational service.[46] In a half century of regulation, it has never denied a license for failure to deliver sufficient news or public affairs programming.

The FCC today is still emphasizing the critical importance of issue-oriented programming (defined broadly in the dictionary sense).[47] Indeed, that is its entire focus for public service programming. Yet its implementation remains just as woefully inadequate.

The commission has eliminated the first prong of the fairness doctrine – the duty to devote a reasonable amount of time to controversial issues of public importance.[48] It has done so on most dubious grounds – that with the elimination of the second prong (the duty to be fair), the broadcaster will now present sufficient amounts of such controversial-issue programming.[49] But what if the broadcaster simply wants to present entertainment fare like MTV or home shopping material? The plain truth is that the FCC now has no policy at renewal that would require a station to present controversial-issue programming.

There remains the duty to present community issue-oriented programming.[50] This programming category is much broader than controversial-issue material and really includes all nonentertainment fare.[51] But on this broad category the commission itself now receives no programming information. It renews stations with only a postcard before it, stating that all required information has been placed in the public file.[52] It is thus placing complete reliance on the public to bring to its attention any case of inadequate public service operation (i.e., insufficient issue-oriented programming). But the public is busy with its own matters; there is no basis, in theory or experience, for the agency to shift this statutory burden to the public.[53]

Incredibly, the FCC at the same time deprived the public of

the information it needed to perform this "watchdog" function. For the commission eliminated its requirement of logs and instead simply required the licensee to list quarterly at least five example issues, with some illustrative programs under each.[54] Such a list shows only a minuscule amount of the station's issue-oriented programming;[55] to determine the overall amount, the public would be put to the extraordinary burden of monitoring the many stations in the area. Under court order, the FCC reluctantly made available sufficient programming material so that an interested person could petition to deny.[56] The final irony is that the licensee does keep records of its public service programming, as it can never tell when it will face a renewal challenge, ordinary or comparative.[57] The records are just not public, as the FCC is really hostile to public participation, despite the statutory command.

The commission itself has no notion of how its deregulatory policies are working; it gets no programming data and conducts no special studies. There has been one such study, conducted by the Radio and Television News Directors Association in 1984. It found that "radio stations across the country are reducing the amount of air time devoted to public affairs and news programming, as a result of Federal deregulation and the broadcast industry's changing economics"; in television, "some cutbacks are also being made, but to a much lesser extent." The research found that public affairs programming – the in-depth treatment of issues – has suffered a "substantial reduction in airtime" since the FCC's deregulatory act of 1981.[58]

There are, I believe, two main solutions to this regulatory botch. The first and most obvious one is to eliminate the comparative renewal, which is supposed to spur substantial as against minimal service,[59] and in its place simply establish percentage guidelines for substantial service for the two critical programming areas – local and informational (including children's informational). The percentage should reflect a reasonable notion of substantial service (i.e., around the median for stations appropriately grouped by their nature – large or small market; VHF or UHF; network affiliate or independent; and for the hours 6:00 A.M. to midnight and prime time). All stations would be required to meet the guidelines or establish good cause for not doing so, with a report to Congress of any waivers.

Sound policy, I believe, strongly calls for the rule rather than the ad hoc approach. The latter disserves the public interest for two reasons. First, it does not inform the broadcaster or the public of what the licensee's responsibilities are in this most important programming area. Terms such as "reasonable" or "substantial" amounts of informational programming are mushy. As former Chairman Dean Burch testified concerning such terms, "These are, in the vernacular, 'marshmallow' phrases – they mean almost nothing in and of themselves or, conversely, almost anything that one wants them to mean."[60] Vagueness, with its consequent "unbridled administrative discretion,"[61] creates a further danger that the renewal evaluation might chill the exercise of licensee First Amendment rights. As the court stated in *Greater Boston Television v. FCC*, "a question would arise whether administrative discretion to deny renewal expectancies, which must exist under any standard, must not be reasonably confined by ground rules and standards."[62]

This point is crucial. It is not a matter of the FCC's avoiding appraisal of the renewal applicant's programming under one approach as compared with another. Under the statutory scheme, the critical issue is the incumbent's record, and programming is the essence of that record. The question is whether in this sensitive area the First Amendment is served by examination of an incumbent's programming without any objective standards that the licensee has had the opportunity to meet.

Second, the ad hoc approach is ineffective. Because terms such as "reasonable" or "substantial" amount of time do not really inform the licensee of its responsibilities, and because the commercial nature of the licensee militates against performance in this area, particularly in public affairs, many stations tend to perform poorly. If the renewal applicant then faces a challenge to its operation on this score, the agency also tends to protect the applicant against the challenge. For broadcasters are operating in the dark because of FCC failure, and the agency is thus a partner to the station's dilemma at renewal. If the FCC moves against the broadcaster in the "subjective" circumstances, there is both unfairness and the serious First Amendment problems noted in *Greater Boston.* In short, there is a wide gap between the promise of the FCC's high-sounding proclamations and its performance in implementing them on an ad hoc basis.

There is a second and much more sweeping reform. As noted, there has been no effective FCC enforcement of these obvious public service requirements for the last half century; the FCC has never denied a license for failure to provide sufficient local, informational, or children's programming. The comparative renewal process is just as great a charade. The incumbent always wins, no matter what its past record, and the court has roundly condemned the commission for failure to discharge its statutory obligation.[63]

Further, the present content regulation strains the First Amendment, as shown by several incidents (e.g., drug lyrics; topless radio; fairness complaints like the *Hecht* one previously discussed).[64]

After more than half a century of failure, it is time to try a different approach. Content or behavioral regulation cannot fill the real gaps in the marketplace, and any attempt to do so would run afoul of the First Amendment.

Common sense establishes that there *are* gaps. The more than nine thousand commercial radio stations do an excellent job in supplying a variety of formats, usually interspersed with brief news and other talk materials. People welcome these services – they stand the test of the marketplace.

But a public trustee should deliver significant amounts of worthwhile programming for children, who listen so much to radio. Commercial radio fails here. Nor will one hear serious drama – Faulkner or Shakespeare or new playwrights – on commercial radio. Commercial radio will not broadcast lengthy public affairs shows; it will not provide a "news magazine" or gavel-to-gavel coverage of great national issues like the Panama Treaty debate.

What I am describing is public radio, which now faces a serious financial crisis in this country. And that brings me to my substitute scheme. Why not eliminate the public-trustee concept (i.e., renewal and the fairness doctrine) and in its place exact a modest spectrum fee – say, 1 percent of gross revenues, fixed for a 35-year term in a contract? The broadcaster volunteered to be a public trustee, and it is now being relieved of that responsibility. But the question then arises, Why is the broadcaster on that frequency, with all others enjoined by the government? Why not selection by lot or auction? Clearly this would be too disruptive in light of the long-established system, but it is not too disruptive to demand a reasonably modest fee for the government-granted and protected privilege of "grazing" on the spectrum range.

The moneys obtained would go to the general treasury and could be appropriated by Congress periodically to accomplish more directly and effectively goals not fulfilled in the marketplace – for example, educational, cultural, dramatic, minority, and in-depth informational programming. This could be done through the Corporation for Public Broadcasting (CPB) for public radio or through funding minority ownership and would be reviewed periodically in the appropriation process.

Congress would thus have ended ineffectual content regulation, with its economic and First Amendment costs, and would now have a rational structure. It would no longer be saying to commercial broadcasters, "You are a business impressed with the public interest and must present educational and informational programming." The commercial broadcaster would be free to act as it does today, and the modest sums taken from it for exclusive "grazing" rights would support the public broadcaster, who *is* motivated to present educational, cultural, in-depth informational service. In this connection, Congress should also act to insulate the public broadcast system better from political interference (as was the case during the Nixon administration); nominees for

CPB should come from a list of five names selected by prestigious special commissions, rather the present method of presidential choice on a purely political basis.

I see little downside to this spectrum fee approach. It is true that a station could then act as WXUR-AM did in Media, Pennsylvania;[65] but the public in the Philadelphia area, with its large number of radio outlets, will survive such partisanship. It is also true that with the end of the fairness doctrine, one side could outspend the other on, say, a ballot issue. But that is true today where the discrepancy can be quite large – 5 to 1 in overall time – before fairness comes into play; significantly, we do not equalize war chests in the political area. In any event, I do not believe that we should hold on to this present scheme, with all its flaws, for this one purpose, when much can be gained by shifting to the alternative approach I have urged.

I would also favor this approach in television, but I recognize that Congress may be reluctant to move so rapidly in light of the much smaller number of TV outlets. Therefore, I would await the experience with radio deregulation and, if it is successful, use the same approach in television about five years later. In the meantime, the regulation of television should be made more effective along the lines I have described.

I would maintain the multiple-ownership rules. When the government bestows a scarce privilege in the mass media area, it makes sense to promote the *Associated Press* principle – to diversify as much as possible the sources of information coming to the people. The most important aspect of diversification is in the local area. Certainly no one entity should own two TV stations in the same market or a local daily newspaper and a local TV station. Because people get their news primarily from TV and secondarily from newspapers, these two powerful media should be in different hands. Note that this does not prevent newspapers from owning TV stations. The *Washington Post* can readily own the TV station on Channel 4 in Detroit rather than Channel 9 in Washington.

The second most important area is regional concentration: One entity should not control the editorial policy of five or more stations in, say, the New York State area, as there are statewide political and ballot issues. The commission erred, therefore, in its refusal to adopt any effective regulation in this area.[66]

GOVERNMENT POLICY AND THE NEW TECHNOLOGIES

The biggest plus in the entire government policy area is the "letting in" process that now holds sway. The FCC will permit all new services to have their chance in the marketplace: Direct Broadcast Satellite (DBS), Multipoint Distribution Systems (MDS, including multichannel MDS), Operational Fixed-Microwave Service (OFS), cable television (by far the most important new technology to challenge television broadcasting), Satellite Master Antenna Services (SMATV), low-power TV, teletext, videotext, and so on. (And significantly, some new developments such as the videocassette and disk wholly escape government regulation.) Although the FCC's authorization processes are flawed (i.e., the use of the lottery technique instead of auctioning), it is seeking to promote new services for the competition and diversity they represent. One need only look at cable TV, with program services like Cable News Network or C-SPAN, to see how much these new services can contribute to attaining the goals listed at the outset of this discussion.

The FCC policy has been reinforced in recent law. In the 1985 FCC authorization legislation,[67] Congress provided that "it shall be the policy of the United States to encourage the provision of new technologies and services to the public," and fixed a twelve-month period for resolution of petitions and applications for such new services.

Direct Broadcast Satellite (DBS)

This is not to say, however, that all aspects of government policy applicable to the new technologies are sound. In the

DBS field, the FCC adopted a "pick 'em" policy – that is, the applicant could choose whether it wanted to conduct its operation as a common carrier, a broadcaster, or a private radio operator, with the appropriate regulatory scheme then being made applicable (e.g., if a broadcaster, then Section 315 – equal time and fairness – would apply).[68] Even more important, if one became a DBS entrepreneur by leasing transponders from a common carrier like RCA or Western Union, no regulation was applicable; the situation is then analogous to conducting an operation over the facilities of a telephone company. When the Court of Appeals considered this issue in 1984, however, it held that the operation fit the definition of broadcasting in Section 3(o) of the Communications Act, and therefore either the DBS entrepreneur or the common carrier must be required to observe the broadcast provisions of the Communications Act.[69]

In my view, this is a flawed ruling. The existence of common-carrier facilities (in this case the large number of transponders available to anyone who wishes to undertake a DBS operation) satisfies the public interest requirement of diversification. There is no need to overlay the area with broadcast requirements. In the future there will be a fiber-optic highway into every home, permitting thousands of TV operations: Would the court insist on broadcast requirements of fairness, and the rest?

The FCC's policy of laying no large "regulatory trips" on a new service like DBS seems to me sound. DBS may struggle along, never achieving very great penetration and thus having little effect on the public. Or it may succeed greatly. If the latter, it will be time to consider, for example, what diversification policies are required to prevent undue concentration. But close regulation today would be premature, perhaps unnecessary, and in all likelihood stifling.

Although the court in the *NAB* case did not express an opinion on Multipoint Distribution Systems,[70] its ruling has obvious applicability to these, where similarly the commission hopes to avoid broadcast regulation. The commission therefore adopted a new tactic – classifying all pay-TV operations as nonbroadcast in nature, however delivered, in order to make sense out of the field.[71]

Teletext and videotext

In 1983, the FCC authorized broadcast teletext under an "open market" approach.[72] Defining teletext broadly, the FCC now permits broadcasters to offer any type of data and any kind of service (point-to-point, point-to-multipoint; service to the public at large, only to segments, advertiser-supported, pay, etc.). This flexible approach is similar to that developed for DBS except that here broadcasters, as the primary licensees, remain responsible for all teletext transmissions. Because of its emphasis on the marketplace, the FCC has declined to specify technical standards. Although the marketplace may eventually sort out the standards issue, this decision may hamper the development of the service (and videotext as well), as it has done in the case of AM Stereo.

As for its regulatory status, the FCC has deemed teletext to be an "ancillary" service. Using this definition, the commission held that as a legal and policy matter, traditional broadcast content regulation (fairness, equal time, etc.) is inapplicable to teletext transmissions. In part, the FCC's decision is based on "teletext's unique characteristics as a print medium,"[73] as well as the fact that Congress did not have this service in mind when it enacted the content provisions.

Upon appeal, the court held that teletext fits the definition of broadcasting, since the vertical blanking interval in which teletext exists is an integral part of the broadcast signal. The court therefore ruled that the commission could not waive *statutory* requirements applicable to broadcasting (e.g., equal opportunities for rival candidates, reasonable access for candidates for federal office). It found that the fairness doctrine is not statutorily required and that the FCC acted reasonably in not applying it to this new service.[74]

Videotext, as opposed to teletext, is a two-way, interactive service transmitted via either telephone lines or cable TV. Although the means of transmission (telephone and to a lesser extent cable TV) are regulated, there is no regulation of the videotext services themselves, either as to entry or content.

One important policy matter needs to be considered here – the role of the divested Bell companies. Under the Modified Final Judgment in the AT&T antitrust suit,[75] the Bell companies are not permitted to offer information services. In a 1987 ruling, the district court relaxed that prohibition to allow them to provide an infrastructure for efficient, nationwide videotext services.[76] The court did not find that the risk of anticompetitive action by the Bell companies is "insignificant"; rather, that risk "is, on balance, outweighed by other considerations."[77] Those considerations are that the United States, like other industrial nations, is entering the information age, that this nation's development of a national videotext service is lagging behind that of countries like France and Japan, and that "the broad scale and the reasonable cost criteria necessary for a successful system can be met only by permitting the Regional Companies to provide the necessary infrastructure components for efficient videotex services on an integrated basis."[78] The court thus allows the Bell companies to provide information services for the "transmission" of information, but not to generate or manipulate content.[79]

This latter restriction prevents the Bell companies from rendering electronic yellow pages service. The companies have been deeply involved in directory assistance as a natural adjunct to running the local network. Under the Modified Final Judgment they continued such print directory assistance, both white pages and yellow pages. There will be a gradual evolution to electronic directory assistance. The district court allowed the Bell companies to engage in electronic white pages but not in yellow pages, because, as noted, that would constitute content generation or manipulation. The court, however, never engaged in any cost-benefit analysis.

The Bell companies and the Videotex Industry of America argued that there would be great benefit from their provision of electronic yellow pages.[80] Videotext is a difficult service to establish, as shown by the experience in the United

States and several countries, and electronic yellow pages may be the necessary "core" element in gaining consumer acceptance. The district court acknowledged that this rationale "does contain a grain of truth,"[81] but never determined how important it is to allow this service – never ascertained whether it is indeed the core service that will facilitate the spread of a nationwide infrastructure for commerce and information. If it is, the benefits to commerce and to First Amendment considerations (upon which the district court places great reliance)[82] are enormous. In short, the Bell companies may well be *the* entities that can effect an electronic yellow pages service. Others, like newspapers, appear today to be phantom competitors. Yet the court seems motivated to protect the newspapers' classified base. Such protectionism is no more warranted here than in the case of the broadcaster–cable television or cable television–VCR.

Considerable controversy also surfaces today over the proposed entry of telephone companies into cable television. The 1984 Cable Television Policy Act[83] sought to implement diversification policy[84] by requiring cable systems with thirty-six or more channels to make 10 percent to 15 percent of their capacity available for leased channel access (i.e., with no censorship by the cable operator).[85] Because of its restrictive conditions, this provision has never been implemented. The cable television operator thus has a monopoly over the many TV channels into the home, in contravention of the *Associated Press* principle. Telcos are increasingly using fiber optics in their systems, creating the potential for competition to the cable systems, and more important, for the entry of a broadband telecommunication entity that will meet the *Associated Press* principle – that is, a true common carrier with a separation of content and conduit. This development – video publishing over a common carrier, like print (magazines) publishing over the Postal Service – is obviously of great benefit to the First Amendment.

However, since any telco entry faces an entrenched broadband competitor, cable, which has already attained 54 percent penetration of U.S. TV homes and passes 85 percent of such homes, it may be necessary to allow the telco, while operating largely as a common carrier, also to "prime the pump" by itself engaging in some video content origination.[86] One such plan might be a limited minority investment in programming operations permitted for a reasonable but specified period, and divestiture at the end of this period. But under the district court's approach, no such telco operation in cable television would be permissible, because it involves content generation. The result might well be the continuation of the present unfortunate situation from the viewpoint of the First Amendment. Again, what is needed is not rigid adherence to a mechanical standard ("content: ergo no") but rather a cost-benefit analysis of detriments as against possible great gains to the nation.

Cable TV

Cable TV is by far the most important of the new video services (with the VCR in second place). As noted, cable has reached 54 percent penetration of U.S. TV households. Modern cable has a large channel capacity, is served by more than sixty cable programmers, and has the ability to render local service. It can therefore make a large contribution toward achieving the goals set out initially. Does government policy assist or hinder cable in making such a contribution?

One threshold issue has to be resolved here: namely, what regulatory model is constitutionally required. This is a difficult question in light of cable's hybrid nature – part broadcaster (in its carriage of distant signals); part common carrier (in its data transmission operations); and part video publisher (in its local originations and carriage of cable programmers). Cable argues that it is a telepublisher, using no part of the spectrum and thus coming under the print model; it is true that it is almost always a monopoly service, but the monopoly newspaper comes under the full benefits of *Miami Herald v. Tornillo*. The courts are divided on this issue, with several recent decisions supporting cable's position.[87] The discussions are to some extent dicta, with countering dicta in other cases. Until the Supreme Court speaks on the issue, it must be regarded as unsettled.

In my view, cable can be subjected to a regulatory scheme in order to promote sound diversification policies. The modern cable operator asserts the right to be the editor in thirty, fifty, or even a hundred or more channels. Such control by cable over content is unsound for two reasons.

First, it flagrantly violates the *Associated Press* principle that the American people should receive information from as diverse and antagonistic sources as possible. Second, cable can be an essential or "bottleneck" facility for a growing segment of video programming. Except for a handful of places, there is only one cable operator in a city (or in a given area of the large cities). To reach the 50 percent to 55 percent of the TV homes on the cable, a pay entrepreneur or a new UHF station, for example, must have access to the cable system. There is no other practical way into the cable homes. And the growing vertical integration of the cable industry – large multiple-system owners developing their own programming networks – exacerbates this bottleneck problem.[88]

Two solutions are obvious. First, require the modern cable operator to set aside some reasonable amount of its large channel capacity on a common-carrier basis – that is, nondiscriminatory access on a first-come, first-served basis, with no right of censorship; and second, on all other channels, except those devoted to the system's own local origination, bar the cable operator from editorial control over individual programs. The operator could decide on these latter channels whether and how to carry HBO or CNN or USA, on what "tier" to place the particular service, and what rate to charge. But it could not censor any program on CNN or the other networks. Because the cable operator is thus not responsible for content, it would be exempt on these and the leased channels from the application of the fairness doctrine or equal time or from libel, slander, or obscenity suits. The programmer would be held responsible for any libel or obscenity transgressions.

As stated, the cable industry argues that it is like print – a telepublisher – because it does not use the radio spectrum, and no one could constitutionally require a newspaper to set aside some percentage of its pages for leased access or tell a publisher that it cannot be the editor on all its pages. Cable concedes that it uses the streets, but – it argues – so also do the newspaper delivery trucks. But unlike the newspaper, cable must obtain a government franchise to conduct its business and this franchise is necessarily limited, both technically and economically. Actually, like telephone, it is bestowed as a de facto monopoly – that is, although it is labeled nonexclusive, only one award is given. But this monopoly aspect is not critical. What is crucial is that no franchising authority will give out an unlimited number of permits to string wires through or under the streets; it is simply too disruptive and, in any event, space on poles or in ducts is limited.

Suppose a telephone company applied for a franchise to use the streets for its wires, but insisted that it had a First Amendment right to pass on the content of intelligence carried on these wires. The franchising authority would obviously demur, stating that its policy was to bestow telephone franchises only on a separation of content and conduit (and note that this would be true even if there were several local phone companies); if the applicant did not want to comply with this sound policy, it should step aside and allow others willing to accede to it to come forward. Clearly the government would be sustained in this position. And just as clearly, in my view, a cable company can be required, as a condition of its franchise, to set aside some reasonable portion of its large channel capacity for common-carrier operation. This strongly promotes the First Amendment.

The cable industry also argues that cable in the major markets is a high-risk business and that it must be afforded control in order to experiment and to innovate. But no one today is arguing for a *complete* separation. Rather, the issue is whether some reasonable percentage of the modern cable system's large capacity should be made available for leased channel access. Surely it is enough if cable controls what programmer or programming is carried on forty-four out of fifty-four channels.

The Cable Communications Policy Act of 1984 implements these concepts. While soundly ruling out programming regulation, the act seeks to foster the public interest through a different, structural (i.e., content-neutral) approach aimed at diversifying the sources of information over cable (the *Associated Press* principle). It thus proscribes local cross-ownership of cable by broadcast or telephone entities; requires that systems with thirty-six or more channels set aside 10 percent to 15 percent of capacity for leased access for video programming; and permits the franchising authority to specify channels for public, educational, and governmental use, with facilities support and a franchise fee not to exceed 5 percent of overall cable revenues. The cable operator is to exercise no editorial control over the leased or public, educational, and governmental channels.

This structural approach is sound – far superior to the broadcast, content-focused scheme. The flaw lies in its incomplete or inadequate implementation in the act. Thus, although the franchising authority may not establish requirements for video programming or other information services, it can enforce requirements in the franchise "for broad categories of video programming or other services."[89] This is not only content regulation but even can become quite specific, because there can be only one news, music, and so on, channel.

Even more important, the new act fails to deal with some existing provisions that make cable subject to broadcast content requirements. In 1972, Congress amended Section 315 to provide that for the purposes of the section, "the term 'broadcasting station' includes a community antenna system."[90] This apparently makes fairness and equal opportunities applicable to cable although there is no discussion of this result in the legislative history (and no implementation because of a dearth of complaints to the FCC). There is also some evidence that Section 312(a)(7), calling for reasonable access for candidates for federal office, applies to cable,[91] although the FCC has now questioned the applicability of the section to cable.[92] These content provisions should not be made applicable to cable, with its abundance of channels; the least intrusive method should be employed to accomplish the diversification goal and that is access, not fairness or similar provisions.

The act also has flaws in implementing the structural (access) approach. Thus, a video programmer complaining that the terms for leased access are onerous is forced to go to court and win against a "presumption" that the terms are reasonable "unless shown by clear and convincing evidence to the contrary."[93] But the programmer needs immediate access; it cannot afford lengthy court proceedings, with the dice so loaded against it. As a practical matter, the leased channel provision is thus apt to be little used. An alternative was suggested: to use compulsory arbitration in the event of a dispute, while the programmer obtains immediate access, but the cable industry strongly resisted this approach.

The provision for public, educational, and government broadcasting also contains a serious flaw. The problem here was never provision of channel capacity on these large modern systems but, rather, financial support. The FCC rule in existence at the time of the act permitted a 3 percent franchise fee (to defray regulatory costs) and an additional 2 percent fee if the funds were used for cable-related purposes, most often for public, educational, and governmental programming. The act, however, allows the cities to have a 5 percent fee with no requirement that revenues be used for cable purposes.[94] The cities insisted that there be no strings, and Congress was indifferent to a proposal that there be 1 percent for national access programming and 1 percent for local. The act is thus a step backward from the previous regulatory scheme. Cable subscribers are being taxed with no assured benefits. Indeed, this raises a most serious constitutional issue.[95]

I believe it is time to look to television on an overall basis, just as the viewer does. If a 3 percent franchise fee (taken from an overall 5 percent fee) were dedicated to production of national programming, and combined with a 2 percent spectrum fee on commercial television revenues, the result would be a sum of $1 billion for the production of programs for distribution over public telecommunications (e.g., public television; cable access or other channels; VCR; disk; etc.). The remainder of a 5 percent franchise fee would be used to defray the cost of regulation (not usually a substantial figure) and to support local access programming, including any "local C-SPAN" effort.[96]

The cross-ownership provisions similarly accomplish little, because the FCC now has such rules. The one sound advance – a bar on cable–newspaper cross-ownership in the same area – was eliminated because of pressures from the newspaper lobby.

LIBEL

I turn now to an issue involving all the mass media – libel. There is no question that libel law is needed. The Supreme Court would clearly so hold, and one can think of several suits where libel law markedly served the public interest (e.g., the John Henry Faulk suit against Aware). Rather, what is called for is a proper balance between two contending public interest considerations: freedom of expression and the strong interest in personal reputation.

The Supreme Court sought to strike such a balance in the seminal 1964 case, *New York Times v. Sullivan*. The Court held that the common law rule making the critic of official conduct guarantee the truth of factual assertions was unconstitutional because it led to self-censorship. If truth must be proved as a defense against libel actions, Justice Brennan wrote, "would-be critics of official conduct may be deterred from voicing their criticism, even though it is believed to be true and even though it is in fact true, because of doubt whether it can be proved in court or fear of the expense of having to do so."[97] Any such rule, the Court concluded, would "dampen the vigor and limit the variety of public debate."[98] The Court found "a profound national commitment to the principle that debate on public issues should be uninhibited, robust and wide-open."[99] The Court therefore held that in libel suits by public officials against their critics, the plaintiff must prove that the allegedly defamatory statement was made with "actual malice," defined in the decision as meaning "with knowledge that [the statement] was false or with reckless disregard of whether it was false or not."[100]

Sullivan, however, has not settled the issue of the proper balance. Plaintiff's attorneys believe that the case goes too far in protecting the press, whereas the press argues that it does not go far enough. A host of problems certainly remains.

First, libel suits seeking hundreds of millions of dollars have been filed by such plaintiffs as General Westmoreland and Ariel Sharon. The press believes that the huge legal costs to defend these suits imperil the very vigor of public debate sought to be encouraged by *Sullivan*. The small press can be wiped out by adverse verdicts, and even the large press can be influenced, albeit unconsciously, to avoid such costs.

Second, it is not clear which plaintiffs must meet the *Sullivan* test of actual malice. The Court, beginning in *Sullivan* with "public officials," extended the malice standard to "public figures" and held that people involved in issues of significant public interest were public figures, regardless of fame; prominence of the issue rather than of the person was controlling. But the Court has since retracted that approach and is now narrowing the definition of "public person."[101]

Third, there is the problem of proving that a defendant has stated a falsehood knowingly or recklessly. To do so, the Court held in the 1979 case *Herbert v. Lando* that a plaintiff can inquire into the defendant's state of mind at the time the piece was being composed.[102] This means turning over internal memoranda and early drafts of the piece, and interviews with all involved, to glean the author's attitudes or thoughts. This procedure, it is argued, undermines the independence of the press and the prepublication editorial scrutiny that should attend investigative journalism.

Finally, there is the extraordinary chasm between results at the trial and the appellate level: Juries find for the plaintiff in more than 80 percent of the cases, and appellate tribunals, finding that actual malice was not proved, reverse in 80 percent. This would seem to indicate the need for summary judgment for the defendant in more cases and, at the least, for better instructions on what actual malice is ("constitutional malice," as used by Judge Sofaer in the Sharon case would appear to be a better term).[103] It might be helpful here to use special questions to the jurors and elicit separate responses by the jurors as they reach their verdicts on each question (again the Sharon suit).[104]

A number of suggestions have been made to alleviate some of these problems. None is perfect, but some are worth noting.

1. A considerable case can be made for eliminating punitive damages in libel suits. Punitive damages are not compensation for injury; rather, they have the sole purpose of deterrence. But deterrence, while normally appropriate, works here against the *Sullivan* goal: The possibility of huge punitive damage awards forces self-censorship, so that reporters say only what they are *certain* they could prove if they were sued. Significantly, in the *Dun & Bradstreet* case, where Chief Justice Burger and Justice White in concurring opinions called for reexamination of *Sullivan*, Justice White also suggested that the judiciary or the legislature might look to controlling the now unrestricted damage awards in libel suits.

2. Congress could authorize a specialized declaratory judgment action that could be invoked by the plaintiff, with the sole issue being whether the statements are true or false. In light of *Sullivan*, there would be no damages, but this would enable plaintiffs to vindicate their reputations; and it would free defendants from the risk of large damage awards and the discovery procedures probing mental processes and internal decisions.

3. Victims could be given a right to reply promptly at the expense of the person or institution responsible for the alleged defamation, with the reply receiving comparable exposure; a lawsuit would follow only if this right were refused.

4. Libel plaintiffs and defendants could be encouraged to use arbitration and similar mediation mechanisms for resolu-

tion of their disputes. Thus, Congress could require that as a prerequisite to access to the federal courts, the parties to a libel action certify that they discussed in good faith the possibility of arbitration.

5. The "English rule" could be used in libel cases, with the loser paying the winner's reasonable legal costs.

6. *Sullivan* could be modified to eliminate "recklessness" and confine liability to purposeful distortion of the truth. Also, a clear distinction could be made between public figures and public officials, doing away entirely with libel actions by public officials.[105]

NOTES

1 *Associated Press v. United States*, 326 U.S. 1, 20 (1945).
2 H. Kalven, "Broadcasting, Public Policy and the First Amendment," *Journal of Law and Economics* 10 (1967): 15, 30.
3 See Section 315(a), 47 U.S.C. 315(a); *Red Lion Broadcasting v. FCC*, 395 U.S. 367 (1969).
4 See *Miami Herald v. Tornillo*, 418 U.S. 241 (1974).
5 See *HBO v. FCC*, 567 F.2d 9, 45–48 (D.C. Cir. 1977), *cert. denied*, 434 U.S. 829 (1977).
6 *National Association of Regulatory Utilities Commissioner v. FCC*, 533 F.2d 601, 608 (D.C. Cir. 1976).
7 *U.S. v. Associated Press*, at 20.
8 See, e.g., *Hynes v. Mayor of Oradell*, 425 U.S. 610 (1976); *Gooding v. Wilson*, 405 U.S. 518 (1972); *Keyishian v. Board of Regents*, 385 U.S. 589 (1967); *Griswold v. Connecticut*, 381 U.S. 479 (1965).
9 See Roper Organization, *Public Attitudes Toward Television and Other Media in a Time of Change* (1985), pp. 10–11: 65 percent of the population rely primarily on TV for news, up from 51 percent in 1959.
10 See *King Broadcasting v. FCC*, Case No. 88–1367, D.C. Cir., decided November 1, 1988.
11 See First Report and Order, 48 FCC 2d 1, at par. 35 (1972).
12 Ibid., at par. 36.
13 See Hearings before the Senate Communications Subcommittee, on S. 2876, 91st Cong., 1st sess., at 34–44.
14 See, e.g., Steven J. Simmons, *The Fairness Doctrine and the Media*

(Berkeley: University of California Press, 1978); Ford Rowan, *Broadcast Fairness* (New York: Longman, 1984).

15 See *Telecommunications Research and Action Center v. FCC,* 801 F.2d 501 *reh'g en banc denied,* 806 F.2d 1115 (D.C. Cir. 1986) (TRAC), *cert. denied,* 107 S.Ct. 3196 (1987).

16 *Inquiry into Alternatives to the General Fairness Obligations of Broadcast Licensees,* 102 FCC 2d 143 (1985).

17 *Syracuse Peace Council,* 2 FCC Rcd. 5043, 5057 (1987), *recon. denied,* 3 FCC 2d 2035 (1988).

18 2 FCC Rcd. at 5048–52; 3 FCC Rcd. at 2039–42.

19 *Syracuse Peace Council v. FCC,* Case No. 87–1516, D.C. Cir., decided February 10, 1989, pet. for rehearing pending.

20 *Meredith Corp. v. FCC,* 809 F.2d 863 (D.C. Cir. 1987).

21 See *Red Lion.*

22 At 367. But see *Miami Herald v. Tornillo,* where the Court invalidated a print fairness approach on the grounds that it would be chilling, with no more evidence before it than in *Red Lion.* In my view, there is no real way to square *Tornillo* with *Red Lion.* See H. Geller and D. Lampert, "Cable Content Regulation and the First Amendment," *Catholic Law Review* 32 (1983): 603, 617–18. Indeed, the proposition that there should be the least intrusive government action is contradicted by the Court's affirmation of the fairness approach in *Red Lion,* because contrary to the Court's observation in *CBS v. DNC,* 412 U.S. 94 (1973), fairness, particularly as implemented by the FCC on a case-by-case basis, represents a deep intrusion into daily editorial decision making, whereas there are less intrusive content-neutral approaches to achieve diversification of sources of information. See Henry Geller, *The Fairness Doctrine,* The Rand Corp., R-1412-FF (December 1973); but see *NCCB v. FCC,* 567 F.2d 1095, 1115–16 (D.C. Cir. 1977), *cert. denied,* 436 U.S. 926 (1977). I believe that the explanation rests on Holmes's aphorism "the life of the life is not logic; it is experience"; the broadcast system had become entrenched with the public trustee–fairness approach for a half century, and the Court would not disrupt this long "experience."

23 *Fairness Report,* 48 FCC 2d, at 8.

24 See *Inquiry into Alternatives.*

25 See comments of Media Access Project, Docket No. 84–262, at 27–37.

26 See Rowan, *Broadcast Fairness,* pp. 71–88.

27 See *Fairness Report, supra; Strauss Communications v. FCC,* 530 F.2d 1001, 1011 (D.C. Cir. 1976); C. Ferris and J. Kirkland, "Fairness: The Broadcaster's Hippocratic Oath," *Catholic Law Review* 34 (1985): 605, 614.

28 *Syracuse Peace Council v. FCC,* at 24.

29 Ibid.

30 Group W comments to the FCC in Docket No. 84–282, at 6.

31 40 FCC 2d 1150 1973.

32 H. Geller, *The Fairness Doctrine.*

33 See *NBC (Pensions),* 44 FCC 2d 1027 (1974), *NBC v. FCC,* 516 F.2d 1101 (D.C. Cir. 1971), vacated, *cert. denied,* 424 U.S. 910 (1976); Simmons, "The Problems of 'Issue' in the Administration of the Fairness Doctrine," *California Law Review* 65 (1977): 546; Steven Simmons, "The FCC's Personal Attack and Political Editorial Rules Reconsidered," *University of Pennsylvania Law Review* 125 (1977): 990.

On personal attack, compare *Strauss Communications, Inc.,* 51 FCC 2d 385 (1975) (calling congressman a coward personal attack) with *Philadelphia Federation of Teachers,* 31 Pike and Fischer, Rad. Reg. 2d 26 (1974) (calling public teacher association guilty of "blackmail" and "blood money" not personal attack); *WMCE,* 26 FCC 2d 354 (1970) (charging persons with "deliberate lie" or being "paranoid" personal attacks); *WMCP Broadcasting,* 41 FCC 2d 201 (1973) (not a personal attack to charge public officials with "hiding" county funds, "hoodwinking" another agency about them, using them for "taxi service"); *University of Houston,* 11 FCC 2d 790 (1968) (stating that group engages in "physical abuse and violence" and "local terror campaigns" personal attack); *J. Allen Carr,* 30 FCC 2d 894 (1971) (calling university a "breeding ground" for "terrorists" and "guerrillas" not a personal attack).

34 In *Public Media Center,* 59 FCC 2d 9 (1976), the commission in effect tried to establish that if the two sides have had roughly the same amount of time, the frequency and audience factors are not to be considered. See, e.g., decision as to *KATY* (at 499–500) (503–4, 519); *KJOY* (505–6, 519); *KPAY* (505–6, 526); and *KVON* (509–23) – where the commission found "reasonable opportunity" relying solely on roughly the same amount of time, despite great disparities as to frequency – 34 to 1, 25 to 1, 14 to 1, and 16 to 1. But see *Clarence F. Massart,* 10 FCC 2d 968 (1967); *George E. Cooley,* 10 FCC 2d 969, 970 (1967), where

the commission found unfairness in two political editorializing cases because of an imbalance in frequency even though overall time was roughly the same. And see *KSRO*, 507–8, 522, where there was a 4-to-1 disparity in total time, so the commission looked to "frequency and audience" and, finding an 8-to-1 frequency ratio, found unfairness – but see *NBC*, 16 FCC 2d 956 (1969), holding a 5-to-1 total time and 8-to-1 frequency ratio to be reasonable. My point is obvious: The area is confused and contradictory. Upon appeal, the court so found and remanded the matter to the commission to clarify its policies. See *Public Media Center v. FCC*, 581 F.2d 1322 (D.C. Cir. 1978). The commission simply ordered the other stations to give time but never clarified its policies, because it is impossible to do so.

35 *Complaint of the Wilderness Society against NBC (ESSO)*, 31 FCC 2d 729, 735–9 (1971). In that case the staff set forth the following "stopwatch" analysis of the material broadcast on the issue (pp. 738–9):

Date of Broadcast	*Pro*	*Anti*
June 7, 1970	4:40	5:35
September 10, 1970	:20	1:00
January 13, 1971	:06	:15
February 14, 1971	–	:10
February 16, 1971	:49	1:05
February 24, 1971	:15	1:30
February 28, 1971	1:32	–
June 4, 1971	1:58	–
July 11, 1971	:27	2:15
August 6, 1971	:45	1:10
August 26, 1971	–	:15
September 15, 1971	–	8:00
Total	10:52	21:15

See also *Sunbeam TV*, 27 FCC 2d 350, 351 (1971).

36 See, e.g., *Complaint of Wilderness Society against NBC*, at 733, 735.

37 See *Lamar Life Broadcasting*, 38 FCC 1143 (1965), reversed and remanded, *Office of Communication of the United Church of Christ v. FCC*, 359 F.2d 994 (D.C. Cir. 1966).

38 *New York Times v. Sullivan* 376 U.S. 254 (1964).

39 See *Letter to Chairman Oren Harris*, 40 FCC 582 (1962).

40 *Fairness Doctrine*, 74 FCC 2d 163 (1979).

41 See Rowan, *Broadcast Fairness*, p. 165.

42 See Geller, *The Fairness Doctrine*, p. 37.
43 See *CBS v. DNC*, 412 U.S. 94, 131 (1973).
44 See Section 315(a); *Red Lion Broadcasting v. FCC*, at 384; *UCC v. FCC*, 707 F.2d 1413, 1428, n. 46 (D.C. Cir. 1983).
45 *Editorializing Report*, 13 FCC 1246 (1949).
46 See, e.g., *Herman Hall*, 11 FCC 2d 344 (1968); *Simon Geller*, 90 FCC 2d 250, 265 (1982), *rev'd*, 737 F.2d 74 (D.C. Cir. 1984).
47 See *Radio Deregulation*, 84 FCC 2d 968 (1981), aff'd in part, rev'd in part, *Office of Communication of the United Church of Christ (UCC) v. FCC*, 707 F.2d 1413 (D.C. Cir. 1983); *Radio Deregulation*, 96 FCC 2d 930 (1984), remanded, *UCC v. FCC*, Case No. 84–1239, D.C. Cir., December 20, 1985 (holding that the FCC must make available to the public a significant accounting of the broadcaster's public service efforts); *TV Deregulation*, 98 FCC 2d 1076 (1984), 104 FCC 2d 358 (1986), rev'd in part on other grounds, *ACT v. FCC*, 821 F.2d 741 (D.C. Cir. 1987).
48 See *Syracuse Peace Council*.
49 The court of appeals affirmed this precatory holding as reasonable, with Chief Justice Wald issuing a strong dissent. See *Syracuse Peace Council v. FCC*.
50 See *UCC v. FCC*, 707 F.2d 1413 (D.C. Cir. 1983).
51 Ibid.
52 See *Postcard Renewal*, 87 FCC 2d 1127 (1981), aff'd *Black Citizens for a Fair Media*, 719 F.2d 407 (D.C. Cir. 1983), *Cert. denied*, 104 S. Ct. 3545 (1984).
53 Ibid. at 434 (dissenting opinion of Judge Wright).
54 See note 45.
55 *UCC v. FCC*, at 1441 n. 95.
56 *UCC v. FCC*, 779 F.2d 702 (D.C. Cir. 1985).
57 See *Broadcasting Magazine*, September 26, 1985, 39–40.
58 See *New York Times*, September 17, 1984 ("radio stations reduce airtime given to news").
59 *Central Florida Enterprises v. FCC*, 598 F.2d 37 (1978).
60 Hearings on Broadcast License Renewal Before the Subcommittee on Communications and Power of the House Committee on Interstate & Foreign Commerce, 93d Cong., 1st sess., Ser. 93–96, pt. 2 at 1120 (1973).
61 Ibid. at 1119.
62 *Greater Boston Television v. FCC*, 444 F.2d 841, 854 (D.C. Cir. 1970), *cert. denied*, 402 U.S. 1007 (1971).
63 *Central Florida Enterprises v. FCC*.

64 *Yale Broadcasting v. FCC*, 478 F.2d 594, 603 (D.C. Cir. 1973), *cert. denied*, 414 U.S. 914 (1973); *Illinois Citizens Committee for Broadcasting v. FCC*, 515 F.2d 397, 407, 427 (Statement of Ch. J. Bazelon) (D.C. Cir. 1975).
65 *Brandywine–Main Line Radio v. FCC*, 473 F.2d 16 (D.C. Cir. 1972), *cert. denied*, 412 U.S. 922 (1973).
66 *In the Matter of Regional Concentration Rules*, 49 Fed. Reg. 19, 670 (May 9, 1984).
67 P.L. 98–214, Dec. 9, 1983.
68 See *DBS*, 90 FCC 2d 676, 708 (1982).
69 See *NAB v. FCC*, 940 F.2d 1190, 1201 (D.C. Cir. 1984) ("broadcasting remains broadcasting even though a segment of the public is unable to view programs without special equipment").
70 Ibid. at 1203–4.
71 See *NAB v. FCC*, 849 F.2d 665 (D.C. Cir. 1988).
72 *Teletext Transmission*, 53 Pike & Fischer, R.R. 2d 1309 (1983).
73 Ibid., at par. 54.
74 See *TRAC v. FCC*.
75 *U.S. v. AT&T*, 552 F. Supp. 131 (D.D.C. 1982), *aff'd Maryland v. U.S.*, 103 S.Ct. 1240 (1983).
76 *U.S. v. Western Electric Co.*, 673 F. Supp. 525, 587–97 (D.D.C. 1987); opinion issued March 7, 1988.
77 Ibid.
78 Ibid.
79 Ibid. at 597, 603–4.
80 673 F. Supp, at 595.
81 Ibid.
82 Ibid., at 585–86.
83 47 U.S.C. Sec. 521.
84 Specifically, the act sought to implement the *Associated Press* principle that the "underlying policy of the First Amendment is that the American people receive information from as many diverse and antagonistic sources as possible." See H. Rept. No. 98–934, 98th Cong., 2d sess., at 30–36.
85 See Section 612, 47 U.S.C. 532.
86 R. M. Pepper, OPP Paper 24, "Through the Looking Glass: Integrated Broadband Networks, Regulatory Policy and Industrial Change," November 1988, p. 105.
87 See, e.g., *Preferred Communications v. City of Los Angeles*, aff'd and remanded, 106 S. Ct. 2034 (1986). *City of Los Angeles v. Preferred Communications; HBO v. FCC*, 567 F.2d 9th Cir. (1977);

Quincy Cable v. FCC, 768 F.2d 1984 (D.C. Cir. 1985); *cert. denied*, 476 U.S. 1169 (1986); G. Shapiro, P. Kurland, and Mercurio, *Cablespeech* (New York: Harcourt Brace, 1983). But see *Community Communications v. City of Boulder*, 660 F.2d 1370 (10th Cir. 1981), *cert. dismissed*, 102 S. Ct. 2287 (1982); *Omega Satellite Products v. City of Indianapolis*, 694 F.2d 119 (7th Cir. 1982); *Berkshire Cablevision of Rhode Island v. Burke*, 571 F. Supp. 976, D. R.I. 1983), dismissed as moot, 773 F.2d 382 (1st Cir. 1985); Geller and Lampert, "Cable Content Regulation and the First Amendment," p. 603.

88 Thus, just to give some anecdotal examples, Ted Turner's Cable News Network (CNN) could not get on the Manhattan Cable system because its owner had a competing cable news network. (Turner sued, but antitrust cases drag on for years: The story has a happy ending only because Turner bought out the rival.) Another large multiple-system cable operator, *Times-Mirror*, developed its own new pay service, "Spotlight," and to give it a boost, ended the carriage of rival services like HBO on its systems. HBO then had no way into these hundreds of thousands of cable homes. Finally, because a cable operator in eastern Oklahoma did not want to present the controversial ABC show *The Day After* (about the aftermath of a nuclear attack), the operator decided to schedule "technical difficulties Sunday night during the show" (*Broadcasting*, November 21, 1983, p. 88).

89 Sec. 624(b) (2) (B)).

90 47 U.S.C. 315(c).

91 *Use of Broadcast and Cablecast Facilities by Candidates for Public Office*, 34 FCC 2d 510, n.2.

92 FCC Report to Sen. Goldwater, *Cable Television and Political Broadcast Laws*, January 1981, pp. 24–6.

93 Sec. 612(f).

94 Sec. 622(h)(3).

95 See *Minneapolis Star & Tribune v. Minnesota Commissioner of Revenue*, 460 U.S. 575 (1983).

96 For further discussion of the concept, see H. Geller, A. Ciamporcero, and D. Lampert, "The Cable Franchise Fee and the First Amendment," *Federal Communications Law Journal* 39 (1987): 1, 24–5.

97 *New York Times v. Sullivan*, at 279.

98 Ibid.

99 Ibid., at 270.

100 Ibid., at 279–80.

101 Compare *Curtis Publishing v. Butts,* 388 U.S. 130 (1967), and *Rosenbloom v. Metromedia,* 402 U.S. 29 (1971), with *Gertz v. Welch,* 418 U.S. 323 (1974), *Hutchinson v. Proxmire,* 443 U.S. 111 (1979), and *Dun & Bradstreet v. Greenmoss Builders,* 472 U.S. 749; 11 Med. L. Rptr. 2417 (1985).

102 *Herbert v. Lando,* 441 U.S. 153.

103 *Sharon v. Time,* 599 F. Supp. 538 (S.D. N.Y. 1984).

104 Even on the appellate level there can be disturbing issues, such as the panel's majority opinion in *Tavoulareas v. Piro,* 759 F.2d 90 (D.C. Cir. 1984), *vacated, rehrng. granted* 763 F.2d 1472 (D.C. Cir. 1985) (en banc).

105 For an excellent review of possible reforms in this sensitive area, see the Annenberg Washington Proposal for the Reform of Libel Laws, October 1988.

Chapter 11

Content regulation reconsidered

T. M. Scanlon, Jr.

INTRODUCTION

For many years I have thought that there was an important and appealing fundamental truth behind Justice Thurgood Marshall's observation that "above all else, the First Amendment means that government has no power to restrict expression because of its message, its ideas, its subject matter, or its content."[1] As the years have gone by, however, this truth has come to seem more elusive, more limited, and less fundamental than it once did. What follows is an attempt to reexamine the impermissibility of content-based restrictions by regarding it as one element within a larger view of freedom of expression as a right.

The idea that there is something especially bad about government regulation of the content of expression, whether this takes the form of prohibiting some contents or requiring others, has obvious relevance to many questions about the regulation of mass media, ranging from restrictions on advertising of alcohol and tobacco products to the fairness doctrine and statutes mandating a right to reply to political editorials. I shall discuss some of these issues briefly, but I shall not be able to explore any of them in detail. My aim is, rather, to provide a general framework within which they can be discussed in a systematic way.

THE STRUCTURE OF RIGHTS

In my view, rights are constraints on discretion to act that we believe to be important means for avoiding morally unacceptable consequences.[2] To claim that a certain action or policy violates a right is to claim: first, that unfettered discretion to act in a certain way (whether on the part of private individuals or those occupying institutional roles) leads to unacceptable consequences; second, that certain constraints on this discretion, which either are or ought to be in force in the situation at hand, are a feasible way of preventing these consequences at acceptable cost to other goods; and, third, that the action or policy in question is forbidden by these constraints.

Our thinking about a right can be analyzed into three components: (1) ends – the goals or values relative to which the consequences of unfettered discretion are judged to be unacceptable and the constraints proposed are held to be justified; (2) means – the particular constraints that the right in question is taken to involve; and (3) linking empirical beliefs about the consequences of unfettered discretion and about how these consequences would be altered by the constraints the right proposes. These include beliefs about the motivation of the relevant actors, about the opportunities to act that are available to them, and about the collective results of the decisions they are likely to make. Also relevant here are facts about the institutional background that determine whether a given constraint is "in force."

To illustrate these components of a right, consider the right to privacy. The idea that there is such a right depends, first, on the belief that unfettered discretion to observe us and investigate our affairs would be unacceptable: We need to be able to conduct part of our lives out of public view, as well as to communicate with others without being overheard by third parties. (This belief reflects judgments both about ends and about linking empirical beliefs.) Many different sets of constraints might provide the protection we need here, some more efficiently than others. In order for our privacy rights to be made determinate, we need institutions and conventions that make a selection from among the sets of morally acceptable constraints – institutions and conventions that indicate, for example, when we may and may not be observed, which of our written and electronic communications are protected and which are fair game for others to read or intercept.

Sometimes (as in the case of the often invoked "right to life") appeals to a right leave the constraints that it is supposed to involve almost entirely unspecified. The claim that there is a right is thus reduced to the claim that a certain factor is of great moral value and must be given great weight in deciding what discretion people have to act. Moral argument involving rights of this kind becomes a process of "balancing" rights against one another by comparing their relative "weight." This strikes me as an unedifying form of moral argument. If appeals to rights are to be useful and informative, these rights need to be understood in terms of some specific limitations on discretion to act, limitations that represent a reasonably clear strategy for avoiding the threatened evils at tolerable cost. When a right is understood in this way, the process of applying it will be largely a process of working out what such a strategy requires in a given situation. If, under normal conditions, the strategy really represents a way of avoiding the threatened evil at tolerable cost, the need to "balance" competing rights against one another will be greatly reduced.

The term "rights" can be used in many different ways. Some claims about the rights we have depend directly on particular laws and institutions: My right to return the used car I have recently bought, for example, may derive simply from the "lemon law" the state legislature has passed; and if you have rented half of my garage, the rights you have to park your car there, to drive in and out of my driveway, and so on, depend simply on the law of property and contracts and on the agreement we have made. The origin of such rights is a relatively straightforward matter. But another, more critical use of the notion of rights assumes that rights are not merely the creatures of particular legal systems but also tell us what those systems ought to be like. It is puzzling what the "existence" of such rights could amount to. What does it mean to say that "there is" a right of this kind? When we disagree about the content of these rights, in virtue of what could one of us be correct and the other mistaken?

The analysis I have sketched is meant as a response to these puzzles. It follows from this analysis that the relation between legal rights and more general moral or political rights is complex. On the one hand, legal institutions can incorporate rights that have an independent existence as critical moral ideals. The speech clause of the First Amendment, for example, needs to be understood in the light of a more general moral idea of freedom of expression, which exists independently of that particular amendment and which we can appeal to in appraising institutions other than our own. On the other hand, as I have just suggested, the exact content of such moral rights often depends on an institutional context. Often, more than one system of constraints is capable of providing the protection that a right holds to be necessary, and it may therefore be difficult or impossible to argue simply from first principles that a particular system of constraints is morally required. In these cases the content of people's rights will depend on the institutional strategy in place in their society (assuming, of course, that that strategy actually provides the needed protection).

It is sometimes said, for example, in the context of argument about the First Amendment, that a newspaper or a television station is a "voice" rather than a "forum." There is no necessity about this: One could operate something like a newspaper as a public forum, and some cable television channels are operated in this way. The point of the claim, I take it, is that in our way of achieving the aims of freedom of expression the function of newspapers and many broadcasting stations is to serve as independent voices reflecting the judgment and opinions of those who own them. The force of this claim is partly a matter of property rights and expectations that are independent of freedom of expression. It derives further protection from that right as well, however, insofar as these functions are part of our strategy for achieving a "system of freedom of expression" (and insofar as that strategy is a reasonably successful one).

This qualification points toward another feature of rights, which might be called their "creative instability." First, because rights as I understand them involve a significant empirical component, our understanding of a right can always be upset by evidence that forces a change in these empirical beliefs. Second, at any given time our understanding of the three elements of a right that I have distinguished – the ends, the constraints, and the linking empirical beliefs – may not (indeed, probably will not) form a coherent whole. That is, the constraints we regard as adequate protection for the values underlying the right may not actually be adequate. It may be that they can be thought adequate only if we adopt linking beliefs that are in fact false. This tension gives rights a dynamic quality that can lead to an almost constant process of revision. New situations or changes in our "linking beliefs" can, as just suggested, lead us to conclude that old constraints are inadequate. Similarly, new cases, or reflection on our reactions to old ones, can lead us to enlarge or redefine the set of values in terms of which existing constraints are justified. I do not mean to suggest, however, that these tensions can always be resolved. It may happen that the values presupposed by a right cannot be adequately served without radically departing from that strategy of constraints in terms of which the right is customarily understood. (I will consider one example of this kind of tension in the right of freedom of expression at the end of the next section.)

FREEDOM OF EXPRESSION AS A RIGHT

To analyze freedom of expression along the lines I have suggested, we need to identify the values it seeks to protect. I begin with the values attached to satisfying certain widely shared private interests. These include, first, interests that we all have, as potential speakers and writers, in having the opportunity to communicate with those who wish to hear or read us and, especially in political life, to have the opportunity to gain the attention of others who have not specifically chosen to hear or see us. Second, there are our interests, as potential audiences, in having access to expression that we wish to hear or read, and even in being exposed to some degree to expression we have not chosen. These interests are diverse. They include interests in being informed, amused, stimulated in a variety of ways, and even provoked when this leads to reflection and growth. Third, there are our interests as bystanders (that is, not necessarily as either participants in expression or audiences). These include such things as, on the one hand, the benefits of living in a society that enjoys the cultural, political, and technological benefits of free expression and, on the other, the interest we all have in not bearing the costs, such as noise and disorder, that expression can entail.

In addition to these categories of private interest, there are more general moral and political values that freedom of expression is also supposed to protect. Most commonly mentioned here is the value of having fair and effective democratic political institutions. In order for the formal process of democratic politics to confer legitimacy on its outcomes, this process must operate under conditions of free and open public debate, and one of the aims of freedom of expression is to prevent these conditions from being undermined. This important public value gives added support to individuals' interests in having access to means of expression. It also adds an important new element to arguments about freedom of expression because fair democratic politics requires an equality – an equal opportunity to participate – that is not necessarily in the interest of particular individuals.

I have described the goals of freedom of expression very abstractly, in terms of the values attached to various categories of activity and opportunities. Individuals will inevitably disagree about the value of particular acts of expression within these categories – for example, about the merits of the various political doctrines, scientific hypotheses, and theological positions that are expressed. Our views about freedom of expression, however, are based on a measure of agreement about the value of having the opportunity to engage in, and to have access to, expression on these topics, whatever the merits of the particular messages we choose to express or receive may be. There are some participant and audience interests, however – such as the interest in learning how to make bombs or in teaching others how to do so, and the interest in cheating others through fraudulent mail-order schemes – to which no such value is attached; and other interests have values intermediate between these extremes, that is, are capable of asserting intermediate degrees of "upward pressure" on the limits of expression.

These categories of expression make it possible to formulate widely shared judgments of value on which argument in favor of freedom of expression can be based, and they do this by abstracting from more specific value judgments that we use our freedom of expression to argue about. I do not mean to suggest that these categories are entirely uncontroversial or that their relative values cannot be questioned. My aim is merely to point out, first, that they are a way of expressing judgments of relative value and, second, that they provide a way of arguing about expression that sets aside even more controversial questions. The distinction between these two kinds of judgments about the value of expression is important for the question of content regulation, because the idea that expression should not be regulated on the basis of its content amounts in part to the idea that regulation must not be based on evaluation of the more specific and controversial kind just distinguished.

I turn now to what I earlier called "linking empirical beliefs" about the motives and opportunities of various agents that lead us to conclude that in the absence of constraints, the values just listed are seriously at risk. Chief among these are generalizations about how governments generally behave. Governments, whether elected or not, have a settled tendency to try to silence their critics. They also tend to be unsympathetic to ideas, values, and points of view that are unpopular in the society at large. As a result they are often reluctant to bear the burden of ensuring that people speaking for these points of view have an opportunity to be heard. Governments tend to overestimate threats posed to the security of the country and to their own policies. In particular, they tend to overestimate the costs of unrestricted expression, which are visible and dramatic and often seem to be easily foreseeable, and to underestimate its values, which make themselves felt gradually and unpredictably over a long period of time. These faults need not be due to evil intent, but are typical of all governments we know of, those whose structure and policies we otherwise admire as well as those we disapprove of.

The empirical assumptions on which freedom of expression is based are not, however, limited to beliefs about the behavior of governments but also include beliefs about the behavior of private agents that we need protection against. We know, for example, that when people believe they can prevent the expression of ideas they strongly disagree with by threatening a violent response, they are likely to employ this tactic. This leads us to a familiar conclusion about the impermissibility of the "heckler's veto," namely, that governments should not be free to ban expression whenever they believe it may lead to public disorder.

It is extremely difficult to state explicitly the constraints that make up the right of freedom of expression even as these are understood at a given time. Our understanding of these constraints is carried mainly by a series of examples that are taken to illustrate the unacceptable consequences of restrictions violating the right. Application of the right to new cases proceeds by a process of generalization from these examples, guided by our understanding of the values at stake and of the general strategies our responses to these examples are taken to involve.

In saying that the right to freedom of expression is composed of "constraints on discretion to act" I do not suggest that it is what is sometimes called a "negative right," in other words, that it only requires that governments refrain from interfering with expression. As the example of the heckler's veto indicates, freedom of expression also requires governments to take positive action to protect speakers, and it can require other costly actions, for instance, that public spaces be made available for expression even when this interferes significantly with other pursuits. Nor does freedom of expression constrain only governmental agents. Governments are not the only threats to freedom of expression, and they are also not the only agents capable of violating it. Suppose, for example, that a large private corporation were to adopt a policy of firing any employee who took a public stand on some controversial issue – say, abortion – with which the company's directors disagreed. This seems to me to represent a clear violation of the employees' right to freedom of expression because such a use of economic power is a standing threat that clearly needs to be constrained. It is a separate question, however, whether such an action would violate the First Amendment, which states only: "Congress shall make no law . . ."

Just as the First Amendment can be seen as involving a narrower range of constraints than the intuitive moral idea of freedom of expression does, it is also important to see that freedom of expression itself is only one part of a larger family of strategies for protecting the same values. The Freedom of Information Act, for example, promotes many of the audience values just listed, but it is not simply a part of the right of freedom of expression (and not simply a corollary of the First Amendment). Similarly, the idea of academic freedom promotes these same values, by protecting important sources of ideas and information and providing for their dissemination. But this idea, again, is not simply a part of freedom of expression: It is not concerned only with expression or with expression generally. Rather, it applies only to those who work within certain institutions, and it derives its authority from the nature and purposes of those institutions.

The rights described by academic freedom are consequences of the ways in which the control of universities from without, and the authority of deans and boards of trustees within them, must be constrained if the institutions are to fulfill their stated function as centers of thought and inquiry.[3]

It might be argued that journalists have analogous rights, reflecting the ways in which the authority not only of the government but also of editors and publishers must be limited if "the press" is to fulfill its function in society. This argument would be more difficult to carry through because "the function and purpose" of publishing and broadcasting companies are less clear. While universities are nonprofit enterprises that are chartered and seek financial support on the basis of their dedication to the aims of scholarship and teaching, publishing and broadcasting companies are in large part commercial enterprises. It might be possible, however, to argue as follows: Insofar as these companies claim that their function in society requires special protection from governmental regulation, they open the door also to claims that authority within them must be constrained in the ways that are required in order to ensure that this function will be served. Even if arguments of this kind were to succeed, however, the special journalistic rights they establish would not be part of freedom of expression but, like academic freedom, ancillary to it.[4]

Insofar as freedom of expression involves only a limited range of strategies for protecting the values with which it is concerned, creative instability of the kind mentioned in the previous section is likely to arise, since these means are almost certain to be insufficient for the full realization of these goals. The natural response is that rights do not promise to ensure the full realization of the values with which they are concerned, but only to ward off certain serious threats to these values. The tension remains, however, because this response leaves open the question of why the range of strategies that the right involves should not be extended.

The problem of equality of access provides a clear example of this instability. One aim of freedom of expression is to provide opportunities for the kind of public discussion that is an essential precondition for fair democratic politics. If the political system is to be fair, however, a significantly widespread equality of opportunity to engage in this discussion is required. The familiar idea that leafletting must be permitted because it is "the poor man's printing press" reflects this commitment. But in a society like ours, one cannot achieve a significant degree of equality of access to effective means of expression simply through the strategies that freedom of expression has traditionally involved (i.e., simply by constraining the power to regulate expression). This generates pressure to find new strategies, but it is not clear where these are to be found.

THE PROBLEM OF CONTENT REGULATION

This brings me to the problem of content regulation. It is common to state the constraints that make up the right of freedom of expression in two parts. Freedom of expression requires, first, that expression not be restricted on the basis of its content, and, second, that it should not be restricted *too much:* Any regulation should leave ample opportunity for (at least the valued forms of) expression. Laurence Tribe states this familiar idea with particular clarity by distinguishing between two ways in which government can "abridge speech":

> *First,* government can aim at ideas or information, in the sense of singling out actions for government control or penalty either (a) because of the specific viewpoint such actions express, or (b) because of the effects produced by awareness of the information such actions impart. . . . *Second,* without aiming at ideas or information in either of the above senses, government can constrict the flow of information and ideas while pursuing other goals, either (a) by limiting an activity through which information and ideas might be conveyed, or (b) by enforcing rules compliance with which might discourage the communication of ideas or information.[5]

Tribe summarizes this distinction by saying that "the first form of abridgment may be summarized as encompassing government actions *aimed at communicative impact;* the second, as encompassing government actions *aimed at non-*

communicative impact but nonetheless having adverse effects on communicative opportunity."[6]

As Tribe goes on to say, First Amendment theory has regarded these two forms of abridgment in a somewhat different light:

> Any government action aimed at communicative impact is presumptively at odds with the first amendment. For if the constitutional guarantee means anything, it means that, ordinarily at least, "government has no power to restrict expression because of its message, its ideas, its subject matter, or its content. . . ." . . . Whatever might in theory be said either way, the choice between "the dangers of suppressing information and the dangers of its misuse if it is freely available" is, ultimately, a choice "that the First Amendment makes for us."[7]

On the other hand:

> Where government aims at the noncommunicative impact of an act, the correct result in any particular case . . . reflects some "balancing" of the competing interests; regulatory choices aimed at harms not caused by ideas or information as such are acceptable so long as they do not *unduly* constrict the flow of information and ideas. In such cases the first amendment does not make the choice but instead requires a "thumb" on the scale to assure that the balance struck in any particular situation properly reflects the central position of free expression in the constitutional scheme.[8]

This "two-track" analysis is extremely appealing, and seems to capture a distinction which is an important feature of our ideas about freedom of expression. The interesting question is why the constraints that make up the right of freedom of expression should have this two-part structure. This is particularly puzzling because, as Geoffrey Stone has pointed out,[9] restrictions of expression based on its content are not always more damaging to our interests in expression than content-neutral restrictions: A law banning discussions of abortion on morning television, for example, does no more harm to these interests than a law banning morning television altogether. Stone points out that content-based restrictions often have a "distorting effect" on public debate: A law banning political advertising on billboards except by candidates of the two major parties would in that respect be worse than a statute banning all billboards. Concern with this kind of distortion and unfairness does seem to have something to do with our antipathy to content regulation, but it does not seem to be the central factor, because, as Stone says,[10] content-neutral restrictions can also have distorting effects, and even when they do, the case against them must, on the two-track analysis, be made by balancing competing concerns, while the presumption is that content-based restrictions are ruled out absolutely.

The analysis of rights sketched in the preceding sections suggests the following alternative explanation, at least as a first approximation: Our ideas about rights are ideas about the constraints on discretion to act that we regard as both necessary and feasible. These ideas are always incompletely formulated, and our understanding of them depends heavily on the "lessons" of particular historical examples. Prominent among these lessons is the idea that general powers of government censorship, and laws against political sedition, are impermissible. These are powers that, I believe, it is not only necessary but also feasible simply to deny to governments. On the other hand, it is clearly not feasible to deny governments all powers to regulate expression; nor does this seem necessary: Laws regulating the use of loudspeakers and the placement of billboards, for example, are clearly acceptable. Because the powers it is clearly necessary to constrain and feasible simply to deny involve the regulation of expression on the basis of its content, whereas many of those that it is not feasible and seemingly not necessary to deny are content-neutral, it is natural to draw the conclusion that the power to regulate on the basis of content is prima facie illegitimate.

This would be an overgeneralization, however. Some content-based restrictions, such as restrictions on libel and false advertising, seem clearly permissible even when the harms they protect against are not overwhelming. But at least we can say this: There are some powers to restrict expression on the basis of its content that it is important and feasible simply to deny to governments. These forms of regulation are distinguished not by the greater seriousness of the threat they present but, rather, by the nature of the appropriate response to that threat, which is simply to deny that such powers can legitimately be exercised. Although there may be some powers to regulate on a content-neutral basis that should also simply be denied, such as the power to forbid the publication of any newspapers at all, this is of lesser importance. Such powers are less of a threat to us because they are less likely to be asserted than powers to regulate on the basis of content are, since every government wants to preserve effective means of mass communication, at least for its own favored ideas.

It follows that while the impermissibility of (some forms of) content regulation has a special place on the "surface" of freedom of expression (i.e. in the constraints that make up the practical content of that right), this does not reflect any special objection to such regulation that is apparent at a more fundamental level. But there has often seemed to be something fundamental about the impermissibility of content regulation. It has seemed to many people that at least certain forms of content-based regulation should be opposed because they allow governments to manipulate public discussion of important issues and are therefore a threat to citizens' "autonomy." In an earlier article[11] I myself took this view. I characterized the power that must be denied to governments as the power to restrict expression on the ground that it would cause harms of certain kinds – namely:

> (a) harms to certain individuals which consist in their coming to have false beliefs as a result of those acts of expression; (b) harmful consequences of acts performed as a result of those acts of expression, where the connection between the acts of expression and the subsequent harmful acts consists merely in

> the fact that the act of expression led the agents to believe (or increased their tendency to believe) these acts to be worth performing.[12]

The idea that these harms cannot be taken to justify restrictions on expression was what I called the Millian Principle. This principle was not intended as a complete account of freedom of expression. Its function was simply to keep certain considerations "out of the scales" of justification. Further components in my theory specified that participant and audience interests in expression are to receive high value among those elements that can be weighed in assessing the justifiability of restrictions on expression, and that opportunities to enjoy these values must be distributed in such a way that general criteria of distributive justice and the special requirements of rights to political participation are fulfilled.

The two parts of this theory – the Millian Principle, which keeps certain harms out of the "scales of justification" altogether, and the positive values, which place a "thumb on the scales" in the subsequent balancing – correspond roughly to Tribe's two tracks.[13] That is to say, the two theories describe a similar set of constraints. There is, however, a significant difference in the reasoning that the theories offer for these constraints. My theory not only proposed a set of constraints that prevented certain kinds of balancing in the application of the right of freedom of expression but also carried this hostility toward balancing into the theoretical justification for these constraints themselves. Accordingly, I claimed that the Millian Principle was a constraint on the justification of restrictions on expression that arose from the idea of autonomy itself and did not depend on judgments about the relative value of different forms of expression. This claim now seems to me to have been mistaken.

The problem with this appeal to autonomy was that it did not allow for the different degrees to which content-based restrictions of expression represent a threat to our ability to make up our own minds about important matters. Governments have no power to restrict expression on the ground that it would undermine respect for law and government or because it questions the institutions of marriage and the family. Such powers would threaten our "autonomy" – our ability to make up our minds about important questions through public discussion. On the other hand, penalties attached to false advertising or to expression that defames or invades the privacy of private citizens present no such threat. The Millian Principle allowed for content-based restrictions of the latter kinds, since the harms they are designed to prevent are not of the types that it screens out. (They do not lie simply in the disutility of false belief or in the harmful actions others will be led to take.) But the real difference between these restrictions and impermissible forms of content regulation lies in factors ignored by the argument for the Millian Principle, namely, the different values attached to free public discussion of different topics, and the different degrees of risk involved in authorizing government to regulate the content of these discussions.

The lesson of all this is that we cannot understand or interpret the idea that content-based regulation is impermissible without ourselves drawing distinctions between different forms of expression on the basis of their content (or at least their subject matter) and making judgments about the relative value of these forms of expression.[14] This may be only a superficial irony, but it is instructive. Bearing it in mind, I shall turn in the next section to a more detailed discussion of some forms of content-based regulation. As a basis for that discussion, it will be helpful to review the standards for appraising restrictions on expression that emerge from the preceding analysis.

In discussions of "autonomy" the emphasis is on audience values. It is important to audiences that they have access to "enough" expression (where this level is determined by the value of expression as compared with competing goods) and that the expression to which they have access should not be distorted. Parallel to these on the participant side, but not exactly coincident with them,[15] are the participant interests in having "enough" opportunities for expression and the value of having these opportunities not be unfairly distributed. This unfairness can be of two kinds. The first is unfairness between representatives of opposing positions on the same issue – for example, between competing political parties, labor unions, or religious groups. The second kind of unfairness is between different topics of discussion. This occurs when, for example, there are ample opportunities for public discussion of religious and political questions but such opportunities are denied to those who wish to engage in artistic expression or to challenge established scientific views. These types of unfairness are analogous to two forms of "distortion" from the point of view of audiences: distortion of the discussion of particular topics, which can lead to the manipulation of people's attitudes on that question, and distortion that leads to emphasis on some topics and neglect of others. The power to regulate expression on the basis of its content is illegitimate when it poses a serious threat of "distortion" or "unfairness" of either of these two kinds.

But what constitutes "distortion" or "unfairness" of the relevant kinds? It would be unrealistic and even dangerous to grant to legislatures or to judges the power to engage in detailed regulation of expression based on their conceptions of perfectly fair and undistorted discussion. This would be unrealistic because we lack a sufficiently clear and widely shared view of what these ideals come to and because, in any plausible view, actual discussion will always fall short of these ideals. It would also be dangerous insofar as it would involve assigning to actual political institutions, for instance, courts or legislatures, the power to prohibit any expression that falls short of their conception of these ideals. Despite these problems, however, we can identify certain clear examples that would count as unfairness or distortion on any account, and it is such cases that we refer to in determining the shape of the right of freedom of expression. This is one example of a way in which that right is "negative," in other words, aimed at warding off recognized harms rather than at realizing an ideal. It does not follow, however, that it is a "negative right" in the more familiar sense of that term, since the prevention of these harms can require "positive" action, as mentioned in discussing the "heckler's veto."

VARIETIES OF CONTENT REGULATION

Let us now consider some specific examples of content regulation in the light of the analysis presented. Statutes allowing for prosecution for false advertising are an instance of content regulation that seems clearly legitimate, and it is easy to see why this should be so. It would be a mistake to deny that "commercial speech" in general serves legitimate and important interests for both participants and audiences. But the participant interest in having the opportunity to try to defraud carries no value, and as long as the standards for what constitutes "falsehood" are sufficiently clear and are not tied up with matters of great political controversy it seems likely that the power to prosecute for false advertising will not become a threat to other participant and audience values.

Restrictions on television advertising of liquor and tobacco are slightly more controversial but still seem justifiable. The participant interest involved is generally regarded as having a greater claim to legitimacy than false advertising does, but it seems clear that no audience interest is threatened. (No one would complain that they have insufficient opportunity to see such advertising.) If there is a worry, it is that there is a greater threat that regulation, if permitted here, might expand into other areas. If advertising can be regulated in this way, why not other aspects of program content? The answer, I believe, is the one just given, namely, that there are few other areas where regulation could be allowed with so little threat to audience interests.

Consider, for example, the power to regulate the portrayal of sex and violence in television programs. Here the problem is not merely one of spillover but of how to define the power itself in a way that does not already threaten important interests of speakers and audiences. This is extremely difficult to do, especially since programs that have the same "amount" of sex or violence can suggest quite different attitudes toward it, and, presumably, have quite different effects on their audiences. It is difficult to see how to frame a power to regulate the worst programming that would not in practice threaten some of the best as well.

I have concentrated so far on what might be called judgmental regulation: regulation that is based on a judgment about what the correct opinions or attitudes are on a given question and is aimed at preventing expression that might mislead or degrade people. I turn now to two forms of content-based regulation that do not have this judgmental character, to consider how the issues they raise are similar to, and how they differ from, those just discussed. These are viewpoint discrimination and subject matter restrictions.

Regulation that discriminates among speakers on the basis of their points of view can reflect the judgment that some of these points of view are mistaken, but it can also have other aims. It can, for example, be aimed simply at favoring speakers who have political power or those whom the governing authorities wish to see prevail in public debate, and this need not reflect any judgment as to the merits of their claims. More benignly, viewpoint-based regulation may be aimed at securing a higher degree of fairness in public discussion by constraining those who already have a great deal of exposure in order to give others a chance to be heard. Our resistance to viewpoint discrimination differs from our resistance to judgmental regulation by having a slightly different empirical basis. It arises from fear of partisanship and partiality rather than fear of paternalism. The speaker and audience interests that are threatened are the same, but because of the nature of the threatening motives our resistance to viewpoint discrimination puts more emphasis on the protection of participant values and the value of fairness.

Unlike the aims that lie behind some judgmental restrictions, motives of partisanship lack even prima facie justificatory weight. They thus present no theoretical problem in our thinking about freedom of expression but only pose a threat to be guarded against. Fairness, however, is a more difficult problem. It seems clearly mistaken to say that freedom of expression never licenses government to restrict the speech of some in order to allow others a better chance to be heard.[16] On the other hand, as I observed in the preceding section, the power to demand what one judges to be a fair and balanced discussion may easily become the power to demand a discussion that leads to what one judges to be the correct outcome (since a discussion that leads to the wrong outcome must fail to give some considerations their due weight). Giving the FCC power to deny license renewal to television stations whose coverage of public affairs it judges to have been "unbalanced" would, for example, be ruled out on this ground. In between these extremes, however, limited powers to prohibit clear and specific forms of unfairness may be compatible with freedom of expression and even required by it. The case for or against such powers must be made out on the basis of their consequences. Statutes requiring that opponents of newspaper or television editorials be given the opportunity to reply are not, on the face of it, inconsistent with the right of freedom of expression. Everything depends on what the consequences of such statutes would be as compared with the likely alternatives. If they pose a serious threat to the relevant interests, they violate that right; otherwise they do not, even though they may be ineffective or otherwise ill-advised. Would they simply discourage controversial editorials and programs and thus diminish the effective "voice" of editors? Or would they provide a chance for other voices to be heard without diminishing the range and liveliness of the debate? It may seem odd to make a question of rights turn on such empirical considerations. But if the role of freedom of expression is simply to safeguard central participant and audience interests how can that right be interpreted without taking these factors into account?

I turn now to subject matter restrictions, which bring me back to the *Mosley* case quoted at the outset. I have stated that it is impossible to argue sensibly about freedom of expression without recognizing the fact that some forms of expression are of higher value than others. We need to distinguish between the values assigned to different categories of expression (because of the differing participant and audience values they serve) and the values assigned to particular acts of expression within these categories. It is mainly discrimination of this latter kind that we want to exclude in ruling out judgmental and viewpoint-based restrictions on expression, and our reasons for this exclusion are brought vividly to mind by Justice Marshall's ringing denunciation of the regulation of expression on the basis of "its message, its ideas, its subject matter, or its content." But these words do not seem to fit the issues in the *Mosley* case, which struck down an ordinance prohibiting picketing near schools except for picketing by the parties to labor disputes at that school. This ordinance does distinguish between acts of expression on the basis of their content, but it does not reflect any judgment of the merits of various messages, nor, on the face of it, does it seem to favor some points of view over others with which they are in competition.

This appearance may be misleading, however. Mosley was picketing the school to protest racial segregation. If we suppose, as seems quite plausible, that the ordinance was aimed at silencing him and others with a similar message, then something more like objectionable viewpoint discrimination emerges. But the fact that the ordinance makes an exception for labor picketing, thus distinguishing between acts of expression on the basis of their content (in this case their subject matter) is irrelevant to this objection. A blanket prohibition of all picketing near schools would also be objectionable, assuming that it had the same aim and no stronger justification. The relevant criticism of those who passed the Chicago ordinance is thus not that they should not have distinguished between categories of expression on the basis of their content but rather that they should have recognized expression of the kind that Mosley was engaged in as having a particularly high value – at least as high as that of labor picketing. Armed with that judgment, we can explain why both the blanket prohibition and the selective one are to be rejected.

What the selective nature of the prohibition does, however, is to offer the court the opening for an ad hominem argument through which it can avoid the need to balance the value of opportunities for various kinds of expression against the value of preserving a peaceful atmosphere near schools. The city council has already determined that the latter value does not outweigh the importance of opportunities for labor picketing, so the court, assuming only that political protest is at least as important, can conclude that there is insufficient justification for denying Mosley the right to picket.

A second way to look at *Mosley* is to see it as raising the question of fair distribution of a scarce resource. If it would be too disruptive to allow anyone who likes to picket near a school, the question is, Who, if anyone, is to be allowed this opportunity? This brings out both a similarity to and a difference from central cases of content-based regulation. The similarity lies in the fact that we are concerned with the question of fairness to participants and with the threat of favoritism on the part of political authorities. (It is reasonable to suppose that the exception for labor picketing in the *Mosley* ordinance reflected the political power of labor unions.) The Chicago ordinance does seem unfair, but it is not clear that fairness rules out drawing distinctions between participants on the basis of the subject matter with which they are concerned. It would not seem unfair, for example, if picketing near schools must be restricted, to limit it to those whose message is concerned in some way with school policy.

CONCLUSION

Does the restriction of expression on the basis of its content represent a particularly clear or particularly serious violation of freedom of expression? The idea that it does seems to me to have two sources. First, our thinking about rights is strongly influenced by a few leading examples, and some of the clearest examples of unacceptable regulation of expression involve regulation on the basis of content. But great care has to be exercised in generalizing from these examples. Second, in contrast to other decisions, which involve messy balancing of competing interests, the conclusion that a form of regulation is illegitimate because it involves distinguishing between acts of expression on the basis of their content has the clear ring of principle. This makes them appealing to the theorist, who likes sharp distinctions, as well as to the judge, who may prefer decisions that do not involve large and obvious elements of value judgment. But this clearness may be an illusion. Distinguishing permissible from impermissible forms of content-based regulation requires us to weigh the value of different categories of expression, and this element of balancing should not be ignored.

The impermissibility of certain forms of content-based regulation plays a prominent role in the constraints that define freedom of expression. This fact is important, but the clarity of this prohibition should not be taken to represent something more fundamental. Like all judgments about rights, it rests on judgments of strategy about the constraints we need to protect us against those outcomes which we have most reason to avoid.

NOTES

1 *Police Department of Chicago v. Mosley,* 408 U.S. 92 (1972).

2 Here and in the following section I summarize a view of rights that I have set out more fully in "Rights, Goals and Fairness," in *Public and Private Morality,* ed. S. Hampshire (Cambridge: Cambridge University Press, 1978). I have applied this view to freedom of expression in "Freedom of Expression and Categories of Expression," *University of Pittsburgh Law Review* 40 (1979): 519.

3 I have elaborated this view of academic freedom in "Academic Freedom and the Control of Research," in *The Concept of Academic Freedom,* ed. E. Pincoffs (Austin: University of Texas Press, 1975), pp. 237–54.

4 They would thus not follow from the "speech" clause of the First Amendment. Whether they would be covered by the "press" clause is, of course, a separate question.

5 Laurence Tribe, *American Constitutional Law* (Mineola, N.Y.: Foundation Press, 1978), p. 580.

6 Ibid.
7 Ibid., p. 581. The first quoted passage is from *Mosley;* the other, from *Virginia State Board Pharmacy v. Virginia Consumer Council,* 425 U.S. 748 (1976).
8 Tribe, *American Constitutional Law,* pp. 581–2.
9 Geoffrey R. Stone, "Content Regulation and the First Amendment," *William and Mary Law Review* 25 (Winter 1983): 197.
10 Stone, "Content Regulation," p. 218.
11 T. M. Scanlon, Jr., "A Theory of Freedom of Expression," *Philosophy & Public Affairs* 1 (1972): 204–25.
12 Ibid., p. 213.
13 Only roughly, because the range of considerations screened out by my Millian Principle is narrower than what Tribe calls "communicative impact."
14 That is, we must make distinctions between categories of expression of the kind described in the preceding section, even though we may be able to avoid drawing more controversial distinctions between acts of expression within these categories. Tribe is quite clear about the fact that these categorical distinctions convey judgments of relative value. See Tribe, *American Constitutional Law,* p. 583. See also John H. Ely, "Flag Desecration: A Case Study in the Roles of Categorization and Balancing in First Amendment Analysis," *Harvard Law Review* 88 (1975): 1482.
15 Not coincident because even perfect fairness to all parties can result in a "distorted" discussion if there are important considerations that none of these parties wishes to mention (perhaps because some of them are unaware of these considerations).
16 As maintained in *Buckley v. Valeo,* 424 U.S. 1 (1976), at 48–9.

Chapter 12

The rationale of public regulation of the media

Lee C. Bollinger

Public regulation of the broadcast media is now under strong attack and may even be fighting for its life. Opposition to regulation has been gaining strength gradually over the last decade, but it has now gathered such force that even the very federal agency that developed the principal regulations at issue and has served as overseer of the regulatory system for the past half century is openly calling for a return to the free market system as the exclusive mechanism for ensuring a rich marketplace of ideas. That politics makes strange bedfellows has long been appreciated, but the alliance of political ideologies that stands behind this opposition to public regulation gives new life to that adage. The Federal Communications Commission's 1985 "Report on the General Fairness Doctrine Obligations of Broadcast Licensees," which issues the call for the abandonment of the fairness doctrine, draws heavily on the writings and opinions of Justice William O. Douglas.

It is, indeed, the fairness doctrine that is now the primary battleground for the war being waged over public regulation of the media. Generally, three arguments are leveled against the doctrine. First, it is claimed that the doctrine chills more speech than it fosters. Because the doctrine imposes a variety of costs on broadcasters – such as the cost of covering opposing viewpoints at the broadcaster's own expense and the costs of resisting fairness doctrine complaints – broadcasters often choose not to cover public issues at all, thus reducing instead of expanding the amount of discussion of public issues on television and radio. Second, it is said that the doctrine is inherently unenforceable in any principled way, because a decision as to what is and what is not a "controversial issue of public importance," and whether a given broadcaster's programming has provided only one side of that issue, is a fundamentally "subjective" decision that inevitably will lead, and indeed has led, to inconsistent decisions with unarticulated premises. And finally, and I think most important, it is said that the fairness doctrine must be repealed because its rationale has disappeared. Traditionally, the official justification for regulation of broadcasting has been the asserted phenomenon of spectrum scarcity, which yields too few broadcast outlets. But changes in the opportunities for entry into both the electronic and print media markets have now removed what had been an essentially oligopolistic market, making it possible to rely on the free market as the sole method of allocation for political information and ideas.

Together these arguments constitute the principal contemporary case against the fairness doctrine, and they enjoy a forceful as well as an official articulation in the commission's 1985 report, which, as I have already noted, calls for an end to the fairness doctrine. But, in my view, the arguments, at least as they have been developed by the current opponents of public regulation, are seriously flawed and, I would even say, do a disservice to thoughtful reconsideration of the wisdom of having public regulation. They do a disservice primarily by being so incomplete. They appear to be ideologically motivated and, as such, they tend to oversimplify the issues they purport to address.

In this essay I say a few words about the first two arguments against the fairness doctrine, which I have already noted, and then consider at somewhat greater length the third argument, namely, the claim that public regulation like the fairness doctrine is no longer needed because the circumstances justifying it have significantly altered. My objective is to point out their incompleteness and to suggest what inquiries ought to be undertaken if we are serious about giving full consideration to the question of public regulation of the broadcast media in particular and of the mass media in general. I use the FCC report as my primary target, although I believe it is really only illustrative of a pervasive way of thinking about public regulation. I should emphasize again that I do not intend here to argue the ultimate issue of whether the fairness doctrine should be abandoned, modified, or retained unchanged. Nor do I wish to argue the case for or against the constitutionality of the present fairness doctrine (which the commission itself similarly says it avoids). My agenda is more limited. I want to argue that the intellectual premises of the anti–public regulation position are incorrect or incomplete and, accordingly, that we should consider alternative theoretical perspectives on regulations like the fairness doctrine before we reach the conclusion that they be abandoned as a matter of public policy.

I

The weaknesses of the claim that the fairness doctrine has an impermissible chilling effect on coverage of public issues seem to me to be sufficiently straightforward, and I do not intend to discuss them at length here. The commission's conclusion rests entirely on an acceptance of the testimonial claims of some broadcasters that they had chosen not to cover public issues out of a fear that coverage would generate the costs of a fairness doctrine complaint and possible response. These statements were credible, the commission found, because they were essentially admissions against self-interest, given the professional embarrassment and risk of an adverse regulatory response involved in admitting that they, as broadcast licensees, had chosen not to fulfill their journalistic and legal obligations to cover political issues. In a footnote, the commission rejected the possibility of using the first part of the fairness doctrine (which independently requires broadcasters to provide coverage of public issues) to overcome this inhibition and consequent chilling effect resulting from the second part of the doctrine for the reasons that such a course would "increase the government's intrusion into the editorial decision making process of broadcast journalists," "enlarge the opportunity for governmental officials to abuse the doctrine for partisan political purposes," and "increase the economic costs that are borne both by broadcasters and the commission."

This position, as developed and expressed by the commission, is insufficient. The question of the credibility of the broadcasters' testimony seems far more open to doubt than the commission assumes. After all, a broadcaster who claims to have been chilled may have his or her professional embarrassment significantly reduced, if not eliminated entirely, by the likely reputational enhancement that presumably comes from having challenged a scheme of government regulation of journalism; and surely the fear of retaliation by the agency must have been viewed as of marginal importance, given an awareness of the commission's unsympathetic predisposition to the fairness doctrine.

Putting aside the matter of the credibility of the testimony, however, it must be said that the commission only considered half of the real question. For even if the fairness doctrine has chilled in the instances asserted, we still must decide how much we can infer from the concrete evidence about the overall level of chilling, and then we must weigh that against the instances in which the doctrine induces compliance and thereby expands the number of voices that would otherwise occur without the doctrine – inquiries the commission wholly ignores. Finally, as to the commission's dismissal of the possibility of enforcing the first part of the fairness doctrine (something the Supreme Court in *Red Lion* indicated was possible should broadcasters prove reluctant to cover controversial issues of public importance because of the costs associated with complying with the fairness doctrine), it should be clear that the potential costs associated with that course cannot reasonably be regarded as decisive until we have considered what benefits we might gain from more rigorous enforcement.

What we really need to know, and do not at this point, is

what benefits people hope to derive from regulation like the fairness doctrine and the extent to which that hope is realized in practice. I intend to discuss the range of possible benefits later in the essay, but I now turn briefly to the argument about the inherent "subjectivity" involved in the implementation of the fairness doctrine.

II

Looking back over the fairness doctrine case law for the past few decades, one finds a number of highly controverted decisions, with commissioners and judges disagreeing about this and that parts of the doctrine, being unable to give convincing reasons for their views and then frequently reversing themselves over time. Thus, in a series of cases beginning in the late 1960s, the commission went from requiring broadcasters who aired cigarette commercials to provide airtime for antismoking messages to considering a number of fairness doctrine complaints about other commercial advertisements – which produced split results – to a position in 1974 of virtually conceding error in having followed the fairness doctrine into the commercial thicket. And in a famous decision in the 1970s, the federal court of appeals in Washington, D.C., split severely on the question whether an NBC documentary program on abuses in pension programs was really only a program about "some abuses in some programs," which nobody believed was a controversial proposition, or an implicit statement that the pension system was rotten to the core and badly in need of major legislative intervention, which everyone believed to be a controversial issue. After pages upon pages of judicial argument and discussion about the meaning of the text of the program, the case was eventually dismissed as moot.

To some people this record demonstrates that a fairness doctrine is inherently unenforceable, in accordance with the usual standard of principled decision making. The doctrine requires balanced coverage of "controversial issues of public importance." But what "issue," or "issues," does any given program address? If you apply the fairness doctrine only to the "explicit" message of a program, you perhaps accomplish some clarity of enforcement, but only at the expense of opening the opportunity for evasion so wide as to render the doctrine useless. On the other hand, if you leave yourself room to look for subtle expressions of viewpoint, you get a doctrine with bite but one also requiring a hopelessly "subjective" evaluation of what the "real" impact of a program was on its audience. Furthermore, because the doctrine applies only to issues of "public importance," the government agency, as well as the courts, are inevitably drawn into making value judgments about which issues are more important than other issues, and that, it is said, is something the First Amendment does not allow.

Much can be said about this line of argument against the fairness doctrine (especially about the difficulties of sorting out workable guiding principles for any new area of law), but we should understand a simple point that puts the issue in proper perspective: The fairness doctrine is no more open-ended, or open to unprincipled, "subjective" decisions, and no more dependent on the development and use of a hierarchy of values in the realm of public issues, than other well-established areas of First Amendment jurisprudence. In the libel area, for example, we now face much the same tasks of deciding, in the public figure cases, what public controversies warrant the most uninhibited debate and, on the matter of distinguishing statements of opinion from statements of fact, what the overall impact is on the general audience. The feature of uncertainty and the need to reach difficult-to-articulate judgments are hardly unique to public access regulations like the fairness doctrine.

III

I turn now to the question of whether changed circumstances have drained the fairness doctrine of its social usefulness. The questions that need to be asked are these: What concerns might lead a society such as this one to have a regulation like the fairness doctrine for the broadcast media? What might the society be seeking to achieve? What benefits can it reasonably expect to derive from such a policy?

The commission's answer to this question follows a commonly heard and quite simple logical line: The First Amendment both embodies and reflects a basic value of this society, namely, that we share a commitment to seeking truth and wisdom, especially in matters of democratic decision making, and a further belief that the best way to achieve this end is to have a rich available pool of information and ideas. With respect to the broadcast media, however, physical limitations on the number of possible outlets has meant, at least in the past, that too few people would be able to control this highly important means of access to the marketplace of ideas; without correction through government regulation, therefore, we would face an unhealthy situation in which broadcasters would manipulate and control public opinion, primarily by presenting one-sided and biased programming. Hence, the fairness doctrine was devised to correct the market failure produced by the physical limitations of the electromagnetic spectrum.

Now, however, because of the proliferation of outlets in the broadcast media (cable, low-power television, and so on) as well as in the print media, the fear of extraordinary concentration in the broadcast media, which gave rise to the extraordinary remedy of government intervention, is no longer reasonable.

To this line of argument, the proponents of the fairness doctrine have generally responded with two arguments. First, they argue that the asserted increase in availability of outlets has not yet been realized. Second, they claim that even if the other media (notably the print media) are open and unconstricted, we should keep our eyes fixed only on the broadcasting market, and on the opportunities for entry there, because broadcasting has a significantly greater "impact" on its audience than other media; that fact, together with the additional one that the broadcast medium is still severely afflicted by physical limitations, is said to compel us to think of broadcasting as a discrete, unique medium. In short, fairness doctrine proponents look only at the broadcast media and continue to point to the peculiar circumstances of market failure traditionally deemed characteristic of those media.

These responses seem to me to overlook a more central defect in the anti–fairness doctrine position. The more critical defect arises from an assumed premise, namely, the idea that the only rationale for public regulation of this kind involves a kind of market failure. The commission's position, in other words, seems to assume that people have no legitimate interest in having public regulation like the fairness doctrine as long as the *total number* of actual or potential outlets in the media rises above a certain threshold. So long as the shelf of information and ideas can be fully stocked to satisfy consumer demand, we have no reason for intervention. I think this is incorrect.

It is true, as a starting point for discussion, that, given the premises of the First Amendment, if only a few people or groups control the access to the marketplace of ideas, then we have great reason to be concerned about the power they wield by virtue of that position. Those individuals may slight or omit discussion of some issues that deserve more attention, and they may do the same to opinions, or viewpoints, about issues they do discuss. Either action on their part may well distort public discussion and decision making and produce unfortunate consequences for the society.

But, assuming this is true, we should recognize immediately that our concern is with power – that is, the ability to command an audience more or less exclusively – and that is a concern undiminished by the way in which such power is achieved. It should make no difference to us, in other words, whether the power is the consequence of physical limitations associated with the use of that medium (the traditional assumption about broadcasting); or the result of limitations of the economic system (the traditional assumption about concentration of power in the daily newspaper market); or – and this is the commonly unrecognized point – the result of clear market success in solidly appealing to a segment or majority of the community. It is the risks associated with power over access to the marketplace that raise the sense of alarm, and not the source of that power. It is, therefore, a great mistake to assume that a large *total number* of entrants, or potential entrants, in the media, however defined, is by itself sufficient to quell that sense of alarm.

But even this does not fully capture the range of our potential concerns, for we may add to the point that we may reasonably be concerned with power however it is achieved, the point that we may reasonably be concerned with the nature, or character, of our own behavior in the discussion of public questions – which means, in essence, a concern with the nature of our demands in the market. We may recognize in ourselves troublesome tendencies: to jump to conclusions from partial evidence without waiting to hear or read the other side; to want to hear only what we are predisposed to believe, and to shelter from our attention ideas and opinions that differ from and challenge our own political values; and so on. Such tendencies may have rather obvious bad effects for the society, not just in yielding misinformed and closed-minded citizens but also in creating subgroups within the society that feel the alienation of exclusion.

The reality that most raises this set of concerns (although it is important to understand that it is not the only possible situation that might) is the one that many would describe, with justice, as today's mass media world. A few networks reaching millions of people at the national level, and a single daily newspaper reaching the most residents in each local community, constitute the primary sources of national and local information for the vast majority of citizens. That these sources of news and information do not by any means exhaust the potential for other entrants is clear, just as it may be conceded that these sources are, in a sense, simply giving viewers and readers what they "want," or demand, through the expression of their preferences in the marketplace. And yet it is hardly unimaginable that we – the same "we" that issue our marketplace votes for what we get – might be very concerned about how we are behaving, about what choices we are making, in that system. And we may, accordingly, decide together, through public regulation, that we would like, to some extent, to alter or modify the demands we find ourselves making in that free market context.

The thought here is, I think, the same that motivates groups of people or institutions to decide that decisions will be made only in the context of a collective meeting. We recognize that if a meeting is not held, and we are instead left to our own free choice about whether and how to inform ourselves on any given issue, too many of us will neglect to undertake the burdens of self-education, choosing instead to pursue more pleasant things, or will only inform ourselves selectively because of a natural inclination to seek out only those who already agree with us, or for any number of other reasons that have nothing whatever to do with the likelihood of acquiring full information.

Thus, even though we may have the *opportunity* to acquire all relevant points of view, in the absence of agreed-upon structures or methods for deciding questions, we may very well end up with poorer decisions than we would otherwise have. It is important, therefore, that we recognize the following: Public regulation requiring the media to grant access under certain conditions need not be thought of as designed only to correct structural defects in the market. That too few people wield too much power over public discussion may be a good and sufficient reason to justify regulation, but it certainly is not a necessary condition for regulation. Other sufficient concerns may come to the foreground in its absence, and we must therefore be careful not to make the mistake of thinking that public regulation hinges only on one possible rationale, and certainly not on the traditionally expressed rationale of market failure.

Does it make sense, though, to impose public regulation only in the context of broadcasting? This is an important question, especially since it seems clear that the concern underlying such regulation, which focuses on the quality or character of our thinking as consumers in a free market, is a general one – that is, one that arises in both print and broadcast media. In the past I have argued that, as a constitutional matter, it makes good sense to allow public access regulation only in the broadcast media, even though there may be no distinction between broadcasting and print for these purposes. If both media, I argued, are afflicted by a common concern, which I then called the problem of excessive concentration of power, it is appropriate to permit partial but not complete regulation to remedy that problem. I do not wish to revive that issue here, but I do want to consider whether, even if one believes that regulation *would be justified* and permissible in the context of print as well as broadcasting, we should be justified in choosing, as a matter of public policy, to impose public access regulation in the broadcast media only. It seems to me the answer is clearly yes.

A partial remedy offers many advantages. The potential costs or risks of the undertaking are, of course, contained. And in the context of public regulation of the media that is especially important. The risk of government abuse is ever present, and it may therefore be thought sensible to limit the reach of government power, as well as to provide an unregulated sector to serve effectively as a guard against abuse. Such a risk, therefore, may be not only contained but also reduced. And the reduction can be furthered by limiting regulation to a new medium, where the sense that the introduction of regulation constitutes a break with tradition is substantially lessened and where the regulators must constantly work in an environment in which they are the exception and the unregulated sphere the norm.

Considering the effectiveness of a partial remedy, it of course offers at least some access to excluded groups or points of view. But perhaps of equal or even greater importance is the potential of the regulation to assume symbolic proportions. It can represent – as, indeed, I think the fairness doctrine does – a public endorsement of the proper professional norms for journalists generally, as well as an expression of what are appropriate demands in the marketplace.

A difficult question remains: it may fairly be asked by people who strongly favor the free market approach exclusively, if there is no market failure and if people have an understanding of what the problems are in getting the information they need and supposedly want, then why should we permit government regulation (especially in the First Amendment area where the concern over government abuse runs high) when it seems entirely possible for people to implement their desires through the market system? If people want balanced discussions of public issues, then let them demand it. And if they don't demand it, then perhaps we should assume they don't want it – a choice that belongs to them and that we should respect.

It must be remembered that the question is not whether "we" should impose an access or a balance requirement on "others," either the minority or a majority, because we see them as needing legal correction. We should not allow the specter of paternalism to be invoked as a means of diverting attention away from the real issue. Rather, as I have stated it, the question is whether the majority may, if it chooses, sensibly turn to public institutions and regulations as a means of altering to some degree the choices they see themselves making in the open market.

The point seems helpfully made by the example I used earlier of the choice to decide questions in the context of a meeting instead of by individual vote. It is true that a meeting saves time and effort in gathering the information needed for a vote on any decision, but the advantages, I think, go well beyond that. Again, we see that it is simply an unavoidable feature of human nature that, if left to an anonymous or private role, we will neglect to inform ourselves or will inform ourselves only partially. We will make different choices and behave differently depending on the context in which the choices are made. The point need not depend on our being disappointed with our behavior in one system; we may simply feel that there are different sides of ourselves, different preferences, and that each side is only satisfied in different structures. The critical issue is whether we are prepared to accept the proposition that people may reasonably want to guard against, or to moderate, certain inclinations they know they have by altering the context in which they will exercise choice.

For most people who oppose public regulation of the media on First Amendment grounds, the above proposition seems to me to be one they simply cannot deny, since they themselves ultimately rely on precisely the same proposition. For them the issue cannot be whether or not it is wise for a society to set up different, or special, social institutions for the purpose of fostering certain values that are thought likely to be undervalued by any other method of social decision making, for that is the common view of the role of the First Amendment and the Supreme Court.

IV

It has been said for several decades now that the original model of freedom of speech and press, which emphasizes the importance of protecting those activities against the power and threat of censorship, is no longer sufficient to deal with the realities of modern life or the aspirations that originally motivated those who fought for that model. Primarily because of the growth of media and the obvious disparity in the power of speech that some enjoy over others, especially in having access to the mass media, many have called for the recognition of an affirmative side of the First Amendment, one that would create opportunities for speech and not just protect against suppression. We ought now to recognize that even that achievement would not leave us bereft of aspirations, for a situation of full equality of access would not, given human nature, necessarily guarantee our best behavior or the best decisions.

Chapter 13

The role of a free press in strengthening democracy

SANFORD J. UNGAR

The United States has always placed a tremendous amount of faith in the ability of free and open communication to bring peace, stability, and justice to its people. It is ironic, then, that the American government has often failed to recognize the fundamental role of a free press in sustaining democracies everywhere, and in helping to build them where they do not exist. This role transcends national borders, ideological fashions, and short-term changes in political climate. Indeed, it is fair to say that the most basic goals of U.S. foreign policy – the promotion of liberty, the fostering of free-market capitalism, and the securing of American political and strategic interests around the globe – cannot truly be achieved without at the same time advocating freedom for the media worldwide.[1]

Unhappily, administrations of both parties have, in the post–World War II era, been willing to accept varying degrees of suppression of press freedom on the part of friendly governments – from Great Britain to South Korea, from Chile to Liberia to Singapore, among many others – as the price of doing business in a world of realpolitik. In judging the degree of freedom in other countries, U.S. leaders preoccupied with elections (preferably conducted American style), often ignore more significant indices of free expression, most notably whether the news media are permitted to offer the people full and truthful information.

Nor have American news organizations been as forthcoming on this issue as they could be. While jealously guarding their First Amendment freedoms at home and fighting for their own access to information overseas, some U.S. media institutions have been slow to understand the importance of supporting similar guarantees for the journalists of other nations.

The point is a simple one: A free press is needed everywhere, no less in developing countries than in advanced industrial societies. In any country where political institutions and opposition groups are not yet – or are no longer – operating freely, a press able to report and reflect popular discontent with the course of national policy or with the government of the moment can serve as an important warning light, identifying early problems that demand solution if political stability is to be maintained. Far from subverting public order in unstable societies, free and robust media can actually promote conciliation by encouraging the discussion of controversial issues before they reach a volatile or explosive stage.

All governments anywhere, whatever their makeup, share a certain antipathy to the press. Notwithstanding their avowals that they are committed to openness and honesty, officials will usually seek to prevent the thorough airing and debate of issues that are uncomfortable or embarrassing. Such instinctive secrecy – particularly in the field of foreign policy – tempts governments to use deception as a tool to achieve their political ends. Abroad as in the United States, it is critically important that the media not permit this to happen, that they intervene to promote public discussion of problems that may not be fully or adequately handled by the normal processes of government.

The promotion of a free press should therefore be a priority in American foreign policy, without regard to which party is in power at any given time. There is a great yearning around the world today for free expression through open media, and it is one of the most significant areas where the United States still has reason to boast of its own record (although, to be sure, press freedom comes under threat in that country all too frequently).

Contrary to conventional wisdom, freedom of the press is one of the institutions of American democracy that is most, rather than least, transferable to other nations – including those of the Communist bloc and the Third World. Once in place, it is an extraordinarily powerful catalyst for other democratic reforms.

Perhaps no leader in recent times has appreciated this more fully than Mikhail Gorbachev. Greater press freedom is one of the central elements in his policies of *glasnost* (openness) and *perestroika* (restructuring), not least because the media have served as a useful weapon in ferreting out corruption in the Soviet system. Newspapers and magazines felt an immediate impact when they began to exploit his reforms. While subscribers flocked to the new Soviet journals and literary periodicals testing the limits, the readership of traditional newspapers calling for a more cautious approach, such as *Pravda*, the official publication of the Communist party, plummeted.[2] Eventually Gorbachev replaced *Pravda*'s editor with one of his personal advisers. Now a committee of the Soviet parliament has drafted a law banning censorship of the mass media. Yet Gorbachev appears to have had second thoughts about the potential consequences of press freedom; when the Soviet Union's best-selling newspaper, the weekly *Argumenty i Fakty*, got too feisty, he put pressure on the editor to step down.

Contrast the trend under Gorbachev with recent events in Deng Xiaoping's China. The spring 1989 student protests were caused, in part, by widespread frustration with corruption and with the fact that economic reforms had not been accomplished by a loosening of political restrictions. Indeed, long before the events in Tienanmen Square, Deng made clear that he would tolerate no challenge to Communist Party rule, and the media were expected to toe the line.

A press empowered to expose the financial abuses that accompanied economic expansion, and to discuss the political ferment that was spreading across China, might well have helped the country avoid the cataclysm of June 1989. It is no accident that one of the strongest and earliest demands of the protesters was for more open and honest media, and no surprise that the pro-democracy movement had many open, bold journalistic supporters at Radio Beijing, the *People's Daily,* and other official outlets.

This is not to say that freedom of the press is easy to establish in countries that have little recent experience with democratic values and institutions. But press freedom is much more likely to be accepted in some nations than other democratic traditions, such as an institutionalized opposition party, that might be seen as too much of a threat to existing regimes. Instead of functioning strictly as an adversary of the government, a free press can provide an effective forum for public debate, a mechanism for precious two-way communication between the people and their leaders. In this role, it can accomplish a great deal. Any country with a genuinely free press, for example, will have a hard time holding a large number of political prisoners without having to explain itself to the public. A free press may, in fact, be more effective than an opposition party in achieving change in an oppressive system.

One of Africa's most persistent problems is the failure of many of its leaders to allow legal opposition movements or to establish a constitutional succession process. This has contributed to the instability of quite a few African countries; so long as political competition and the opportunity to participate in public affairs are so restricted, ordinary people are bound to distrust their government.

But although African leaders may not tolerate an institutionalized opposition party, they can sometimes be persuaded to accept the existence of an opposition press. Kenya is a case in point. Granted, to say that Kenya has been home to some of the freest media in Africa is not to say much; President Daniel arap Moi has imprisoned some journalists in recent years, and many editors do, in effect, censor themselves. But Moi "does allow wide criticism and discussion of social issues at a certain level" in the press.[3] Not coincidentally, Kenya "is one of the few newly independent countries in the world to enjoy an unbroken run of political stability since independence" and has "one of the most thriving economies in Africa."[4] To be sure, Moi's latest assaults on human rights, including press freedom, have called Kenya's record – and its future stability – into question; yet the last remaining fragments of open opposition to his regime find expression not in the country's Parliament, but in its outspoken newspapers and magazines.

Leaders who are intolerant of press freedom may soon find themselves powerless to prevent it, as new technologies are making it much easier to launch and sustain independent media. Governments that reject the notion of a legal opposition press will find an illegal one increasingly difficult to control. This became especially apparent in Panama. Except for a brief period in February 1988, that country's independent media were shut down beginning in the summer of 1987, as military leader Manuel Antonio Noriega struggled to maintain his monopoly on power. Yet a Panamanian exile who has taught at Davidson College in North Carolina and Lehigh University in Pennsylvania managed to produce an underground newspaper, *Alternativa.* He transmitted the paper over telephone lines to the Panamanian News Center in Washington, D.C., which then forwarded it to a number of facsimile receivers located in banks, law offices, and travel agencies in Panama. Within hours, up to thirty thousand photocopies of the paper were on Panama's streets.[5]

One could argue that the rarity of press freedom, especially in Third World and Communist-bloc countries, is proof of how difficult it is for this democratic value to take hold. But the fact that it has traditionally been one of the first liberties to be denied by totalitarian governments demonstrates the significance and power of a free press and is further reason for making its promotion a priority of U.S. foreign policy. Even when a free press does not lead to the establishment of other parallel institutions, it inevitably reinforces democratic ideals. Invariably, with freedom of the press, people "are in a position to participate in the decision-making process. The result of this shift is to redistribute power, which in the long run results in a different form of government."[6]

Less than a year after Nicaragua's *La Prensa* – the newspaper that once opposed the Somoza regime and later became a thorn in the side of the Sandinistas – was allowed to reopen in October 1987, after having been closed for sixteen months, one reporter commented, "Nicaragua's news outlets currently constitute the country's most vital arena of political activity."[7] The wife of slain *La Prensa* editor Joaquin Chamorro, Violeta Chamorro, who became the Nicaraguan democratic opposition's presidential candidate, has asserted that "freedom of the press is a basic criterion for determining if there is democracy in a country."[8]

Certainly there are cases in which freedom of the press has been difficult to establish, or reestablish. If a regime is brutally repressive and does not even pretend to be accountable to its people, it will never willingly tolerate a free press; it simply would not be in its best interest to do so. In Chile, for example, the repressive regime of General Augusto Pinochet succeeded for well over a decade in suppressing the previously independent print media; by the time of its downfall, it had constructed a network of thirty-four laws and regulations restricting the press.[9] Even as late as 1988, while building up to the plebiscite he conducted as a referendum on his rule, Pinochet brought thirty-one journalists to trial, most of them in military courts, on charges of "offending the armed forces." Around the time of the October 1988 plebiscite, some twenty-four Chilean and foreign journalists were physically attacked, in what appeared to be a carefully calculated strategy of assault on the media.[10] Only after Pinochet had lost the plebiscite did the Chilean press finally begin to come back into its own.

(The United States, alas, has a particularly sorry history of involvement on the wrong side of this issue in Chile. During the Nixon administration, the Central Intelligence Agency [CIA] provided funds to help *El Mercurio*, Chile's leading national newspaper, undermine the leftist regime of Salvador Allende, who was overthrown by Pinochet in a bloody military coup in 1971. This was a case of American prestige and money being used to promote press manipulation rather than freedom.)

The Sandinista government in Nicaragua and Moi's regime in Kenya can hardly be called democracies at this point. Yet both allow, if not a completely free press, at least an overt opposition press. This may be because they recognize that independent media, while they often agitate and cause controversy, may in fact be a crucial component in achieving stability. Shrewd (if repressive) leaders realize that whatever their own propaganda may say, there is always opposition, and that this opposition will inevitably express itself – through wall posters in China; graffiti in Chile; jazz and rock music in Czechoslovakia; tape cassettes smuggled into the bazaars and mosques of the Shah's Iran; and the unions, legal or otherwise, in Poland.

If press freedom is denied, this opposition may turn to other, more violent forms of expression. While *La Prensa* was closed in Nicaragua, Violeta Chamorro said, "By closing down the last reserve of civic opposition in Nicaragua, the Sandinistas reveal they have decided on a military solution, although they preach the opposite. They have closed the doors to dialogue and opened the doors to war."[11] After *La Prensa* was reopened, Sofia Montenegro, a senior editor at the official Sandinista newspaper, *La Barricada,* seemed to concur when she observed, "The war has changed from the military front to the political and ideological one. And the media are the battleground."[12]

The regime in South Africa would do well to look at the Sandinista example in allowing *La Prensa* to resume its independent reporting. The country that once prided itself on having the freest media in Africa has, since it first declared a nationwide state of emergency in June 1986, initiated some of the most severe censorship laws in the world. The South African home-affairs minister has the power to ban publications for three months, to install resident censors in newspaper offices, and to require prepublication approval of articles.[13] The government of former President P. W. Botha used this power with abandon, to stifle any coverage deemed too critical of the regime. Two black weeklies, *The New Nation* and *South,* as well as the country's most prominent white-run antiapartheid newspaper, *The Weekly Mail,* were temporarily suspended in 1988. The complex, ambiguous censorship laws and the constant threat of suspension have failed miserably as attempts to stabilize the country, however, and the regime probably made conditions worse by its actions. One observer has pointed out that in South Africa "the danger . . . is that by silencing the media and removing the last of the few non-violent options left to apartheid's opponents, history could take its course in ways bloodier than the West can imagine."[14] It is too early to know whether the new South African president, F. W. de Klerk, will choose press freedom as one of the areas in which he will institute reform; the fact that his brother was a longtime Afrikaans-language newspaper editor may, however, be a hopeful sign.

In the years before his death, the Ayatollah Ruhollah Khomeini may finally have recognized the dangers of government control of the media, even in a theocracy. Although the Iranian press was nationalized after the Islamic revolution of the late 1970s, and no criticism of the Ayatollah himself or of fundamentalist Islamic ideology was allowed, a few years ago there began to be occasional open discussion in the media of government actions and policy. In late 1988, for example, debate raged in the Iranian press over whether the country should seek foreign investment; one Muslim intellectual argued in a series of editorials in the Tehran daily *Ettlaat* that Iran should enter a new age of Islamic modernism.[15] It is possible that Khomeini and his associates realized that the total lack of freedom of expression in Iran under the Shah may have made the latter's downfall more traumatic.

One observer of Iran says, "Now everyone talks more openly; grumbling has become a national pastime, as it is in Western societies."[16] These grumbles are not necessarily a sign that the regime is collapsing, however. They demonstrate, in fact, a certain amount of stability: "Freedom to criticize is a safety valve, something that people consciously appreciate. Even the most unrevolutionary people say that it is one way in which life is better now than it was under the Shah."[17] Life might be better still if this freedom of expression were truly widespread in the Islamic Republic of Iran; several formerly prominent editors are missing and feared dead, presumably because of what they wrote or published.

The late Philippine president Ferdinand Marcos was another leader who, although he certainly was no beacon of democracy, nevertheless appreciated the stabilizing power of press freedom and became quite adept at opening and closing this safety valve. One Filipino reporter said before Marcos's downfall that he was "in fact a very good politician to realize that people need to let off steam. So he is allowing them to do that, but not on substantial matters. The problem is that by loosening up a bit, Mr. Marcos has succeeded in dividing the opposition."[18]

One could argue that this kind of manipulation of press freedom serves to keep tyrants in power. But a freer press only buys a dictator breathing space, not long-run survival. Marcos's charade obviously was not effective for long; he did not loosen up enough to win the trust of independent voices in the Philippine media.

Poland is a good example of the ultimate price states may pay if they muzzle the local press. Under the system that evolved under Communist rule during the postwar period, press censorship was scarcely necessary. Journalists advanced their careers and increased their incomes by censoring themselves, and for the most part they reliably transmitted the message of the rulers to the people, blatantly propagandizing and, at times, helping to ferret out "enemies of the state." The system backfired, however, in the early 1980s under former Party Secretary Edward Gierek. As one analyst of the situation has described it,

> Gierek had insisted on a press that served as a transmission belt from the leaders to the people about the success of the regime's programs. He had closed the official channels of com-

munication to those who had any evidence to the contrary. He therefore had cut off opportunities to develop a dialogue with the people and persuaded himself that they were unaware that he was lying to them.[19]

Ironically, Gierek's tactics prevented him from realizing that he and his policies were in trouble. Furthermore, his insistence on a "propaganda of success" did not ensure the regime's legitimacy, as he had hoped, but, as Albright points out, "created a frustrated, disoriented, and restive population." The media kept telling the Polish people that the economy was steadily improving, when in fact they found themselves standing in ever longer lines to obtain basic goods and had to share apartments with other families. Among the graffiti that began to appear was an especially significant complaint, *Prasa klamie* ("The press lies").[20] This was not difficult to understand, given the high literacy rate in Poland and the foreign broadcasts and publications that penetrated the country and told the truth about conditions there.

With the growth of the Solidarity labor union, however, came public access to types and levels of information that had long been denied. Solidarity developed its own press, uncensored bulletins and pamphlets appeared in factories and offices, and even journalists working for the official press began to behave in a less restrained manner.[21] The demand for information rose with the supply. Newspaper kiosks in cities and towns were swamped early in the morning; in some places newspapers sold for ten times their normal price. Western reporters published and broadcast a version of events that confirmed Solidarity's view of the Polish reality.

This ad hoc press freedom, which quickly grew out of control, obviously brought pressure from the Soviet Union and contributed to the imposition of martial law by Wojciech Jaruzelski in 1982. It might be argued that if Gierek had not allowed such press freedom, stability could have been maintained and the Communists would still be firmly in power in Poland today. This, however, is unlikely. Gierek allowed too little freedom, and he allowed it too late. The boiling point had long since been reached in Poland, and the independent press was hardly the only force working against the regime.

Subsequent events in Poland have proved the point. By the late 1980s Poland faced energy and housing shortages, staggering debt, and a continually falling real income. Solidarity had not gone away when outlawed, it had simply gone underground – and the underground press helped coordinate union strategy.[22] Jaruzelski tried to defuse violent opposition by allowing a certain level of criticism of his regime in the press. The tactic worked, as it had for Marcos, for the time being: In 1987 one observer wrote, "Faced with a firm but tolerant government, the Polish opposition has lost momentum."[23]

But by 1988 this strategy had failed. Poland continued to decline economically, and when the local Communist leadership looked to the Soviet Union, it found no backing from Gorbachev for the traditional kinds of solutions. In February 1988, Solidarity adviser Jacek Kuron observed in the main underground weekly, *Tygodnik Mazowsze,* "The specter of a social explosion is haunting the country."[24]

In 1989 the Poles achieved reform beyond even the Solidarity activists' wildest imaginations. The results of semifree elections in June made it clear that the Communist party could no longer hope to persuade the people to make the sacrifices necessary to restore the nation's economy. Instead after much haggling, Tadeusz Mazowiecki, former editor in chief of Solidarity's weekly newspaper, became Poland's first non-Communist prime minister in forty years. That a journalist had more credibility and maneuvering room as a new political leader than the internationally known father of the Solidarity movement, Lech Walesa, speaks volumes on the importance of press freedom in the circumstances. Indeed, one of Mazowiecki's first and most important decisions was to name another Solidarity journalist to run Poland's state-owned radio and television service. Ending the Communists' postwar monopoly over state broadcasting had been one of Solidarity's key goals in its drive toward power.

Poland's dictators, like so many others, learned that it is impossible to use the media as a tool of manipulation indefinitely. Societies cannot be frozen or anesthetized to the point where the public will believe everything it is told. Too much change is taking place too quickly in this era, whether above or beneath the surface, and the press is better able than any other institution to reflect the pressure points, to show where the pain is being felt and explain what must be done to relieve it. Wise leaders will get the message and adapt in meaningful ways. The rest will be removed, constitutionally or otherwise. Whatever happens, the media will play a central role in the political transition.

None of this is to suggest that countries in the Communist bloc or the Third World are the only ones in which a free press serves as a catalyst for democratic reform. Even in the United States, where press freedom is probably more highly developed than anywhere else in the world, the media must sometimes act as the conscience of the nation, and that role may require them to function as a lonely adversary of the government in power.

To take one example from recent U.S. history, major institutions in the American press performed this controversial but necessary role in 1971, when they made public the "Pentagon Papers," a classified Defense Department history of the American role in Southeast Asia.[25] At the moment when the *New York Times*, the *Washington Post*, and other newpapers published articles based on these top-secret documents, Congress was still far behind the American public in its attitudes and actions in relation to Vietnam; the legislature, and for that matter the executive branch, had to be shocked by the press into recognizing certain realities and taking certain steps. By revealing that American governments of both parties had systematically lied to the public about the circumstances in Vietnam for several decades, these articles made it easier to effect a change in American policy. When finally the Supreme Court had upheld the right of the newspapers to publish articles based on the documents, it was clear that the media had made a significant contribution to the vitality of the American system through this dramatic episode.

(The Pentagon Papers, as it turned out, also figured prominently in the Watergate affair. The original reason for creating the White House "plumbers" was to investigate Daniel Ellsberg, the former government official who leaked the documents to the media; they broke into his psychiatrist's office, looking for his medical records, long before moving on to the Democratic National Committee.[26] Here again, the press played a crucial part in safeguarding democracy by exposing these illegal acts by government agents.)

It would be comforting to believe that the lessons of the Pentagon Papers case have been well recognized by subsequent administrations. But even as Ronald Reagan accused the American media of being influenced by Communist disinformation, it was revealed that the Office of Public Diplomacy for Latin America and the Caribbean in the U.S. State Department had surreptitiously written or underwritten articles intended to promote American aid to the antigovernment Contra rebels in Nicaragua. The Bush administration, like so many before it, vowed to ferret out the sources of unofficial leaks of government information; but Attorney General Richard Thornburgh put a new bite into the issue by reviving an old Nixon administration threat to subpoena reporters' telephone records in order to discover their sources.

Freedom of the press has come under disturbingly frequent attack in recent years in other Western democracies. The close ties between Britain and the United States make it a delicate subject for American officials to raise, but the fact is that the British media – and the public officials who may deal with them – have been repeatedly restricted during the more than a decade that Margaret Thatcher has been prime minister. Piece by piece, the Thatcher government has pressed a vigorous attack on British civil liberties. This goes far beyond what has long been possible under the Official Secrets Act.

The crisis in Britain has caught many people by surprise. But *Index on Censorship*, a magazine published in London expressly dedicated to tracking threats to freedom of expression around the world, devoted its entire issue of September 1988 to the problem. "Liberty is ill in Britain," wrote Ronald Dworkin, professor of jurisprudence at Oxford University and of law at New York University, in the magazine's introductory essay. "Censorship is no longer an isolated exception, in which the nation grudgingly gives up some of its liberty, with great regret and a keen sense of loss, in the face of some emergency. . . . The sad truth is that the very *concept* of liberty . . . is being challenged and corroded by the Thatcher government."[27]

Recent changes in the Official Secrets Act strongly encourage the prosecution of British civil servants who engage in "whistle-blowing" – telling the press and the public about corruption or other official misconduct in government. And under a new clause of the local government bill, officials are forbidden to express opinions on the rights of homosexuals that diverge from government policy.

Thatcher's government has continued to move in this direction despite some notable setbacks. One was the failure to prevent newspapers and magazines from discussing the contents of *Spycatcher*, by Peter Wright, a former member of the British secret service, or, indeed, to prosecute Wright under the Official Secrets Act for writing the book. But this was no victory for free speech. Britain's courts ruled against the prime minister largely because Wright's book had already been widely published in other countries, including Australia and the United States. "I would stress," said Lord Keith, senior judge of the five law lords hearing the Wright case, "that I do not base this [ruling] upon any balancing of public interest, nor upon any considerations of freedom of the press, but simply on the view that all possible damage to the interest of the Crown has already been done."[28]

Shortly after the *Spycatcher* decision, Thatcher struck at broadcasters. In October 1988, her government announced that radio and television would be prohibited from airing interviews with members or supporters of "terrorist" organizations. The edict was an obvious effort to silence Sinn Fein, the political arm of the Irish Republican Army, which had caused so much trouble in Northern Ireland. During election campaigns, broadcasters are free to quote Sinn Fein as a legal political organization; but when the election ends, Sinn Fein representatives again become taboo.[29]

Israel, which prides itself on being the only democracy in the Middle East and purports to share Western values of free expression, has also come under criticism recently for the restrictions it has imposed on reporters covering the Palestinian *intifada* (uprising) in the West Bank and the Gaza Strip. Israeli military censors have long imposed limits on the foreign and domestic media in the territories occupied since the 1967 war, but awareness of the phenomenon has been much more widespread since December 1987, when the *intifada* began. (In fact, many Israelis and supporters of Israel have attempted to deflect blame for the uprising to the press, a common ploy once used by segregationists in the American South to explain their bad public image.)

There were earlier incidents that made Israel uncomfortable. In 1984, for example, the tabloid *Hadashot* broke ranks with other newspapers and published a story that the then defense minister, Moshe Arens, had appointed a respected Israeli general to investigate the deaths of two Arab terrorists after a bus hijacking. Photographs had come to light showing that at least one of the hijackers was alive for a time after his capture by Israeli security officers. Relying on emergency regulations originally promulgated during the British mandate over Palestine, Arens ordered *Hadashot* closed for four days for printing the story against government wishes.[30]

The *intifada* has exacerbated tense relations between journalists and Israeli soldiers. As it dawned on the Israelis that they were losing the television war – that they were ironically being portrayed as Goliaths arrayed against stone-throwing Davids – the soldiers came to view the press as an enemy.[31]

This attitude was unfortunately reinforced by at least one influential American. In February 1988, former Secretary of State Henry Kissinger reportedly advised that "Israel should bar the media from entry into the territories . . . accept the short-term criticism of the world press for such conduct, and put down the insurrection as quickly as possible – overwhelmingly, brutally and rapidly."[32]

It must be added, of course, that the press standards of Britain and Israel are much higher than those of most other nations in the world. If Israel's Arab neighbors were held to those standards, most of them would overwhelmingly fail the test. Restrictions on the press are common throughout the Middle East, and if an Arab government wants to impose its will on restive citizens, it tends to do exactly as Kissinger allegedly advised the Israelis to do: It bans the media and works its will. Witness Syria's brutal massacre of an estimated ten thousand people in the city of Hama in 1982, with no meddlesome press coverage.[33]

Some might suggest that press freedom under authoritarian regimes can only benefit the people at the expense of their leaders, and therefore that it would be difficult, if not impossible, to convince most unrepresentative rulers to grant a liberty that is against their own interests. But in fact, because economic and social changes in almost all societies are so fast-paced, those in control have as great a need to learn the truth as those they are trying to control, and so they may come to see the value of a free press as a better source of information than the secret police or some other intelligence agency. And outside countries with a stake in the course of another country's internal events, for political, economic, or humanitarian reasons, also need a dependable version of reality, lest they be led into erroneous assumptions and bad policy choices by the irresponsible rulers of client states.

Few countries exemplify so completely the explosive consequences of turning the press into a one-way "transmission belt from the leaders to the people" as Iran under the Shah.

From the time when the Central Intelligence Agency restored him to his Peacock Throne in 1953, the Shah set off on a course of rapid modernization and Westernization of a country whose people were still very traditional in their beliefs and their life-style. As Iran's oil wealth boomed and caused millions of persons to move to the cities from the countryside, there was great tension over the impact of technology. The majority of the people were increasingly alienated from the elite. But one never would have known any of this from the Iranian press. For that matter, one could not have gleaned any useful information from Iran's media, which were totally dominated by the Shah's court and his social circle. As one Iranian scholar teaching in the United States pointed out,

> Despite the overall growth in the population, literacy rate, and purchasing power of the Iranian people, the circulation of the daily press did not keep pace with the industrial and socio-demographic expansion. The majority of Iranian journalists, writers, and poets were denied access to the media, while those few who remained in the mainstream of politics were reduced to orchestrating the "Great Civilization" of the government policy. The provincial newspapers and magazines, which [had once] formed the main integrating force in the political and cultural life of Iran, also disappeared. Major cities such as Isfahan, Tabriz, Mashad, and Shiraz had no press of their own.[34]

What was published or broadcast in the officially sponsored or tolerated media was widely disbelieved, as much by the more cynical members of the elite as by the mass of the people.[35] Under the circumstances, there were few formal, reliable internal sources of information about what was truly happening in Iran – about the growing abuse of power by Savak, the Shah's secret police; about the ferment developing in the bazaars; and about the spreading dissent, expressed largely by Shi'ite Muslim religious leaders and disseminated primarily by cassette tapes and other artifacts of Western technology. The rumor network became a far more reliable source of information than Iran's media.

Meanwhile, the Shah monopolized most other channels through which the U.S. government might have learned more about what was happening in Iran. He was himself the primary contact and informant for the CIA, and his government successfully discouraged American diplomats from developing relations with opposition groups. Although British and French intelligence seemed to maintain better access to the opposition, American officials distrusted them because of their distance from the Shah. As a result, the reports on Iran that came to Washington from the U.S. embassy in Tehran were unduly glowing about the Shah's successes and his future prospects.

Foreign correspondents working in or visiting Iran were inevitably more skeptical. Although they too were often drawn in by the grandeur of the Shah's court, they did seek out the opposition and report the use of torture by Savak. As one former American official with responsibility for Iran noted, "the Shah was very sensitive to the growing tide of uncomplimentary reporting in the U.S. media" and worried especially about its effect on American-Iranian relations. During the period just before the 1976 U.S. presidential election and in the first year of Jimmy Carter's administration, the Shah tried to avoid embarrassing the United States, by cutting back on the use of torture, reducing the number of political prisoners, and introducing some reforms into the Iranian judicial system.[36]

But still the Shah did not allow the government-controlled Iranian press to function more freely, and he continued to be insulated from critical opinion within his own country. Finally, the publication of an officially sanctioned article ridiculing the Ayatollah Khomeini unleashed the wave of mass demonstrations that brought down the Shah.

It is interesting to speculate now on how things might have been different – for the Shah and for American political fortunes in his country – if Iran had had a free press. This is to suggest not that change, even drastic change, would not have occurred, but that the process might have been more gradual, less violent, and, for the United States as well as the Iranian people, less traumatic.

Certainly the transition was more benign in the case of another traditional American client state, the Philippines.

There the work of a relatively free domestic press, along with the active involvement of the foreign media, was a crucial factor in bringing about the fall of a dictator, Ferdinand Marcos, and his replacement by a president who enjoyed popular support, Corazon Aquino.

For more than two decades after receiving its independence from the United States in 1946, the Philippines was regarded as having the freest press in Asia, and perhaps one of the freest in the world. The Americans, who had governed the Philippines as a colony from 1901 until independence, made sure of this, leaving behind a constitution with a U.S.-style bill of rights that prohibited any laws abridging freedom of the press. But in September 1972, the day after a television news report portrayed an aborted ambush of Marcos's defense minister as a government-staged event intended to stir concern over subversion, Marcos declared martial law and, among other measures, temporarily closed down all the print and broadcast facilities in the country. He attacked "lawless elements, their cadres, fellow-travellers, friends, sympathizers and supporters" for using the Philippine media to distribute "deliberately slanted and overly exaggerated news stories and news commentaries as well as false, vile, foul and scurrilous statements, utterances, writings and pictures."[37]

For more than a decade, the previously proud Philippine media were forced into a position of outrageous submission, notwithstanding Marcos's periodic and insincere scolding that the press was being too servile. Some journalists actually went to work for the government, helping implement draconian censorship; an Office of Media Affairs in the Malacanang Palace told the press how to handle events in the news and which stories it should emphasize. The recklessly independent Manila television stations were quickly brought under control by making them part of the financial empire of the Marcos family and their friends. Even after martial law was lifted in 1981, there were still stringent restrictions on the press; to make "disparaging remarks" with the purpose of undermining the government was a serious crime.

But the assassination of opposition leader Benigno Aquino, as he returned in August 1983 from self-exile in the United States, changed all that. Convinced that the Marcos government was responsible for killing the much loved Aquino, middle-class Filipinos staged massive demonstrations. And having seen the story of Aquino's return and assassination played down or ignored altogether, except by one small Catholic radio station and a newly emboldened society magazine, they made greater freedom of the press one of their key demands.

Remarkably, the Philippine business establishment, which was itself embarrassed by Marcos's behavior, organized an advertising and circulation boycott of the largest newspapers in the country, all of which were controlled by Marcos's associates; before long, those papers' coverage of the Aquino story and the government's cover-up became more balanced. At the same time, new opposition publications emerged, some with financing from the same businessmen. Within a few months, there were at least ten new nonestablishment newspapers on the stands, and there was no turning back.[38]

The return to a Philippine tradition of robust and lively dialogue in the press – and the fact that the United States and other nations were fully aware of the ferment, courtesy of the international media – obviously contributed to Marcos's decision to hold presidential elections early in 1986 and to take seriously the challenge of Benigno Aquino's widow, by then the leader of an opposition coalition. Indeed, Marcos's capacity to continue to control most of the broadcast media – and to orchestrate television coverage of the election campaign, which was absurdly biased in his favor – only angered the public further. The day before the election, his Office of Media Affairs distributed a thirty-page collection of "talking points," advising radio and television personalities on how to convince the public that there was nothing questionable about the balloting or the tabulation of votes. At the one Manila station that could claim nominal independence from the Marcos government, the woman who was news director and principal anchor person decided to abandon election-night coverage altogether rather than follow the guidelines.[39]

Some two weeks after the election, it was Marcos's loss of control over the Manila television stations that finally sealed the collapse of his regime. As it became ever clearer that he had stolen votes and that the public did not support him, Marcos lost the loyalty of the military, and detachments of troops took over one television station after another; antigovernment journalists moved in behind them. The final indignity came when Marcos insisted on going through with his own inauguration for a new term as president and demanded that it be televised, but was unable to keep the one station carrying it on the air for the full ceremony. Corazon Aquino's inauguration, held at the same time, was taped by a station whose loyalties had changed, and it was broadcast to the public later. That same night, Marcos left the country for exile in Hawaii.[40]

The American media – particularly the commercial television networks – also played a key role in the ultimately peaceful Philippine revolution. Perhaps out of vanity more than anything else, Marcos permitted the foreign press to work unencumbered during his final campaign, and Americans got an unprecedentedly thorough inside view of a foreign nation's politics. In fact, the only one-on-one debate that Marcos and Aquino were ever scheduled to have was supposed to be on ABC News's *Nightline,* with Ted Koppel as moderator; that fell through because of last-minute conditions imposed by Marcos, but the two candidates did appear on the program in consecutive interviews with Koppel. The extent of American network coverage of the Philippine election campaign and of Marcos's last-ditch effort to stay in power – the anchors of the three U.S. evening news programs all broadcast directly from Manila at one time or another – clearly put Congress and the American public on Aquino's side. As in many other cases over the years, the American press was ahead of the U.S. political system on a critical issue of foreign policy.

President Reagan finally had no choice but to withdraw his backing from Marcos. As one media critic observed, "In a precarious few days, it was the total collapse of Marcos' American support that sped the end. TV proved its awesome power."[41] Another way to put it would be that a free press, Philippine and American, provided both warning lights and a safety valve. One might argue that Marcos would have held on longer if he could have retained control of the Philippine media. But the media were only a mirror of public opinion: Marcos, like the Shah, was doomed in part because manipulation of the press had kept him in a cocoon of ignorance. The difference is that the somewhat freer media of the Philippines made it possible for the inevitable Marcos–Aquino transition to occur with little violence.

As a postscript to the Iranian and Philippine cases, it should be pointed out that a government-controlled press is often a useless press; the public recognizes it as the purveyor of propaganda. One African journalist commented on African governments that censor:

> Even governments are sometimes worried because the public is jaded with the usual hackneyed coverage of events by the government media. And there is growing unease in official circles that many people have lost interest in watching and listening to news reports on television and radio or reading them in the print media. In some countries newspaper sales have fallen and those who buy them do so because they have found them a cheap substitute for wrapping paper and toilet rolls.[42]

The traditional argument commonly advanced by Third World representatives, and by many of their friends in the West, is that press freedom is a luxury that developing societies cannot afford. It is often explained that "given the conditions of scarce resources, a colonial legacy, a poorly educated population, tribal and ethnic rivalries, and a subservient position in the world economic and information systems, a free press can too easily lead to an inability of government to function and to internal chaos" in Third World countries.[43] Commonly, the importance assigned to the task of building confidence in national leaders and institutions, as well as to creating a consensus around central elements of government policy, is thought to transcend any ideas of independence that might be entertained by local journalists. Indeed, the usual syndrome in some parts of the Third World is for political leaders – especially those who are corrupt and repressive – to regard any comment from the press that does not toe the party line as subversive.

In reality, the existence of a free press is not entirely rare in developing countries. One 1988 survey listed some thirty Third World countries – as diverse as Colombia, India, Trinidad, and Botswana – as enjoying a "generally free" press.[44] Yet such classifications are not clear-cut; the governments of some countries considered to enjoy a free press, such as India, have been making subtle and not so subtle threats to that freedom.[45]

A free press can be easily undermined in the Third World. If, like Pinochet's regime in Chile, a government is more concerned with staying in power than with addressing the needs and criticisms of its people, and if it is brutally repressive, then a free press certainly stands little chance of survival. At the same time, if a press that is free is not also responsible, it has the power to bring down a government that is in fact operating in the public's best interest – or at least to cause needless bloodshed. One author who addressed these problems pointed to an incident in Pakistan: A short time after Zulfikar Ali Bhutto began to allow some press freedom in that country in 1972, he decided to make Sindhi the official language of the central province. In reaction to this, the Urdu-speaking owners of the local press began to publish "dramatic stories proclaiming the decision to be the death of their language." The stories sparked three days of street fighting with stones and sticks, in which a dozen people were killed and scores were wounded.[46]

The public itself can also undermine the operation of a free press in the Third World. People who are not sufficiently educated about the inherent problems their country faces, simply by virtue of its underdevelopment, are liable to attribute these problems to a government that is in fact doing everything it can with its limited resources. This, along with press irresponsibility, is the argument most Third World leaders use to justify press censorship. One Pakistani reporter said of his countrymen, "People are not sophisticated, they are apt to explode over small issues."[47]

These arguments may have validity in particular cases. But it is important to remember that the existence of a free and independent press does not preclude the existence of an official or progovernment press at the same time; the government will always be free to counter any criticism, and the public will have an opportunity in this open marketplace of ideas to educate itself and decide which criticisms of the government are legitimate and which are not. Kenya has offered an example of this kind of system: A ruling-party newspaper and government-controlled television and radio exist alongside independent print media. But Third World governments expressing these concerns are frequently insincere: "Too often . . . it is not economic survival at stake, but the survival of the regime in power. As the country's problems become harder to control, the government controls the reporting of them instead."[48]

This assessment certainly holds true for Chile. The country's widely reported economic boom of the late 1980s was not enjoyed by much of the society. The struggling independent press reported on the ever broadening gulf between the rich and the poor at its peril; it was ceaselessly harassed by the Pinochet regime, which obviously found truth to be destabilizing. Yet Pinochet, despite the government's near monopoly of information, was defeated in the October 1988 plebiscite. Perhaps lies are, in the long run, even more destabilizing than the truth.

If one insists on arguing that the importance of a free press is overridden by other values, such as stability and economic development, one must then explain why so few of the countries that deny press freedom are stable or prosperous. Poland, Panama, and Chile have hardly enjoyed stability, although press restrictions (along with other repressive measures) were certainly given time to work their professed magic. South Africa, although it has not yet faced the severe economic difficulties of some other countries, continues to be plagued by instability of a different kind, and no amount of press restriction has helped.

Finally, it must be acknowledged that in many Third World countries, the only entity that can afford to run a newspaper or a radio or television station is the government. But these governments would do well to permit the expression of all views, or, as in the case of Britain's BBC, to fund the media through a license tax and allow independent operation. Under government control, the quality of journalism usually sinks, since reporters who do nothing but repeat the government line "tend to lose their inspiration. The papers become sterile, dull."[49] The public turns away from the press and becomes more cynical and alienated. Under these conditions, people are hardly likely to respond to the government's calls for austerity, or other sacrifices, in the name of nation building, which is usually the pretext for government control in the first place.

It should by now be apparent that the promotion of a free press serves certain narrow American self-interests in addition to the idealistic desire to foster democratic change abroad. With few exceptions, the stability that a free press brings to a country also makes U.S. relations with that country more comfortable and honest. With the enormous amount of Third World debt owed to the United States, it is certainly in the American interest to promote any mechanism that would foster stability in underdeveloped countries. Most dictatorships in which all forms of expression are repressed have failed miserably in their attempts to revive their economies; press freedom could hardly make matters worse, and it stands a good chance of making them considerably better, from the standpoint of both Third World citizens and U.S. creditors.

The information other countries' leaders receive from a free marketplace of ideas also benefits the formulation of U.S. foreign policy. The lack of reliable information about internal events in Iran under the Shah, for example, obviously contributed to the lack of foreknowledge of, or preparation for, the Iranian revolution on the part of the United States; the contrast with the Marcos–Aquino transition is sharp. Democratic change in other countries is invariably beneficial to U.S. interests. One need only look at the effects that Gorbachev's reforms in the Soviet Union, engineered through a new openness and honesty in the Soviet media, have had on U.S.-Soviet relations and, as a result, on international peace and stability.

All too often, however, American leaders have only paid lip service to the need for international press freedom, and even that has sometimes been missing. A search of the speeches of U.S. presidents since World War II reveals that Harry Truman was the last one to make a major issue of the free flow of information in the world – at least until Ronald Reagan discovered this issue as a basis for withdrawing the United States from UNESCO at the end of 1984. In several speeches in 1947, Truman specifically included freedom of information in his personal concept of human rights.

Since the late 1970s, the State Department has had a vehicle for comment on the condition of human rights in various countries, in the annual reports required by Congress on this subject. Unfortunately, violations of press freedom have played a relatively minor role in most of these country reports, especially during the Reagan administration, which tended to highlight the abuses of its adversaries and overlook those of its friends. For example, the 1988 reports ignored the Pakistani government's control of the distribution of newsprint, understated the official manipulation of the print and broadcast media in Singapore, omitted discussion of terrorist attacks on the opposition press in Guatemala, and settled for a description of the heavily censored Liberian media as "lively."[50] (Liberian journalists expressed amazement when Secretary of State George Shultz declared, on a visit to Monrovia in January 1987, that "there is freedom of the press here.")

A succession of administrations have understated threats to freedom of the press in such places as South Korea and Taiwan, apparently on the grounds of their importance to U.S. national security, and have tended to minimize the problems in others, such as Haiti and Somalia, where the collapse of client regimes might have unpredictable consequences for the United States. When the journalistic heroes of the 1989 revolt in China disappeared from view, the Bush administration was too busy with other matters to stand up for them. The inevitable impression is that official American comment on issues of press freedom is far more expedient than idealistic. Reagan's well-deserved attacks on UNESCO for promoting a scheme to license journalists as part of a "new world information order" would have had more credibility internationally if he had not appeared to be looking the other way while authoritarian friends of the United States, including the South African government, jailed individual reporters who displeased them.

As a result, much of the burden of standing up for American principles has fallen on the media themselves – the ultimate example of the free-enterprise defense of liberty. South Africa's plan to license journalists was rescinded only after independent organizations such as the World Press Freedom Committee and the Committee to Protect Journalists mounted a coordinated international campaign. Even so, the managers of American news organizations often seem to believe that speaking up on behalf of endangered colleagues in other countries would somehow compromise their distance from, and objectivity toward, the news from those countries. They are far too timid in the face of tragedy.

The United States has taken some steps in the right direction in recent years. The National Endowment for Democracy's financial assistance to Nicaragua's *La Prensa* may yet be a helpful precedent; but the danger is that foreign news media funded by the United States may become – or at least be perceived as – American propaganda tools. When that happens, the Sandinistas and others in their position may feel threatened and once again shut down these media as intruders on national sovereignty.

It is time to go much farther and to be more forceful. Leading American newspapers and magazines, the commercial networks, and public broadcasting could sponsor and conduct practical training of journalists from other countries in the kind of hard-hitting, no-holds-barred reporting that makes the press such an essential component of the democratic system in the United States. This could take place both in America and abroad, with schools of journalism and communication providing an academic framework where appropriate. The U.S. Agency for International Development and other donors could spend less time in the often patronizing field of "development communications" and more in simply helping Third World media become more independent of their governments. The Voice of America, with its superb technical facilities, could do more overseas to help professionalize radio, often the most direct and cost-effective means to inform people who live far from capital cities and commercial centers in the Third World. Journalists everywhere, when free to do their work properly, understand each other well; and more frequent exchanges of people and ideas would benefit all sides. A few months on the firing line in certain countries, living not as privileged foreign correspondents but as local reporters struggling to do their jobs, would certainly help American editors and producers understand better what is at stake.

On the moral plane, there is a great deal to be done. The U.S. government and private human-rights and journalistic organizations should raise issues of press freedom routinely in international forums. Since independent media are among the most effective tools with which to fight corruption, international financial organizations such as the World Bank and the International Monetary Fund must be urged to begin conditioning their loans on these factors, too. Certainly press freedom is as legitimate as economic reform as a precondition for further U.S. military or economic assistance to key countries. The insistence on a free flow of ideas must be just as strong a factor in American foreign policy as the reliance on a free flow of capital. Indeed, the former eventually might well lead to the latter.

NOTES

Parts of this chapter were originally presented at the Third Argentine-American Forum in San Carlos de Bariloche, Argentina, in March 1986. Excerpts appeared in *Foreign Policy* magazine. The author is grateful to John Mies, Kevin Matthews, and Michael Blumfield for their assistance with research on this topic.

1 The terms "press" and "media" are used interchangeably here to apply to organs of both print and broadcast journalism.
2 Ulrich Meister, "Soviet Readers, Spurred by Glasnost, Look for the Truth in the Press," *Neue Zurcher Zeitung*, July 5, 1988.
3 Radiala Onim, "Kenya: Subtle Self-Censorship," *New African*, May 1988, 39.
4 Blamuel Njururi et al., "25 Years On," *New African*, December 1988, 25.
5 Ron Chepesiuk, "Faxing the News into Panama," *The New Leader*, August 8–22, 1988, pp. 7–9.
6 Madeleine Korbel Albright, *Poland: The Role of the Press in Political Change* (Washington, D.C.: Center for Strategic and International Studies, Georgetown University, 1983), pp. 128–9.
7 Michael Massing, "Nicaragua's Free-Fire Journalism," *Columbia Journalism Review* (July–August 1988): 29.
8 Violeta Chamorro, "The Death of *La Prensa*," *Foreign Affairs* (Winter 1986–7): 385.
9 Sanford J. Ungar, "How Chile Muzzles Its Press," *Washington Post*, January 3, 1988, p. B5.
10 Peter Galliner, "New Threats in the Democracies," *World Press Review* (February 1989): 52–3.
11 Chamorro, "Death of *La Prensa*," p. 385.
12 Massing, "Nicaragua's Free-Fire Journalism," p. 10.
13 Peter Galliner, "Freedom Gains and Losses," *World Press Review* (February 1988): 55.

14 Charlene Smith, "The Death Rattle of Freedom," *World Press Review* (September 1986): 62.
15 Patrick E. Tyler, "Voice of Moderation Emerges as Iran Edges into New Era," *Washington Post*, October 24, 1988, p. A1.
16 Michael Field, " 'Revolutionizing' a Middle-Class Society," *World Press Review* (May 1987): 20.
17 Ibid.
18 Joel Dresang, "Authoritarian Controls and News Media in the Philippines," *Contemporary Southeast Asia* (June 1985): 40.
19 Albright, *Poland*, pp. 15–16.
20 Ibid.
21 Ibid., p. 2.
22 Anna Husarska, "One More Round in Poland," *The New Leader*, May 2, 1988, 6.
23 Adam Bromke, "Jaruzelski Walks a Fine Line," *World Press Review* (June 1987): 37.
24 Husarska, "One More Round in Poland," p. 7.
25 See Sanford J. Ungar, *The Papers and the Papers: An Account of the Legal and Political Battle over the Pentagon Papers*, rev. ed. (New York: Columbia University Press, Morningside Books, 1989).
26 Ibid., p. 3.
27 Ronald Dworkin, "Devaluing Liberty," *Index on Censorship* (September 1988): 7–8.
28 Andrew Neil, "Britain's Unfree Press," *Washington Post*, January 15, 1989.
29 Robin Lustig, "Margaret Thatcher's 'Non-Persons,' " *The Observer*, October 22, 1988.
30 Nicholas B. Tatro, "Israeli Authorities Clamp Down on the Press," Associated Press, May 2, 1984.
31 Glenn Frankel, "Why the Israelis Lifted My Press Card Last Week," *Washington Post*, May 1, 1988.
32 Robert D. McFadden, "Kissinger Urged Ban on TV Reports," *New York Times*, March 5, 1988, p. 5.
33 Jonathan Alter, "A Maze of Double Standards," *Newsweek*, January 11, 1988.
34 Hamid Mowlana, "Technology Versus Tradition: Communication in the Iranian Revolution," *Journal of Communication* (Summer 1979): 108.
35 Hamid Mowlana, "The Press and National Development in the Middle East," *Intellect* (March 1976): 468.

36 Gary Sick, *All Fall Down: America's Tragic Encounter with Iran* (New York: Random House, 1985), p. 23.
37 Dresang, "Authoritarian Controls," p. 34.
38 Ibid., p. 39.
39 Jonathan Kolatch, "Uprising in the Philippines: Could There Have Been a Revolution Without Television?" *TV Guide*, May 31, 1986, 5. A second article in this excellent series is "TV and the Philippines: For the First Time the People Could See What Was Happening," *TV Guide*, June 7, 1986.
40 See Kolatch, June 7, 1986.
41 Thomas Griffith, "Newswatch: The Visuals Did Marcos In," *Time*, March 17, 1986, p. 72.
42 Niyii Alabi, "Publish and Survive," *New African*, May 1988, p. 36.
43 David H. Weaver, Judith M. Buddenbaum, and Jo Ellen Fair, "Press Freedom, Media, and Development, 1950–1979: A Study of 134 Nations," *Journal of Communication* (Spring 1985): 104–5.
44 Leonard R. Sussman, "Communications: Openness and Censorship," in *Freedom in the World: Political Rights and Civil Liberties, 1988–89*, ed. Raymond D. Gastil (New York: Freedom House, 1988), pp. 132–5.
45 Darryl D'Monte, "Ghandi Bullies the Press," *The New Leader*, February 8, 1988, pp. 11–12.
46 Joanmarie Kalter, "The Fourth Estate in the Third World," *Bulletin of Atomic Scientists* (November 1983): 14.
47 Ibid.
48 Ibid., p. 12.
49 Kalter, "The Fourth Estate," p. 15.
50 For these and other examples, see *Critique: Review of the Department of State's Country Reports on Human Rights Practices* for 1988, published by Human Rights Watch and the Lawyers Committee for Human Rights (New York 1989).

Index